Storming the Eagle's Nest

Jim Ring's 1996 debut, *Erskine Childers*, won the Marsh Prize for biography. It was followed by *How the English Made the Alps* which was described as 'fascinating' by the *Daily Telegraph* and 'evocative and entertaining' by the *Financial Times*. His collective biography of Britain's leading Cold War submariners, *We Come Unseen*, won the Mountbatten Prize and was called 'a welcome acknowledgement of one of the Cold War's little known aspects' by the *Sunday Telegraph*.

Praise for *How the English Made the Alps*, also by Jim Ring:

'Cannot be bettered.' *Daily Mail*

'A comprehensive, well-written account of a fascinating subject.' *Guardian*

D0988012

Storming the Eagle's Nest

Hitler's War in the Alps

JIM RING

faber and faber

First published in 2013
by Faber and Faber Limited
Bloomsbury House
74–77 Great Russell Street
London WC1B 3DA
This paperback edition published in 2014

Typeset by Donald Sommerville
Printed by CPI (UK) Ltd, Croydon, CR0 4YY

A CIP record for this book
is available from the British Library

ISBN 978-0-571-28239-5

FSC
www.fsc.org
MIX
Paper from
responsible sources
FSC® C101712

2 4 6 8 10 9 7 5 3 1

For Peter Alexander Ring, MS, FRCS,
orthopaedic surgeon.

Contents

List of Plates

Hitler in the Alps. *Keystone-France/Gamma-Keystone via Getty Images*
Olympic skier Christl Cranz. *FPG/Getty Images*
Chamberlain at Berchtesgaden. *Press Association*
Hitler and Mussolini. *Mary Evans Picture Library*
German alpine soldier. *J. R. Eyerman//Time Life Pictures/Getty Images*
General Henri Guisan visiting Davos. *Familienalbum Vogel-Rupp/Dokumentationsbibliothek Davos © Dokumentationsbibliothek Davos*
Swiss troops in the mountains. *Familienalbum Vogel-Rupp/ Dokumentationsbibliothek Davos © Dokumentationsbibliothek Davos*
Allen Dulles. *Keystone-France/Gamma-Keystone via Getty Images*
Wilhelm Gustloff. *Fotoalbum Wieland-Grisebach © Dokumentationsbibliothek Davos*
Alain le Ray. *© Collection Musée de la Résistance et de la Déportation de l'Isère*
Matteus Guidon. *By kind permission of Matteus Guidon*
Two of the Jewish refugees escorted by Matteus Guidon. *By kind permission of Matteus Guidon*
Survivors of the Ebensee concentration camp. *Courtesy of the National Archives/Newsmakers*
Göring's art collection in Allied hands. *Keystone-France/ Gamma-Keystone via Getty Imagess*

American tanks in Garmisch-Partenkirchen. *Horace Abrahams/ Keystone/Getty Images*

American troops in the ruins of the Berghof. *Keystone-France/ Gamma-Keystone via Getty Images*

List of Maps

Preface

Everybody knows the Alps. Nobody knows how Europe's play-ground became its battlefield.

Virtually from the Fall of France in June 1940 to Hitler's suicide in April 1945, the swastika shadowed the peaks of the Haute-Savoie in the western Alps to the passes above Ljubljana in the east. The Alps as much as Berlin were the heart of the Third Reich. 'Yes,' Hitler declared of his headquarters in the Bavarian Alps, 'I have a close link to this mountain. Much was done there, came about and ended there; those were the best times of my life . . . My great plans were forged there.'

In 1940, Mussolini's troops pitched battle with the French on the Franco-Italian Alpine border, skiing resorts all over the Alps were turned into training centres for mountain warfare, and Switzerland prepared to be invaded. Concentration camps were seeded in the Alpine valleys, Gauleiters were installed in the resorts, and secret rocket factories established; in the southern Alps of Switzerland, St Moritz and Zermatt welcomed escaping Allied PoWs, whilst further north Berne grew fat on looted Nazi gold, and guards turned away Jewish refugees at the country's borders.

Yet as the war progressed, the occupied Alps became the cradle of resistance to totalitarian rule. Backed by Churchill's brainchild, the Special Operations Executive and its US equivalent, the Office for Strategic Services, the mountain terrain spawned the French maquis and the Italian and Yugoslav partisans. From Slovenia to the Savoie, ski-runs became battlegrounds, the upper and lower stations of téléphériques fell to opposing forces, and atrocities were committed with Mausers, bowie knives, mortars and grenades where once winter sports enthusiasts sipped Glühwein. In the spring of 1945, with the Red Army nearing Berlin, Goebbels propagated the myth of the Reich's Alpine Redoubt. Here, Hitler and his diehards would supposedly hold out for years. Eisenhower's armies were diverted south away from the German capital, leaving the city open to Stalin. After the Führer's death the Allies discovered hoards of looted Nazi treasures, banknotes and bullion secreted in the Bavarian and Austrian Alps.

I was attracted to this story partly because in its entirety it had been told only tangentially and parenthetically before in broader studies of the European war; partly because of the paradox of fascism engulfing such a potent symbol of freedom as the Alps; and partly because of the richness of the personalities it involves, its sheer human drama.

Adolf Hitler, the Luftwaffe chief Hermann Göring, the SS mastermind Heinrich Himmler and the prototypical spin doctor Joseph Goebbels are familiar enough; less so are the Nazis' leader in Switzerland Wilhelm Gustloff, the Alpine concentration camp commandant Obersturmführer Otto Riemer, and the perpetrator of the Glières tragedy, Waffen-SS Sturmbannführer Joseph Darnand. Similarly, the figures of Churchill, Roosevelt and Eisenhower are complemented by the Swiss general Henri Guisan who stepped in where his country's politicians feared to tread, Conrad O'Brien-ffrench (the model for James Bond), the German spy Fritz Kolbe, the hundreds of charismatic Frenchmen who rose above the country's 1940 fall – one of whom rejoiced in the fanciful name of Emmanuel d'Astier de la Vigerie – and the US spymaster and Don Juan, Allen Welsh Dulles. There are also those with two faces: Josip Broz aka Marshal Tito, the 'good Nazi' Albert Speer, and France's Charles de Gaulle. The General was the man who accepted such large quantities of Anglo-American blood and treasure – resulting in the freeing of his own country – with such admirably regal disdain. 'La France, c'est moi!'

There were also the everyday people of the Alps drawn by the vortex of fascism into the denouncements, betrayals and atrocities that rendered them inhuman: the agents, above all, of the Holocaust. These were countered by tales of courage, heroism and self-sacrifice, of the ordinary people doing extraordinary things, that characterise conflict wherever and whenever it occurs.

For the Alps, the years under the swastika really were both the best and the worst of times. This is the story that – for the first time – this book tells.

Burnham Overy Staithe,
June 2013

PART ONE

ONE

Plan Z

*From this surrender at Berchtesgaden, all else
followed.*

WILLIAM L. SHIRER

I

On 14 September 1938 an Englishman was getting ready to leave
London for the Alps.

There was nothing unusual in this as such, for the English, as
well as other Europeans and North Americans, had been seeking
adventures in the Alps for more than two hundred years. First
as Grand Tourists en route to the classical remains of Italy and
Greece; then as 'scientific travellers', trying to unravel puzzles
like the movement of glaciers and the impact of altitude on
human physiology; later, in the wake of the Napoleonic wars, as
artists. The Romantic poets – Percy Shelley, Lord Byron, William
Wordsworth – had defined Romanticism in their response to the
Alps; J. M. W. Turner and Caspar David Friedrich did likewise
in paint; Mary Shelley had created *Frankenstein* on the shores of
Lake Geneva. There came, too, the mountaineers who were the
first to actually climb the high peaks of Europe's great mountain
range: from Mont Blanc in the west, the Matterhorn and the
Monte Rosa towering above Zermatt, the famous trio of the
Eiger, Mönch and Jungfrau in the Bernese Alps high above the
Swiss capital of Berne, to the Piz Bernina, the Ortler and the
Grossglockner in the east. In the second half of the nineteenth
century the clean, dry Alpine air was identified as a palliative
and even a cure for tuberculosis. Sufferers from a disease at the
time widespread flocked to the mountains for the 'Alpine cure'.
Amongst them were Thomas Mann, A. J. A. Symons, Robert Louis

Stevenson and the wife of Arthur Conan Doyle, her husband in train. With the coming of the railways, the travel entrepreneurs Thomas Cook and Henry Lunn introduced tourism to the summer Alps. In the early years of the twentieth century, Henry's son Arnold for the first time brought skaters, tobogganers and skiers to the Alps in winter, hitherto closed season. By the outbreak of the First World War a handful of remote villages had won worldwide fame as Alpine holiday resorts. Amongst them were Chamonix, Cortina d'Ampezzo, Davos, Grindelwald, Kitzbühel, St Anton, St Moritz, Wengen and Zermatt. After the war skiing established itself as a major international sport, and in 1936 the Bavarian resort of Garmisch-Partenkirchen joined the winners' circle as the venue for the Winter Olympics. In an age defined by industrialisation, the Alps had become the playground of Europe. Here the upper and – later – the middle classes escaped from their dark satanic mills to a purer, older and less material world.

For Switzerland in particular at the heart of the Alps, the English had an affection based on shared liberal constitutional principles and a tradition of personal freedom. Charles Dickens, writing to Walter Savage Landor at the height of the vogue for European revolutions in 1848, declared of the Swiss: 'They are a thorn in the side of the European despots, and a good and wholesome people to live near Jesuit-ridden kings on the brighter side of the mountains. My hat shall ever be ready to be thrown up, and my glove ever ready to be thrown down for Switzerland!'[1] Yet the appeal of the Alps ran deeper. In an age that was beginning to question the conventional tenets of Christianity, thinkers like John Ruskin seized upon the Alps as a visible expression of the work of a deity. The Alps were 'the best image the world can give of Paradise'.[2] This was echoed in 1878 by Mark Twain:

I met dozens of people, imaginative and unimaginative, cultivated and uncultivated, who had come from far countries and roamed through the Swiss Alps year after year – they could not explain why. They had come first, they said, out of idle curiosity, because everybody talked about it; they had come since because they could not help it, and they should keep on coming, while they lived, for the same reason; they had tried to break their chains and stay away, but it was futile; now they had no desire to break them. Others came nearer formulating what they felt; they said they could find perfect rest and peace nowhere else when they were troubled; all frets and worries and chafings sank to sleep in the presence of the benignant serenity of the Alps. The Great Spirit of the Mountain breathed his own peace upon their hurt minds and sore hearts, and healed them; they could not think base thoughts or do mean and sordid things here, before the visible throne of God.[3]

Switzerland, though often taken as a byword for the whole eight-hundred-mile range, was of course buttressed to the west by the massif forming the border with France that included Mont Blanc, the greatest peak in western Europe; to the east and south by those ranges that formed the frontiers with and between Austria, Italy, Germany and – in 1938 – Yugoslavia.

Here, in the 1930s, dark forces were at work. It was true that Switzerland was still a democratic state whose permanent neutrality had been reaffirmed at Versailles in 1919; true that France, under Prime Minister Édouard Daladier, was the democratic Third Republic. But Yugoslavia under the regent Prince Paul was riven by vicious rivalry between its constituent parts, the Banovinas; the de facto dictator King Alexander had been assassinated in 1934. Italy had fallen under the shadow of Fascism as early as 1922 under the leadership of Benito Mussolini – dubbed by his Chief of General Staff Pietro Badoglio 'Dictator Number One'. Free speech, freedom of association and political opposition had been abjured. Austria became a fascistic state on the Italian model after the end of the First Republic in 1933 and the accession of Chancellor Engelbert Dollfuss. Germany, the southern province of which was largely Alpine, had become a totalitarian state after Adolf Hitler became chancellor in 1933 – for Badoglio 'Dictator Number Two'. The Bavarian capital of Munich was the ideological centre of Nazism, the Hauptstadt der Bewegung, and the first of the concentration camps was opened in the Munich suburb of Dachau on 22 March 1933. A year later came Hitler's purge of Ernst Röhm, the leader of the Nazis' militia, the SA (*Sturmabteilung*, storm battalion), and his confederates at the Alpine resort of Wiessee. This was the 'Night of the Long Knives' on 30 June 1934. Wiessee lies between Munich and the Tyrolean capital of Innsbruck. For Winston Churchill, at the time out of office and languishing as a backbencher in the House of Commons, it was also the road to Damascus:

This massacre . . . showed that the new Master of Germany would stop at nothing, and that conditions in Germany bore no resemblance to those of a civilised State. A Dictatorship based upon terror and reeking with blood had confronted the world. Anti-Semitism was ferocious and brazen, and the concentration-camp system was already in full operation for all obnoxious or politically dissident classes. I was deeply affected by the episode, and the whole process of German rearmament, of which there was now overwhelming evidence, seemed to me invested with a ruthless, lurid tinge. It glittered and it glared.[4]

Even the mountains themselves saw trouble. As a surrogate for war, they were exploited for the purposes of national vainglory. The conquest of Alpine peaks became less a sporting achievement than an expression of Aryan 'racial' pride. The most notorious case was the north face (Nordwand) of the Eiger, in Switzerland's Bernese Oberland. Wall was the right word for a 5,900-foot face much of which was angled at 85 degrees, some overhanging, the climb bedevilled with ice, snow and rockfall. In 1935 two young German climbers, Karl Mehringer and Max Sedlmeyer, froze to death in an attempt on the face. In 1936 another group of Austrian and German climbers made an assault that left four of them dead. In July 1938 the wall was finally beaten by an Austro-German team. Their leader was Heinrich Harrer, later to win fame for *Seven Years in Tibet*. The four were given heroes' welcomes by Hitler as heralds of the New Germany.

This was the shadow under which the 'visible throne of God' had fallen by 1938. It was to Munich that the Englishman was heading.

He had been advised that September can be a wonderful month in Bavaria, but that it is often wet. An umbrella was as likely to be as useful as a panama. He was a dressy man who so affected stuffy Edwardian costume that he was nicknamed by some of his colleagues 'the coroner'. As to getting to the German Alps, he chose to fly. Commercial aviation was a sickly child of the years after the First World War, and the height of the Alps – in places they rose to 15,000 feet – challenged the early passenger aircraft. The first commercial flights between England and Switzerland were established in 1923 and by the summer of 1938 the enthusiasm of the English for Alpine pleasures justified two flights a day to both Basel and Zurich. Still, flying was far from commonplace and the Englishman had taken nothing other than a joyride before. A train would have brought him from London to the Alps in a day and a half. Time, though, was of the essence.

He called his adventure 'Plan Z'. He wrote to his sisters Ida and Hilda melodramatically: 'If it comes off it would go far beyond the present crisis and might prove the opportunity to bring about a complete change in the international situation.'[5] The news of the plan was broken on the evening of 14 September 1938 at a banquet attended by one of his contemporaries, Henry 'Chips' Channon. Ecstatically, the diarist recorded: 'It is one of the finest, most inspiring acts of all history. The company rose to their feet electrified, as all the world must be, and drank his health. History must be ransacked to find a parallel.'[6] The Poet Laureate John Masefield was moved to write a poem on the mission published in *The Times*.

The Englishman, bearing his umbrella, was duly cheered by crowds en route to the airport at Heston in west London. His party took off at 8.36 a.m. in a ten-seat Lockheed Electra. Four hours later on his arrival in Munich he was met by a gaggle of German diplomats. They were the German ambassador to the Court of St James's, Dr Herbert von Dirksen, and his superior the foreign minister Joachim von Ribbentrop. This was a man vilified by Dirksen himself as an 'unwholesome, half-comical figure'. An open car took the party from the airfield to Munich station. A special train on which Ribbentrop presided over a lunch took the group ninety miles south from Munich to their final destination of Berchtesgaden.

This was a picturesque little resort of a few hundred souls, nestling at 1,500 feet in the south-eastern Bavarian Alps. Its quiet streets were cobbled, its houses painted with Luftmalerei frescos in the traditional Bavarian style, and it was surrounded by the high mountains that lift the human heart. The Untersberg lay to the north, the Kehlstein to the east, and to the south soared the Watzmann – at almost 9,000 feet the third-highest peak in Germany. There was skiing in the long winter and in the summer mountain hiking in the surrounding mountains and at the Königssee to the south. At the newly enlarged station at Berchtesgaden the party was met by a black Mercedes and whisked the few hundred yards to the Berchtesgadener Hof, the resort's principal hotel. Here the delegates were allowed just half an hour's respite before being collected once again and driven across the river Ache a mile uphill to a mountain plateau: Obersalzberg. Their host stood awaiting them on the steps of a mountain chalet called without much originality the Berghof.

The Englishman was the British Prime Minister, Neville Chamberlain. He observed of his host, 'His hair is brown, not black, his eyes blue, his expression rather disagreeable, especially in repose and altogether he looks entirely undistinguished.'[7] These were Chamberlain's first impressions of Adolf Hitler, chancellor of Germany and leader of the Third Reich. Mahomet had come to the mountain.

2

Berchtesgaden might have seemed an odd choice. Hitler's new Chancellery in Berlin was a more obvious venue for the sort of meeting that Chamberlain's parliamentary colleague Winston Churchill would later dub a 'summit'. In practice, the palace in Vossstrasse – constructed quite literally regardless of cost – was at present unfinished. In any case, Hitler, like Mark Twain, drew inspiration from the Alps. It was in Berchtesgaden that legend placed Barbarossa. There in the Untersberg overlooking Berchtesgaden lay the medieval German Kaiser in an enchanted sleep, awaiting the day on which he would awake to bring Germany back to its golden age. Barbarossa was a Teutonic King Arthur and a secular messiah. Wagner, Hitler's favourite composer, had popularised the myth in the Ring Cycle, and the Führer had identified himself with it. 'You see the Untersberg over there,' he once remarked in conversation at the Berghof. 'It is no accident that I chose my residence opposite it.'[8]

Hitler had first visited Berchtesgaden with his sister Paula in April 1923. This was a few months before the failed putsch in Munich, the first milestone of his political career. After his release from Landsberg prison in 1925 – a spell that had been the upshot of the putsch – the politician spent two years living in the Deutsches Haus in Berchtesgaden. Displaying the sensibilities of the failed artist that he was, Hitler described this as 'a countryside of indescribable beauty'.[9] Here he wrote the second volume of his prospectus for the Third Reich, *Mein Kampf*. In 1928 he first rented and then bought Haus Wachenfeld. This was a small chalet situated on the Obersalzberg plateau halfway up the Kehlstein, across the valley from Berchtesgaden. Two years after Hitler became chancellor in January 1933, the Haus Wachenfeld was considerably enlarged by the architect Alois Delgado. A terrace was added to the front and the roof was raised to provide an additional floor. Garages and storage rooms were created in the basement, above which was a large conference room with a huge picture window – twenty-five feet by twelve – opening onto the Alps of Berchtesgadener Land. On the second floor were Hitler's study, bedroom and living room, and several rooms for guests; above were a further fifteen rooms. The Berghof was garnished with the most expensive materials, including marble from Carrara and the Untersberg itself. It was Hitler's Camp David, his Chequers, his dacha – or in Churchill's case, his Chartwell.

Soon the Berghof became the centre of a Nazi settlement. Hitler's acolytes – Reichsleiter Martin Bormann, Reichsmarschall Hermann Göring, Reichsleiter Joseph Goebbels and the architect cum arms and war production minister Albert Speer – had chalets within call of the Führer. For Hitler's fiftieth birthday in 1939 a lofty retreat known as the Kehlsteinhaus – dubbed 'the Eagle's Nest' by the French ambassador to Germany, André François-Poncet – was constructed by Bormann at the 6,017-foot peak of the Kehlstein. An SS barracks, guest hotel and assorted subsidiary buildings created a community that would eventually number 4,000. Obersalzberg had its own kindergarten, school, swimming pool, theatre and fire station. Guards were provided by the SS (Reichsführer Heinrich Himmler's Schutzstaffel) and the Reichssicherheitsdienst (RSD, Reich Security Service). Their members preferred service at Obersalzberg to elsewhere. The local girls were much attracted to uniforms. Although Hitler also had houses in Munich and Berlin, it was the Berghof that he regarded as his real home. On 17 January 1942 he declared, 'There are so many links between the Obersalzberg and me. So many things were born there and brought to fruition there. I've spent up there the finest hours of my life. It's there that all my great projects were conceived and ripened.'[10]

It was fitting, then, that on 19 November 1937 came a meeting there that ushered in Neville Chamberlain's Alpine mission. This was Hitler's encounter with Lord Viscount Halifax, former Viceroy of India and shortly to replace Anthony Eden as Britain's foreign secretary. Halifax was a traditional representative of England's ruling classes. He leavened inherited wealth, a country estate, Eton and Oxford with a predilection for field sports and High Anglicanism. The latter inspired Churchill's punning nickname, 'the Holy Fox'. Under the cloak of attending one of Luftwaffe chief Hermann Göring's garish hunting parties – shooting foxes in Pomerania – Halifax had been dispatched by Chamberlain to the Berghof. There in the Alps he was to establish better relations with a renascent Germany, and to attempt to reconcile Hitler's ambitions for the Third Reich with the interests of a country that in 1937 remained a world power, her empire largely intact.

Hitler was of course an adherent of racial theories about the supremacy of the 'Aryan' people that demanded the reunification of the German-speaking 'Volk' of Europe into the Reich. The result would be a Grossdeutsches Reich – Greater German Reich. The difficulty in this modest proposal was that such a plan required existing national borders to be torn up. The Alpine republic of Austria was predominantly German-speaking; so too was the Sudeten area of Czechoslovakia – with some 3 million German speakers; so too some 400,000 residents of the Baltic city of Danzig in Poland; so too the majority of the citizens of Switzerland. Hitler was also looking further east for Lebensraum – living space – for his people. Given the experience of France, Great Britain and the United States in the First World War, the Versailles Treaty specifically proscribed the unification or Anschluss of Germany and Austria; it established Danzig as a 'Free City' under League of Nations control; it created the new state of Czechoslovakia. It was Germany's ambitions to rearrange these affairs that Halifax was to explore with Hitler in the Alps.

The meeting at Berchtesgaden nearly began with misfortune. Arriving at the Berghof, the gangling Halifax mistook the 5' 8" Hitler for a footman, and was on the point of handing the Führer his hat and coat. Happily the gaffe was avoided by a member of the diplomatic corps standing on his tiptoes urging in the Viscount's ear, 'Der Führer! Der Führer!' Thereafter Hitler had very much his own way. He rehearsed the injustices of Versailles and the partiality of the British press. He protested – apparently without irony – that 'Germany sets great store by good relations with all her neighbours'. Halifax reciprocated by playing what amounted to the opening card of Chamberlain's policy of appeasement. He made it clear that Britain was prepared to contemplate reinterpretations of Versailles on the questions of Danzig, Austria and Czechoslovakia. Providing, of course, such alterations came through 'peaceful evolution' rather than 'methods . . . which might cause far-reaching disturbances'. For Hitler this opened a prospect – a mountain path, a Wanderweg – to the high sunlit uplands of a Grossdeutsches Reich. Everything seemed possible. Thus Halifax at Berchtesgaden – in the words of his most recent biographer Andrew Roberts – 'let Hitler see his chance'.[11] The Führer then relaxed and took it upon himself to advise the former Viceroy of India on the problem of the national aspirations of the subcontinent. 'Shoot Gandhi,' he proposed.

3

On his return to England, Halifax reported on the meeting to the British Cabinet; he 'would expect beaver-like persistence in pressing their claims in central Europe, but not in a form to give others cause – or probably occasion – to interfere.'[12] For his part, Hitler dismissed Halifax as 'the English parson', sacked a couple of generals – Blomberg and Fritsch – who amongst other lapses he felt lacked an appetite for war, consolidated his hold over the armed forces, and on 20 February 1937 made an inflammatory speech at the Reichstag dismissive of British concerns. According to Winston Churchill, Hitler now 'regarded Britain as a frightened, flabby old woman, who at worst would only bluster, and was, anyhow, incapable of making war'.[13]

On 12 March 1938 Hitler duly invaded Austria, replacing the nationalist chancellor Kurt Schuschnigg with the Nazi Arthur Seyss-Inquart. This was Anschluss, as forbidden by Versailles. The American war correspondent William L. Shirer was in the Austrian capital, covering the story for Columbia Broadcasting System (CBS) radio. The thirty-four-year-old Chicago-born Shirer was one of the 'Murrow's boys', CBS journalists hired by the legendary Ed Murrow. He has much to tell us of the first months of the Nazis in the Alps, not least in his classic account of the era, *The Rise and Fall of the Third Reich*:

I had emerged from the subway at the Karlsplatz to find myself engulfed in a shouting, hysterical Nazi mob which was sweeping towards the Inner City. These contorted faces I had seen before, at the Nuremberg party rallies. They were yelling, 'Sieg Heil! Sieg Heil! Heil Hitler! Heil Hitler! Heil Hitler! Hang Schuschnigg! Hang Schussnigg!'[14]

When Versailles brought the curtain down on the old Austro-Hungarian Empire, it was joked that the rump republic of Austria comprised an imperial city and a handful of Alpine valleys. Amongst the vestiges of the empire were the two western Alpine provinces of the Vorarlberg and Tyrol. They hinged on the Tyrolean capital of Innsbruck, the gateway to Italy. Together, the provinces boasted two resorts with international reputations: St Anton am Arlberg, close to the border with Switzerland, and Kitzbühel, the medieval Tyrolean town patronised by the Duke of Windsor in his earlier days as the playboy Prince of Wales. With Anschluss, these resorts became the southern outposts of the Third Reich, their streets decked in swastikas and their chalets cleared of political opponents, the disabled, gypsies and Jews alike. The Gestapo soon moved in.

As the French and the British, the guarantors of Versailles, did little but wring their hands at this turn of events, Hitler matured his plan for the invasion of Czechoslovakia. This was a scheme much more practicable via neighbouring Austria than from Germany. In late May 1938 the shooting by a Czech official of two Sudeten farmers precipitated the Czech crisis. It bubbled throughout the summer, stoked by pronouncements from both the British and the French in favour of redrawing the Czech border to the benefit of Germany. At the annual Nazi rally in Nuremberg on 12 September 1938, Hitler declared, 'I have stated that the Reich would not tolerate any further oppression of these three and a half million Germans, and I would ask the statesmen of foreign countries to be convinced that this is no mere form of words.'

On 13 September the Czech government under Edvard Beneš was obliged to declare martial law; the Czechs themselves, France and Britain mobilised. Europe seemed closer to a general war than at any time since 1918. Chamberlain, feeling – with his gift for cliché – that desperate times called for desperate measures, unveiled Plan Z to Foreign Secretary Halifax. Conceived by the Director of the Conservative Research Department Sir Joseph Ball, this was in the days long before 'shuttle diplomacy', G8 and G20 conferences, and long before the world's leaders met on anything other than a very occasional basis – normally at the League of Nations in Geneva. The plan, according to the Prime

Minister, 'was so unconventional and daring it fairly took his [Halifax's] breath away'.[15]

4

At the time Chamberlain was almost seventy, and had been Prime Minster since May 1937. He was part of a political dynasty: the son of the Cabinet minister Joseph Chamberlain and half-brother of Austen Chamberlain. His premiership was defined by the European crisis brought about by the Depression and the rise of fascism, and in fathering the policy of appeasement he was the counterpoint to Churchill, who summarised his rival's position: 'The Prime Minister wished to get on good terms with the European dictators, and believed that conciliation and the avoidance of anything likely to offend them was the best method.'[16] For Lloyd George, Chamberlain would have made 'a good mayor of Birmingham in an off year'; it was also said that he 'looked at Foreign Policy through the wrong end of a municipal drainpipe'.

Chamberlain's Berchtesgaden party comprised himself, a senior civil servant and adviser, Sir Horace Wilson, the British ambassador to the Reich, Sir Nevile Henderson, and a secretary. Foreign Secretary Halifax had been left in London because his presence – in terms of protocol – would demand that of his counterpart Joachim von Ribbentrop at the meeting with Hitler. The former wine salesman was not regarded by the British as a constructive contributor to debate. Halifax had remarked that he was 'so stupid, so shallow, so self-centred and self-satisfied, so totally devoid of intellectual capacity that he never seems to take in what is said to him'.[17] Collected at the Berchtesgadener Hof, the British party was driven fifteen minutes through the rain up to the Berghof. There they were greeted by an eighty-man black-uniformed SS guard of honour and, at the bottom of the flight of steps leading up to the chalet's terrace, by Hitler himself. The Führer was flanked by Generaloberst Wilhelm Keitel, resplendent in field grey. Here was a symbol of Germany's renewed military prowess. Chamberlain was clutching his hat and umbrella, but did not try to give them to the Führer. The party then entered the Berghof. Traudl Junge, Hitler's secretary at Obersalzberg, remembered:

The place had a strange, indefinable quality that put you on your guard and filled you with odd apprehensions. The only comfortable room was the library on the first floor, which in the old house had been Hitler's private sitting room. It was rustically furnished, with beer mugs placed here and there for decoration. The books at everybody's disposal were of no great interest: world classics that nobody seemed to have read, travel atlases, a large dictionary, albums and drawings, and of course copies of *Mein Kampf* bound in gold and morocco leather.[18]

Tea was served in the reception room with its great window looking across to the Untersberg. Hitler had a limited aptitude for small talk. The preliminary conversation concerned the room, the splendours of the view – marred by the rain – and the idea of the Führer visiting England. Chamberlain's priggish eye was caught by the paintings of nude women scattered around the chalet, and he raised the subject with the Cabinet on his return to England. The Prime Minister and the chancellor then removed themselves with the Führer's interpreter, Dr Paul Schmidt, to the study upstairs in which Hitler had entertained Halifax the previous year. The room, Chamberlain later complained, was bare of ornament. 'There was not even a clock, only a stove, a small table with two bottles of mineral water (which he didn't offer me), three chairs and a sofa.'[19]

Hitler's approach with Chamberlain was much the same as with Halifax: a litany of the injustices served on Germany and a complementary catalogue of demands. As Schmidt recorded, Hitler declared that he 'did not wish that any doubts should arise as to his absolute determination not to tolerate any longer that a small second-rate country should treat the mighty thousand-year-old German Reich as something inferior . . . he would be sorry if a world war should arise from this problem . . . [but] he would face any war, even world war, for this'. He worked himself into a lather. Such, indeed, was the Führer's tenor that the Prime Minister asked him why he had agreed to the visit if he was so determined to take action – most immediately against Czechoslovakia. 'I soon saw', wrote Chamberlain to his sisters, 'that the situation was much more critical than I had anticipated. I knew that his troops and tanks and guns and planes were ready to pounce, and only awaiting his word, and it was clear that rapid decisions must be taken if the situation was to be saved.' Hitler's precise formulation, in the words of the debonair Sir Nevile Henderson – twiddling his thumbs downstairs as the rain and darkness fell – was that 'the only terms on which he could agree to a peaceful solution were on the basis of the acceptance of the principal of self-determination'.[20]

This Chamberlain provisionally accepted. Because the results of a plebiscite in the Sudetenland were a foregone conclusion, he went considerably further than Halifax. He effectively told Hitler that Britain was prepared to see the dismemberment of Czechoslovakia. Chamberlain concluded by agreeing to seek consent to this concession from the British Cabinet, the French and – last and least – the Czech government itself.

Business concluded, dinner was served. The British party was joined by some of Hitler's neighbours in Obersalzberg: the convicted murderer Reichsleiter Martin Bormann and his wife Gerda, Margarete, the wife of the Reich's architect Albert Speer, and Hitler's mistress Eva Braun. This was an honour for the Prime Minister. Braun was normally kept under wraps – indeed confined to her room – when dignitaries were visiting the Berghof. It was pitch-dark before Chamberlain got back to the Berchtesgadener Hof, and close to midnight before his short report to the Cabinet in England had been drafted, enciphered and telegraphed.

As Hitler reflected on another occasion, 'Those rainy days at Berchtesgaden, what a blessing they were! No violent exercise, no excursions, no sunbaths – a little repose! There's nothing lovelier in the world than a mountain landscape.'[21] How fortunate that Chamberlain had brought his umbrella.

5

The Prime Minister flew back from the Alps the next day well satisfied with his efforts, and with another meeting with the Führer in his diary. 'It was impossible', he reported, 'not to be impressed by the power of the man . . . his objectives were strictly limited . . . when he had included the Sudeten Germans in the Reich he would be satisfied.' All in all, he was a man with whom Chamberlain felt 'I can do business'.[22]

The Prime Minister still needed the Cabinet's endorsement of his proposals. He also required the support of the French, who, following the reoccupation of the Rhineland on the Franco-German border in March 1936, had every reason to fear Hitler's expansionist policies. There were the Czechs too. Reporting the matter in the American *News Chronicle*, the paper's European correspondent related that the elevator operator in the paper's New York headquarters had asked, 'Mr. Waithman, can you tell me why Britain should have any right to give Czechoslovakia to Hitler?'[23] The French Prime Minister Édouard Daladier saw no such difficulty, perhaps because France had a pact of mutual support with Czechoslovakia that she was ambivalent about honouring. The Czech leader Edvard Beneš saw little alternative to the Anglo-French proposals, however unpalatable.

Returning to the Rhineland resort of Bad Godesberg on 21 September 1938, Chamberlain expected to be congratulated by the Führer for achieving the compliance of the French and the Czechs. On the morning of 22 September he was somewhat surprised to hear from the Nazi leader that the proposal was no longer sufficient. Now the Sudetenland was to be handed over on 1 October, to be transferred directly to German troops, without due process, a commission, and the normal paraphernalia of bureaucracy. For the British that was enough.

Chamberlain flew back to England and the country prepared for war. The fleet was mobilised, the public issued with gas masks, and air-raid trenches dug in Hyde Park. On 27 September, Chamberlain famously told the nation, 'How horrible, fantastic, incredible it is that we should be digging trenches and trying on gas-masks here because of a quarrel in a far-away country between people of whom we know nothing.' On 28 September, the US ambassador to Britain, Joseph P. Kennedy, reported to the US State Department that 'failing acceptance of the German ultimatum by 2:00 p.m. today, Germany may attack Czechoslovakia tomorrow'.[24] The French army mobilised and 1.5 million Czech soldiers manned the border with Germany. In Switzerland all the roads leading into the country from her neighbours were mined.

That evening it fell to the Prime Minister to update the House of Commons on the crisis. As Chamberlain was reaching the climax of an hour-long speech chronicling these events, he was handed a note. He read it in silence. He then turned again to the benches of the Commons, both to his own followers and to the Opposition. In response to a proposal from Mussolini, he announced, Hitler had agreed to postpone German mobilisation for twenty-four hours and to meet Chamberlain himself, Mussolini and Daladier in Munich. The Commons broke into uproar. The huge crowds assembled outside in Parliament Square wept with relief. A telegram arrived from the White House in Washington. It was worded simply, 'Good man! Franklin D. Roosevelt.' In Munich, it took only hours to agree the formal dismemberment of Czechoslovakia. Chamberlain, moreover, induced Hitler to sign a flimsy piece of paper declaring that Germany and Britain would never again engage in war. On his return to Heston he pulled this out of his pocket and told the crowds, 'Here is a paper that bears his name. It is peace for our time.'

This was Munich, but it would be better named Berchtesgaden. For it was at the Berghof that the Rubicon had been crossed. Here Chamberlain had embraced the belief that the sacrifice of Czechoslovakia could satisfy Hitler's demands. Thereafter, the dominoes fell. In Berchtesgaden the fate of Europe, and with it the Alps, was sealed. Hitler not unreasonably concluded that France and England would not stand in the way of his ambitions in eastern Europe. As Shirer summarised, 'From this surrender at Berchtesgaden, all else followed.'[25]

6

Having achieved his ambitions in Czechoslovakia, Hitler turned to the Polish question. An agreement created by Halifax for France and England to support Poland should she be invaded was regarded by Hitler as a dead letter. The Molotov–Ribbentrop Pact between the Reich and the Soviet Union signed on 23 August 1939 negated his concern of fighting a war on two fronts: Zweifrontkrieg. At dawn on Friday 1 September 1939 German troops invaded Poland.

Cicely Williams's family was on holiday in Zermatt, the Swiss resort catapulted into international fame by the tragedy that followed the first ascent of the Matterhorn by the Englishman Edward Whymper in 1865.

On Friday morning we wandered down to the station to get a paper – an excited little crowd was gathered round the kiosk. We got a copy of *La Suisse* and on the front page in thick black type we read a proclamation by the British Consul in Berne ordering all British tourists to leave by the night train – the last to leave Switzerland for the coast. This was a command that could not be ignored.[26]

Two days later, Chamberlain was forced to take to the airwaves once more to recant the bargain struck a year earlier in the Berchtesgadener Alps. The Anglo-French ultimatum to Hitler had been ignored. At 11.15 a.m. on 3 September Chamberlain told the nation:

This morning the British Ambassador in Berlin handed the German Government a final note stating that unless we heard from them by 11.00 a.m. that they were prepared at once to withdraw their troops from Poland, a state of war would exist between us. I have to tell you that no such undertaking has been received, and that consequently this country is at war with Germany.

This was the ultimate result of Chamberlain's trip to the Alps. The speech was the epitaph of appeasement and the epitaph of Plan Z. Europe was at war, and with Europe the Alps.

The Alps of Germany, Austria and Italy were already in thrall to fascism. Those to the east in Yugoslavia and to the west in

France now fell under the shadow of the Reich. As to Switzerland, the Alpinist Arnold Lunn – the son of Henry Lunn, who had done so much to create Swiss tourism – commented on the prospect with perhaps understandable partiality: 'Second only to the supreme horror of Hitler's evil face gloating over conquered London from the balcony of Buckingham Palace was the possibility that the swastika might fly from the roofs of Berne.'[27] For Lunn and many other lovers of the Alps, possibility was becoming probability. Certainty loomed. Cicely Williams recalled, 'On Sunday morning, September 3rd 1939, shortly after eleven o'clock, the general mobilisation call sounded in Zermatt.'

TWO

'I need a few thousand dead'

*I need a few thousand dead so as to be able to
attend the peace conference as a belligerent.*

BENITO MUSSOLINI

I

'When will it be Switzerland's turn?'[1] So asked William Shirer
nine months later on 13 May 1940. With his wife Tess living
in Geneva with the couple's daughter, the fall of the Alpine
republic to Hitler's forces was a matter of paramount personal
interest – not just high-octane copy for Ed Murrow. On 14 May
both the Swiss government itself and the Allied high command
at Vincennes in Paris assumed that the time had now come.
The invasion of the Alpine republic was imminent. That night,
General Henri Guisan, the sixty-five-year-old commander of the
Swiss army, issued orders telling his troops to expect the German
attack in the early hours of 15 May. Blitzkrieg, the mechanised
lightning war that the Wehrmacht* had practised so spectacularly
in Poland, was coming to the Alps.

Four days earlier, on 10 May 1940, forces under the commands
of Generalobersts Gerd von Rundstedt, Fedor von Bock and
Wilhelm Ritter von Leeb had finally executed Fall Gelb – Case
Yellow. Neutral Luxembourg and Belgium had been invaded to
outflank from the north the fixed defences on the border between
France and Germany. This was the eighty-seven-mile Maginot
Line of fortresses that ran from Luxembourg to Switzerland, and

---

* Wehrmacht is commonly used as the term for the German Army, but
actually means 'defence force' or 'armed forces'. When used in this latter
sense it covers all three armed services – Heer, Kriegsmarine and Luftwaffe
– but excludes the Waffen-SS.

by which the French set such store. Now, though, after the it helter-skelter of the first seventy-two hours, it seemed to General Maurice Gamelin in Vincennes that the Wehrmacht advance was faltering. At Hannut in Belgium on 12 and 13 May the French had inflicted a tactical victory on Generaloberst Erich Hoepner's XVI Panzer Corps. The following day this was repeated when Hoepner defied orders and again tried to break the French line. In the light of this reverse, Gamelin speculated that the next move of the German armed forces high command, the Oberkommando der Wehrmacht (OKW), would be an attack on Switzerland.

This fresh tactic would outflank not the northern but the southern end of the Maginot Line, and so reach France by the back door. The way to the Channel ports would then be open. Freiburg in Baden-Württemberg, just thirty miles north of the Swiss border at Basel, was the HQ of the German 7. Armee-oberkommando (Seventh Army). Swiss intelligence reports indicated a massive concentration of thirty German divisions of the Seventh on the northern banks of the Rhine where it forms the Swiss–German border. Landing craft were spotted further east along the border on the shores of Lake Constance. It was going to be Switzerland's Anschluss, the annexation to which her Alpine neighbour Austria had been subjected more than two years before.

Guisan had already mobilised 700,000 men, nearly one in five of the Swiss population. On 14 May many of his units were positioned on this northern frontier. Urs Schwarz was the commanding officer of an anti-aircraft battery at Olten in Canton Solothurn, just twenty miles south from the German–Swiss border at Basel:

As far as I could see when observing the officers and soldiers under my command, beneath their calm exterior was an excited expectation, coupled with a kind of incredulity. This was easy to understand in an army that had trained and trained, yet had never seen a war. Some of the men seemed to look forward to a real fight, some seemed to think that such a thing simply could not happen to us, but nobody looked scared.[2]

General Guisan was similarly phlegmatic. A nipped, jockey-like figure who often graced a horse, he came from Switzerland's French-speaking community in Canton Vaud. Originally a farmer, he had distinguished himself as a militia artilleryman, turning professional soldier in 1926. Thirteen years later in August 1939 he had been elected by the Swiss Federal Assembly to a position filled in Switzerland only in times of war. This was to obviate the regrettable tendency of the military to usurp civilian political power. His HQ was at Gümligen Castle close to the capital of Berne. Swiss intelligence had picked up a story that the castle was to be raided by German saboteurs. Removing himself to a nearby chateau, he had a final meeting with his Chief of Staff and the head of the intelligence service, Colonel Roger Masson. The prospect of the Wehrmacht attack was confirmed. The invasion was on. 'See you tomorrow,' Guisan remarked at this conclusion. 'Good night.'[3]

The following morning, 15 May 1940, the British Prime Minister was woken at 7.30 to take an early morning phone call by his bedside in 10 Downing Street. This was now Winston Churchill, who had replaced Neville Chamberlain as the country's leader just five days earlier. It was not General Guisan asking for help. It was a call entirely unexpected. It was Churchill's opposite number in France, Prime Minister Paul Reynaud. Churchill recorded, 'He spoke in English, and evidently under stress: "We have been defeated. We are beaten; we have lost the battle."'[4] Churchill was dumbfounded.

2

For Hitler, brooding over his maps in Berchtesgaden as his troops did battle in the Low Countries, Guisan's Switzerland was almost as tempting a plum as Reynaud's embattled France.

At a glance, this tiny Alpine country of 4.2 million people and 16,000 square miles – just half the size of Scotland – was beneath his notice. It was neither a potential source of Lebensraum for the 80-million-strong Reich nor, as in the case of France, a plentiful source of labour, raw materials and daily bread. Switzerland depended on her neighbours Italy and France for around three-quarters of her food and on Germany herself for energy. Without the Reich, Swiss lights would dim, her stoves grow cold, her factories close. Yet standing at the crossroads of Europe, sharing borders with France, Germany, Austria and Italy, the Alpine republic was a kingpin, a hub around which all Europe revolved. Critically, she cut off the northern European countries from the Mediterranean. She divided France from Austria and the Danube basin, and Germany from her Axis partner Italy. In the days when Autobahns were in their infancy, Switzerland's transalpine railway tunnels – principally the twelve-mile Simplon and the nine-mile St Gotthard – were the arteries of central Europe. Where the Alps divided, they united, forming the lifelines between the central European states. On 21 March 1938, in the aftermath of Anschluss, the Swiss Federal Council declared by way of a warning to Hitler that it was 'Switzerland's secular mission in Europe to guard the passage of the Alps in the interests of all'.[5]

This was hardly sufficient to discourage the Führer's ambition to unite all German-speaking peoples within the Grossdeutsches Reich. 'Common blood must belong to a common Reich,' he had declared on the first page of *Mein Kampf*. This had dictated Anschluss with Austria and the destruction of Czechoslovakia and Poland. In 1940 about two-thirds of Swiss spoke German, so the inference was obvious. Politically, too, Switzerland was distasteful. Whereas the Swiss and the English had much in common, for the Führer the Helvetic touchstones of democracy, freedom of expression, independence and co-operation between language groups were anathema. Switzerland also had a near world monopoly on the tiny jewel bearings used in the manufacture of watches and all sorts of precision instruments used by the military, particularly for aircraft navigation; she was the home of the state-of-the-art anti-aircraft gun manufacturer Oerlikon. These wares were prized both by the Reich and by the Allies. It was Hitler, though, who – naturally enough – was most concerned about Switzerland as a source of military intelligence placed at the disposal of the French and the British, principally concerning the Reich. All in all, Switzerland's very existence was an affront. To Mussolini and the Italian foreign minister Galeazzo Ciano, Hitler dismissed the Swiss as 'the most despicable and wretched people and national entity . . . mortal enemies of the new Germany'.[6]

A German plan for the invasion of Switzerland was circulated in the Swiss press as early as September 1933. The Swiss viewed Hitler's remilitarisation of the Rhineland in March 1936 with foreboding; Anschluss two years later in March 1938 with alarm. The cantons of St Gallen and Graubünden formed the Swiss frontier with western Austria. After Anschluss, the Reich was one step nearer. She was now on both Switzerland's northern and eastern doorsteps. On the day Hitler entered Vienna in March 1938, a statement endorsed by Hitler's Reich minister of propaganda Joseph Goebbels appeared in the *Frankfurter Zeitung*, 'No branch of the German race has the right or possibility of withdrawing from the common destiny of all Germans.'[7] Then the stout and strutting Luftwaffe chief Hermann Göring published a map of the Reich with Switzerland comfortably within her borders. Switzerland was just a province of the Reich, a Gau, to be ruled by a regional leader, a Gauleiter.

This was enough for the Swiss. They had begun rearming in 1933 when Germany withdrew from the League of Nations. After Anschluss military service was extended. The frontiers both with Italy and Austria were reinforced with new emplacements and pillbox fortifications. Munitions were brought up to various putative front lines. The Swiss gold reserves were removed from Zurich to vaults secreted in the high Alps in southern Switzerland near the St Gotthard Pass. Plans to mine the Simplon and St Gotthard tunnels as a means of deterring the German army's adventures were hatched: without the tunnels, Switzerland was not a conduit but a full stop. After Anschluss, these plans were repeatedly advertised to the Reich.

In the early days of Fall Gelb, with his forces thrusting through the supposedly impenetrable Ardennes into Belgium, Hitler thought Switzerland could wait. If the campaign were to falter, things might take quite a different turn. On the map of Europe so often used at the Berghof, Hitler could see easily enough that from Baden-Württemberg in the south-west of Germany, Swiss territory could be used as a short cut to Paris and the Channel ports. The Maginot Line barred the most direct route, and the forcing of the Ardennes was the northern way. The alternative route, through Switzerland, posed surprisingly few problems.

'And we are here as on a darkling plain . . . Where ignorant armies clash by night.' So sang Matthew Arnold, and plains are indeed fine for armies. Troops prefer a level playing field and their commanders favour terrain where they can observe and control their troops. Mountains are different, for they swing the balance dramatically in favour of the defender – or at least to those who hold the higher ground against an advance. Such forces can observe their attackers' movements with far greater ease and – perched on ridge or crest – they enjoy a far better field of fire. This in turn greatly diminishes the impact of any superiority of numbers. A small force can defeat a much larger one. The Swiss themselves instanced the Battle of Morgarten Pass in 1315, where 1,400 Swiss peasants ambushed 20,000 Habsburg knights in a narrow defile, decimating the knights at the cost of twelve Swiss. Mountain warfare also favours those with knowledge of all the ridges, passes, gullies, spurs, screes and buttresses that constitute a mountain system – the local understanding normally in the possession of the defenders alone. Up hill and down dale also set at naught the fast-moving mechanised warfare developed in the 1930s, partly by the Germans, partly the French. In mountains, to have was to hold.

Yet Switzerland was a country with her back rather than front to the Alps. Her southern and eastern frontiers with Italy and Austria were defined by Alpine ranges; so too was her south-western flank with France south of Geneva. To the north-west, though, the Rhine valley and the Jura provided relatively few obstacles to hostile armies. As to the north and north-east, where Switzerland had her frontier with Germany running from Basel to Lake Constance, here were the rolling plateaus that were perfect for the blitzkrieg motorised warfare practised to such effect by the Heer and the Luftwaffe. And here, too, were the principal Swiss cities of Basel itself, Zurich and the capital Berne.

So to a man like Hitler fluent in the language of maps, albeit those of a small scale, the Swiss northern frontier was porous. Should the thrust to the north of the main Maginot Line indeed falter, the Swiss excursion was a perfectly viable option. Bernard Biner was a guide in Zermatt, a friend of the Williams family who had holidayed in the resort for years. To the family he wrote in spring 1940 of the day when he met a boy at the Britannia Hut, a mountain refuge high above Zermatt's neighbour Saas-Fee. The lad had been sent up from the village with a notice of general mobilisation. 'Then the guardian of the hut told me that Holland and Belgium were invaded and that things were going badly for the Allies. Already people were beginning to talk of the invasion of Switzerland.'[8] Such, it seemed, was the explanation of the Seventh Army activity on the frontier spotted by the Swiss in mid-May 1940, and which caused such alarm.

Back in Berlin, on 14 May William Shirer was notified that the US government had advised Americans living in Switzerland to leave immediately. The League of Nations closed its Geneva offices. British Consul officials in Zurich burned all their files and fled the city. The British legation in Berne swept up its archives and headed west. Three British officials – Ena Molesworth, Richard Arnold-Baker and Marguerite Winsor – cycled all the way to Bordeaux. Tens of thousands of citizens of Basel, Schaff-hausen and Zurich piled their cars with household furniture and mattresses – a shield from aerial gunfire – and headed south to the safety of the mountains. Others rushed to the railways. It was less a retreat than a rout, a panic, an exodus and a flight.

Then a yet more disturbing rumour reached Swiss ears. The Swiss had long believed that Mussolini, the leader of their southern neighbour, did not see it in his interests to have the north of his country surrounded by the Reich. Italy, like France, could be relied on to help maintain the Swiss buffer. But now a tale that had first started to circulate in early May 1940 reached a crescendo. Italian mountain troops were massing on the Swiss border just south of Canton Ticino. It seemed that the country faced attack from all sides: the 80 million Germans and 43 million Italians against 4.2 million Swiss. While the Swiss army was dealing with the Wehrmacht in the north, the Italians would sneak in the back door. Switzerland was going to be gobbled up by the Axis.

In those grim mid-May days of 1940, Switzerland held its breath.

3

If Italy meant Mussolini and Rome, it also meant a good deal of the Alps. They formed Italy's border with Switzerland herself, France, Austria and Yugoslavia, a cap over the top of Italy's leg. They ran in an arc west to east from the Gulf of Genoa in the Ligurian Sea to just north of Trieste on the Adriatic. The western range bowled north from Nice to Mont Blanc, the central from the Brenner Pass into Austria via the Matterhorn, and the eastern from the Brenner to Trieste via the strange, sculpted limestone Dolomites.

For centuries these stone frontiers had provided a focus for national rivalries. The 15,761-foot Mont Blanc might have been the highest peak in western Europe but according to the Italians it was not French but Italian. It was Monte Bianco. The Swiss Matterhorn was Monte Cervino from the Italian side, and the 1865 cross-border race to make a first ascent had decidedly chauvinist overtones. Further east, the historical rivalry was between Italy and the Habsburg monarchy. Between May 1915 and November 1918, the 'white war' in the Dolomites claimed the lives of nearly three-quarters of a million Italians and around half that number of Austro-Hungarian troops. In 1919 the Treaty of Saint-Germain-en-Laye gave Italy some of the spoils due to the victor by way of Trieste, the Alpine provinces of Friuli and Trentino, and the German-speaking Alpine South Tyrol.

The latter became a bone of contention between Hitler and the man on whom the German leader modelled himself: Il Duce,

Benito Mussolini. It was Mussolini's march on Rome in October 1922 that had established the thirty-nine-year-old in power and inspired Hitler's failed Munich putsch of thirteen months later. Mussolini's Fascism also gave Hitler ideas like militaristic uniforms, the use of paramilitaries to perpetrate violence against political opponents, orchestrated rallies for propaganda purposes, pageantry, and the straight-armed Roman salute. The very word Duce meant leader or, in German, Führer. Both dictators also found the Russian Revolution a ready source of pleasingly illiberal ideas. When Galeazzo Ciano visited the Berghof in Berchtesgaden on 24 October 1936, Hitler tactfully declared, 'Mussolini is the leading statesman in the world to whom none may even remotely compare himself.'[9] This did not wash with the foreign minister, who was rabidly anti-German. Ciano's father-in-law, the bullet-headed Mussolini, was himself ambivalent about the newly muscular Germany. Germans generally he regarded as bullies and pederasts. Hitler's long-cherished and widely publicised ambition to reunite Austria and Germany would put the Reich on his doorstep. The recently acquired South Tyrol might follow into the maw.

When the pair of dictators first met in Venice in June 1934, Mussolini whispered to an aide: 'I don't like the look of him.'[10] Neither did he like the sound. Hitler subjected Mussolini to a tirade, talking without pause for an hour. The Führer left little opportunity for his Italian counterpart to vent his own well-rehearsed opinions. Mussolini complained to his Chief of General Staff, Pietro Badoglio, that 'Hitler was simply a gramophone with seven records, and that when he had played them all he began again at the beginning'.[11] His self-importance was outrageous. When Hitler's propaganda campaign for the reunification with Austria reached a peak in 1934, the Austrian chancellor, Engelbert Dollfuss, turned to Mussolini for help. On 25 July 1934, Austrian Nazis murdered Dollfuss, seized the Vienna Chancellery and attempted to proclaim a government under the Nazi Anton Rintelen. Mussolini massed his troops on the Brenner Pass that divided the North Tyrol from the contended

South Tyrol and formed the Austro-Italian border. His point was made. Hitler was obliged to repudiate his Austrian followers and the Catholic nationalist Kurt Schuschnigg became Austrian chancellor. Back down marched Il Duce's troops.

But when Britain poured cold water on Italy's colonial ambitions over Abyssinia in 1936, Mussolini was forced into Hitler's arms. The Rome–Berlin Axis was established on 25 October 1936. On the occasion of Anschluss in March 1938, Mussolini thought better of ordering his troops once again up to the top of the Brenner. It was this forbearance that elicited from Hitler the famous exclamation 'Tell Mussolini I shall never forget him for this, never, never, come what may.'[12] On 22 May 1939, Italy and Germany signed their military alliance, the Pact of Steel. In the general dismemberment of Europe Il Duce anticipated, he was greedy for the former Italian possession of Nice, France's second city of Lyons, the Italian-speaking Swiss canton of Ticino bordering on Italy, perhaps his north-eastern neighbour, Yugoslavia. Still, despite the Pact, Italy remained neutral when Hitler invaded Poland in September 1939 and Germany found herself at war with France and Britain. By the following spring it was apparent at least to Mussolini which way the wind was blowing.

On 13 May 1940, when Switzerland was believed to be on the point of an attack from the north by the Seventh Army, the rumour circulated the southern cantons of Switzerland like an avalanche. Mussolini's Alpine soldiers were coming up from Lombardy to invade the canton of Ticino and the city of Locarno on the verdant shores of Lake Maggiore. At two o'clock in the morning of 14 May 1940, the Swiss army contingent at Zermatt was turned out and ordered to patrol the passes from the Weisshorn to the Dent d'Hérens, the great peaks that marked the frontier, beyond which lay Italy.

Although such invasion plans certainly existed, Mussolini's thoughts were actually elsewhere. He had followed events in northern Europe from his headquarters in the Palazzo Venezia in

Rome with a mixture of admiration for the blistering triumphs of the Wehrmacht and a daily increasing concern that his place at the victor's banquet might not be laid. On 13 May 1940, Chief of General Staff Badoglio and Marshal Italo Balbo were called into Mussolini's office for a special audience. Badoglio recalled:

He did not speak at once and silently transfixed us with his penetrating stare. Finally he decided to speak and with an air of inspiration, he announced, 'I wish to tell you that yesterday I sent a messenger to Hitler with my written declaration that I do not intend to stand idly by with my hands in my pockets, and that after 5 June I am ready to declare war on England.'

When I was able to speak, I said, 'Your Excellency, you know perfectly well that we are absolutely unprepared. We have about twenty divisions with 70% of the necessary equipment and training; and about another twenty divisions with 50%. We have no tanks. The air force . . . is grounded. This is to say nothing of stores – we have not even sufficient shirts for the army. In such a state of affairs how is it possible to declare war? It is suicide.' Mussolini did not answer for a few minutes and then said quite calmly, 'I assume that the war will be over in September and that I need a few thousand dead so as to be able to attend the peace conference as a belligerent.'[13]

Badoglio then tottered across to the Ministry of Foreign Affairs to discuss the matter with Ciano, the foreign minister who cared so little for Germans, Hitler or a war. According to Badoglio, Ciano 'commented several times, "Mussolini is absolutely mad"'.[14] Nevertheless, four weeks later, Italy duly declared war on England and her ally France. President Roosevelt commented from Washington, 'On this tenth day of June 1940, the hand that held the dagger has struck it into the back of his neighbor.'[15]

England was a distant target for the Regia Aeronautica – the Italian Royal Air Force – which had been hastily declared airworthy. France was a different matter, for Italy shared with the Third Republic the Alpine border that ran north from the Riviera to Mont Blanc. Beyond the frontier in the south lay the prizes of Lyons and Nice. Here in the southern Alps were stationed two Italian armies under Prince General Umberto di Savoia. They supposedly numbered 700,000 in thirty-two divisions. These forces were ranged against just 35,000 French at the disposal of General René Olry. These were the remnants of the Armée des Alpes, much depleted by reinforcements sent to northern France and Norway. The result was surely a foregone conclusion.

4

Contrary to the supposition of both the Allied high command in Vincennes and the Swiss, by this time the thrust of Hitler's blitzkrieg forces in the Low Countries and France had entirely regained its momentum. It was just as Reynaud had told Churchill so early in the morning of 15 May. France was defeated.

After the spearhead of the 2nd Panzer Division had reached the Channel coast at Abbeville on 20 May, it turned north. There followed the deliverance of the British Expeditionary Force at Dunkirk, the collapse of the Weygand Line, the flight of the French government to Bordeaux, and the push into France by the Wehrmacht dubbed Fall Rot – Case Red. Paris fell on 14 June 1940, and the Maginot Line on the German border was gradually outflanked. On 16 June Generalleutnant Heinz Guderian's Panzers reached the Swiss border near Pontarlier, driving before them the French XLV Army Corps. On 19 June, the French requested permission to cross the Swiss border. Observing the Hague Convention, the Swiss complied. Forty-two thousand French and Polish soldiers – together with 5,000 horses – crossed the frontier into Canton Neuchâtel. There they were disarmed and interned. The sight of this bedraggled, bleeding and broken army did little for Swiss morale.

In the light of this devastating news from northern France, there seemed – at first glance – little prospect of General Olry's Armée des Alpes holding firm.

In the north, the fixed defences of the Maginot Line on the Franco-German border had simply been outflanked by the Wehrmacht. In the Alps, there was another line of fixed defences known as the Ligne Alpine or the Petit Ligne Maginot. This comprised a series of small forts or *ouvrages* – concrete strongpoints linked by tunnels. The largest of these, the *gros ouvrages*, were manned by between two and three hundred specialist fortress infantry: the Brigade Alpin de Forteresse. Unlike the more concentrated line of the Maginot further north, the forts were placed only where it was strictly necessary to defend: at the few passes in the Alpine wall that could be breached by an army. From the north downwards: Bourg-Saint-Maurice in the Tarentaise valley stood sentinel at the Little St Bernard Pass, Modane in the Maurienne defended the Mont Cenis, Briançon guarded the Col de Montgenèvre and the road up from Turin, and Barcelonnette the Col de Larche and the high road to Lyons. Close to Nice, where the Alpes-Maritimes dropped down towards the sea, the terrain was easier and the forts were more closely grouped: both to the north in the mountains and along the coastal road – and railway line – east to Italy.

This natural barrier, fortified by man, should have given Mussolini pause for thought. These *ouvrages* might be invested by highly trained mountain troops like the Wehrmacht's Gebirgs-jäger, not by a regular army. Moreover, despite their huge numerical advantage over the French, the Italian armoured units were equipped with light tanks entirely ill-suited to the terrain. Finally, although the Italians did have shirts, most had just thin summer uniforms. Some had cardboard shoes. Only the Alpini mountain specialists were actually equipped for fighting in the Alps. It was high summer, but in the Alps even in high summer it can snow and it can also rain.

It was in the Italians' favour that because of the local idio-syncrasies of the terrain there were a number of places where their positions overlooked those of the French. Towards the northern end of the Ligne Alpine the medieval walled town of Briançon on the road to Grenoble in the Dauphiné was threatened by Fort Chaberton, built on the very peak of Mont Chaberton's 10,272-foot summit. Its battery of eight turreted guns was often wreathed in clouds. It was here that on 17 June the Italian fort, manned by units of the Fourth Army, opened fire on the defending *ouvrage* of Fort de l'Olive, garrisoned by the French XVI Corps. On the same day, General Bertin's II Army Corps ventured a series of probing patrols across the Col de Larche. They were met with heavy fire from the French Roche la Croix *ouvrage*. Right at the north of the line, the Little St Bernard Pass was defended by the deceptively named Redoute Ruinée. It was manned by just forty-seven men under the command of the bespectacled Sous-Lieutenant Henri Desserteaux. The Italians here had some success before Desserteaux's men found their range.

A young French mountain soldier gave a sense of the strangeness of the conflict in the high Alpine world:

I remember one night in June 1940, standing on watch at an altitude of 7,500 feet with the thermometer at 16 degrees Fahrenheit; the wind was blowing wildly through the pass and there was an infinite void on both sides of the ridge. Below me, four square yards of snow and rocks; in front of me, beyond my Tommy gun, a desert of ice, where, in the deceptive light of the moon, each crevasse looked like a man advancing towards me. With ice-cold hands, a flask of brandy inside my anorak and my feet tight with cold inside boots that were too wide for me, I was longing for dawn while peering into the night. The slightest touch of my finger on the trigger would have started a roar of gun-fire in every direction.[16]

To the south of the Line in the foothills of the Alpes-Maritimes, the campaign was no more fruitful. Here, where the Italian First Army was facing the French XV Corps, the Italian Cosseria Division began advancing along the Riviera coastal road from just beyond the border at Ventimiglia. The Italians came under fire from the *ouvrage* Cap Martin, garrisoned by the 96th Brigade Alpin de Forteresse. In the next few days the 96th Brigade repelled without much difficulty the probing patrols of the Italian First Army. Indeed, so slow was progress that General Umberto was obliged to turn to the Germans for help. General-oberst Erich Hoepner's XVI Panzer Corps – survivors of the Battle of Hannut – was advancing south down the Rhône valley towards Lyons. They were ordered by OKW to advance with all speed to engage General Olry's forces from the rear.

*

For Mussolini, who less than a month before had appointed himself Italy's Supreme Commander of the Armed Forces, this was not the blitzkrieg he had envisaged. Neither was it a report he relished making to Hitler when the pair met on 18 June 1940, in Munich. The performance of his forces was belittled by the Wehrmacht in the north of France. Hitler refused his request to jointly discuss the terms of the forthcoming armistice with the French, or the idea that the Italians should be entitled to the Rhône valley as their share of the spoils. Ciano recorded in his diary that Mussolini left the meeting 'very much embarrassed'.[17] To relieve his feelings the Duce tersely ordered General Umberto to redouble the efforts in the Alps.

So in the north came fresh attacks right up to the Little St Bernard. On 19 and 20 June the Assietta Division was making slow progress towards the French lines in Briançon. The French responded by bringing up the mortars of the 154th Position Artillery Regiment. On 21 June these knocked out seven of the eight turrets of Fort Chaberton. On the Col de Larche, a series of advances between 20 and 22 June produced heavy Italian casualties and the retreat of the Acqui Division to whence it came. Then came snow. Not terribly unusual for the time of year but unusually heavy. It had to be cleared to allow firing positions to be used, and the ill-equipped Italians suffered from frostbite.

In the south, the weather was also appalling: thick mist, snow above the snow line, heavy rain below. On 20 June, infantry of the Cosseria Division on the south coast attempted a frontal assault on the Casemate du Pont St Louis outside Menton. This was manned by Sous-Lieutenant Piedfort and eight others, armed with just a 37 mm anti-tank gun and twin machine guns. The Italians were driven back by the tiny garrison of the casemate itself and by covering fire from the main *ouvrage* at Cap Martin and two adjoining *ouvrages* at Saint-Agnès and Mont Agel. The following day the Italians called up air support and an armoured train. This damaged one of Cap Martin's 75 mm guns. On 24 June two more armoured trains were brought in support. The Italian infantry infiltrated above the casemate – failing to take it – and managed to capture the Riviera resort of Menton. Italian units also reached Cap Martin, but were forced to retreat by French artillery.

At the same time, events further north took a decisive turn. In the immediate vicinity of the fighting, Hoepner's XVI Panzer Corps had now advanced lower down the Rhône valley and was beginning to outflank Olry's forces, forcing the French general to face two ways at once. On 19 June, Hoepner's 13th Motorised bridged the Rhône at Lyons and headed east into the mountains towards Annecy, Aix-les-Bains, and Grenoble. Olry's forces blew up all the bridges across the Isère river which barred the way to Grenoble. Further away in northern France, with Paris in the hands of the Nazis, on 22 June the armistice was signed between the French and the Germans at Compiègne. This in turn prompted the French to come to terms with the Italians. Further resistance was clearly futile.

At 7.35 p.m. on 24 June in Olgiata, near Rome, the second armistice was signed. When it came into effect six hours later, the French tricolour was still flying above Sous-Lieutenant Piedfort and his eight men at the casemate at Pont St Louis and – in the northern section of the Line – Sous-Lieutenant Desserteaux and his forty-seven men in the Redoute Ruinée. The Petit Maginot Line had held. The English painter Neville Lytton was living in a village just north of Lyons. He remembered the return of the French troops. 'Those who came from the Italian front had their tails right up. They said, "Why were we not allowed to go for these macaronis? We would have made one mouthful of them. If we had been allowed to attack, we should by now have been half-way to Rome."[18]

Mussolini had hoped for 'a few thousand dead'. Here he was disappointed. Only 631 Italians were killed. Still, with another 616 missing, 2,361 wounded and more than 2,000 cases of frostbite, the Italian tally was not so bad after all. On the other hand, General Umberto's forces had hardly covered themselves in glory. Ciano commented, 'Mussolini . . . is quite humiliated because our troops have not made a step forward.'[19] Churchill's verdict was that 'the French Army on the south-eastern borders saved its honour'.[20] Certainly the terms of the armistice granted Mussolini only the French territory his three-quarters of a million troops had managed to capture from 35,000 French, together with a modest demilitarised zone imposed on the French side of the Alpine border. It was not blitzkrieg, barely a victory.

5

France had fallen, and with it the Third Republic; yet Switzerland was still unscathed.

On the night of 14–15 May when the invasion had been expected, General Guisan's slumbers went undisturbed. So too on subsequent nights. For the massing of the Seventh Army on the Swiss border turned out to be a feint. By day, the troops were marched up to the Swiss border, where they were all too visible. By night, the very same troops were marched straight back again – quite unseen. The following day the exercise was repeated. The impression was of an army moving south to cut through Switzerland to outflank the southern end of the Maginot Line. The Swiss thought they were about to be invaded. The French drew precisely the conclusion intended by OKW, that they should reinforce their southern flank. This they duly did with nineteen divisions sorely needed in the north around the Meuse. Meanwhile, the units of Kleist and Guderian attacked in the north around Sedan, crossed to the west bank of the Meuse and opened the way to the Channel. The northern border with Switzerland was left untouched. So, too, was the southern frontier between Canton Ticino and the Italian province of Lombardy. Mussolini's energies were focused further south in the Alps.

Yet for the Swiss, the situation was still dire. The Fall of France left the country a democratic oasis in a fascist desert. On 4 July 1940 Shirer was visiting his family in Geneva and took the opportunity to gauge Swiss opinion:

They see their situation as pretty hopeless, surrounded as they are by the victorious totalitarians, from whom henceforth they must beg facilities for bringing in their food and other supplies. None have any illusions of the kind of treatment they will get from the dictators . . .

now that France has completely collapsed and Germany and Italy surround Switzerland, a military struggle in self-defence is hopeless.

Mont Blanc from the quay today was magnificent, its snow pink in the afternoon sun.[21]

This pessimism was understandable. The Wehrmacht, revelling in victory, was at the height of its powers. In six weeks it had accomplished what the Kaiser had failed to achieve in four years. On 18 June 1940 there was a thanksgiving service held in Notre Dame Cathedral in Paris. The following day a victory parade was staged on the Brandenburger Tor in Berlin. It was the first such parade since 1871 when the Second French Empire had been defeated and the Second German Reich founded. On 24 June, the day the armistice between the French and Italians was signed, Swiss intelligence reported that Hitler had once again discussed the invasion of Switzerland with Göring, Keitel, Ribbentrop, Hess (Hitler's deputy) and Goebbels. The following day a new plan for the invasion of Switzerland was drafted by the OKW staffer Captain Otto Wilhelm von Menges. Operation Tannenbaum – Christmas Tree – envisaged a pincer movement between the Germans in the north and the Italians in the south. It was just as the Swiss had feared in May.

This was also the momentous day on which the Swiss federal president, Marcel Pilet-Golaz, addressed the Swiss nation. The fifty-year-old was a bureaucrat who had made his name putting the Swiss railways in order. Affairs of state were less his *métier*. He sported a toothbrush moustache, reminiscent of Hitler's, and his tone, if not his precise message, was clear. 'The time for inner renewal has come. We must look forward, determined to use our modest but useful strength in the reconstruction of the world in the state of upheaval.'[22] The Swiss took this to mean they should accept the New Order in Europe. Henceforth, the country would be a satellite of the Third Reich. The President told the government that Switzerland should seek a pretext for breaking off diplomatic relations with Great Britain so as to facilitate an accommodation with the Reich.

Europe's New Order had arrived in the Alps.

THREE

Triumph of the Will

*'These are not dark days; these are great days – the
greatest days our country has ever lived'*
WINSTON CHURCHILL

I

On 13 July 1940 Hitler was once again entertaining at the
Berghof. In addition to the generals whose exploits since the
spring had so dazzled the world, he was attended by the head
of the Kriegsmarine, Grossadmiral Erich Raeder. It was high
summer in Berchtesgadener Land, and the Alps were perhaps
at their most enchanting. Though the May flowers were over,
the scent of mown hay wafted up from the meadows below the
Berghof, there were drinks on the terrace overlooking Berchtesgaden under shady parasols and – beyond – the glories of the
Untersberg tomb where Barbarossa dozed, vying for attention
with Eva Braun in her summer dirndls. The skylarks sang. For
Hitler, too, the world might have seemed at his feet. Poland,
Norway, Denmark – now Belgium, Luxembourg, Holland and
France – had fallen to his forces. Russia, Italy, Spain, Bulgaria
and Hungary had come to terms that were largely his own. Of
England, Churchill would say of this July tsunami in European
history, 'We were done, almost disarmed, with triumphant
Germany and Italy at our throats, with the whole of Europe
open to Hitler's powers.'[1] For William Shirer, too, in Berlin, there
was a sense of finality: 'As I recall those summer days, everyone,
especially in the Wilhelmstrasse and the Bendlerstrasse, was
confident that the war was as good as over.'[2] Soon the generals
were taking wagers with him on when the swastika would be
flying over Trafalgar Square.

Paradoxically, the warlords in their summer uniforms – the heavyweight Göring in pearl grey – at the Berghof found Hitler bemused and frustrated. Contrary to the forces of destiny shaping the new European order, two leaders with a combined age of 132 were defying his wrath and steel by attempting to rally their peoples to resist the onward march of the Reich: Winston Churchill in England and Henri Guisan in Switzerland.

The Führer had assumed that once France fell, England would have no appetite to continue the struggle. On 1 July 1940 he had remarked to the Italian ambassador in Berlin that he 'could not conceive of anyone in England still seriously believing in victory'.[3] Five weeks earlier on 20 May when Guderian's Panzer spearheads had reached Abbeville on the Channel coast, Hitler had begun drafting a peace treaty with England. It was a labour of love, for the Führer was a great admirer of the British Empire. Daily in the last two weeks of June and in the early days of July he had expected a dove from Whitehall. Instead, all he got was an eagle. Nothing had changed since 4 June, when Churchill had spoken at length to the House of Commons – later to the nation – of the country's desperate plight. He had summed up by saying,

We shall not flag or fail. We shall go on to the end, we shall fight in France, we shall fight on the seas and oceans, we shall fight with growing confidence and growing strength in the air, we shall defend our Island, whatever the cost may be, we shall fight on the beaches, we shall fight on the landing grounds, we shall fight in the fields and in the streets, we shall fight in the hills; we shall never surrender.[4]

Hitler, second only to Churchill as an orator, doubtless appreciated the technical merits of the speech, the Prime Minister's flair, chutzpah and showmanship, irrespective of its unpalatable contents. By 11 July, when Grossadmiral Raeder arrived in Berchtesgaden, it was nevertheless beginning to dawn on the Führer that the British Prime Minister meant what he said. The Admiral had been summoned to Obersalzberg to counsel on ferrying the land forces to England's beaches to do battle. His colleague, Army Chief of Staff Generaloberst Franz Halder, arrived with his senior staff a couple of days later to advise – amongst other things – on the implications of the more equivocal policies of Switzerland. The Swiss people had been much stirred by Churchill's speech. It had been reported in the republic and was echoed by Guisan himself in various speeches and orders, much to the annoyance of Hitler. Then, on 25 June, had come Federal President Marcel Pilet-Golaz's speech which preached accommodation, indeed hinted of collaboration. Just what were the Swiss up to?

On these two matters and many others – not least Operation Barbarossa in the east – Hitler's advisers advised. Raeder believed the invasion of England was neither desirable nor practicable. He thought the British could be made to come to heel by a U-boat blockade of their merchant shipping and by letting loose the Luftwaffe both on their Atlantic convoys and on their industrial heartland. Hitler wavered. It was lamentable that the matter had not been properly considered by OKW beforehand. As to the Swiss, they were a pimple on the face of Europe. Hitler pondered. When the meeting broke up on 13 July 1940 he wrote testily to Mussolini declining the Duce's considerate proposal of Italian help for the invasion of England. 'I have made to Britain so many offers of agreement, even of co-operation, and have been treated so shabbily that I am now convinced that any new appeal to reason would meet with a similar rejection. For in that country at present it is not reason that rules.'[5] By 16 July the Führer's mind was made up. On that day he issued Directive No. 16, 'on the Preparation of a Landing Operation Against England'. He had finally registered Britain's will to resist and acknowledged Churchill's 18 June Commons statement of the country's 'inflexible resolve to continue the war'. Unternehmen Seelöwe (Operation Sea Lion), the invasion of England, was put in hand, and with it the requirement for the Luftwaffe to clear the skies of the RAF. The Battle of Britain – for Hermann Göring Operation Eagle (Adlerangriffe) – was at hand. In the time he could spare from building up a collection of the artistic treasures of Europe that he hoped would rival that of the Louvre, the fat man of the German air force would direct the destruction of its British counterpart, the RAF.

On the other matter of the invasion of Switzerland, Hitler remained ambivalent. Would the adherents of Pilet-Golaz or those of General Guisan hold sway? Switzerland was clearly divided. Invasions were a troublesome and uncertain business, greedy of blood and treasure. If the Swiss President triumphed, it might save the Wehrmacht a good deal. He had already rescinded the ban on Nazi newspapers and released interned Luftwaffe aircrew. In the case of both countries, Hitler was mindful that invasion was a seasonal sport. Snow in the Alps and storms in the Channel made winter the closed season.

With that thought, the warlords departed the sunny Berghof and made their way back to Berlin.

2

So to Davos, where lay the seeds of President Pilet-Golaz's speech of two weeks earlier.

Davos was 230 miles south-west of the Berghof. It was a 5,120-foot resort in the Canton Graubünden in the south-east of Switzerland – right on the Italian and Austrian borders. It had established itself in the 1870s for the 'Alpine cure'. The resort's high valley set crosswise against the prevailing winds created a remarkably dry microclimate that proved a prophylactic against, sometimes even a cure for, tuberculosis. Drawn by this reputation, it had been patronised by scores of prominent writers including A. J. A. Symons, Robert Louis Stevenson, Erich Maria Remarque, Thomas Mann, Erich Kästner and Arthur Conan Doyle. It was Doyle who introduced skis to Davos in 1895, the author prophetically remarking that 'I am convinced the time will come when hundreds of Englishmen will come to Switzerland for the skiing season between March and April.'[6] By the twenties his dreams had come true, and Davos had added to the tuberculosis sanatoria in which it abounded the facilities of an international skiing resort. In the early thirties Davos was one of the first resorts to pioneer cable railways – Seilbahnen – for hauling skiers up the slopes of the Jakobshorn, Weissfluhjoch and the Parsenn. Hitherto they had climbed. Less creditably, at much the same time the resort had become the centre of the Nazi Party in Switzerland.

It would have been strange if the Swiss had been entirely deaf to the call of National Socialism. The economic crisis epitomised by the Wall Street Crash of October 1929, in Europe by the collapse of the Weimar Republic, reduced Swiss exports over the next five years by two-thirds. In 1936, in England the year of the Jarrow March, in the United States of the second New Deal, there was in Switzerland similarly drastic unemployment – 13.2 per cent. The Schweizerische Nationalbank (SNB) devalued the franc by 30 per cent and wages plummeted. All this caused unrest. Switzerland, traditionally liberal though she was, could not entirely rise above the tide of belief that parliamentary government had been foisted on central Europe as a result of defeat in the Great War; that the political and social order so clearly absent in – say – Weimar Germany and in the young Austrian republic could only be restored by the single-minded and autocratic state. Postwar Switzerland was very different – much more stable – from her immediate neighbours, fractious places that teetered on the brink of revolution; yet she was not an island. As the largest language group in Switzerland was German, the Swiss could also hardly avoid the story of the rise of Hitler and its implications.

Hitler's policy from the beginning of his ten-year rampage was always to attack both from without and within: in Austria, Czechoslovakia, the Sudetenland and Danzig he had fomented internal unrest and then used this as a pretext for intervention. So too in Switzerland. Fascism had taken root here as early as 1918 with the foundation of the Schweizerischer Vaterländischer Verband – the Switzerland Fatherland Association or SVV. By the 1930s more than thirty-six fascist 'fronts' were established, all enthusiasts to a lesser or greater degree for the Reich's National Socialism. Their membership was around 40,000. According to the Simon Wiesenthal Center, 'Few other countries have had such a great number of extreme right-wing associations per capita and size of their geographical territory as had Switzerland during the Hitlerian era.'[7] They were festering in Basel, Geneva,

Lausanne, Montreux, Zurich, Schaffhausen and the capital Berne – in all the major centres of industry and population in Switzerland's twenty-one cantons. They were also in the high Alps: in Interlaken in the Bernese Oberland, in Leysin in Canton Vaud, together with Arosa, St Moritz and Davos itself in Canton Graubünden.

Amongst these fronts was the Swiss branch of the Nazi Party for German residents in the country – the Landesgruppe Switzerland. It had been founded in 1932 by a German, Wilhelm Gustloff, whose wife Hedwig had once apparently been Hitler's secretary. Born in Schwerin in Mecklenburg in 1895, Gustloff had moved to Davos in 1917 as a tuberculosis patient, joining the large (four-figure) German colony in the resort. He was less an adherent of the Nazi movement than a fanatic, once remarking brightly to his doctor, 'I would murder my wife if Hitler commanded.'[8] Hedwig's response is not recorded. All the Swiss branches of the Nazi Party paid homage to Davos, and it was tasked by Berlin to agitate for Anschluss with the Reich. Soon Gustloff was working as a meteorologist. In the time he could spare from keeping an eye on the weather – like St Moritz, Davos was a very good place for winter sun – Gustloff staged debates, organised cultural programmes and screened Goebbels's propaganda films. These included Leni Riefenstahl's 1935 *Triumph des Willens*, her lyrical chronicle of the Nazi congress in Nuremberg. Gustloff also inflamed anti-Semitism by energetically distributing *The Protocols of the Elders of Zion*, the fabrication that purported to be a plan for Jewish global domination.

Then, on 4 February 1936 – right at the height of the skiing season – Gustloff received a visitor in his apartment in Davos Platz. The door was opened by Frau Gustloff, the caller announcing himself as David Frankfurter. As her husband was on the phone in the corridor, Hedwig Gustloff asked Frankfurter to wait. He took a seat. When Gustloff hung up, Frankfurter rose to his feet, produced a small 6.35 mm pistol, aimed it at him and pulled the trigger. It failed once before wounding Gustloff fatally in the neck and chest. Frankfurter, a twenty-seven-year-old Jew from Daruvar in Yugoslavia who was studying medicine in Berne, then thought better of his notion of turning the gun on himself. Instead he surrendered himself to the police. He acted, he later said, to 'avenge persecution of Jews in Germany'.[9]

The assassination at once became an international cause célèbre. On 11 February 1936 a special train took Gustloff's body on a progress from Davos back to Schwerin via Stuttgart, Würzburg, Erfurt, Halle, Magdeburg and Wittenberg. The state funeral the following day was attended by the galaxy of Goebbels, Göring, Himmler, Bormann, Ribbentrop and Hitler. The Führer himself gave the funeral oration: 'behind every murder stood the same power which is responsible for this murder . . . the hate-filled power of our Jewish foe, a foe to whom we have done no harm, but who nonetheless sought to subjugate the German people and make of it its slave'.[10] Gustloff became a Blutzeuge, a martyr, for the Nazis. Reichsminister Goebbels pressed for the death sentence for Frankfurter, at the time proscribed in Switzerland. Put on trial on 9 December 1936 in Canton Graubünden's capital of Chur, the assassin was sentenced to the maximum possible term of eighteen years in jail.

The assassination of Gustloff crystallised the choices facing the Swiss people. The Federal Council had already taken the opportunity – on 18 February 1936 – to ban the Swiss Nazi Party. Yet the government could scarcely control the influence of its pernicious neighbour, not least because of the readership in Switzerland of the German press, and because of what the British post-war Prime Minister Harold Macmillan supposedly called 'Events, dear boy, events'. After all, some of the Swiss found there was something to admire in Germany's economic renaissance under Hitler; even in Hitler's legerdemain in acquiring the Rhineland, Austria, and the Sudetenland without a shot – or not too many shots anyway – being fired. After war was declared and the events of the autumn of 1939 unfolded with the Sitzkrieg (for the British, the 'Phoney War'), the following year with Operation Weserübung and the fall of Denmark and

Norway, Fall Gelb and Fall Rot, a sense of fatalism had emerged in the Swiss people. As her great neighbours fell to the Reich, as she was hemmed in on all sides by the fascists, even the staunchest critics of the Nazis began to wonder what point there was in resistance. As the confidence of the German community in Davos and elsewhere grew with each Reich victory, so too did Swiss morale fall. The conundrum for the villagers was whether to prepare for resistance or inevitable defeat.[11]

This was precisely the issue faced by Federal President Marcel Pilet-Golaz, and exactly the issue he addressed in his speech to the Swiss nation on 25 June 1940.

3

It was fortunate that General Henri Guisan, though by training a soldier, was by instinct a politician.

No sooner had Guisan heard Pilet-Golaz's speech than he seized his pen. The following day – it was 26 June 1940 – the Federal Council received the General's request to confirm that his mission remained as originally drafted on the occasion of his appointment ten months previously: 'de sauvegarder l'indépendance du Pays et de maintenir l'intégrité du territoire'.[12] This adeptly put the equivocators on the defensive. It was a question that they could not judiciously answer no. The consequences would have been Guisan's resignation, a loss the Council knew that neither country nor Council could afford. Early on the evening of 4 July a courier arrived at Guisan's Gümligen Castle HQ bearing a letter. It was the Council's necessary affirmation. The General smiled. He now had the laissez-passer to a radical plan. This he had been incubating since his appointment, and had been brought to fruition as Reynaud's and Weygand's France collapsed. It was for the Alpenfestung, the Réduit National for the country's speakers of French, or for the many Anglophiles the Alpine Redoubt.

There was little that was entirely novel about the idea, but the implications of the Redoubt strategy were explosive, and its ultimate manifestation breathtaking.

*

When Guisan was appointed Commander-in-Chief of Swiss forces on 30 August 1939 he was astounded to discover that there existed no overall plan for Switzerland's defence. Not a draft of any nature, nor any contingency plans for the likelihood of a German invasion – let alone one from Italy in the south; conceivably an attack from France to the west. There was no systematic doctrine manifested in a pattern of defence, tank traps, machine-gun nests, pillboxes, earthworks or strongpoints. In terms of armament there was a collection of nineteenth-century 84 mm and 120 mm museum pieces, together with – in all – eight antiquated and thirty-four modern Oerlikon anti-aircraft guns. In the dawning age of motorised warfare, the Swiss army boasted 50,000 horses borrowed from the civilian population, and the facility to requisition civilian motorised transport. Contemporary photographs show small pieces of field artillery towed by taxis. The Swiss professional army amounted to a fraction of the total of around 500,000. Of this militia, the Elite were aged between twenty and thirty-six, the Reserve thirty-six and forty-eight, the Home Guard forty-eight and sixty. They were good marksmen, for tradition maintained that each man kept his arms at home and practised regularly. These were the tools with which Guisan was to fight the blitzkrieg.

The events of May and June 1940, of Fall Gelb and Fall Rot and the spinelessness of Marshal Pétain, showed Guisan all too clearly the fragility of his position. It was natural enough for a country to defend its own borders. Yet despite the Maginot Line, France had discovered that its frontiers were indefensible to the Wehrmacht's combination of infantry supported by a motorised army and the Luftwaffe. Given that Switzerland's northern frontier with Germany was at least as porous as that of France, Guisan realised that it was similarly impossible to defend. He noted the aphorism of Frederick the Great: 'He who defends everything defends nothing.'

So Guisan's first move as the country's military leader was to withdraw troops from the 1,200-mile border to any feature of the terrain that could be an ally. A river, canal, lake, wood, hill

– or indeed a mountain. Yet if May 1940 had lowered his hopes, June in some respects raised them. On the Franco-Italian Alpine border he had been given the clearest conceivable demonstration of Switzerland's salvation. His staff summarised the French performance in the Alps: 'Un chef décidé, des troupes de qualité, un terrain alpestre extrêmement bien fortifié, une météorologie détestable, sont parvenus à arrêter un ennemi.'[13] The Alps were indeed the country's natural – as opposed to political – frontiers. They constituted a lozenge-shaped block dropping down to the Italian border from a line heading north-east-east from the eastern tip of Lake Geneva to the eastern end of Lake Zurich. This was an area intrinsically defensible – and indeed had been long recognised as such before the heady days of Stukas and Panzers. It was akin to England, a fortress built by Nature for herself.

Like the Alps on the Franco-Italian border, the Swiss massif needed additional fortification only at the doors into the higher ground: the passes. For such purposes, fortresses had been constructed in the last quarter of the nineteenth century. They guarded the St Gotthard railway, the Oberalp, and the Furka and Grimsel passes in the central Alps. Guisan's plan – developed in a series of meetings with his general staff as France was falling – was to lightly defend the border and more heavily defend what he called the army line. This ran from west to east in the middle of the country, following natural features of the terrain. These positions were merely to delay the invading force sufficiently to allow the main body of the army to retreat to the Alps. It was a strategy that attracted the name Verzögerungskrieg or delaying war. Beyond would be established an impregnable zone in the high Alps. There – as both the Swiss and the Germans recognised – the defending force would be a much tougher nut to crack. The army would also control the country's key strategic assets of the St Gotthard and Simplon transalpine railway tunnels. In their absence – should they be mined – the incentive to invade evaporated.

However, the Redoubt strategy had profound implications. On the day on which the German–French armistice came into effect, Guisan met with members of his general staff to finalise the strategy. Later he wrote, 'I had to be clear now . . . to what extreme degrees we must be prepared for all possible consequences of the reduit policy'.[14]

4

The most obvious of these was logistical. The framework or infrastructure of the Redoubt was already – albeit very lightly – in place. It took the form of three great fortresses at the perimeter of the massif: at Sargans in Canton St Gallen in the east in the Rhine valley; at St Gotthard in the south on the main route between Zurich and Milan; and at St Maurice in the far west, guarding the entrance to the upper Rhône valley. St Gotthard – Fort Airolo – dated from 1887; St Maurice – the subterranean Fort Dailly – was started in 1892; Sargans was begun in the immediate aftermath of Anschluss in the late spring of 1938. Each was designed for a garrison of about 1,000 soldiers, and had to be duly stockpiled with victuals and ammunition.

These, though, were merely the foundations of a ring of citadels that would need to be built on the fringes of the Redoubt. At this stage Guisan's staff could not detail what would be required. They had an agreed outline and the three key fortresses. Until a survey had been completed, it was impossible to say precisely what strongpoints would be required where. In the end, the *réduit* would comprise no fewer than seventy medium-sized fortresses and around 10,000 smaller bunkers, command posts, observation positions and pillboxes. One of the medium emplacements – the Vitznau Artillery – was quarried into the side of 5,896-foot Mount Rigi, overlooking Lake Lucerne and the Rütli meadow. As the *New York Times* reported in 1999 when – for the first time – this swarm of secret emplacements was thrown open to the public, 'It has a kitchen, with spotlessly clean oversized pots and pans to feed large numbers, an infirmary, toilets modern by 1940 standards and separate sleeping quarters for officers. It also has a radio room, war room, huge water tank, disinfection area in case of a chemical attack, generator, ammunition storage areas and two 105-millimeter cannons.'[15]

As the French discovered when building the Maginot Line, a chain on a comparable scale to the Swiss redoubt, emplacements like these were immensely greedy of resources. The Maginot Line cost 2–3 billion French francs, and took nine years to construct. If it was to be of any value to the Swiss, their own Redoubt needed to be completed in months not years. It also needed to be constructed in secret so that the precise location of the emplacements was hidden. Arthur Joller was a boy at the time of the construction of the Vitznau Artillery. 'When I was young we would hear dynamite, and we'd see the earth move down from the mountains. The work was always guarded, and we never dared come. It was absolutely forbidden.' When construction was completed, the fortresses still needed to be concealed. Festung Gütsch on the Oberalp Pass had its turrets camouflaged as boulders. At Magletsch in Canton St Gallen the fort dug into the mountainside had its 105 mm gun turrets disguised as Alpine chalets. There was also a story – unverified – about an airstrip built into a mountain face with an opening in the rock large enough for planes to fly in and fly out. Time, materials, skill, men, money were needed just to build the redoubt, let alone provide it with a stockpile of war materiel and food for the fortress guard corps – the Festungswachtkorps. According to some estimates the cost in today's terms was $13 billion. All this in a country of 4.2 million souls. It was as though Switzerland had planned to put a man on the moon.

The second problem was also logistical in one sense, but human and political too. There was every logic in Guisan and the army defending only what could be defended. Yet it meant leaving to the good offices and tender mercies of the Nazis all the country's major cities – Zurich, Geneva, Basel, Berne, Lausanne, Winterthur, St Gallen, Lucerne and Lugano. That is, the vast majority of the country's industrial assets, and just about four-fifths of her population. It was as if the British army had proposed, in the face of Operation Sea Lion, withdrawing to the Scottish Highlands and so leaving London, Manchester, Birmingham, Leeds, Sheffield and Bristol to fend for themselves. In a sense, this was a counsel of despair that might reasonably have been expected to have fallen on stony ground with the country's politicians and the public.

Guisan judiciously described the Redoubt to his political masters less as a practical strategy than as a deterrent. Rather like the Western nuclear deterrent in the Cold War, if the strategy had been executed it would already have failed. As Guisan put it to the Federal Council on 12 July, just as Hitler, Raeder and Halder were meeting at the sunny Berghof:

Switzerland cannot escape the threat of a direct German attack unless the German high command, while preparing such an attack, becomes convinced that a war against us would be long and expensive, would uselessly and dangerously create a new battleground in the heart of Europe, and this would jeopardize the execution of its other plans . . . If we must be dragged into this struggle, we will sell our skins as dearly as possible.[16]

The Federal Council was duly persuaded of this argument. On 17 July 1940, it gave its stamp of approval.

Here again Guisan was adroit. The plan was presented not as his own but as the brainchild of the head of the Military Department, Rudolf Minger. The equivalent of Britain's secretary of state for defence was well regarded by the six other members of the Federal Council. They were reluctant to gainsay a senior colleague. They might well have contradicted a mere soldier. Whether even the Council was aware of the full implications of the plan is still not clear, even today.

The public of course could not be kept ignorant of the strategy, for its essence was that it was a deterrent of which the Germans were made entirely aware and of which they were constantly reminded. Guisan was far from insensitive to this issue and to the point that the army itself needed persuading. What exactly would his men be fighting for in the Redoubt if their wives and daughters in Zurich, Basel and Schaffhausen were already in the hands of the Nazis? As Jon Kimche puts it in *Spying for Peace: General Guisan and Swiss Neutrality*, 'it had become clear to Guisan that the reduit would be little more than a hollow shell if it were not filled with the spirit of a people united, determined and prepared to resist'.

When Guisan talked of the consequences of the Redoubt strategy, this was the most important that he had in mind. Had his troops the will to resist the Reich?

Here, Guisan again had to hand an object lesson from recent events all too close to home. France fell for many reasons, not least the courage, skill and tactics of the Wehrmacht. Yet it also collapsed because of the absence among a good deal of the French army of the will to resist. In the course of the 'Sitzkrieg' there was a good deal of contact between General Gort's British Expeditionary Force and the French, then still led by General Gamelin. The British high command – at the time headed by the chief of the Imperial General Staff, General Edmund Ironside – was perturbed by what it discovered. Some French units were excellent, others less so. Lieutenant General Alan Brooke, later to become Churchill's Chief of Staff, recalled a march past of a French unit in November 1939: 'Men unshaven, horses ungroomed, vehicles dirty and complete lack of pride in themselves or their units. What shook me most, however, was the look in the men's faces, disgruntled and insubordinate looks . . . although ordered to give the "eyes left", hardly a man bothered to do so.' In the eyes of some of the British commanders, this was less than surprising, given the quality of the leadership of the French. Air Marshal Arthur Barratt, the commander of the RAF in France, thought Gamelin a 'button-eyed, button-booted, pot-bellied little grocer'.[17]

Vividly aware of the threat to morale, when the Germans crossed the Meuse on 15 May 1940, Guisan issued an order in which he observed that if the French had resolved to stop the Wehrmacht, they would have done precisely that. Guisan told his troops that they themselves were *never* to surrender.

Everywhere, where the order is to hold, it is the duty of conscience of each fighter, even if he depends on himself alone, to fight at his assigned position. The riflemen, if overtaken or surrounded, fight in their position until no more ammunition exists. Then cold steel is next . . . As long as a man has another cartridge or hand weapons to use, he does not yield.[18]

Once France had actually fallen, morale in Switzerland became ever more critical. Defeatism was commonplace both in the general population and the army. In these circumstances Guisan decided to stage a rally for the benefit of his officers, their subordinates and – ultimately – the Swiss people. He chose a location of great symbolic significance for the Swiss: the Rütli meadow on the eastern shore of Lake Lucerne. Here, in 1291, tradition placed the foundation of Switzerland on the occasion of the forging of the alliance between the cantons of Uri, Schwyz and Unterwalden. On 25 July 1940 there was to be a repeat performance. There the General mustered his Chiefs of Staff and the entire 650-strong officer corps. Grouped in a semicircle facing the silver lake in which were reflected the glories of the surrounding peaks of Mount Pilatus and Mount Rigi, Guisan told his officers, 'We are at a turning point of our history. The survival of Switzerland is at stake.'[19] Excerpts from the speech were printed and broadcast on that day, and it was announced that the Redoubt was to be manned by eight infantry divisions and three mountain brigades.

After the Rütli speech Guisan toured the whole country, becoming just the sort of national hero that politicians deplore: a Nelson, Wellington or a Bonaparte. As Swiss historians remark, the battle had begun between Guisan and the political classes for the Swiss soul. Through the blissfully hot summer of 1940, as the fate of Switzerland hung in the balance, the General became the human embodiment of the resistance spirit, the Widerstandsgeist.

5

Six days after the Rütli rally, on 31 July 1940, Hitler once again gathered his warlords at the Berghof. It was just a fortnight after their last meeting. By this time they were used to the tiresome journey from Berlin: either a flight from the capital's Tempelhof airfield to Salzburg, or an eight-hour train journey via Munich. Raeder was present once again to report on the developing plans for invading England, with the army leaders – Brauchitsch, Halder, Keitel and Jodl – to advise on the land war in all its aspects. Army Commander-in-Chief Generalfeldmarschall Walther von Brauchitsch was earmarked as Churchill's successor, the man who would take the Prime Minister's seat in Downing Street, though probably not in the House of Commons.

Invasion was certainly the order of the day, with plans afoot to invade Germany's new ally, the Soviet Union, as well as England and Switzerland. On Operation Sea Lion, Raeder was pessimistic about the weather prospects for the early autumn, the lack of German shipping – which could restrict the landings to the fairly well-defended coast between Dover and Eastbourne – and the efficacy of the Luftwaffe. In these circumstances he proposed May 1941 as the best time for the adventure. Hitler, mindful of the time this would allow Britain to re-equip Gort's Expeditionary Force evacuated from Dunkirk, was in more of a hurry. In the end the conference agreed to aim for 15 September 1940, subject to the efforts of Hermann Göring's Luftwaffe and the success of Unternehmen Adlerangriffe. On 1 August Hitler issued Directive No. 17. This required preparations for this invasion to be completed by 15 September 1940, with the invasion itself to be set for a day between 19 and 26 September.

The first of August 1940 – the date of the Berghof meeting – was also the Swiss National Day, the 649th anniversary of the Rütli accord in 1291. It was marked by thousands of beacons set blazing on the country's Alpine peaks, so sending a message of defiance to would-be invaders. This was timely, for the OKW had been reviewing its plans for invading Switzerland; Captain Otto von Menges had been busy once again. On 12 August 1940 his staff submitted a revised plan to Generaloberst Franz Halder. The Chief of Staff was himself busy overseeing the first-draft plans for the invasion of the Soviet Union. Menges proposed a simultaneous

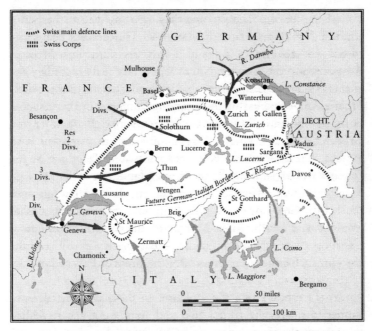

Captain von Menges's plan for the invasion of Switzerland

attack on Switzerland from both Germany and occupied France. Halder thought a feint, much like that carried out in May by the Seventh Army, would be more effective. An infantry attack in the Jura would draw in the Swiss army, and then a second attack in the south would attempt to cut off the army's line of retreat to the Alps. Halder allotted eleven divisions for the attack, some 150,000 men. Yet when he came to undertake a reconnaissance of the Swiss operation by driving along the French and German sections of the border, he had second thoughts. 'The Jura frontier offers no favourable base for an attack. Switzerland rises, in successive waves of wood-covered terrain, across the axis of an attack. The crossing points on the river Doubs and the border are few; the Swiss frontier position is strong.'[20]

In any case, Operation Sea Lion was proving a distraction. In the absence of what the Führer himself called 'complete air superiority', on 14 September 1940 Raeder, Halder and the

Führer had been obliged to meet again – for once in the Berlin Chancellery rather than the Berghof. Hitler conceded, 'The enemy recovers again and again.'[21] Three days later he postponed the invasion. The German Naval War Diary drily records, 'The enemy Air Force is by no means defeated.'[22] Reluctantly, Hitler ordered the dispersal of the shipping gathered in the Channel ports to transport the invading Heeresgruppe A and B (Army Groups A and B). They had been subjected to persistent RAF attacks. On 4 October, Hitler and Mussolini again met at the Brenner Pass. Ciano was again in attendance, the Italian foreign minister noting, 'There is no longer any talk of landing into the British Isles'. After his humiliation of three months earlier over the fiasco in the Alpes-Maritimes, this put Mussolini into a transport of delight. Ciano commented, 'Rarely have I seen the Duce in such good humour as after the Brenner Pass today.'[23]

On 19 October 1940, Guisan announced that home defence soldiers aged between forty-two and sixty were being recalled to relieve younger troops who had been on duty since the war began. This was tacit acceptance that, with winter drawing in, the threat of invasion was over for the year. After the breathtaking successes of the early summer, Hitler had met with failure over the Channel and frustration in the Alps. The German historian Joachim Fest commented, 'In Churchill Hitler found something more than an antagonist. To a panic-stricken Europe the German dictator had appeared almost like invincible fate. Churchill reduced him to a conquerable power.'[24] As many reflected, it was a strange, paradoxical, quixotic turn of events. Hitler had written to Mussolini that 'in that country at present it is not reason that rules'.

Henri Guisan in Switzerland had taken a similar line, albeit in a lower key. 'It's not their war,' reflected Shirer. 'But they're ready to fight to defend their way of life. I asked a fat businessman in my [train] compartment whether he wouldn't prefer peace at any price . . . "Not the kind of peace that Hitler offers," he said. "Or the kind of peace we've been having the last five years."'[25]

In Zermatt, shortly after the Fall of France, the mountain guide Bernard Biner had been sheltering in the Schönbühl Hut on the old trade route between the Swiss resort and Sion in the Rhône valley. Hearing a tremendous roar, he rushed outside, thinking the chimney was on fire. He saw, low over the Theodule Pass, a lone British bomber heading south towards Milan. 'I knew then that England would fight back. I was happier than I'd been for weeks.'[26]

FOUR

The Alps under the Swastika

All during the last months they [the Nazis] had in
the most shameful manner persecuted, killed and
imprisoned thousands of Jews from all over the
country.

MARIA VON TRAPP

I

By mid-October 1940 it had become clear to Shirer in Berlin
that the invasions of both Great Britain and Switzerland had
indeed been postponed for the remainder of the year. When the
spring snows melted, General Guisan might have to remobilise
his army. In the meantime, most of his troops could revert to
their normal occupations as – in Hitler's eyes – herdsmen and
cheese-makers with some armaments manufacture and spying
thrown in. It was a stay of execution, and Shirer won his bets
with the Wehrmacht top brass who had been so confident of
flying the swastika in Trafalgar Square before the clocks went
back. 'I shall – or should – receive from them enough champagne
to keep me all winter.'[1] The reprieve, though, had consequences.
On 15 October 1940 Shirer noted, 'This winter the Germans,
to show their power to discipline the sturdy, democratic Swiss,
are refusing to send Switzerland even the small amount of coal
necessary for the Swiss people to heat their homes. The Germans
are also allowing very little food into Switzerland, for the same
shabby reason. Life in Switzerland this winter will be hard.'[2]

It was the same throughout the Alps. Six years hence Churchill
would remark in his epochal speech in Fulton, Ohio, 'From
Stettin in the Baltic to Trieste in the Adriatic, an iron curtain
has descended across the continent.' For the present just such

a totalitarian pall had fallen on the Alps from Mont Blanc to the Grossglockner, the highest peaks in France to the west and in Austria to the east. Only the Alps in Switzerland remained politically free – but they were scarcely unfettered. On 24 October 1940, Shirer was himself in Switzerland on a visit to Berne. 'A sad, gloomy trip up from Geneva this afternoon. I gazed heavy-hearted through the window of the train at the Swiss Lake Geneva, the mountains, Mont Blanc, the green hills and the marble palace of the League that perished.'[3] Darkness had fallen on the Alps, the 'visible throne of God'.

The shadow had fallen over Switzerland's neighbouring Alpine republic of Austria two and a half years previously. In the Alpine city of Salzburg overlooked by Hitler's Berghof, a member of the Austrian gentry recalled:

It was March 11, 1938. After supper we went over to the library to celebrate Agathe's birthday. Someone turned on the radio, and we heard the voice of Chancellor Schuschnigg say:

'I am yielding to force. My Austria – God bless you!' followed by the national anthem.

We didn't understand, and looked at each other blankly.

The door opened and in came Hans, our butler. He went straight to my husband and, strangely pale, said:

'Herr Korvettenkapitän, Austria is invaded by Germany, and I want to inform you that I am a member of the [Nazi] Party. I have been for quite some time.'

Austria invaded. But that was impossible . . . At this moment the silence on the radio was broken by a hard, Prussian-sounding voice, saying: 'Austria is dead: Long live the Third Reich!'.[4]

So the breaking news of Anschluss was remembered by Maria von Trapp in the city of Mozart.

As the film *The Sound of Music* portrays with, for Hollywood, surprising fidelity to fact, the von Trapp family was aghast at this turn of events. At first the singers were in a tiny minority. One reason for the invasion was a referendum on Austria's independence planned by Chancellor Schuschnigg for 13 March 1938. Fearing a pro-Austrian result, Hitler sent in his troops. But when on 15 March the Führer spoke from the balcony of the Hofburg Palace, the seat of the old Habsburg monarchy in Vienna, he was fêted by around a seventh of the country's population – perhaps a quarter of a million people; when the plebiscite on Anschluss was held three weeks later on 10 April, 4,453,000 of an electorate of 4,481,000 turned out. Of those, 99.73 per cent supported the dissolution of their nineteen-year-old republic.

There were various mitigating circumstances. Not least amongst these was the absence of any opposition party, or indeed support for Austria's independence from neighbouring Italy or the mother of democracies, Great Britain. It is also more than doubtful as to whether the vote was 'free and fair' – as the Austrian resistance leader Fritz Molden later pointed out in his memoirs.[5] Still, 99.73 per cent is 99.73 per cent.

The Nazis – both German and Austrian – then began to put the lamentable affairs of the new Alpine province of the German Reich into order. First came the arrest and imprisonment of those deemed by the new chancellor Arthur Seyss-Inquart as unsympathetic to the Nazi cause. Around 20,000 were seized on the night after Anschluss. Some of these enemies of the Reich would eventually find their way to Dachau in Bavaria. As this was 300 miles away from Vienna, that very month Heinrich Himmler – in his capacity as Reichsführer-SS – had the idea of establishing something comparable on Austrian soil. Since 1934 the SS had managed the concentration camp system under a formation known – after their skull-and-crossbones insignia – as the 'death's head unit': SS-Totenkopfverbände. A granite quarry at the confluence of the Danube and Enns was identified as a possible site. The quarry could usefully provide the raw materials for the rebuilding of the Reich along the grandiose lines envisaged by Hitler and his tame architect Albert Speer. The city fathers in Vienna duly endorsed the idea of a camp to accommodate up to 5,000 prisoners. The one proviso was that it would provide cobblestones for the streets of the city of Mahler, Strauss, Wittgenstein and Freud. Work proceeded apace and the site received its first 300 inmates on 8 August 1938. The camp was Mauthausen, which would spawn a series of subcamps all over the Alps of Austria and Bavaria.

Many of their inmates were of course Jews. The Nuremberg Laws of 1935 had deprived Semites of their citizenship, banned marriage between Jews and other Germans, and forbidden them to practise various professions, so preventing many of them from earning a living. With Anschluss, these laws applied in Austria. Here there was a Jewish population of around 192,000. Shirer recalled their treatment in Vienna in the immediate aftermath of Anschluss:

There was an orgy of sadism. Day after day large numbers of Jewish men and women could be seen scrubbing Schuschnigg signs off the sidewalk and cleaning the gutters. While they worked on their hands and knees with jeering storm troopers standing over them, crowds gathered to taunt them. Hundreds of Jews, men and women, were picked off the streets and put to work cleaning public latrines and the toilets of the barracks where the S.A. and the S.S. were quartered. Tens of thousands more were jailed. Their worldly possessions were confiscated or stolen.[6]

At this stage in its gestation, Nazi policy on the Jewish question was to encourage emigration. The focus of this programme was the Zentralstelle für jüdische Auswanderung (Central Office for Jewish Emigration). This was set up on 22 August 1938 by the notorious architect of the Holocaust, the thirty-two-year-old Adolf Eichmann, suitably located in the former Rothschild Palace in Vienna, home of the Jewish banking dynasty. In Salzburg, 250 miles west of the capital, the matriarch Maria von Trapp remarked of that summer, 'All during the last months they [the Nazis] had in the most shameful manner persecuted, killed and imprisoned thousands of Jews from all over the country.'[7]

Still, some Austrians undoubtedly supposed that the Nazis' crushing of civil liberties in 1938 was compensated by material advancement. Fascism was a child of the Depression that for Austria was epitomised by the collapse of the Creditanstalt Bank in May 1931. The von Trapps themselves were victims of another bank collapse in 1935, the spur to their careers as professional singers. Inflation and unemployment – Arbeitslosigkeit – were the two great evils of the day. In Austria, unemployment at its height stood at one million out of a population of only six million. At the time of Anschluss, about 10 per cent of the workforce or 400,000 were unemployed. Two years later the figure had fallen to 250,000. Amongst the beneficiaries of the economic upturn were the resorts in which Alpine Austria – Carinthia, Upper Austria, Salzburgerland, Tyrol, Vorarlberg – abounded. Here, visitors from within Austria began to return; so too did those from Germany. Hitherto the Nazis had done their best to strangle tourism in Austria by requiring German citizens – the country's principal visitors – to buy a 1,000-mark visa. This was dropped, and an exchange rate was agreed between Seyss-Inquart and Hitler that made the major resorts attractive destinations. In the winter and summer seasons that immediately followed Anschluss – winter 1938–9, summer 1939, winter 1939–40 – the resorts flourished.

Frau Inge Rainer was born in the Tyrolese resort of Kitzbühel in 1929, and brought up in the pension run by her family. Her memories are vivid of the poverty of the valley in the thirties. 'Not everyone had a pair of shoes, and I remember one day my father cutting up a small piece of boiled beef on his plate into five pieces. One for himself, one for my mother, and the three remaining for myself and my siblings.' Anschluss for her was like day after night. 'When Anschluss came everything changed for the better. Immediately everyone had a job and I joined – you had to join – the Hitler Youth. This was a lovely thing to do. There were competitions in sport, singing, dancing. We had a uniform, went camping, did things that had never happened before.' For Frau Rainer, the popular enthusiasm for Hitler was entirely understandable. He brought full employment. 'That's why everyone voted for him.'[8] The resistance leader Fritz Molden commented, 'a great many Austrians regarded Hitler as a liberator, if not actually a Messiah'.[9]

*

For some, though, Austria in her new manifestation remained untenable. Georg Ludwig von Trapp – the Captain in *The Sound of Music* – had been a distinguished submariner in the old Austro-Hungarian Navy. In the course of the First World War, he completed nineteen war patrols and sank 45,669 tons of shipping. Much of it was British.

In 1936 he was approached by the Kriegsmarine to command a new U-boat, and eventually to establish a submarine base on the Adriatic. This he had the courage to turn down. Then in August 1938, the family was told they had been chosen as representatives from the new Ostmark to sing to the Führer on the occasion of his fiftieth birthday in April 1939. In a sense this was wonderful news. As Maria von Trapp candidly recorded: 'This meant we were made. From then on we could sing morning, noon and night and make a fortune!'[10] The family spurned the honour. Contrary to Hollywood's account, they did not set off at night over the Alps to Switzerland – which were inconveniently 180 miles away. To avoid arousing suspicion, they did in fact leave the house in Salzburg in their traditional Austrian garb of lederhosen and dirndls, saying they were going climbing in the Tyrol. In fact they took the train to Italy, then to England. In October 1938 the von Trapps set sail on the SS *American Farmer* from London for New York, fame and fortune.

They were the lucky ones. When war broke out in September 1939, the Austrians' unbridled enthusiasm for Hitler had somewhat cooled. A mass anti-Nazi protest of 10,000 in Stephansplatz in Vienna on 7 October 1939 was the beginning and end of such demonstrations. The rally was broken up and the leaders ended up in Mauthausen and Dachau. A year later, as the reality of war began to settle on the Austrian people, a carpenter's apprentice in Herzogenburg was brave enough to tell the Gestapo, 'The English have never lost a war, and they are going to win this one as well.'[11]

2

Back in Berlin, Shirer was beginning to be of the same opinion, for there was wonderful news from the United States. On 6 November 1940 Franklin D. Roosevelt was re-elected as President for a third term.

It is a resounding slap for Hitler and Ribbentrop and the whole Nazi regime . . . because Roosevelt is one of the few real leaders produced by the democracies since the war . . . I'm told that since the abandonment for this fall of the invasion of Britain, Hitler has more and more envisaged Roosevelt as the strongest enemy in his path to world power, or even to victory in Europe.[12]

For Shirer, the news was particularly welcome because of a story that had been brought to his ears the previous month and which he was now investigating. It had horrified a man inured to the evil of the country he was covering, and it was entirely emblematic of the Nazis' rape of the Alps.

Irmgard Paul was born in 1934 and brought up in Berchtesgaden. In 1930 her father had taken a job in the Bavarian resort in a workshop for hand-painted porcelain. Her mother had followed him there, and the couple married in 1932. At the time, the place where they settled – Obersalzberg – knew Hitler and his Berghof but had yet to become subsumed into the Nazi HQ. In 1933 Hitler became chancellor and the Nazis' grip on the country tightened very quickly. Irmgard remembered that

when I was born into our mountain paradise the Nazis were in full control of all branches of government, the military, and the media. And they had begun to infiltrate all aspects of life and to dictate the everyday details of family decisions: our education, the books and the news we read, how we greeted one another – even the names parents gave their children.[13]

As a three-year-old in the summer of 1937 Irmgard was taught by her father the straight-armed Nazi salute and the greeting 'Heil Hitler'. This was fortuitous. That autumn the family took the opportunity of a blissfully warm day to walk up to Obersalzberg to see the newly enlarged Berghof. When they reached the fence that divided the Führer from his people, they joined a crowd of pilgrims hoping for a glimpse of their leader.

An expectant murmur was in the air, a sense of anticipation, and everyone was ready to raise his arm and scream 'Heil mein Führer!' at a moment's notice.

Then it happened. Hitler came out and I ended up sitting on his lap and family history was made. I remember being ill at ease perched on his knee and suspiciously studying his moustache, his slicked-back, oily hair, and the amazingly straight side part, while at the same time acutely sensing the importance of the moment and of the man.[14]

Naturally enough, the young Irmgard was thrilled by this encounter and felt herself lucky to live so close to the Führer. Yet there were disturbing undercurrents. Her parents and her grandparents were deeply divided over Hitler. Reichsleiter Martin Bormann, the squat, bull-necked convicted murderer who had cast himself as Hitler's secretary, had had Obersalzberg cleared of many of its old settlements – and inhabitants – to create the Führersperrgebiet, the 'leader's territory'. Eighteen farms, three inns, a hospital for children, several hotels and dozens of private homes and small businesses were cleared at the shortest of notice, their owners offered a pittance in compensation. Irmgard's grandfather saw this as a symbol of the Nazis' greed and power; her father regarded it as a scheme for creating jobs for the Obersalzberg locals: building the new SS barracks, refurbishing the Hotel Platterhof and – down in Berchtesgaden itself – entirely remodelling the railway station on resplendent lines suited to the residence of the head of state.

The story of the Dehmel family played to the grandfather's side of the argument. The Dehmel children were neighbours and playmates of Irmgard. There were four of them. The youngest was mildly disabled, a 'somewhat peculiar-looking, slow child with very small eyes and seemingly little response to the world around her'.[15] This was Hildegard, who was treated with great patience and kindness by her two sisters. Another young sibling was too sickly to be allowed out. One day, Irmgard overheard her mother and aunt gossiping: 'One of the Dehmel children, the mongoloid one that's never outside, was picked up by the Health Service a few weeks ago, and now they've said she's dead from a cold.' This was the story that Shirer had heard in Berlin. Irmgard continued, 'What I did not know, and what the adults refused to believe or face, was that Hitler's euthanasia program, while still shrouded in secrecy and as much as possible hidden from the general public, was up and running.' On 25 November 1940 Shirer noted, 'I have at last got to the bottom of these mercy killings. It's an evil tale. The Gestapo, with the knowledge and approval of the German government, is systematically putting to death the mentally deficient population of the Reich.'[16] It was the beginnings of the Nazis' child euthanasia scheme that would eventually lead to the deaths of up to 6,000 children.

The Dehmels at Obersalzberg were prudent and courageous. After August 1939 doctors were obliged to register with a Reich committee those with serious hereditary and congenital illnesses. Having lost one child in suspicious circumstances, the Dehmels were determined not to lose another. By avoiding sending their remaining disabled daughter to school, using public health facilities, or doing anything else to draw her to the attention of the state, they succeeded. Under Hitler's nose in Berchtesgaden, Hildegard survived.

As to Irmgard, she will have much to tell us of the next five years.

3

In the French Alps, many found themselves in comparably precarious positions.

By the terms of the June 1940 armistice between Germany and France, the country was to be governed by Marshal Pétain from Vichy, the spa town in the Auvergne. The watchwords of the revolution – Liberté, Egalité, Fraternité – were discarded and in their place came Travail, Famille, Patrie: Work, Family, Fatherland. Pierre Laval commented, 'Parliamentary democracy has lost the war; it must disappear, ceding its place to an authoritarian, hierarchical, national and social regime.'[17] His objective, said his rival and sometime Prime Minister Léon Blum, 'was to cut all the roots that bound France to its republican and revolutionary past'.[18]

As well as the centuries being rolled back, the country was hacked in two. The extent of the German advance in the north in the summer of 1940 dictated her division along a line drawn between Tours and Dijon. The Atlantic coast – and its strategic ports soon to be used by U-boats – came under direct Nazi rule. This was the Zone Occupée, representing about three-fifths of France. The southern zone or Zone Libre included the Mediterranean coastline, the Rhône valley, and the Alps to the east that ran from Nice on the Riviera coast to Geneva. In both zones, the free press disappeared overnight, civil liberties went the same way, the phone network was cut, and the cost imposed by the Franco-German armistice of paying for the occupying army led at once to the rationing of foodstuffs; motorised transport became a thing of the past and cities and villages that were once neighbours became isolated once more. As to the people, Shirer commented, 'There was a complete collapse of French society and of the French soul.'

In the Alps themselves, Vichy joined forces with the Italians. As part of the Franco-Italian armistice that had followed Mussolini's Alpine campaign, a ten-mile demilitarised zone was set up along the 300-mile Alpine border of the Rhône-Alpes and the Alpes-Maritimes, and the Italians were allowed to retain the modest advances into French territory that they had made. For many of the French in the Alps, faced with the cataclysm of defeat and these two new grim faces of authority, it was a time for the deepest of soul-searching. In the Dauphiné capital of Grenoble it was observed that 'Il s'établit alors sur Grenoble et sa région, une sorte de grand calme, où vont s'étouffer les échos du dehors. La stupeur de l'effondrement national dissipée, la plupart des jeunes hommes retenus captifs, toute vie obéit à une tentation de repliement, à un besoin de méditation, peut-être de pénitence.'[19]

To the Alps also came the Jews. In the early days of the occupation, to be Jewish in France meant the confiscation of property, denial of the use of radios and visits to the cinema or theatre, and the requirement to wear a yellow star. Following the granting by the Reich of full powers to Pétain on 10 July 1940, this had precipitated a great exodus from the Occupied Zone to the Zone Libre; of the 350,000 Jews then living in France, around four out of five fled to where they supposed they would be safer under the jurisdiction of Vichy. Nice, capital of the Alpes-Maritimes, was the seaside city that at the time still retained some *belle époque* charm; it was also a port, an emergency exit to North Africa and the French Arab colonies of Syria, Algeria, Tunisia and Morocco. Likewise, the settlements further north up the Alpine chain in the Rhône-Alpes – Grenoble, Chambéry and Annecy – were conveniently close to Italy and Switzerland. For the French Jews, the Alps seemed to mean safety.

Then, in the autumn of 1940, Pétain had met Hitler at Montoire-sur-le-Loire. It was from here that the Marshal made his infamous broadcast of his intention to co-operate – collaborate – with the Nazis. Indeed, by the time of the meeting on 30 October 1940, his new regime had already begun to show itself in its true colours. Jews had been denaturalised in the first few days of Vichy. The Statut des Juifs, promulgated in the month of the meeting, excluded Jews from the press, commerce, industry, and government administration. For some Frenchmen this was a perfectly welcome development, a riposte to the failure of the Third Republic, liberalism and the Left. Shortly after France's capitulation, one of the men who would lead the resistance in Nice, Ange-Marie Miniconi, overheard a comment in the city's railway station that was not unrepresentative: 'Thank Christ we lost the war – otherwise we might still be governed by those left-wing motherfuckers of the Front Populaire.'[20] For others the new authoritarianism was far less welcome. From the centre of Orthodox Jewry in Nice, the Hotel Roosevelt, a newspaper reported: 'One could see rabbis in their traditional apparel walking through the streets, listen to Talmudic discussions and hear the old tunes of Hebrew prayer and Talmudic study.'[21] By November of 1940, these people in the Alpes-Maritimes and their co-religionists further north in the Rhône-Alpes felt, day after day, the steady closing of a vice.

4

Shirer was now reaching the end of his tether as a war correspondent in Berlin. His experience of covering the rise to power of the Nazis since 1934 had given him what he described as a 'deep, burning hatred of all that Nazism stands for'.[22] As a foreign correspondent and US citizen he was not in principle in danger, but the Nazis kept a close and increasingly watchful ear on his CBS broadcasts. His wife and daughter in Geneva seemed equally vulnerable, especially as rumours of the invasion plans of OKW for Switzerland ebbed and flowed over the summer and autumn of 1940. There was also the increasing difficulty of day-to-day life in Switzerland. As elsewhere in the Alps, life in the democracy was indeed getting hard.

Here, Switzerland had much in common with Britain. Both populations consumed considerably more than they produced, and both were dependent on supplies from elsewhere to keep the body and soul of their populations together; Switzerland was also deficient in virtually all raw materials. With Europe now closed for business, Britain became dependent on the Atlantic convoys for sustenance, Switzerland on her – now uniformly hostile – neighbours. Coal was the country's principal source of energy. Before the war, Switzerland had bought almost 300,000 tons per annum from Britain, some 1.8 million tons from Germany. Immediately war broke out, the Allies instituted a blockade against the neutral European countries, assuming that anything that reached the neutrals would or could eventually find its way to Germany. Trade to these countries was controlled by requiring that all shipments destined for them were issued with a stamp of authority known as a navigation certificate. Allied agents in the world's ports enforced this regime. Coal supplied from Britain to Switzerland ceased, and the Swiss became wholly dependent on the Germans.

Like the Allies, the Reich used this situation as a tactic in warfare. On 18 June 1940, just as France was falling, the Reich cut off coal supplies to Switzerland entirely. This was a negotiating move to get the Swiss to settle on terms favourable to Germany. Ultimately the Reich would supply coal to Switzerland because it needed the products of that energy, not least in the form of armaments, chemicals, precision instruments. The results of the Allies' and the Axis's combined efforts were nevertheless as Shirer predicted. The Swiss that winter of 1940–41 were cold. Paul Ladame was a Swiss army officer whose job was to boost morale by producing weekly newsreels. 'My wife, Andreina, who was then a young mother with two babies, remembers that coal was so severely rationed that they [herself and her neighbours] would not heat their houses any more, and that their children were freezing. They remember how difficult it was to heat the kitchen oven with paper and wood – there was no gas, no electricity.'[23]

Like the British, the Swiss also went hungry. This was an issue addressed by the distinguished Swiss agronomist Friedrich Wahlen in a speech in Zurich on 15 November 1940. Before the war the Swiss nation had imported about half its food, largely from willing partners in trade at its borders: France, Italy, Germany and Austria. Now the Swiss were in danger of starvation, and were obliged to dig not so much for victory as for neutrality. Wahlen proposed increasing the area under cultivation from 180,000 to 500,000 hectares, so raising the country's self-sufficiency from 52 per cent to 75 per cent over a period of five years. When the plan was unveiled in Zurich it was billed as the Anbauschlacht or growing battle. Football fields, town squares, public gardens, private yards and even window boxes were to be put under the plough; flower beds were to be turned into tomato or potato fields; hens, rabbits and goats were to be found lodgings on balconies and verandas in cities; and labour from cities was to be drafted to the fertile central midlands and to the Alps. With many of the men drafted into the army, some of the workers would be women, the equivalent of the British Land Girls.

In due course, Wahlen's plan would blossom. In the meantime there was rationing. It had begun on 30 October 1939, when coupons were introduced for commodities including sugar, pasta, rice, wheat, flour, oats, butter and oil. On 1 December 1940, shortly after Wahlen's speech, textiles, shoes, soap and detergent were added. When Wahlen's plan began to bite, cheese, eggs, fresh meat and milk would follow. Ladame recalled, 'Everything was so severely rationed to about a third of regular peacetime consumption. Rations went down to one pound of meat a month per person, one egg every two weeks, one pound of black bread a week, no sugar, no salt, no fruit.'[24] This was privation rather than starvation, but it had a psychological impact too. As Shirer noted in Berlin on 12 November 1940, 'Coffee, ever since it has become impossible to buy it in Germany, has assumed weird importance in one's life. The same with tobacco.'[25]

With rationing came the blackout. Like the country itself, Swiss airspace was technically neutral. In practice it was violated by both the Luftwaffe and the Allies. During the Battle of France in 1940 there were a series of encounters between the Luftwaffe and Messerschmitt Bf 109 fighters rather rashly sold by the Germans to the Swiss before the war. Planes on both sides were shot down in real or imagined violations of Swiss airspace. By the autumn the RAF had begun small-scale raids on targets in both Germany and Italy. A flight of Whitleys bombed Italy on 10 June 1940, on 23 September 119 bombers hit Berlin, and on 16 November 131 bombers targeted Hamburg. The bombers occasionally overflew Switzerland partly because it was the most direct route, and partly because her still illuminated cities were aids to navigation. Naturally the Luftwaffe objected, demanding a blackout. In the course of the autumn RAF overflights became more numerous and German demands became noisier.

Eventually, on 9 November 1940, President Pilet-Golaz gave in. For Paul Ladame:

Then came the total darkness into which the whole country was plunged every day as soon as the sun had disappeared . . . no outside lights were allowed to shine at night across Swiss territory . . . not one road, not one street, not one place was illuminated . . . every window of every house was covered with black paper so that not one ray of light could be detected from outside . . . the few official emergency vehicles that still were permitted on the road drove with headlamps so dimmed that they lit only about 200 metres ahead.[26]

The Swiss resorts were no different. In Zermatt, right on the Italian border, the villagers were required to cover their windows with black paper at night – and to store enough food to last for six months.

The final thing rationed was truth – proverbially the first casualty of war. Naturally enough, Switzerland was awash with newsreels, magazines and newspapers produced by its German, Italian and French neighbours. With the borders closed by the Wehrmacht from the summer of 1940, British and American papers and newsreels – which told a very different story – became virtually unobtainable. Switzerland's own press was censored as early as 1934, when the federal government had caved in to German demands. It issued a decree enabling the Council to sanction any newspapers that endangered relations between Switzerland and other countries: expressions deemed offensive to foreign leaders were banned. In practice, this was to an extent ignored. With the outbreak of war, the Council redoubled its efforts and directed the army's division of press and radio to monitor such output, to warn, impose sanctions and if required to suppress publication. The upshot was effectively the suspension of a free and independent press.

For Shirer, as the winter of 1940–41 got under way, the situation was worse.

Reichsminister Goebbels's propaganda ministry officials controlled the production facilities that enabled him to broadcast, and had the power to expel him if he was unduly critical of the regime. On the outbreak of war, they introduced a regime of censorship preventing the dissemination of material that might compromise military operations. When the Luftwaffe's bombing of England and the reciprocal RAF raids on Germany got going, the position deteriorated. Whereas Shirer's colleagues in London – notably his boss Ed Murrow – were free to broadcast details of the Blitz, Shirer was unable to report the raids on German cities or to question the veracity of statements issued by the Nazis: for instance, about Luftwaffe and RAF losses during the Battle of Britain, bombing casualties in Hamburg and Berlin – or infringements of Swiss airspace.

As the autumn of 1940 progressed, Shirer was pressurised to broadcast material issued by Goebbels he knew to be misleading; he was also tipped off that the Gestapo was attempting to ensnare him on a charge of spying. This carried the penalty of death. With his family in jeopardy in Geneva and the emasculation of his job in Berlin, the game was no longer worth the candle. 'I think my usefulness here is about over. Until recently, despite the censorship, I think I've been able to do an honest job of reporting from Germany. But it has become increasingly difficult and at present it has become impossible . . . You cannot call the Nazis "Nazis" or an invasion an "invasion." You are reduced to re-broadcasting the official communiqués'.[27]

On 23 October 1940, his wife and daughter left Geneva for the United States, via Lisbon. On 5 December, Shirer himself left Germany for good. Following an emotional reunion with Ed Murrow in London, on 13 December he returned to a United States just a year away from Pearl Harbor.

5

Early in the New Year of 1941, with Berchtesgaden slumbering under a winter blanket of snow, Hitler summoned his three service chiefs to the Berghof. In the rarefied atmosphere of the Bavarian mountain, he was in a bullish mood. He was anxious to help Italy, embroiled in the Axis campaign in Greece at the southern end of the Balkan Peninsula. Then there was England. Despite the Reich's failure to invade Britain in the autumn, the Führer was convinced she was at the end of her tether: she would never regain any position on the Continent and was only hanging on in the vain hope of the United States or the Soviet Union entering the war on her side. Hitler thought this situation had grave implications. His own ally Stalin he saw as a pragmatist who would throw Germany to the lions if he regarded it as advantageous to the USSR.

The Balkans, then, were uppermost in Hitler's mind; after the Balkans, Russia. Curiously enough, these two concerns keep us in the Alps.

Since the golden years of the winter sports movement, St Moritz had been the doyen of the resorts. Famed for its waters since the sixteenth century, the little lakeside village in the Engadine in eastern Switzerland had won fame as a climbing centre in the 1850s, and as one of the pioneering winter resorts ten years later. By 1873 the winter season rivalled the summer and in 1885 the famous Cresta toboggan run was founded. In the winter of 1913 the Cresta was patronised by the Kaiser's son, Crown Prince Wilhelm. After the war the village reached the apogee of its fame, welcomed Americans exploring Europe in large numbers for the first time, and in 1928 hosted the Winter Olympics.

Now it was Christmas 1945, and at the Palace Hotel in Via Serlas the sun was back in the heavens and all seemed right with the world. Outside the foyer stood a young man in a brass-buttoned outfit who might have been taken as a porter – and certainly was by the American who was driven up in the taxi from the railway station. According to the historian of the Palace Hotel:

'Hey there!' snapped the new arrival. 'Don't stand there doing nothing. Can't you see those bags need to be taken in?' The young man dutifully carried them through the revolving doors and put them down in the lobby. The American handed him a tip and was surprised when it was refused. 'Why won't you take it?' he asked. 'Because', replied the young man, 'I am the King of Yugoslavia.'[28]

Yugoslavia was created on 1 December 1918 by the union of a ragbag of provinces of the dissolved Austro-Hungarian Empire and the kingdoms of Serbia and Montenegro. It bordered on Italy and Austria in the north, Hungary, Romania and Bulgaria to the east, Greece and Albania to the south. It was here that the Alps ceased to be a continuous range but rather became a series of eruptions that ran through what are now Croatia, Slovenia, Bosnia-Herzegovina and Albania: the Balkans. When the young King Peter encountered the American in St Moritz, he had just been deposed by the begetter of some of the bitterest fighting in the Alps in the course of the entire war. This was Marshal Tito, otherwise Josip Broz.

It had all begun in the Berghof.

There the regent of Yugoslavia, Prince Paul – Peter's uncle – had been summoned by the Führer on 4 March 1941. The Prince was an Anglophile, educated in Oxford, married to a sister of the Duchess of Kent, and a close student of *Tatler*. Yugoslavia, he knew, was like Switzerland: it lay between the Reich and an object of its interest, in this case Greece. There, British forces were threatening both the Italian troops in Albania and the joint Italian and German forces in North Africa. Hitler also feared that an Allied front above Salonika in northern Greece could jeopardise the grandest of his designs, Barbarossa: the plan to invade the Soviet Union.

With just such threats and blandishments as Chancellor Schuschnigg had been subjected to on the eve of Anschluss, the regent reluctantly agreed to join the common cause of the Axis. On 25 March 1941, in Vienna, the agreement was duly signed by the Yugoslav Prime Minister, Dragiša Cvetković.

Yet not all was well in the state of Yugoslavia. Twenty-four hours after the signing, the regency found itself deposed by the seventeen-year-old King Peter, who had led a popular uprising supported by the air force and the army – and largely engineered by the British. He had escaped the attentions of his uncle's conspirators by sliding down a drainpipe. 'Chips' Channon was an old friend of the regent. His diary for 27 March reads:

News reached the Foreign Office of more extraordinary events in Belgrade. There was a coup d'état in the small hours of this morning. Little Peter was proclaimed King [in reality as opposed to merely nominally], the Ministers who signed the pact have been arrested and the three Regents have resigned: Paul is reported to have fled; some say he has been arrested too. No-one knows what to think but there is much jubilation here. I can see the dramatic happenings in that Palace which I know so well; the boy King awakened; the generals taking control; the Regent at bay; it is pure Ruritania; and certainly a blow to German prestige.[29]

Although King Peter's new regime proposed a non-aggression pact with Germany, it would not be a puppet of Hitler's desires. Hitler was beside himself with rage at the coup, and rushed out Directive No. 25 on the invasion of Yugoslavia, Operation Marita. Executed on 6 April 1941, the Luftwaffe razed Belgrade to the ground, killing thousands. Within a week the Wehrmacht – allied to Italian and Hungarian forces – had secured the capital, the country, and the twenty-eight-division Yugoslav army. The King escaped to Greece, and his country was divided. Croatia became a Nazi state ruled by the fascist Ustaše, the Wehrmacht occupied Serbia, Slovenia, Bosnia and Herzegovina, and the sweepings were taken by Italy, Bulgaria and Hungary.

In this way the eastern outworks of the Alps fell to Hitler, and his domination of the chain became virtually complete. With it came the cold, hunger, repression, persecution, restriction of freedom of expression, speech and movement, concentration camps and euthanasia programmes that the Reich had already brought to much of the Alps. Yet one of the consequences of Operation Marita was less expected. 'The beginning of the Barbarossa operation', Hitler informed his warlords, 'will have to be postponed for up to four weeks.'[30] It was a delay of incalculable and perhaps even fatal results for the Third Reich.

PART TWO

FIVE

'The lifeboat is full'

*The world seemed divided into two parts – those
places where Jews could not live and those where
they could not enter.*

CHAIM WEIZMANN

I

On 19 November 1942 Hitler was once again at the Berghof. The
first snows of the year had fallen and – as ever – cast a blanket of
peace over the enchanted Alpine landscape. From the terrace the
eye was seized by the crystalline masses of the Watzmann and
the Untersberg – where Barbarossa still dozed. In the valley the
dusk came early, and from Obersalzberg the lights of Berchtesgaden glittered warmly below. There was no blackout here, and
from the night sky the constellations of Orion, Sagittarius and
Cassiopeia shone down on the narrow valley.

Yet the recent weeks had been disturbing for the Führer. Indeed
the whole tenor of the war had changed since his precipitate
decision to invade the eastern Alps, those of Yugoslavia, twenty
months earlier in April 1941. Operation Barbarossa, delayed
partly because of the operation in the Balkans, had begun with
such high hopes and dazzling victories. The fall of Kiev, Kharkov
and Odessa, the besieging of Leningrad, the spearheads of the
7th Panzer Division in the suburbs of Moscow. Then had come
the setbacks, culminating in a most reluctant Hitler suspending
the assault of Heinz Guderian's Panzers on the Soviet capital.
This was coupled with the entry of the United States into the
conflict in the aftermath of Pearl Harbor in December 1941, the
final abandonment of the plan to invade Great Britain, the first
USAAF bombing raids on Germany, and Grossaktion Warschau

of the summer of 1942. This had seen more than a quarter of a million Jews dispatched from the Warsaw ghetto to Treblinka, the extermination camp sixty miles north of the Polish capital. Then had come the shocking news of Generalfeldmarschall Erwin Rommel's defeat at El Alamein. After this maelstrom, more than ever Hitler relished the restorative powers of his Alpine retreat. The Germans called it Bergfried, the peace of the mountains.

Thirteen days earlier he had been at his eastern HQ in Rastenburg, Prussia, directing the deteriorating situation around the industrial centre of Stalingrad in south-western Russia. It was at this point – 6 November 1942 – that the first intelligence had filtered through of a large Allied naval force setting sail from Gibraltar. It was steaming east. Two days later Hitler was scheduled to be in Munich, the fount of the Nazi movement, to address the Party on the nineteenth anniversary of the Beer Hall Putsch. Setting out in the command train after lunch on 7 November, Hitler arrived in the Bavarian capital at 3.40 p.m. – much delayed by stopping at every major station to hook up the train to the railway telegraph system to glean the latest news from the Mediterranean. By the time the Führersonderzug reached Munich's main station, the Allied landings in French North Africa had begun. This was Operation Torch, under the overall command of the fifty-two-year-old from Kansas, General Dwight D. Eisenhower.

Opposition should have come in the form of 120,000 Vichy French troops under Admiral François Darlan. Their loyalty was questionable, the Allies even supposing that some Vichy elements would support the landing. Resistance in Morocco and Algiers proved tenacious in some places, sporadic elsewhere, but enough to see a death toll of just under 2,000 accruing to the two sides, the sinking of a number of ships, and Darlan himself declaring for the Allies, before the bridgeheads were established.

For Hitler, as he was driven to the Löwenbräukeller to address the Party faithful, the implications of the landings were obvious. With Rommel in retreat after Montgomery's desert victory, the Axis forces in the whole North African theatre were now threatened: the balance of power in the Mediterranean had shifted dramatically in the Allies' favour. Seven hundred miles away in Downing Street, Churchill took a similar line. On 10 November 1942 he famously told the Lord Mayor's Luncheon at the Mansion House in the City of London, 'Now this is not the end. It is not even the beginning of the end. But it is, perhaps, the end of the beginning.'[1] Both leaders saw that even Germany herself was imperilled if the Allies seized the opportunity to invade unoccupied southern France, the Zone Libre under the control of Pétain's Vichy administration. From Algiers, the French Riviera was just a hop across the wine-dark Mediterranean. From the Riviera, Germany was virtually in sight.

Fall Anton – Operation Anton – had been thoughtfully developed by OKW for just such a contingency. This was the completion of the Third Reich's occupation of France, the seizing of the Zone Libre, the margins of which were the country's tempting Mediterranean coast and her Alpine border with Italy.

Now Hitler at once directed the plan to be dusted off. At 8.30 on the morning of 10 November – just as Churchill was rehearsing his speech – the Führer gave the order for Axis forces to defy the terms of the armistice with Vichy and occupy the Zone Libre. He excused the action by declaring, 'After the treachery in North Africa, the reliability of French troops can no longer be guaranteed.'[2]

The implications for the French Alps along the border that zigzagged north from Nice to Geneva were far-reaching. The Italians had already occupied the fringes of this frontier area during the faltering campaign of June 1940. They had remained there under the terms of the Franco-Italian armistice. Now the Italian Fourth Army under the balding, bespectacled fifty-four-year-old Generale Mario Vercellino marched a further seventy-five miles west to Avignon in the south and Vienne in the north. The Italians assumed control of Nice itself, capital of the Alpes-Maritimes; further north in the Rhône-Alpes they took the capital of the ancient province of Dauphiné, Grenoble; Chambéry, the capital of Savoie; and Annecy, capital of the Haute-Savoie. In all, this was an area comprising eight *départements*.

Occupied Zones in France

Further north in the Alps, Vichy France's border with Switzerland between Geneva and Basel – the *départements* of Ain, Jura, and Doubs – was seized by the German Seventh Army, so closing the fascist ring on the tiny democracy.

Having brazenly assured the junketing Nazis in the Löwenbräukeller that Stalingrad was firmly in the hands of Generalfeldmarschall Friedrich Paulus's Sixth Army, Hitler had retreated south to the Berghof. Generalfeldmarschall Keitel, head of OKW, and his deputy Generaloberst Jodl were in attendance; also Albert Speer. The quartet ruminated on recent developments. The Allied landings – Operation Torch – were the culmination of the Reich's setbacks in North Africa that had begun with the defeat of Rommel's hitherto unvanquished Afrika Korps in the Western Desert at the Second Battle of El Alamein. On the Eastern Front, a counteroffensive from the Red Army was anticipated – though not on a scale that required the presence of Hitler and his entourage at Rastenburg.

It was on 19 November that a phone call came through to Obersalzberg from Rastenburg. The new Chief of Staff General-oberst Kurt Zeitzler called with grave news. The forecast Russian attack – Operation Uranus – had begun. It was on a much greater scale than OKW had envisaged. Three armies under General Nikolay Vatutin were driving south on a 250-mile front in a transparent attempt to encircle Paulus's Sixth Army in Stalingrad. The choice, said Zeitzler, was stark. Either a retreat to the west or be cut off. Hitler was outraged – not least because the forty-seven-year-old Zeitzler had been chosen to replace Generaloberst Franz Halder on the grounds that he would be both more robust and less dogmatic. Keitel, Jodl and Speer were also aghast.

The thirty-seven-year-old Albert Speer was the man unex-pectedly spotlit by Hitler when he saw the architect's designs for the 1933 Nuremberg party rally. It was Speer's idea to hold the rallies at night to disguise the fact that many of the leading Nazis were overweight. Soon he became the principal architect to the Reich, the man who would blueprint Hitler's dreams for a brave new Germany. The Reichskanzlei (Reich Chancellery) in Berlin was his first major triumph, Hitler having dismissed the old building in the Wilhelmstrasse as only 'fit for a soap company'. Having so distinguished himself, Speer was singled out for a further remarkable promotion to the Reich's arms and munitions minister. His supposed ignorance of the Final Solution to the Jewish question later led to the cognomen 'the good Nazi'; and his astutely self-serving memoirs provide an intriguing insight into the upper echelons of the Reich as its narrative steadily unravelled.

On this occasion Speer pictured Hitler pacing back and forth like a caged animal in the great hall of the Berghof:

Our generals are making their old mistakes again. They always over-estimate the strength of the Russians. According to all the front-line reports, the enemy's human material is no longer sufficient. They are weakened; they have lost far too much blood. But of course nobody wants to accept such reports. Besides, how badly Russian officers are trained! No offensive can be organized with such officers. We know what it takes![3]

The matter simmered for three days as the news from the east became worse and worse. Then Hitler, Keitel and Jodl once again entrained at Berchtesgaden on the Führersonderzug and rushed back to Rastenburg.

It was 22 November 1942. Ahead lay the siege of Stalingrad.

2

So to Switzerland. The complete closing of the Swiss border by Operation Anton ten days earlier meant that the republic was now completely surrounded by the Axis, all its frontiers effectively closed. This brought a series of problems in the country to a head. Principal amongst them was that of the Jewish refugees.

Like Great Britain, Switzerland had a long tradition of offering asylum to the oppressed. This was partly as a consequence of her geographical position at the crossroads of Europe, partly because of her traditional neutrality, partly – perhaps – because of the humanity of the Swiss people. The state had given sanctuary from religious persecution to the Huguenots and the Waldenses in the sixteenth and seventeenth centuries, Geneva becoming known as the 'Protestant Rome'. In the years of the French Revolution she had provided homes for her western neighbour's royalists. In 1815 the international guarantee of her neutrality by the Congress of Vienna had cemented her reputation as the capital for asylum; in 1848, the European year of revolution, she had given sanctuary to politicians of all colours – this despite having undergone her own turmoil in the form of the Sonderbund civil war the previous year. In the twentieth century, Russian revolutionaries including Vladimir Lenin had found exile in the mountain state.

Yet despite this record, and despite being a multilingual and multicultural nation, it was often said that the Swiss had a strong sense of their own identity and no particular enthusiasm for outside influences or people. Alexander Rotenberg was a twenty-one-year-old Jew from Antwerp who escaped to Switzerland at the time of Operation Anton in autumn 1942. For Rotenberg, 'The Swiss were not particularly anti-Semitic, but they tended to be xenophobic. They liked their own ways; foreigners, with the exception of tourists, made them feel uncomfortable.'[4] Much more recently, in 2002, this perspective was echoed by Switzerland's own landmark Bergier commission into the country's wartime record: 'Anti-Semitism was mostly unspoken and kept below the surface, but clearly ingrained in the social fabric.'[5] This low-grade xenophobia, at the time commonplace throughout Europe, was manifested in a concern about 'foreignerisation', Überfremdung.

This debate was given increasing force as the number of refugees grew in the years preceding the outbreak of war. After the passing of the Nuremberg Laws in 1935 that deprived German Jews of their citizenship, the Reich had actively encouraged Jewish emigration. By 1938, one in four German Jews – some 150,000 – had left Germany, fleeing to where they could. Great Britain took 50,000, France 30,000, Poland 25,000, Belgium 12,000, the Scandinavian countries 5,000. Switzerland herself accepted 5,000. With the annexation of Austria in March 1938, Nazi policy became more concerted, and saw the establishment of ghettos and forced emigration. Pressure on Switzerland grew.

In the face of this policy and the practical implications for the liberal democracies that might be inclined to accept the Jews, in 1938 President Roosevelt had called an international conference on the question. Switzerland, at the time still the host country of the League of Nations, and in the immediate proximity of Germany, was the obvious venue. The Swiss declined the suggestion, supposedly fearing to offend Hitler. Évian-les-Bains, the French Alpine watering-place south across Lake Geneva from

Lausanne, was chosen as a substitute. It was hoped that charity and justice would be dispensed along with the mineral water.

Here, from 6 to 14 July 1938, the liberal democracies disgraced themselves. The French hosts set the tone by stating that their country had reached 'the extreme point of saturation as regards the admission of refugees'. Lord Winterton, leading the British delegation, followed suit: 'the United Kingdom is not a country of immigration. It is highly industrialised, fully populated and is still faced with the problem of unemployment.' The United States could do no better: it would not relax its strict immigration quota. The Swiss head of the police force responsible for foreigners, Dr Heinrich Rothmund, unapologetically told delegates that 'Switzerland, which has as little use for these Jews as Germany, will take measures to protect herself from being swamped by Jews.'[6]

The consequence was that – at least officially – the enlightened democracies would do precious little to find new homes for the displaced Jews. In their defence, the extermination of the race first threatened by the Nazi SS chief, Reichsführer Heinrich Himmler, before the end of that year of 1938 was hardly an outcome imagined by the delegates. Nevertheless, the fact was that after Évian, as Chaim Weizmann, later Israel's first head of state, commented, 'The world seemed divided into two parts – those places where Jews could not live and those where they could not enter.'[7]

With the outbreak of war the pressure of Jewish refugees on the Swiss borders had risen.

In the Alps, Bavaria had been profoundly hostile to Jews since the promulgation of the Nuremberg Laws. In the resort of Garmish-Partenkirchen anti-Jewish posters were removed only on the occasion of the Winter Olympics in February 1936 – when they might be seen by international visitors; the twin towns' remaining forty Jews were expelled at two hours' notice during Kristallnacht on 9/10 November 1938. Two of them, turned back at the Swiss border, committed suicide. Austria's

Alpine provinces had kowtowed after Anschluss in March 1938, the resort of Kitzbühel seeing its Jewish community disappear virtually overnight. After the Fall of France, Vichy had required no prompting from Berlin to pass the Statut des Juifs: the internment camp in the Paris suburb of Drancy had opened on 21 August 1941. Following the Wannsee Conference in January 1942 in Berlin which formulated 'die Endlösung der Judenfrage' (the Final Solution to the Jewish question), the persecution of the French Jewish population became more concerted. The Vel d'Hiv round-up of Jews in central Paris in July 1942 saw the first 13,000 of a total of 67,400 sent to Auschwitz. The French Alpine regions of the Rhône-Alpes and the Alpes-Maritimes soon followed. Nice lost 600 Jews on 26 August 1942; in Grenoble, capital of the Dauphiné, the community of around 3,000 Jews also found themselves persecuted, then – eventually – deported. In the Italian Alps, Mussolini's pale imitation of the Nuremberg Laws, the Manifesto della razza, held sway from September 1938. In Piedmont, persecution was sufficient to drive families into hiding in the surrounding mountains; deportations to Auschwitz began in 1942. In the Yugoslav Alps, Nazi anti-Semitic policies were pursued with their usual vigour after the Axis invasion of April 1941, though those parts of the country held by the Italians were less harsh in their treatment. By 1942, much of the Alps had become a place where Jews could not live.

Switzerland therefore became the obvious destination for the persecuted. Yet despite its tradition of offering asylum for the oppressed, the Swiss were cautious. They categorised those trying to enter Switzerland as Evaders (military personnel in plain clothes), Internierten (military personnel clothed as such) and Flüchtlinge – civilian refugees. They filtered and they sifted. In the aftermath of the Évian Conference the Swiss successfully petitioned the Nazis to stamp the passports of Jews with a J, a decision approved by the Federal Council on 4 October 1938. This was to enable them to be singled out at the border. As the Bergier commission pointed out, this meant that Switzerland was 'making anti-semitic laws the basis of its entry practices'.[8]

By 1941 the country was playing host to 19,429 Jews, of whom 9,150 were classed as 'foreign'. Some were en route to other countries, others had nowhere else to go. As the consequences of Wannsee became apparent, the refugees' problem became desperate. By the summer of 1942, the fate of Jews sent east in the railway cattle cars – the story of Treblinka – had found its way into the press. Both the *Daily Telegraph* in England and the *Washington Post* in the United States carried stories of the mass exterminations. On 25 August 1942 the story was splashed all over the Swiss newspapers, and the Swiss found themselves besieged. Already, in late July 1942, Heinrich Rothmund had written to his superior, the Justice and Police Minister Eduard von Steiger,

What are we to do? We admit deserters as well as escaped prisoners of war as long as the number of those who cannot proceed further [to other countries] does not rise too high. Political fugitives . . . within the Federal Council's 1933 definition are also given asylum. But this 1933 ordinance has virtually become a farce today because every refugee is already in danger of death . . . Shall we send back only the Jews? This seems to be almost forced upon us.[9]

To avoid the appearance of persecuting the Jews, on 13 August 1942 Steiger agreed to Rothmund ordering the closing of Swiss borders to *all* refugees, irrespective of nationality or race. In a speech at the end of the month, von Steiger explained,

Whoever commands a small lifeboat of limited capacity that is already quite full, and with an equally limited amount of provisions, when thousands of victims of a sunken ship scream to be saved, must appear hard when he cannot take everyone. And yet he is still humane when he warns early against false hopes and tries to save at least those he has taken in.[10]

This was generally interpreted in the headline 'DAS BOOT IST VOLL' (The boat is full), a phrase used both by the Swiss President and by Rothmund himself.

The judgement of history on this decision has been harsh. The Bergier commission noted the democracy's failure to distinguish between war and genocide. It also judged that the country 'rarely chose' to use its position 'for the defence of basic humanitarian values'.[11]

For the Swiss, Operation Anton, less than three months after Steiger's August decision, was a body blow. From 1940 onwards the republic's ambivalence towards refugees had been coupled with the practical difficulty of the shortage of food for an increasing number of mouths, together with fears of social and political unrest. While the refugees remained birds of passage, this was not an overwhelming problem even for a small country with limited food for its own population. The closure of the border caused by Operation Anton exacerbated the crisis, both in terms of perception and reality. It was one thing to be a staging post for refugees. It was another to accept them at the frontier without any prospect of their eventual departure. As Alexander Rotenberg put it, when Switzerland was encircled, 'Refugees, at first a novelty, were also by now streaming in from wherever they could find leaks in the border . . . And now, surrounded and closed off from free world trade, sharing short rations with illegal foreigners was not a popular option.' Switzerland would soon be full, *complet, besetzt, pieno*.

In the autumn of 1942, in a country averse to strangers, in a nation whose very existence was in jeopardy, in a land where the population was on rations, they were the unwanted.

3

In practice the reception of Jews of any age or status often depended on the charity – or otherwise – of the border officials whom they encountered. Some refugees were turned away at the Swiss frontier and sent to their deaths. Others were formally admitted. To yet others a blind eye was turned. Rotenberg recorded his experience in *Emissaries: A Memoir of the Riviera, Haute-Savoie, Switzerland, and World War II*.[12]

In 1940 he had flown a Nazi round-up of Jews in his newly occupied home city of Antwerp. He had escaped first into occupied northern France, subsequently to the first port of call for many European Jews that summer: the Alpes-Maritimes capital of Nice. Here he lived for eighteen months working for the Jewish underground. Forewarned of the general round-up of Jews in the city of 26 August 1942, he took a train north into the Haute-Savoie in the Rhône-Alpes.

Then, as summer turned to autumn, he and a companion, Ruth Hepner, took the steep, rough mountain paths that led up to the Franco-Swiss border close to the French hamlet of Barbère. This was ten miles north-east of the famous old Savoie resort of Chamonix, at the foot of Mont Blanc, and at a height of more than 4,000 feet. It was a bleak and forbidding place, a world of bare rock and broken stones, bereft of vegetation, of human habitation and of pity.

Sucessfully avoiding the Swiss police patrols on the frontier, the pair scrambled down the mountainside towards what they hoped would be the safety of the Swiss village of Finhaut, Canton Valais. There they intended to throw themselves on the mercy of the occupants of the first chalet they could find. This, as they knew, was risky, for – in Rotenberg's words – 'The border patrols had grown more hardened.'[13]

As it so happened, Rotenberg and Hepner chanced upon the home of an army officer, First Lieutenant Emile Gysin. His wife Marguerite was welcoming and plied the pair with café au lait in front of the fire; when her husband returned – complete with a giant mastiff – he was furious. He at once assumed the refugees were German spies and threatened to turn them back to Vichy. 'Why shouldn't I arrest you right now? Can you prove to me you are not spies? And even at that – if you are refugees as you claim – I am supposed to turn you back.' Rotenberg was cornered. How could Gysin be convinced? With a flash of inspiration, the answer came to him. He burrowed in his knapsack and brought out two prizes. These were a Hebrew prayer book and his tefillin, the set of phylacteries – boxes containing parchment inscribed with verses from the Torah – with which he prayed. 'Have you seen these before?' demanded Rotenberg of his host. 'Do you know what they are?'

Gysin did indeed know. The ceremonial objects convinced the lieutenant of the bona fides of the pair, and he at once relented:

My orders are to arrest you, to return all single people to the French. But I will not. No. Absolutely not. I have seen what has happened in the valley, in Le Châtelard, at the border, where Jewish people have been forcibly handed over to the Vichy gendarmes, servants of the Boches, knowing full well what would happen to them. Inhuman indeed. It cannot be believed.[14]

Rotenberg was sent by these two good Samaritans to Montreux on the northern shores of Lake Geneva. Here he would be safe because the Swiss authorities would only expel Jews caught within five miles of the frontier. As he had sought sanctuary in Switzerland he was categorised as a 'Flüchtling'. This meant he would be sent to a labour camp: initially at Girenbad in Canton Zurich.

Rotenberg was lucky. He joined a group of foreign Jewish refugees in Switzerland that by the time of Operation Anton in November 1942 totalled 14,000. 'For each one of us,' Rotenberg wrote of that time, 'there were tens, hundreds, thousands who we knew had been hounded, tricked, duped, caught, torn from families, killed on the spot . . .' As he learned in the course of his stay in the Swiss work camps, his mother and sister Eva were amongst them.

4

Rotenberg had managed to escape to Switzerland over the Alps. Other Jews in France at the time of Operation Anton found refuge in the mountains themselves.

In the south-east of France on the Riviera, the operation had seen the Germans seizing the territory to the west of the Rhône, taking their local headquarters at Marseilles on the river mouth. As we have seen, the Italians had taken over to the east of the river along the coast to Nice itself, and the Alpine border running north to Geneva. This arrangement seemed a very welcome development to the Jewish community in the Alpes-Maritimes and Rhône-Alpes, for it freed them from the strictures of Vichy's Statut des Juifs that had already seen persecution and deportations. If it was true that some amongst the Italians were themselves anti-Semitic, anti-Semitism was not the centrepiece of Italian Fascism, and Italy's anti-Semitic laws were relatively lenient. Moreover, in the Alpes-Maritimes the law was exercised without a great deal of vigour: its strictures were tempered both by the humanity of the Catholic Church and the desire of the Italians to have their own way in France. 'The arrival of Italian soldiers in the departements east of the Rhône was generally received with satisfaction and with a feeling of relief among Jews in southern France.'[15]

At first this sentiment seemed well founded. In the first few weeks after Operation Anton, the Italian Carabinieri protected Nice's Jewish monuments and even broke up a march of French anti-Semites on a synagogue. Yet it soon emerged that the situation was not as clear-cut as it seemed. The demarcation between the Italian and German authorities on the one hand and the remaining Vichy officials on the other was vague, ill-defined and – very shortly – quarrelsome.

No sooner had the Germans settled themselves in Marseilles in the early winter of 1942 than they began rounding up the local Jewish population. They also urged their Italian counterparts in Nice to do likewise. The Italians proved resistant. On 17 December 1942 Mussolini had heard the simultaneous declaration from the Allies in London, Washington and Moscow condemning the Nazis' 'bestial policy of cold-blooded extermination',[16] and drew the logical conclusion. That same month the Italian authorities prevented Vichy attempts in Nice to have the Jews' passports stamped with the letter J for Juif or Juive; they then began interfering with the round-ups being undertaken by the Germans. On 22 February 1943 the Pusteria Division of the Italian Fourth Army had stopped the prefect of Lyons arresting 2,000–3,000 Polish Jews in the Grenoble area to the southeast of France's second city. There was also an extraordinary stand-off between the Axis allies in Annecy. Here the Vichy authorities had rounded up a group of Jews in the local prison for deportation. The Italians set up a military zone in the prison precincts and got them released.

This was all too much. Reich foreign minister Joachim von Ribbentrop was obliged to call a meeting with Mussolini, complaining of this outrageous partiality. This was held on 17 March 1943. Il Duce, mindful of the Allies' views on the extermination camps, diplomatically appointed the former police chief of the Adriatic city of Bari, Guido Lospinoso, as 'Inspector General of Racial Policy'. His job was to deal with the Jewish question. This, believed Lospinoso, was a matter for the Italian authorities, not the Germans. In any case, he found little to be said in favour of forced deportation of the Jewish inhabitants to 'the east'. The Allies' declaration meant that no one could plead ignorance of the likely fate of such people; it was now increasingly uncertain that Italy would continue the struggle on the side of the Axis; and the Sixth Army had been all but annihilated at Stalingrad. Caution was wise.

Accordingly, on his arrival in Nice, Lospinoso adopted the Vichy practice of 'assigned residence', 'résidence forcée'. This required individuals to live in a particular location under police surveillance. Lospinoso's difficulty was to find somewhere within his area of jurisdiction where the Jews could be accommodated without excessive preparatory effort, expenditure of human resources and monetary expense. He hit upon the idea of the high Alpine resorts on the Franco-Italian border. These were places that – as the Swiss had realised – had the additional advantage of being prisons without walls. They were remote enough and in inhospitable enough terrain for escape to be impracticable for all but the most determined.

Lospinoso's first choices that spring were Megève and nearby St Gervais in the Haute-Savoie. Part of the ancient Duchy of Savoie, this was the Alpine *département* lying 250 miles north of Nice in the Rhône-Alpes, on the southern side of Lake Geneva. Megève, a 3,369-foot resort ten miles east of Mont Blanc, in a sense selected itself. It was a medieval farming village developed as a skiing resort by the Rothschild family. The Jewish banking dynasty had tired of St Moritz in the years immediately before and after the First World War. Megève showed some promise as a substitute. It commanded a large, sunny bowl below the flanks of Mont Blanc that flattered the skiing of beginners, and it was easily accessible from Geneva. As skiing snowballed in the 1920s, the resort flourished. It attracted just the sort of set to whom St Moritz itself appealed: aristocrats, financiers and film stars: *haute volée* – high society. Now, in a turn of events not anticipated by the Rothschilds, the bankers were going to be supplanted by refugees.

The next challenge for Lospinoso was to move the 400 Jews from Nice to the Haute-Savoie. Rail was the obvious option to transport the thousands the Inspector General needed to resettle. However, to avoid the gradients of the Alpine terrain, the line from Nice ran west along the coast through the honeypots of Antibes, Cannes and St Raphael to Marseilles, before turning north to Grenoble and thence north-east to Savoie. All three sides of this rough oblong would take the Jews through territory held by German forces. Neither the Italians nor the refugees themselves would run this risk. Nobody knew how the Germans would react. Morale in the Wehrmacht had been badly hit by the final destruction of Paulus's Sixth Army in Stalingrad at the end of January 1943.

Fortunately, a committee had been established in Nice to look after the refugees' affairs and represent the community to the local authorities – now including the Italians. The Comité d'Assistance aux Refugés had provided the Jews with the papers necessary for survival in wartime Europe: identity cards, ration books and housing permits. Now it was able to secure the funding from the community itself to pay for lorries to take the refugees north by road to the Haute-Savoie. These were lumbering gazogènes, developed to run on charcoal in the absence of very heavily rationed petrol. Going uphill, passengers had to get out and push. The first convoys arrived in Megève on 8 April 1943. Just four days previously, a new crematorium – the fifth – had opened at Auschwitz.

As the days lengthened and the snows melted in the mountains, as the spring flowers blossomed, Lospinoso established similar communities in other Alpine resorts as far from the Germans and as close to the Italian border as possible. These were roughly on the north–south line between Megève and Nice: at Barcelonnette, Vence, Venanson, Castellane and Saint-Martin-Vésubie.

The last of these was only half a day's drive north of Nice, a remote 2,346-foot settlement where the village and its stone houses seemed to cling to the edge of a precipice. Between the wars Saint-Martin had been fashionable among the English escaping from the heat of the summer Riviera; in nearby Roque-billière in 1939, Arthur Koestler wrote his masterly critique of totalitarianism, *Darkness at Noon*. Now, courtesy of Lospinoso, the 1,650 locals were joined by more than 1,200 Jews. In the words of a Polish refugee:

Saint Martin, a small settlement in the mountains some sixty kilometres from Nice, was before the war a holiday and convalescence resort. There the Italian occupation authorities have set up one of the places of résidence forcée for the Jewish refugees who have reached France during the war from countries occupied by the Germans. Here the refugees were accommodated in houses and villas. Twice daily they have to report to the police officers; they are also not allowed to go outside the village or to leave it ... They are well organized: a Jewish committee elected by the refugees is responsible to the Italian authorities. They have schools for their children and there is also a Zionist youth movement. Despite the state of emergency life goes on normally, and thanks to the young Zionists cultural life is very well developed. Of course the refugees do not have the right to take jobs. The rich ones live off the money they have succeeded in saving from the Germans and the poor receive assistance from the committee.[17]

Somehow these communities maintained a sense of normality, even happiness, in the face of death. They had been dispatched like the unwanted goods they were into the high Alps to eke out an existence in that epic country, never knowing when a change in the fortunes of war would bring catastrophe.

There was another warning just as the first of the refugees

settled into Megève in that spring of 1943. Following the extraordinary stand-off in February in nearby Annecy, the Italians had prevented a similar round-up of Jews in Chambéry in the Savoie. Should the French or indeed the Germans gain the upper hand, the refugees would obviously be on their way to Auschwitz. Who could tell what might happen next?

5

Over the nearby border in Switzerland, Alexander Rotenberg in his work camp was in a place of greater safety, but that spring of 1943 Switzerland was once again by no means secure.

In March 1943, four months after his abrupt departure from Berchtesgaden to save Paulus's army at Stalingrad, Hitler was to return from Rastenburg to Bavaria. In preparation for his stay in Obersalzberg the Berghof was given a spring clean, the terrace that overlooked the Alps of Berchtesgadener Land was cleared of snow, and the colourful parasols were dusted off. The Führer would be accompanied by his entourage: Generalfeldmarschall Keitel and Generaloberst Jodl were to be joined by the staffs of Göring, Himmler and von Ribbentrop. With patchy snow still on the ground, the Nazi leaders would settle themselves into Obersalzberg, spreading out into the nearby resort of Bad Reichenhall and the city of Salzburg. Here, warming themselves in front of blazing log fires, they would once again plot Switzerland's demise.

Yet first – on their arrival – they discovered that Obersalzberg was beginning to reflect the deteriorating course of the Reich's war. It was no longer quite the sanctuary they sought. Berchtesgaden, hitherto considered inviolable, was now thought to be increasingly vulnerable to Allied air raids. By the time of Hitler's return to the Berghof that March of 1943, Reichsleiter Bormann was already drawing up plans for an elaborate bunker system. The underground accommodation included quarters for the Führer's Alsatian, Blondi. (According to Speer, 'The dog probably occupied the most important role in Hitler's private life; he meant more to his master than the Führer's closest associates

. . . I avoided, as did any reasonably prudent visitor to Hitler, arousing any feelings of friendship in the dog.')[18]

Equally unsettling were the wounded. The pressure on army hospitals throughout the Reich was now such that the Hotel Platterhof, intended to accommodate dignitaries visiting the Führer at the Berghof, had been converted into a hospital. Irmgard Paul, the girl who, as a three-year-old, had been dandled on Hitler's knee, was one of the Kindergruppe invited to put on a play that spring for the injured. The children performed *Sleeping Beauty* to great applause, but Irmgard remembered that she 'could not take my eyes off the young men with their thick, white head bandages, moving along slowly on crutches, arms in slings and legs in casts or missing entire limbs. I felt slightly sick and hoped fervently they would all get well, but wondered what on earth they would do with only one arm, one leg, or no legs.'[19]

It was in this atmosphere that Hitler's general staff began to scheme and plan.

After the calamity at Stalingrad of barely a month previously, and with Anglo-American forces from the Operation Torch landings now pushing back strongly against Rommel's Axis forces in Tunisia, the German army was in retreat. On 14 March – just before his return to Obersalzberg – Hitler had voiced his fear that 'the loss of Tunisia will also mean the loss of Italy'.[20] This in turn might give the Allies easy access to the Alps – and thence to Germany herself.

His staff had accordingly conceived the idea of a strategic retreat into those parts of central and western Europe that could be easily defended. This was the notion of 'Fortress Europe'. Of this, Switzerland and her mountains formed an integral part. The plan would incorporate the Swiss Alps into a defensive system joining General Guisan's Alpine Redoubt with the Black Forest, the Austrian Arlberg with the Bavarian Alps, the Brenner Pass with the Italian Dolomites. As to its practical execution in terms of seizing Switzerland, one imaginative option dated from July 1941. This was Operation Wartegau.[21] It called for a commando force assembled in flying boats on the Bodensee (Lake Constance) to be flown south-west the short distance to the Swiss lakes of Lucerne, Thun and Zurich. That would surprise the Swiss!

The Swiss had a source of intelligence actually within the German high command. On 19 March 1943, the agent known as the 'Wiking line' dispatched the most alarming of news to Berne. General Guisan was immediately alerted. German mountain troops, the Gebirgsjäger, were massing in Bavaria; General Eduard Dietl, a mountain warfare specialist, had been flown from occupied Finland to a specially established HQ in Munich to mastermind the operation. Invasion yet again seemed imminent, and Guisan at once mobilised his civilian army. The Swiss called it the *März-Alarm*.

SIX

Setting the Alps Ablaze

Guerrilla warfare is even more cruel than
conventional war, the chances of surviving slimmer.
Whoever joined up as a patriot or partisan signed
their own death warrant.

MAX SALVADORI

I

In the spring of 1943 Switzerland was once again teetering on the brink of invasion. At the same time to the south-east of the republic in Yugoslavia and to the south-west in France, other Alpine dramas were unfolding. Long heralded and coming to pass much later than Churchill – amongst many others – had hoped, this was the story of resistance in the Alps.

It had begun with the ignominious evacuation from Dunkirk of the British Expeditionary Force in 1940, the first summer of the war. Thence, in Hitler's eyes, there would be no return of a British army to Continental shores. General Gort's forces would sit impotently on the sidelines of Nazi-occupied Europe for the next thousand years.

Even during the chaotic days that followed the Fall of France, the British thought otherwise. If it was true that the Wehrmacht's blitzkrieg victories in Poland, Norway, Denmark, Holland, Belgium and France had been delivered through military might, they had been aided and abetted by fifth columnists in the defeated countries. These were the agents of sabotage, propaganda and subversion who had bombed civilians in Vienna, faked the attack on the radio station in Gleiwitz that had given Hitler the pretext for invading Poland in September 1939, and spread defeatism in France on the eve of her Fall. Commonplace today, at the outbreak of war these tactics were something of a novelty. It was true that in the wake of Anschluss, Britain's Secret Intelligence Service or MI6 had created a special unit for just such a purpose. Section D was based in Caxton Street in the medieval lanes around Westminster Abbey. It had dreamed up some wonderful schemes. They included sabotaging Swedish iron ore exports to the Reich, blowing up the oilfields in Romania and – best of all – blocking the blue Danube. None had come to fruition.

The Fall of France focused minds wonderfully. On 16 July 1940, the same day that Hitler signed Directive No. 16 ordering the invasion of Britain, a midnight meeting was held by Churchill in Downing Street. A plan was agreed to foment sabotage, subversion and resistance throughout Europe. Hugh Dalton, the blustering and belligerent Minister of Economic Warfare, was to be the political chief of the top-secret agency. It was to be called Special Operations Executive or SOE. Churchill's parting shot to Dalton as he left Number 10 through a haze of cigar smoke has passed into legend: 'Now set Europe ablaze.'

This was indicative of the high hopes that Churchill himself, Dalton and many others entertained at the time. The Executive was classed with strategic bombing and the naval blockade as amongst the country's most powerful weapons, its role to foment popular uprisings in Europe of which a new expeditionary army would merely be a guarantor.[1]

In practice, nurturing resistance proved far more difficult than envisaged. In due course there grew sufficient will to resist in the occupied countries of Europe. It was rarely to be found in 1940. The populations of France, Belgium, Holland, Norway, Denmark and Poland were shocked, cowed, subdued and generally sub-missive to their new masters – be they Nazis, Italians or puppet governments. The Alps themselves, remote though they might be, at first seemed little different. As to what Churchill dubbed the 'Ministry of Ungentlemanly Warfare', SOE had to begin at the beginning. In 1940 this was not necessarily a very good place to start. Lord Selborne, a Tory grandee who replaced Dalton in 1942, recalled, 'Underground warfare was an unknown art in

England in 1940; there were no text-books for newcomers, no old hands to initiate them into the experiences of the last war . . . lessons had to be learned in the hard school of practice.'² There was also the problem of MI6. Section D had been folded into SOE at its inception, and the intelligence service saw the new organisation as an upstart. This was understandable given that the two agencies' interests were perpetually at odds. Clandestine activities were undercover: silent, secret and inconspicuous. Sabotage and subversion were the polar opposites. A bomb here, a derailed train there, an assassination 'pour encourager les autres'. Visibility was all.

At once this conflict arose in the Alps.

As Switzerland's General Henri Guisan regularly made clear, the republic's very existence hinged on the Alpine railway tunnels that welded Italy and Germany into the Axis. When the British discovered that a third of Mussolini's coal requirement was trucked from the Ruhr and Saar coalfields through the St Gotthard and Simplon, they became an obvious object of interest to SOE. An operation was drawn up to destroy the marshalling yards, sabotage the bridges and block the railway lines. The Executive claimed that such an action 'might conceivably result not only in holding up [Italy's] coal deliveries but also military supplies or even, in certain circumstances, offensives'. It would shake the foundations of the treaty between Italy and the Reich. Dalton was delighted. 'So act!' he told his staff. 'I will gladly snap for this!'³

The plan was duly tabled with the Foreign Office and MI6. Both gave somewhat qualified support. MI6 regarded Switzerland as its own backyard and the FO pointed out that the operation might perhaps compromise Anglo-Swiss relations. The Swiss were protective of their tunnels, even if their railway had been an English idea. Moreover, both agencies had a general embargo on operations that might endanger Swiss neutrality. On 8 October 1940 it was nevertheless agreed that an SOE officer, John 'Jock' McCaffery, should be sent to reconnoitre.

McCaffery was a thirty-eight-year-old Glaswegian of Irish extraction. A Catholic who trained for the priesthood in

Rome and subsequently settled in Italy, he married, retrained as a teacher and ultimately found himself head of the British Council in the Ligurian port of Genoa. The Council peddled British culture and acted as a cover for intelligence operations. McCaffery, with his grasp of the intricacies of central European politics, was briefed to explore the practicality of the railway scheme, source explosives, and recruit Swiss railway workers. This took time. It was spring 1941 before the Scot had been sent to Switzerland, discovered quite how much dynamite would be needed, quite how closely the Swiss policed the tunnels, and quite how reluctant were the railway workers to blow up their own country's infrastructure. By then the mood in London had also changed. The pressure on Italy had briefly eased because of Hitler's momentous decision to invade the Balkans, the move that buttressed the Italian forces in Greece. The chance of detaching Mussolini's state from the Axis had temporarily slipped away. At the same time, over the winter MI6 agents in Switzerland had unearthed a rich vein of intelligence. This London was loath to lose. In these circumstances the FO and MI6 confirmed that no exception was to be made to the general policy about compromising Swiss neutrality. Dalton stopped snapping.

Yet in other ways the passage of time played into the hands of the SOE. By the summer of 1941, the Executive had settled into its secret headquarters at 64 Baker Street in London's West End, parachuted its first agents into France, and established a modus operandi. 'SOE's objects', related its historian M. R. D. Foot,'included discovering where these outbursts [of resistance] were, encouraging them when they were feeble, arming their members as they grew, and coaxing them when they were strong into the channels of greatest common advantage to the allies.'[4] Likewise, the more enterprising, courageous and resourceful inhabitants of the occupied countries had familiarised themselves with the Nazis and their agents and determined to get rid of them.

In the Alps, principal amongst the naysayers were the French in the west, and in the east the patriots and the partisans of Yugoslavia.

2

In France, as in all the occupied countries, resistance began in the form of virtually spontaneous and very largely incidental activity; only later did it coalesce into a unified, national resistance 'movement' of any substance.

Its figurehead was of course General de Gaulle. Born in Lille in French Flanders in 1890, Charles de Gaulle was an officer who had distinguished himself in the First World War in the trenches, in the thirties as an exponent of motorised warfare, and in combat once again during the brief period of fighting before the Fall of France in June 1940. In those torrid weeks he was promoted first to brigadier general, on 5 June 1940 to under-secretary of state for war. A fervent patriot, he was horrified by Pétain's proposal to seek an armistice with the Reich. On 17 June 1940 de Gaulle and a handful of other senior French officers flew to London. The following day the General issued his great rallying cry on the BBC from his London exile, the *appel du 18 Juin*. This called on the French people to reject the proposed armistice, to fight on, and to form the Free French Forces which – very soon – would oppose those of collaborationist Vichy. 'Whatever happens, the flame of the French resistance must not be extinguished and will not be extinguished.' Few heard this bidding in the darkness of France's Occupied Zone, and fewer still responded.

In the French Alps, the range that ran from Nice to Geneva, the *appel* fell on rather more fertile ground. North of the Jewish sanctuary of Nice and the Alpes-Maritimes lay the Alpine province of Dauphiné; further north beyond Dauphiné, the Alps that reared up to Mont Blanc overlooking the southern shores of Lake Geneva. This was the Haute-Savoie, where in 1943 Guido Lospinoso's Jewish charges would find sanctuary in Megève and St Gervais. From July 1940 these eastern borders of France had been designated part of the Zone Libre. Here homage was nominally paid to Vichy, but Pétain's way of collaboration was by no means to everyone's taste, and political persecution had proved scarcely less virulent under Vichy than under the Nazis in the Occupied Zone. Moreover, in the same way as

Switzerland lived under the constant threat of Nazi invasion, so too did France's Zone Libre – something that throughout France was more conducive to resistance than passivity. In the Alps the people were also of an independent spirit, not always as regardful as they surely should have been of directives from Vichy or Paris or Berlin.

After the initial shock of the events of 1940 had subsided, the Alpine people began to stir. If not all had heard or registered de Gaulle's original appeal of 18 June 1940, many now began to listen to his regular broadcasts from London on the BBC; in August 1940 it had done the General a power of good to be sentenced by Vichy to death for high treason. In Savoie, the Dauphiné and the Alpes-Maritimes the people also began to realise how admirably their surroundings lent themselves to the purpose of the *réfractaires*: those who refused to submit to the Vichy regime. They might be combed out in street-to-street, house-to-house searches in France's towns and cities; they were far more difficult to track down in her mountains. These offered levels of cover that made it very difficult for the Wehrmacht to find, let alone to attack any erring *réfractaires*. They were bandit country.

One day in the summer of 1941 – it was the glory days of Operation Barbarossa when the Wehrmacht swept the Red Army before it – a small group of men gathered in the Café de la Rotunde near Grenoble station. Its immediate environs were grubby, but beyond lay the inspiration of the great mountains of the Rhône-Alpes towering over the Alpine city: the Chartreuse to the north, the Belledonne to the east, and to the south-west the Vercors. This was a limestone plateau sixty miles long and thirty broad, the size – say – of the county of Surrey: less populous, though, less stuffy, more rugged, more wooded, and at the time still supposedly the home of wild bears.

Among the men in the café were a forty-one-year-old engineer called Pierre Dalloz, and forty-seven-year-old Eugène Chavant. Dalloz was a distinguished Alpinist and pioneer of winter mountaineering who had climbed extensively in the Vercors. Chavant was a cobbler's son, born in Colombe just north of Grenoble. Both saw the plateau as a sanctuary, for it was accessible only by a few steep and narrow roads, easily blocked and readily defended. The pair's idea was to turn this to advantage. They would set up camps to provide refuge for those persecuted by Vichy.

Like most of the resistance in occupied Europe, they also had an ulterior motive. The Third Republic had failed. Chavant was a socialist who wanted to build a more just society on its ruins. The Soviet spy H. A. R. 'Kim' Philby, who had worked briefly for SOE before joining MI6, commented that the aim of the SOE, 'in Churchill's words, was to set Europe ablaze. This could not be done by appealing to people to co-operate in restoring an unpopular and discredited old order.'[5]

Chavant screened candidates for the haven. Those selected were then taken up to the plateau. By the beginning of 1942 there were around a hundred distributed in makeshift camps situated in the woods within reach of the scattered villages. They came to be known as the Montagnards, a subspecies of the rural resistance throughout France beginning to be called the maquis. Funding was obtained through the SOE in London's Baker Street, a system of food distribution set up, and a sentinel system arranged using the plateau's electricity station. If the lights went on and off three times, trouble was on its way. Many of the Montagnards were French and foreign Jews who would otherwise be bedded down in Auschwitz.

Three events added impetus to the affairs on the plateau.

First came Operation Anton, the invasion by Axis forces of the Zone Libre. As we have seen, in the south and west of France this had meant takeover by the Wehrmacht; on the eastern Alpine border by General Vercellino's Italian Fourth Army. The Pusteria Alpine Division detrained in Grenoble in November 1942. The result might have been anticipated: the eruption of a plethora of resistance organisations of various political shades:

Combat, Franc-Tireur, Armée secrète, Organisation de résistance de l'armée. Second came the perception that – with victory at El Alamein and the Allied landings in North Africa that had precipitated Operation Anton – the tide of the war was now turning against the Reich. Third, in the New Year of 1943, there came Service du Travail Obligatoire (STO). Set up by the Vichy government on 16 February 1943 to provide workers for German industry, STO entailed dispatching skilled workers to the Reich in exchange for French prisoners of war in Germany. It proved an excellent agent of recruitment for the maquis among those presented with the choice of working for the Nazis or joining the resistance, of turning themselves in or escaping to the mountains. This, it should be said, was no casual choice. As the senior SOE liaison officer Max Salvadori later put it, 'Guerrilla warfare is even more cruel than conventional war, the chances of surviving slimmer. Whoever joined up as a patriot or partisan signed their own death warrant.'[6] In the first few months of 1943, the numbers in the Vercors camps nevertheless doubled or tripled.

The Pusteria Division soon realised that they had a problem on their doorstep. From the maquis established in the Vercors, the Belledonne and the Chartreuse came a steady drip of sabotage and subversion throughout the Dauphiné. *Les Allobroges* – the ancient term for the Alpine inhabitants of both the Savoie and the Dauphiné – was the resistance news-sheet started in the spring of 1941. Eighteen months later, explosives were being stolen, power lines and transformers being destroyed, and the personal details of prospective STO victims were being seized and burned. Something needed to be done. During winter, with snow on the narrow roads that accessed the plateau, the Vercors was virtually inaccessible, an island more than a plateau. With the spring thaw of 1943 came calling the Organizzazione per la Vigilanza e la Repressione dell'Antifascismo (the Organisation for Vigilance and Repression of Anti-Fascism or OVRA). Founded in 1927, this was Mussolini's equivalent of the Gestapo, indeed the organisation that provided a model for Heinrich Himmler's Secret State Police.

In mid-March 1943 the OVRA seized fourteen of the Montagnards on the Vercors. They talked, one of them induced to do so by being forced to sit on a red-hot frying pan. A second series of raids followed in which the OVRA headed straight for the secret camps. The electricity station warning system worked, and in each case the Italians found the camps deserted. In May, disaster followed. An attempt by the Montagnards to seize a petrol tanker at Pont de Claix, at the bottom of the plateau's eastern escarpment, was botched. A dozen men were seized, tortured, and talked. In the purge that followed the plateau's unofficial system of administration collapsed, six tons of explosive were seized, a number of the camps were broken up, and the survivors had to retreat to the most remote parts of the Vercors.[7] The Montagnards needed professional help.

This came in the form of Capitaine Alain Le Ray.

Born in 1910 in Paris, Le Ray was an ambitious young officer and an expert skier and mountaineer. Once commissioned, he was attached to the elite Chasseurs Alpins mountain light infantry, headquartered in Grenoble. Captured in northern France in June 1940, he had escaped from his first POW camp and was sent to Colditz. The legendary 'escape-proof' castle in Saxony held him for three weeks. Following his flight on 11 April 1941 he became the first Colditz prisoner to make it to freedom, to achieve a 'home run'. Le Ray's track record and his familiarity with Grenoble made him a good choice as the first military leader of the Vercors. He was also good-looking, bold and courageous, and he had the impeccable social credentials of being the son-in-law of François Mauriac. He took charge in May 1943, just as the plateau lurched into crisis. In summer 1943, as the maquis emerged once again from their refuges, Le Ray began turning them into a fighting force.

He also did something more. For Operation Montagnards, as it would soon be called, was little less than a secret plan to turn the whole course of the war in Alpine France.

*

At the same time, the maquis further north in the Rhône-Alpes were acting under the same stimuli in similar ways.

In the Savoie, the maquis leader was Colonel Jean Vallette d'Osia. Born in 1898, Vallette d'Osia was a professional soldier who had been decorated in the First World War, wounded three times, and ended up graduating from the elite military academy at Saint Cyr. Captured during the Battle of France in 1940, he escaped twice. He then turned to General Weygand, who had replaced Gamelin as the French military leader too late in the day to prevent the Fall of France. Weygand persuaded d'Osia to follow the call of de Gaulle and take a hand in the renaissance of the French nation. In August 1940 d'Osia became commanding officer of the 27th Mountain Infantry Battalion in Annecy. This was part of L'armée d'armistice, a force of 100,000 that Vichy retained under the armistice terms. The post was a cover that enabled the Colonel to establish links with the nascent maquis in Savoie.

After Operation Anton in 1942 and the dissolution of L'armée d'armistice that Anton entailed, d'Osia became the formal leader of the resistance in Savoie. A small, fiery man and a fierce disciplinarian, he conceived the idea of creating a secret Alpine army as a response to the occupation of the Zone Libre. This meant not simply assembling the maquis – as had been done in the Vercors – but properly training them in the way that his colleague Alain Le Ray would soon be doing on the Grenoble plateau. For this purpose d'Osia set up an instruction camp on the Col des Saisies, a 5,436-foot pass close to what is now the skiing resort of La Saisies. This dated from March 1943, the very beginnings of STO. It was the germ of a series of training camps in the Savoie and Haute-Savoie where maquis leaders were inculcated into the theory and practice of mountain warfare. To many of the recruits brought up in the highlands of Savoie on the flanks of Mont Blanc, the basics of climbing and skiing were second nature. They were now taught how to deal with glaciers, cut steps in ice slopes, use ice axes and crampons: to become proficient, professional mountaineers. Once again, this maquis was armed and funded by the Allies, both by the SOE and, later, its fresh-faced US equivalent, the OSS – the story of which appears in the next chapter.

From March 1943 the BBC, at the behest of the SOE's Baker Street propaganda section, began to talk of major groups of maquisards in the Haute-Savoie. Swiss radio also began to run stories of risings in the Savoie – which adjoined the republic's Canton Valais. It was this activity – and publicity – that gave the movement in the Haute-Savoie a reputation that inspired resistance throughout France. Similarly, from the summer of 1943 onwards, such was the extent of the resistance around Grenoble that it became known by both General de Gaulle's Free French Forces and – critically – the BBC as the 'capital of the maquis'.

The resistance in the French Alps had arrived.

3

Meanwhile, only a few miles to the north-east of the Savoie, Switzerland survived. The March Alarm that had sounded on 19 March 1943 had again proved false.

Four weeks earlier, Generalfeldmarschall von Manstein had launched a fresh attack on the Eastern Front. By the end of March, the Soviet Voronezh Front was back on the east bank of the Donets river, the Red Army had abandoned nearly 6,000 square miles of the territory it had won after Stalingrad, and the cities of Belgorod and Kharkov were once again in the hands of the Wehrmacht.

In the Berchtesgaden Berghof, Hitler's warlords celebrated; every day the sun in the deep valley rose earlier and set later; every day the snow receded and sometimes the warm föhn wind blew from the south. Now there was spring in the air and – with this news from the east – all thoughts of Fortress Europe and the invasion of Switzerland were shelved. General Guisan's forces in Switzerland, hastily mobilised, were once again stood down.

In the place of the invasion of Switzerland, quite another plan was conceived in Berchtesgaden. This was Operation Citadel, the Wehrmacht's ambitious plan to destroy the Soviet Central and Voronezh Fronts 280 miles south of Moscow in the Kursk salient.

Yet if Hitler could once again look with satisfaction to the Eastern Front, he was less happy with his southern flank, with Italy. Here, Il Duce's regime was clearly crumbling. The Italians had entered the war trailing on the coat-tails of the Nazis. They had done so without enthusiasm, hoping at best for some ill-gotten spoils. As it so turned out, the country had gained little and lost a great deal in the conflicts in the Alps, the Balkans, in the Soviet Union and in North Africa. Casualties would soon amount to over 204,000. Of these, 67,000 had been killed, 111,000 were missing and 26,000 had died of disease. Hungry workers in Milan and Turin were now demonstrating for 'bread, peace and freedom'; Venetian women now spurned the propaganda suggestion that they looked their best in coats made of tabby cats' fur.[8]

Il Duce needed support. Now firmly ensconced for three months in the Berghof, the Führer summoned Mussolini up from Rome to the Reich.

On 7 April 1943 Hitler drove down from the Berghof to meet Mussolini in Salzburg. In the city's baroque Schloss Klessheim the Führer unfolded his plans for two operations intended – among other things – to put heart into his ally. The first was Operation Citadel in Kursk; the second Fall Schwarz. This was the Axis's fifth offensive against the resistance in Yugoslavia, Mussolini's north-eastern neighbour. According to Goebbels, the enthusiasm and energy with which Hitler set out these operations won over the faltering Mussolini. 'By putting every ounce of energy into the effort, he succeeded in pushing Mussolini back on the rails . . . The Duce underwent a complete change . . . When he got out of the train on his arrival, the Fuehrer thought he looked like a broken old man; when he left he was in high fettle, ready for any deed.'[9] At the end of the meeting Mussolini exclaimed, 'Fuehrer, the Berlin–Rome Axis will win.'[10]

Nevertheless, Hitler thought it wise to put in place a contingency plan. If Italy withdrew from the Axis, the Reich would at best have a neutral country on its southern doorstep; at worst it would have one newly contracted to the Allies. After all, as 1914 approached Italy had been the third player in the Triple Alliance of Germany and Austria-Hungary; she came into the war in 1915 allied to the Triple Entente of Britain, France and Russia. There was little to stop her doing something similar now. Should that happen, disaster beckoned for Germany. The Alpine passes of Italy were the southern gateways to the Reich. Obviously, neither the passes nor northern Italy could be allowed to fall into enemy hands. On 21 March 1943 Hitler summoned Generalfeldmarschall Erwin Rommel, the hero of the Afrika Korps, to the Berghof.

Hitler briefed Rommel to set up a new army group to take control of northern Italy in the event of Mussolini's collapse. The lightning seizure of the Alpine pass routes was critical to the whole operation: the Brenner, the Reschen forty miles to its west, and the Tarvis seventy miles south-east. Rommel – as experienced in mountain as desert warfare – accordingly sketched a plan to infiltrate four army divisions into Italy to hold these passes. The spearheads would be followed by sixteen more divisions ready to penetrate beyond the triangle of Italy's industrial heartland of Turin, Milan and Genoa. The scheme was to be called Operation Achse (Axis). To his wife Rommel wrote succinctly, 'It is better to fight the war in Italy than at home.'[11]

In the course of developing these plans with Hitler, Rommel would present himself at noon at the Berghof for the daily war conferences. From the picture window in the great hall that overlooked Berchtesgadener Land, the General enjoyed a scene that he found breathtaking every time he turned to it: a paradise of serrated peaks, green valleys, tumbling streams, gingerbread houses and bright blue skies. The red marble conference table told a very different story. The meetings brought Rommel up to date with the position on the various fronts on which the Reich's forces were operating: the trouble in North Africa, the aftermath of Stalingrad, the destruction of German cities by the USAAF and RAF, the U-boat losses running at thirty a month in the Battle of the Atlantic. This was the regular warfare. Now, resistance – irregular warfare – was showing its hand in the French and Yugoslav Alps in the hitherto subdued occupied countries. Where would it all end?

One day Rommel drew Hitler aside and volunteered an appreciation of the military situation, the *tour d'horizon* of which the Führer himself was a master. 'Hitler listened to it all with downcast eyes,' Rommel later told his family.[12] 'Suddenly he looked up and said that he, too, was aware that there was very little chance left of winning the war. But the West would never conclude peace with him – at least not the statesmen who were at the helm now. He said that he had never wanted war with the West. But now the West would have its war – have it to the end.'[13]

On 1 July 1943 Hitler flew back to Rastenburg to oversee Operation Citadel. Rommel headed the ninety miles north to Munich, where, away from the prying eyes of the Italians, he completed his preparations for Operation Achse. If they were to be executed Rommel would be sent a codeword. The infiltration of the Reich's forces into northern Italy was the first task; the second was to turn on the Italians in the event of Italy decamping to the Allies. The word was 'Achse'.

4

This was timely, for it coincided with the failure of one of the two operations over which Hitler had enthused with such effect to Mussolini: Fall Schwarz, the fifth offensive against the partisans in Yugoslavia.

When the Axis forces had invaded the Balkan state in April 1941, Croatia had been hived off as a Nazi satellite under the fascist Ustaše; the remainder of the country had been divided between German, Hungarian and Italian forces. In this ragbag of provinces and statelets riven with age-old racial and religious rivalries, resistance had emerged almost at once.

Josip Broz, who went under the *nom de guerre* of Tito, had set up a resistance cell in Belgrade in June 1941. Born in 1892 in modest circumstances in Croatia, Tito had trained as a mechanic, worked briefly as a test driver for Daimler, was conscripted, and in 1915 became the youngest sergeant major in the Austro-Hungarian army. Wounded and captured by the Russians, his imagination was fired by the Bolshevik revolution. On his return to Yugoslavia after the war he joined the tiny Yugoslav Communist Party. On 27 June 1941 the Party's Central Committee appointed him commander-in-chief of the liberation forces. He dubbed his supporters the partisans.

They were rivalled by the Chetniks, a Serbian group led by Colonel Dragoljub (Draža) Mihailović. A year younger than Tito, Mihailović was a Serb with a similarly distinguished military record to Tito's but with diametrically opposed political opinions. He supported the exiled King Peter, and his followers were mainly drawn from the Royal Army. Based in the mountains of Ravna Gora in western Serbia, Churchill called them the patriots.

With King Peter's government in exile in London, Churchill's sympathies, British policy, and the parsimonious delivery of war materiel by the RAF lay with the Chetniks. Goaded by the SOE in Baker Street, the RAF eventually began dropping more arms to Mihailović. Then, in the course of 1942 the question arose in London as to which of the two resistance groups was doing most on behalf of the Allied war effort to pin down the Axis. In 1941 SOE had set up a station in Cairo, where the British still maintained bases in the former protectorate, to co-ordinate its activities in the Balkans and Middle East. In the autumn of 1942 – the autumn of Operation Torch and its consequence, Operation Anton – word reached Cairo that the partisans were greedier of Axis resources than the Chetniks. Cairo was also told of fighting in places amounting to civil war between the Chetniks and the partisans. Was Mihailović really the best man to set the Alps of Yugoslavia ablaze? To answer this question, on Christmas Day 1942, an SOE colonel, S. W. ('Bill') Bailey, was parachuted into Italian-occupied Montenegro to make an assessment of Mihailović.

Colonel Bailey was somewhat surprised to encounter a man who set himself above the sartorial and tonsorial standards of Sandhurst. There was a tradition in the Serbian Orthodox Church of its adherents neither shaving nor cutting their hair until the country had been rid of its current invaders. This Mihailović followed: his long hair, beard and thin wire spectacles made him look like an elderly cleric. He and his staff also dispensed with uniform in favour of a homespun outfit that included slippers. They did not dispense with plum brandy, or rather they dispensed the local *eau de vie* so liberally that Mihailović – in Bailey's presence – roundly denounced the British for failing to supply him with sufficient arms. The Colonel was a formidable figure: a metallurgist, gifted linguist, excellent at handling explosives. He reported to Cairo that there was little prospect of prodding Mihailović into action against the Axis and less of him co-operating with Tito.

A bitter war now broke out in London and Cairo over whether support should be withdrawn from the right-wing Mihailović and extended to the left-wing – nay, communist – Tito. Basil Davidson was a peacetime journalist on the *Economist* who had joined MI6 at the outbreak of war. By late 1942 he was heading SOE's Yugoslavia station. He wrote: 'Something like battle lines were drawn . . . and soon the opposing sides began to face each other with all the passion that set the Children of Light against the Children of Darkness. Fighting alliances were made, recruits were sought, morality wavered, truth lowered her head. Paper came into its own again. Squadrons of memoranda were loaded up and launched.'[14] In short, there was a fine old row. One of the supporters of the partisans was Davidson's number two, Captain William Deakin. An Oxford don who before the war worked as Churchill's research assistant on his life of Marlborough, he naturally had the Prime Minister's ear. The upshot was that Churchill ordered Lord Selborne – now leading SOE – to find out exactly what Tito's partisans were up to. In the end, on 28 June 1943, Deakin himself was parachuted into Tito's headquarters; or, as it so turned out, into a maelstrom.

From the very beginning of the resistance movement in Yugoslavia in 1941, the Axis had mounted major operations against both Tito's partisans and Mihailović's Chetniks. These had begun in the autumn of 1941 with an attack on Užice, a territory in western Serbia liberated by Mihailović. There followed major offensives in January 1942, in spring 1942, and in the first four months of 1943 – the Battle of Neretva. This segued into the Battle of Sutjeska, into which Deakin plunged. This was the fifth of the major Axis offensives, otherwise called Fall Schwarz.

Here, in the Alpine area close to the Sutjeska river in southeastern Bosnia, were encamped 22,000 of Tito's forces. Though numerous, they were poorly trained, poorly armed, and incapable of holding off a major assault. Against them, under Generaloberst Alexander Löhr and Generalleutnant Rudolf Lüters, were ranged almost 130,000 Axis troops.

The Axis offensive began on 15 May 1943. Tito's forces soon found themselves largely encircled on the Durmitor massif, an Alpine eruption with forty-eight peaks over 6,000 feet. This lent itself well enough to defence, but entailed a month's long battle in the mountain terrain. Two days after Deakin's arrival the Germans were on the cusp of descending from the mountains above Mratinje and cutting off the partisans' last exit. '[O]ur lives', remembered Vladimir Dedijer – Tito's biographer – 'hung by a thread'.[15] The drama culminated on 9 June 1943. The weather cleared and Tito's party was located by a Luftwaffe spotter plane and bombed in the Sutjeska gorge. Tito was injured, his bodyguard and dog were killed. (The latter was credited with saving Tito's life.) Deakin's radio operator, Captain William Stuart, also died, and Deakin himself was hit in the foot. Yet the partisans then managed to break out across the Sutjeska river through the lines of the German 118th and 104th Jäger Divisions, and 369th Croatian Infantry Division. The leading partisan units were trailed by three brigades and 2,000 wounded. In the tradition of the vicious Balkan engagements, Löhr ordered that all should be killed, including unarmed medical orderlies. Yet although this left more than a third of the partisans dead or wounded, the main force had escaped to fight another day. The German field commander Lüters described his opponents as 'well organized, skilfully led and with combat morale unbelievably high'.[16]

The Axis failure here marked the turning point in the war in Yugoslavia. In the first half of 1943 the two major campaigns in Neretva and Sutjeska to eliminate the heart of the partisan forces had failed. There would be further offensives, but none so ambitious. In the Alps of Yugoslavia the resistance – in a sense the whole notion of guerrilla warfare – had come of age.

The episode was also the crux of British policy in the Balkans. Deakin, despite his narrow escape, was as fulsome as Lüters about the virtues of the partisans. On 23 June 1943 Churchill met with his chiefs of staff in London to discuss the Balkan question. Henceforth, the British could not doubt the wisdom of the SOE supplying materiel to Tito; they did not as yet decide to stop supporting the Chetniks. It would take another mission to Tito in the autumn of 1943 to achieve this turnabout. This was an adventure that made the name of Brigadier Fitzroy Maclean and spawned his best-selling account, *Eastern Approaches*.[17]

5

Meanwhile there was more trouble brewing for Hitler further west in the Alps, in Italy.

Within hours of the Axis opening its Fall Schwarz offensive on Tito's forces in Sutjeska, its troops in North Africa were laying down their arms. In Tunisia, on 13 May 1943, the final surrender of Axis forces to the British Eighth Army yielded 275,000 prisoners of war. No sooner had this operation been completed than – on 10 July – Anglo-American forces led by General Eisenhower invaded Sicily. The island was defended by a force of 200,000 Italians and 62,000 German troops and Luftwaffe. In the Berghof, reports soon reached Hitler of the collapse of morale of the Italian army. Mussolini was once again summoned to see the Führer. This time the meeting was to be on Italian soil, in the Alpine garrison town of Feltre in the Dolomites. It was set for 19 July 1943.

The Duce proved to be in despair, scarcely capable of words, and the Führer as usual was left to do the talking. Once again he did his best to rally his demoralised ally. 'If anyone tells me that our tasks can be left to another generation, I reply that this is not the case. No one can say that the future generation will be a generation of giants. Germany took thirty years to recover; Rome never rose again. This is the voice of history.'[18] It was no use. Mussolini's mood was blackened further when the news came through of the first heavy Allied bombing raid on Rome. A force of more than 500 Allied aircraft had caused extensive damage and thousands of casualties. The Duce could not steel himself to tell the Führer that Italy would – could – fight no longer. The tonic that the Führer had given him with such apparent success in Salzburg three months previously now failed utterly.

On his return to Rome from the Alps, Mussolini found his fate sealed. The Fascist Grand Council had not convened since December 1939. It met on the night of 24–5 July 1943. The Council demanded the restoration of power to the monarchy, the return of parliamentary democracy, and the reversion of the leadership of the armed forces from the Duce to the King himself: Victor Emmanuel III. On the following evening Mussolini was summoned to the royal palace, dismissed by the King, arrested and carted off to a police station to spend the night in a cell. The King asked General Pietro Badoglio to step in as Prime Minister.

News of the Council's deliberations first trickled through to Hitler's Rastenburg headquarters on the afternoon of 25 July 1943. 'The Duce has resigned,' Hitler tactfully told his astonished staff at the 9.30 p.m. war conference. 'Badoglio, our most bitter enemy, has taken over the government.'[19]

Italy, Hitler assumed, would at once switch sides. Badoglio, in the glory days the Duce's Chief of Staff, was indeed negotiating with the Allies. Hitler's response was immediate, for he knew how vulnerable this made the German forces engaging Eisenhower's invaders in Sicily. If the Italians blew the Alpine bridges and tunnels, the Wehrmacht lines of communication would be severed, the forces trapped. This was the contingency that Hitler had foreseen and on which he had briefed Rommel. Operation Achse needed no dusting off. Generalfeldmarschall Rommel stood at the shortest of notice to put it into effect. The only word he needed was 'Achse'.

SEVEN

Spy City Central

Overnight Switzerland was transformed into the centrepiece of Britain's intelligence effort against Nazi Germany.

NEVILLE WYLIE

I

On the afternoon of Tuesday 17 August 1943, three weeks after the fall of Mussolini, a short, balding man with big ears could be seen walking circumspectly up to the front door of the British legation in Thunstrasse, Berne. He rang the bell, and was duly admitted. Soon he found himself being shown into the office of the military attaché, Colonel Henry Cartwright VC. The Colonel was a veteran of the First World War, a former POW, author of numerous escape attempts. He thought himself a good judge of men. Cartwright's visitor was clutching a briefcase and seemed nervous. Well he might be. He was a German diplomatic official about to declare his willingness to share state secrets with the Allies.

Fritz Kolbe was a forty-three-year-old official at the Foreign Office in Berlin's Wilhelmstrasse. His job as an assistant to Ambassador Karl Ritter entailed screening and distributing top-secret messages between the ambassador's office and various diplomatic posts abroad. As Ritter was himself Joachim von Ribbentrop's right-hand man, Kolbe was exposed to a great deal of highly sensitive intelligence. Deploring the activities of the Nazis – he was a fervent Roman Catholic – he determined to use this information to help the Allies win the war. In the summer of 1943, Kolbe wangled the job of taking some sensitive documents to the German embassy in Berne, the Reich's window on freedom. He filled a briefcase with samples of his wares. These were mimeographs of signals intelligence. Some were from western Europe, some from the Eastern Front, some from the Far East. On reaching Berne, he arranged an introduction to Cartwright through a friend, a German Jew called Dr Ernst Kocherthaler. Once in the attaché's presence in Thunstrasse, Kolbe steeled himself to say his piece. The risks were very high and the consequences were likely to be momentous. Failure would mean the Gestapo, torture and the concentration camps. Success would mean defeat for Germany, the Fatherland. The choice was stark and Kolbe was a man of tremendous courage. He explained to Cartwright who he was, what he wanted to do, why he wanted to do it, and – by way of a climax – plucked a handful of the copies from his case and thrust them in front of the attaché.

From the start of the interview, Cartwright had been unimpressed. This was Switzerland. The intersection of Europe was the one place where the agents of the Allies and the Axis could live with relative impunity in close proximity to their counterparts, subsisting on the currency of information. This information might be available anywhere, but Switzerland was by far the best place to barter and exchange such goods – preferably for ready Swiss francs. This was nothing new. Since the 'discovery' of Switzerland in the nineteenth century, her great peaks had drawn the well-heeled and well-informed from all over Europe and beyond. What could be more natural than the exchange of gossip, information, ideas that would later be dignified by the term 'intelligence'? The Swiss cities and resorts became hotbeds of spying. Indeed the profession came of age in Switzerland during the First World War when the country acted as the neutral ground where all parties to the war met, talked and struck deals. In 1920 the establishment of Geneva as the League of Nations Headquarters put the finishing touches to the country's status as a bring-and-buy stall for international secrets. In 1928, Somerset Maugham, one of the most popular novelists of his day, published a highly influential spy novel. *Ashenden* proved a prototype for Ian Fleming, Graham Greene and John le Carré. The book was based on Maugham's own experiences of working for MI6 and was naturally set in Switzerland.

If this was Switzerland, this was also the summer of 1943. No sooner had Generalfeldmarschall Erich von Manstein's brilliant initiative seen the retaking by the Wehrmacht of Kharkov than a counteroffensive from the Soviets had culminated in the Battle of Kursk. Operation Citadel had ended in the middle of July with the Wehrmacht losing 550 tanks and more than half a million men killed, wounded or missing. The Allies had just invaded Sicily, and Italy was clearly on the cusp of abandoning the Axis. With the war on a knife-edge, the Allies and the Reich were both desperate for intelligence that might turn its course. What could be more valuable than to know what the enemy intended to do and how he intended to do it?

Intelligence gleaned in Switzerland about German preparations for the Kursk offensive was the crown jewels of a network known as the Lucy Ring. The information was arguably decisive in the Wehrmacht's defeat. The Abwehr – the German army secret service – had been alive to the prospect of an Allied landing on the vulnerable shores of Italy. A brilliant British deception plan involving fake papers suggested the landings would take place in Greece and Sardinia. Operation Mincemeat (wonderfully set out in Ewen Montagu's *The Man Who Never Was* and Ben Macintyre's *Operation Mincemeat*) had fooled the Abwehr and the assault had already come in Sicily. Now the Allies had got wind of a rocket research centre somewhere on the Baltic. Here, what Goebbels would later christen the revenge weapons – Vergeltungswaffen – were being developed. What more could be discovered in Switzerland? The battleship *Tirpitz* was lying low in a Norwegian fjord. A British plan was developed to attack her using midget submarines. By what underwater defences was she protected? Hundreds of such questions puzzled the minds of military planners on both sides of the war. Switzerland was the place where such intelligence could be bought. The place was awash with spies, saboteurs, turncoats, chancers, agents and every sort of agent provocateur. It was once said that the whole of Switzerland was one clandestine conversation.

The Swiss themselves could hardly be excluded from the dialogue. They were anxious, though, not to be seen to promote spying lest it compromise their neutrality. Hitler regarded Switzerland as a fire hydrant through which gushed the secrets of the Reich. Foreign Minister von Ribbentrop thought this alone sufficient reason to invade the republic. The Swiss secret service – Nachrichtendienst – accordingly had to be seen to keep a strict and impartial eye on all foreign agents irrespective of their hue: French, Italian, British, German, American, Soviet and indeed Chinese and Japanese. In early 1940 this even-handedness went as far as penetrating the Zurich station of the British secret service, MI6. Still, the head of the Nachrichtendienst, Brigadier General Roger Masson, judiciously maintained friendly relations with his Allied counterparts and selectively exchanged intelligence.

Meanwhile the warring parties maintained counter-intelligence operations to hamstring their enemies' clandestine activities. The Gestapo trailed Allied agents, earmarked some for possible assassination – including Cartwright himself – and kept a twenty-four-hour watch on Allied premises. The Allied stations reciprocated. Missions of all nationalities had to be very sensitive to counter-intelligence operations both by the Swiss and their enemies. Agents provocateurs were aplenty. Several attempts had already been made to foist them on Cartwright.

This was precisely what Kolbe was taken for by the Colonel. The attaché was in any case under strict orders to turn away anyone purporting to be an anti-Nazi volunteer. He refused even to look at the papers Kolbe had strewn over his desk. 'Sir,' declared Cartwright, 'you take me for an utter fool. I am not an utter fool. I know that you are sent as a plant to get me into trouble but in the remote possibility that you are not a plant, then, sir, you are a cad. And I do not deal with cads.' With that Kolbe was dismissed and shown the door.[1]

Nevertheless he persisted. The German presented himself at

the private residence of the legation's head of chancery. Again he was given a very British cold shoulder. Only at this point did Dr Kocherthaler suggest to Kolbe that he might try the Americans. After all, the Allies were allies. The US legation in Berne was long established and had its own military attaché in the form of Brigadier General Barnwell Legge – a robust and rubicund figure who just happened to be on excellent terms with his opposite number, Cartwright. Moreover, shortly before the Swiss borders were entirely closed by Operation Anton, a specialist in security matters had arrived in Berne via Spain and France. His name was Allen Welsh Dulles, his cover name the very British 'Mr Bull'. A meeting was set for 19 August at which Dulles would be able to form his own opinions of Cartwright's reject.

2

From the point of view of the British spymasters in Berne, the Americans had come rather late to the party and overdressed.

Although intelligence-gathering is the world's second-oldest profession and proverbially just as respectable as the first, states had not set up professional organisations for such purposes until the First World War. Britain's Secret Service Bureau was founded in 1909 and is 'the oldest continuously surviving foreign intelligence-gathering organisation in the world'.[2] It developed into a number of separate sections. Of these, MI6 – also known as the Secret Intelligence Service or SIS – concentrated on espionage overseas. It established itself under Sir George Mansfield Cumming ('C') during the First World War, and employed agents as diverse as the MP and novelist John Buchan, the celebrated cricketer Colonel Freddie Browning, and the future children's writer Arthur Ransome. It achieved just enough to avoid disbandment at the end of hostilities. Only just: 'In the 1920s the British Secret Service, with a worldwide remit, had a total complement of fewer than two hundred people, sixty-odd at home and approximately twice that number abroad.'[3]

With the re-emergence of the threat of Germany in the thirties, attention was focused by its new chief Sir Hugh Sinclair on the Nazi threat. The logistics of the organisation meant it was natural that it should work hand in hand with the Foreign Office. This liaison took the form of the establishment of a Passport Control Officer within embassies, a function that provided a degree of cover – and diplomatic immunity – for clandestine activity. Such a system depended on the good will of the ambassadors concerned, and in this respect Berne proved problematic. Despite the proximity of Switzerland to Germany and her familiar advantages as a market for intelligence, the head of the British legation was intransigent. This was Sir George Warner, appointed to the Berne mission in 1935. Born in 1879, educated at Eton and Balliol, Sir George was a punctilious gentleman of the traditional diplomatic persuasion who regarded intelligence-gathering with distaste. Tampering with mail and tapping phones he thought a violation of Swiss neutrality and an abuse of its hospitality. It compromised his stance with his hosts and he shunned the presence of the grubby mackintoshed men from the intelligence service in his legation in Thunstrasse. Soon he was to be outshone by his colleagues in MI6.

Claude Dansey was one of the few people who justified the moniker of a legend in his own lifetime. Born in 1876, Lieutenant Colonel Sir Claude Edward Marjoribanks Dansey sprang from a family of country squires. He had been educated at Wellington and subsequently seduced by Oscar Wilde's lover 'Robbie' Ross. After the sort of experiences that England could offer her children in the heyday of her empire – the Matabele Rebellion in 1896, an insurgency in Borneo, a lieutenancy in the Boer War – he joined MI6 at Cumming's personal request in August 1917. Twenty years later one of his recruits, Lieutenant Commander Kenneth Cohen, described him as a '"copybook" secret service man. Dapper, establishment, Boodles, poker-playing expression, bitterly cynical, but with unlimited and illogical charm available, particularly for women'.[4]

Dansey became increasingly critical of his employers. He once described his chief, Admiral Sinclair, as 'a half-mad paranoid who preferred to communicate with his people exclusively via messages left in a locked box – to which only his equally half-mad sister had the combination'.[5] He felt that as the MI6 workforce was virtually unpaid, it lacked the incentive to excel. He observed that all the taxi drivers in any given city in the world knew the address of the head of MI6 operations as the Passport Control Office. It was an open secret. And he believed – correctly as it turned out – that MI6 knew precious little about what was going on in the armed camp of thirties Europe. Nevertheless, it was with Sinclair's blessing – or at least agreement – that in 1936 Dansey was tasked with setting up a shadow or tandem operation to MI6. This worked on rather different principles and was – amongst other things – an insurance policy against the exposure of its parent. Dansey's Organisation Z specialised in gathering intelligence in Germany and Italy (where Dansey was stationed to keep an eye on Mussolini). It employed industrialists and businessmen as agents. It paid them for their trouble. Cover was commercial rather than diplomatic. The HQ in Bush House on the Aldwych in central London appeared in the guise of Geoffrey Duveen & Co – export department. Another façade was an export–import company called Menoline, its offices a mile north at 24 Maple Street, off Tottenham Court Road. Very Ian Fleming, very Claude Dansey. The spy Kim Philby described Z very simply as 'designed to penetrate Germany from bases in Switzerland'.[6]

Conrad O'Brien-ffrench was Dansey's Agent Z3. Born in 1893 as the second son of the Marquis de Castelthomond, he had joined the Canadian Mounties as a seventeen-year-old, fought in the Battle of Mons, joined the secret service, become a highly distinguished mountaineer, then turned professional painter. In the early thirties he had been asked by Dansey to rejoin the secret service as Agent Z3. His mission was to set up a travel agency in Kitzbühel, offering tours of the Tyrol. This enabled him to develop a network of anti-fascists in the Tyrol itself, Bavaria and the northern Italian Alps. A friend of Ian Fleming – also resident in Kitzbühel – the handsome, dashing, multilingual womaniser was one of the inspirations for James Bond. On 11 March 1938 Conrad was alerted by one of his agents to Wehrmacht troops heading south from Bad Tölz and Rossenheim in Bavaria towards the Austrian border. This heralded Anschluss. Realising the potency of the intelligence, Conrad broke cover by phoning the news from Kitzbühel directly to the Foreign Office in Whitehall. He then warned all his local contacts: 'I met Louis de Rothschild . . . hastening towards the station.' The following day, Conrad made his escape to Switzerland. He was just in time. 'I caught the train that night and by next morning fanatical Austrian Gestapo officials were ripping the soles off passengers' shoes in the search for money and incriminating documents.'

Switzerland being Switzerland and George Warner being George Warner, it was necessary that a number of Z personnel were designated to cover the republic. The official MI6 station was tactfully located in Geneva under the usual cover of Passport Control Officer. When the outbreak of war in September 1939 finally caused Warner to relax his stance on spies, Organisation Z was able to slip into the shadow of MI6. Dansey himself and his principal staff at once decamped to the Peterhof hotel in Zurich. Here Dansey was styled consul. At the end of the year his promotion to assistant chief of MI6 dictated a return to the London headquarters at 54 Broadway, a quarter of a mile from the House of Commons. Now, despite the presence of Organisation Z, the British tended to rely on the French for Allied clandestine presence in Europe. In the spring of 1940 this was a policy that unravelled disastrously with the fall of Norway, Denmark, the Low Countries, France and the loss of almost all Allied agent networks across northern, eastern and western Europe. No one had foreseen the sudden collapse of these countries. The inability of MI6 to identify the lack of political will in France to fight the good fight was later regarded as its greatest wartime failure. In June 1940, minds were concentrated in London. The consequence was that 'Overnight Switzerland was transformed . . . into the centrepiece of Britain's intelligence effort against

Nazi Germany.'[7] When Warner was replaced shortly before the Fall of France by Sir David Kelly – a First World War intelligence officer – Thunstrasse became Britain's most important base for secret operations on the Continent.

Its operatives were a colourful crew. Following Dansey's departure, the MI6 station head in Zurich was Count Frederich 'Fanny' Vanden Heuvel. Son of a papal count, he had excellent connections with the Vatican, had been brought up in Berne, spoke Schweizerdeutsch to perfection. Tall, dressy, languid and famously courteous, he was the caricature not of a spy but of a diplomat. He was a figure out of P. G. Wodehouse who liked to sport lavender spats with his morning suit: a Catsmeat Potter-Pirbright, Gussie Fink-Nottle or Bingo Little. His number two was Andrew King, later exposed as a communist and homosexual at a time at which Bolshevism was beyond the pale and intercourse between those of the same sex illegal. King had been a couple of years below the spies Kim Philby and Donald Maclean at Cambridge. The agent, who knew nothing of film-making or films, worked under the commercial cover of Alexander Korda's famous London Films company. It was said that Korda, a Hungarian by birth and Englishman by choice, supplied agents in the form of refugees while Dansey supplied the cash. The military attaché was Colonel Cartwright, a veteran of the Kaiser's POW camps. The air attaché, Group Captain Freddie West, was a First World War Royal Flying Corps ace and VC to boot. Losing a leg in the conflict had not deprived him of his *joie de vivre*. Transferred from Rome to Berne after the outbreak of war, his nocturnal swimming parties in the summer of 1940 scandalised the upright citizens of the sleepy Swiss capital. Well informed about the Regia Aeronautica (the Italian air force), West discovered the existence of its Swiss counterpart only after his arrival in the capital. It was said that the legation's standing with General Guisan's representatives was much compromised by the lamentable standard of the Allied military attachés' skiing. An exception was presumably made in the case of the one-legged West.

After the Fall of France, Dansey's Swiss section was under pressure to deliver. Deliver it did. From the earliest days of the Axis, the Foreign Office in London had doubted Mussolini's commitment to an alliance with Hitler. After the disastrous Alpine campaign of June 1940, the similarly disappointing adventure in Greece the following autumn, and the beginnings of the RAF bombing campaign of Italian cities, the British Foreign Office deemed intelligence on the country's morale vital. Replete with his old contacts in Rome, West excelled himself. Between the end of summer and the end of the year he delivered more than seventy reports. These covered every aspect of Italy's domestic, political, social and economic situation. This was gold dust. In the view of the Foreign Office it confirmed the importance of Switzerland as 'the easiest and most natural channel leading into Italy . . . [for] establishing contact with dissident and revolutionary elements'.[8] As a consequence, the consulate in Lugano in Canton Ticino (adjoining Italy) was expanded to provide a base for more MI6 operatives in Italy. By this time, to the human intelligence of agents worldwide had been added the signals intelligence derived from the rapidly developing science of cryptanalysis, later epitomised by the work of the code-breaking centre at Bletchley Park in Buckinghamshire. This was of immense value in its own right, did much to turn the Battle of the Atlantic in 1943, and conceivably turned the course of the war. However, it did not replace but rather complemented human intelligence. For human intelligence (HUMINT) dealt with different issues from those of signals intelligence (SIGINT). It trafficked things like morale, industrial production levels, domestic shortages, issues in the Axis leadership and so on. By the middle of 1942, the Joint Intelligence Committee was rating the Swiss human product as 'the most valuable and amongst the best reports received from any quarter'.[9] Nine months later in the spring of 1943, Dansey reported that MI6 was running agents from Switzerland in Germany itself, Italy, France, Belgium and the Netherlands.

3

So by the time Dulles had got his feet underneath his desk in his apartment in Herrengasse 23, Dansey was cock o' the walk and not necessarily particularly welcoming to what might be regarded as competition. Competition, too, that had the funds to compete for the services of agents, the stock-in-trade of intelligence services. The Americans quickly won a reputation for free spending. One of Dansey's 'attachés' recalled their arrival as 'like a man with a loud hand-bell which he rang as loud as he could in the town square while shouting for wares and calling his customers'.[10] An MI6 agent in Geneva was horrified when a newly arrived American operative threw open his suitcase and revealed that it was literally packed with currency. Cash, the American helpfully explained, to buy agents and information. Dansey knew Dulles from the intelligence community in Berne in the First World War but from the first regarded him as a trespasser on his own territory. He instructed Vanden Heuvel to be uncooperative; 'above all', Vanden Heuvel was told, 'keep his nose away from our files'.[11] Shortly after Dulles's arrival in Berne in November 1942, a note appeared in the *Journal de Genève* flagging his arrival as 'a personal representative of President Roosevelt' for 'special duties'.[12] This barefaced advertisement was the antithesis of Dansey's approach to his profession and confirmed his worst suspicions. Dulles was an opportunistic rival, not a colleague. Duly and dutifully lunched by Vanden Heuvel, the return match in which Dulles outdid the Briton on the quality of wine and food did perhaps not endear him to his new colleagues. It was a relationship whose ambiguities would soon be compounded by the Kolbe affair.

Dulles himself knew Switzerland from his days as a junior diplomat in the First World War. Born in 1893, his maternal grandfather was secretary of state under President Benjamin Harrison. His elder brother John Foster Dulles would do the same job for Dwight Eisenhower from 1953 to 1959. Graduating from Princeton in 1916, the younger Dulles joined the diplomatic service and was attached to the US legation in Berne. Here he distinguished himself one quiet spring afternoon in April 1917. He was duty officer at the legation when the phone rang. The caller announced himself as Vladimir Ilich Lenin. Here was an informant known to the legation as an authority on the rapidly unravelling situation in Russia. Tsar Nicholas had abdicated on 15 March 1917 and there was revolution in the air. Lenin said he was en route to Berne and must speak to a member of the legation staff on a matter of utmost urgency. Dulles, tall, good-looking, with a well-developed interest in women, had a date. He firmly declined the opportunity and told Lenin that no one else would be available to see him until ten o'clock the following morning. 'Tomorrow', Lenin told Dulles, 'will be too late. I must talk to someone this afternoon. It is most important. I must see someone.' As far as Dulles was concerned there couldn't be much that would not wait till the following morning. 'Ten o'clock tomorrow,' he countered.[13] By then, though, Lenin was already returning to Russia on the famous 'sealed train', rather like, as Churchill put it, 'a plague bacillus'.[14] Arriving at Petrograd station on 17 April 1917, he at once instigated the mischief that would lead to the October Revolution. It was this that he wished to disclose to Dulles, forewarning of Russia's exit from the First World War.

Dulles's career survived this embarrassment, not least because he turned out to be the right man at the right time with connections in the right place. Given the isolationist stance of the United States in the 1930s, the country had given little thought and fewer resources to intelligence-gathering in Europe. After Pearl Harbor in December 1941 and – more significantly – the Arcadia Conference later that month in Washington, all changed. At the White House Roosevelt and Churchill had made the key strategic decision of placing the war in Europe as a priority above that in the Far East. The powerhouse that was the USA accordingly turned its energies to the matter of intelligence-gathering on the Continent. This meant Switzerland. Formed on 11 July 1941, the nascent US foreign intelligence-gathering organisation was given the snappy name of the Office of the

Coordinator of Information (COI). It was headed by another old friend of Claude Dansey, a maverick millionaire lawyer called 'Wild Bill' Donovan. Of Irish extraction, Donovan's nickname was acquired on the football field and followed him to the US 165th Regiment. He led the regiment's 1st Battalion on the French Western Front in the autumn of 1918 and won the coveted Medal of Honor. His subsequent career as a lawyer showed all the gusto that he had hitherto displayed. He made things happen. 'Switzerland', he wrote to President Roosevelt, 'is now, as it was in the last war, the one most advantageous place for the obtaining of information concerning the European Axis powers . . . information from Switzerland is far more important than from any other post.'[15] What was needed was a station there and the right man at its head: 'we need badly a man', Donovan continued, '. . . to tap the constant and enormous flow of information that comes from Germany and Italy'. In Donovan's opinion, the forty-nine-year-old Dulles was just that man. A lawyer like Donovan, Dulles spoke French and German, knew the intelligence ropes, was a hands-on spymaster, and familiar with Berne. Roosevelt was persuaded and in the autumn of 1942 Dulles was asked to set up a secret service office that would cover all the occupied territories and the Third Reich itself. For this purpose the COI was renamed the Office of Strategic Services (OSS). It comprised a secret intelligence service, the equivalent of MI6, and a secret operations service, a counterpart to the SOE. After the war, it would evolve into the CIA. Dulles would be its first civilian director.

On 7 November 1942, Dulles caught the last train up through the Vichy border town of Annemasse before Operation Anton closed the Swiss frontier. He carried on his person a large sum of ready cash, reputedly as much as $1 million. In the winter of 1942–3, as Paulus's army collapsed in Stalingrad, Dulles settled into his apartment in Herrengasse 23, a fourteenth-century house in the cathedral quarter in Berne. One of the OSS staff, Cordelia Hood, recalled that it was 'a beautiful apartment with a big terrace in the back that overlooked the Aare, then you looked up and saw the whole Bern Oberland mountain range, the Eiger, and the rest of the mountains. It was almost kitschy it was so postcard perfect.'[16] It was also practical. As Dulles himself wrote, 'Between my apartment and the river below grew vineyards which afforded an ideal covered approach for visitors who did not wish to be seen entering my front door on the Herrengasse.'[17] This was sensible, for the Gestapo were soon watching the premises day in, day out. Here Dulles set about reviving old contacts and cultivating new ones. Almost the first of these efforts got him into a tangle with the British.

4

In February 1943, Dulles was approached by a gangling German Abwehr officer called Hans Bernd Gisevius. Formerly of the Gestapo, Gisevius was an able bureaucrat who had risen to work for the head of the military intelligence service, Admiral Wilhelm Canaris. Born in 1887, Canaris himself had joined the Kriegsmarine as a seventeen-year-old. He had seen action against the British in the Falkland Islands in the light cruiser *Dresden*. Subsequently he was trained as a submariner, commanded a U-boat, and by 1932 was commanding officer of the battleship *Schlesien*. On his forty-eighth birthday in 1935 he was appointed head of the Abwehr. Never a member of the Nazi Party, it was later said that Canaris – a wiry little intellectual – hated not merely Himmler and Hitler, but the whole Nazi political system. He certainly surrounded himself with those of a similar bent, Gisevius included. Moreover, his position was an excellent one for turning his beliefs into practice, into plots. As Dulles was later to put it,

An intelligence service is the ideal vehicle for a conspiracy. Its members can travel about at home and abroad under secret orders, and no questions are asked. Every scrap of paper in the files, its membership, its expenditure of funds, its contacts, even enemy contacts, are state secrets. Even the Gestapo could not pry into the activities of the *Abwehr* until Himmler absorbed it. He only succeeded in doing so late in 1943.[18]

It was this pull that enabled Canaris to appoint the lanky Gisevius as vice-consul at the German legation in Zurich. Here Gisevius's talents and inclinations might be put to best use. He might also keep Canaris in touch with MI6. This was an organisation with which he had surprisingly long-standing contacts, so much so that some have suggested that Canaris was an MI6 double agent. Gisevius duly made contact with MI6 in Berne in the form of the spry and suave Vanden Heuvel. On introducing himself to Dulles on 9 January 1943, Gisevius disclosed his identity and questioned Dulles as to the Allies' likely attitude towards Germany in the event of Hitler's removal. He omitted, though, to mention his contacts with MI6. Vanden Heuvel had taken the precaution of installing his own agent in Herrengasse to keep an eye on Dulles. This was the British butler with the irreproachably English name of Henry Baldwin. Vanden Heuvel was duly tipped off by Baldwin, who could scarcely fail to have noticed the striking, shambling figure of the 6' 6" Gisevius. Vanden Heuvel warned Dulles of MI6 suspicions that Gisevius was a Nazi plant. Nevertheless, on 14 January 1943, Dulles again met Gisevius at the Herrengasse appartment. Dulles duly reported this meeting to Washington on a cipher.

This was all well and good. However, Canaris had a mistress in the form of a Polish woman called Halina Szymanska, the wife of a Polish officer imprisoned by the Soviets. Vanden Heuvel's successor, Nicholas Elliot, recalled:

Madame Szymanska was a formidable lady. Canaris used to come to various neutral countries to lay her. And in the course of the pillow talk be used to talk to her freely and once told her about the secret meeting between Franco and Hitler. It is clear to me that Canaris knew exactly what he was doing and that she would pass this on.[19]

Whether in bed or elsewhere, what Madame Szymanska did discover was that the Germans had broken the Americans' code. This was duly passed to Andrew King, Vanden Heuvel's number two, who ran the Polish agent. Dulles was of course himself informed. Three months later in the course of another meeting with Gisevius in Berne, Dulles was told a splendid story. It concerned the building of forty huge seaplanes in Nazi-occupied Rotterdam. They were to be manned by suicide squads and used to bomb London. Despite the Szymanska warning, Dulles passed this back to Washington not in one but two telegrams. Dansey, who remained highly sceptical of Gisevius, thought this a piece of misinformation or disinformation, designed to deceive. Dansey was beside himself. He told Vanden Heuvel: 'could you report to the fool [Dulles] who knows his code was compromised if he has used that code to report meetings with anyone, Germans probably identified persons concerned and use them for stuffing. He swallows easily.'[20]

All this merely formed a prelude to the Fritz Kolbe affair, the second act of which appears to have taken place on 18 August 1943, just as Italy was falling into chaos. This was the day after Kolbe's rejection by Cartwright and – as it so turned out – the day after an air raid that showed the power of intelligence: the RAF bombing of the rocket research centre at Peenemünde (Heeresversuchsanstalt Peenemünde) in the Baltic that set back the production of the V-2 rockets by anything up to a year.

According to one account, Kolbe attended mass in Berne cathedral before being taken under the convenient cover of the vineyard up to the Herrengasse apartment – away from the prying eyes of the Gestapo. Ushered into Dulles's large ground-floor office, he held his briefcase in such a way as to catch the American's eye. His line with Dulles was just as with Cartwright. 'I want to see Germany defeated in this war,' Kolbe declared. 'It is the only way to save my country. I think I can help in securing that defeat. I am an official of the German Foreign Office and I see all the telegrams that pass through the Department. I have copies of them in this briefcase. I brought them into Switzerland in the diplomatic bag, and I am willing to turn them over to you. There are more where these came from.'[21] Kolbe drew a key from his watch chain, unlocked the case, and opened it on Dulles's desk. Dulles lit his pipe and picked up two reports at random. One was a detailed account of the Japanese army's plans for an offensive in Burma. The second – rather topical on that day – was plans for the use of V-weapons against England. 'Your experts', Kolbe told Dulles, 'will need to study them to make sure they are genuine.'[22] Dulles concurred. The only problem was that the experts were British.

The documents duly found their way to Claude Dansey's desk in London. Dulles had of course been duped. A colleague speculated that Dansey concluded: 'It was clearly impossible that Dulles should have pulled off this spectacular scoop under his nose. Therefore he had not. The stuff was obviously a plant, and Dulles had fallen for it like a ton of bricks.'[23] This particular colleague was Kim Philby, who had by now – in his own words – drifted from the SOE to MI6. Philby, among others, counselled caution, suggesting the documents should be checked. Dansey was outraged. It was out of the question to let Dulles and OSS 'run riot all over Switzerland, fouling up the whole intelligence field. Heaven knew what damage they wouldn't do. Such matters had to be handled only by officers with experience of the pitfalls that beset the unwary.'[24] The documents were nevertheless passed on to Philby for verification by the counter-espionage section. This was done by finding if any of them matched intelligence from a different source – in this case from the Ultra decrypts from Bletchley Park. 'I chose for his scrutiny', recalled Philby, 'a striking series of telegrams from the German Military Attaché in Tokyo to the German General Staff which had been transmitted through diplomatic channels.'[25] Commander Alastair Denniston headed up the Code and Cipher School at Bletchley Park. Two days later Denniston called Philby. The telegrams matched.

Dansey of course was appalled. He was only mollified when Philby explained he had not credited the documents to the OSS and that as head of the Swiss section credit might reasonably be attributed to Dansey himself. 'Carry on,' Dansey told Philby. 'You're not such a fool as I thought.'[26] According to Philby, his motive in verifying the material and ensuring that credit was given where credit wasn't due was to get himself promoted to a role of greater value to his Soviet masters. 'I regarded my SIS appointments purely in the light of cover-jobs, to be carried out sufficiently well to ensure my attaining positions in which my service to the Soviet Union would be most effective.' Needless to say, the secrets also found their way to Moscow.

Kolbe, though, was a find and a huge one. His second visit to Berne on 7 October 1943 was followed by many. He would later be regarded as one of the most important spies of the Second World War. His rejection by Cartwright and acquisition by Dulles helped the American's make his mark in the nest of spies in Berne in the early autumn of 1943. Once having done so, the pipe-smoking, avuncular Dulles turned to the matter of conducting extra-marital affairs.

Mary Bancroft was a highly intelligent fellow American who had been living in Switzerland since 1934. The thirty-eight-year-old spoke French and German fluently, and had befriended the pioneer Swiss psychologist Carl Gustav Jung. She was working for the US legation in Berne on psychological analyses of the speeches of Hitler, Göring and Goebbels. On first meeting Dulles in the Herrengasse, she disclosed to the spymaster that the legation had discovered a homosexual network operating across the foreign offices of Britain, the USA, Switzerland and Greece. Through this fraternity, information was disseminated even more quickly than through the Catholic Church or – in her own words – various Jewish organisations.[27] She was also able to enlighten Dulles on what homosexuals actually did in bed. Bancroft, bored with her second marriage, wanted a job from Dulles and soon rather more. Dulles, separated from his wife Clover by the Atlantic Ocean and temperamentally unfaithful, was of a like mind. He propositioned her with a line well worth remembering by those contemplating office affairs, 'We can let the work cover the romance and the romance cover the work.'[28] Bancroft complied. Soon, the OSS with its ample money, *joie de vivre* and lax morals began to be called 'Oh So Social'. Particularly by the British.

EIGHT

Operation Achse

At any moment, a pedestrian would be asked to get into a car . . . The car went to the synagogue. There the victim was undressed and, if he was circumcised, he automatically took his place in the next convoy to Drancy.

LEON POLIAKOV

I

When Hitler had met Il Duce at Feltre in the Italian Alps on 19 July 1943, it had been clear to the Führer how close to the end of his tether was his old ally. Yet even Hitler was caught by surprise by the speed of subsequent events in the Italian capital that led to the dismissal of Mussolini. By 24 July he had been replaced by the seventy-two-year-old Pietro Badoglio, former Chief of Staff of 'Dictator Number One'. Soon the news from Rome filtered through to Hitler in Rastenburg.

On 27 July 1943 Rommel was summoned to attend the noon conference at the Führerhauptquartier. 'The Italians are obviously planning to betray us!' Hitler declared.[1] It was hardly a controversial opinion. He gave the Afrika Korps veteran his top-secret orders to return to his HQ in Munich and prepare for Operation Achse: the infiltration of the Alpine passes, the occupation of northern Italy and – if need be – the disarming of Italian forces. On 29 July Hitler gave the necessary order to Rommel for the first stage of the plan to proceed. The following day, 30 July 1943, a spearhead of the 26th Panzer Division headed south from Innsbruck up towards the Brenner Pass, the 'great gate of Italy', the border between the Reich and her increasingly nominal ally. The Italian border guards watched in astonishment as the motorised infantry column ground its way slowly towards the railway station that marked the border itself, a frontier hemmed in by the high ridges of the Eisack valley. The spearhead was a squadron of Tiger tanks. The column's weapons were trained, its guns cocked and the turrets of the tanks were traversing. It was ready for anything.

What should be done? Clearly a reference must be made to higher authority.

General Alessandro Gloria was in command of the XXXV Corps at Bolzano, the Alpine capital of South Tyrol. This was some thirty miles south of the Brenner Pass into Italy, a handsome medieval city dominated by the 10,968-foot Marmolada, the highest peak in the Dolomites. The General himself, a veteran of the Italians' disastrous North African campaign, was as undecided as his border guards on the Brenner. Suspicious though he might be about the purpose of the Panzer division, resistance by force of arms could be personal and professional suicide. By the time he had telephoned Rome to check whether the Wehrmacht had the necessary permission to pass, the 26th Division already held the border. Fait accompli. Forty-eight hours later, on 1 August 1943, the 44th Infantry and the 1st SS Panzer Divisions followed. Rommel had given his commanders strict orders to provoke the Italians no more than the very presence of his troops dictated. General Gloria's patience had been tried and it was tested further when the 44th Infantry arrived in Bolzano itself. Here Germans and Italians were forever at loggerheads. It will be remembered that the German-speaking inhabitants had been placed under Italian control when the South Tyrol was gifted to Italy after the First World War by the Treaty of Saint-Germain. Now the tables had once again been turned. Gloria protested vehemently and vociferously to Rommel but he restricted himself to words. The Desert Fox was unyielding. As a fighting force he regarded the Italians with contempt. What had they done in North Africa? Nothing. In the end the Axis generals came to terms. Whatever the future might hold, Italy and Germany were not yet at war.

*

A month later they were. On 3 September 1943 General Giuseppe Gastello signed an armistice with the Allies in Cassibile, Sicily. At 6.30 p.m. on 8 September this agreement was published by the Allies as the Badoglio Declaration. Dwight Eisenhower's Kansas drawl declared on Radio Algiers, 'The Italian government has surrendered its armed forces unconditionally.'[2] The breaking of this news on that stifling airless evening was premature, for it caught the three million men of Italy's armed forces by surprise: Badoglio had yet to inform the Regia Marina, the Regia Aeronautica and the Regio Esercito of the armistice. Orders are the sine qua non of the military. The Italians had none. The three Italian armed services were poleaxed. The Wehrmacht was not. At 7.50 p.m. the OKW phoned the codeword 'Achse' to Rommel's headquarters, a special command train simmering in a siding just south of Munich. The second part of Operation Achse swung smoothly into action.

The very evening of Eisenhower's announcement, Rommel's forces seized the French Alps occupied by the Italians. In a lightning operation, all points of strategic importance were taken. These were the Alpine passes of the Little St Bernard, the Great St Bernard, the Mont Cenis, the Col de Montgenèvre and the Col de Larche – all the passes in the Rhône-Alpes and the Alpes-Maritimes where the Italians had fought the French in the Alpine campaign of June 1940. The occupying Italian Fourth Army, amounting to about 100,000, largely disintegrated. In Albertville in the Savoie, in the happier times of 1992 host to the Winter Olympics, the Italians resisted all night. Other units had the initiative to mine the Fréjus tunnel leading from France to Italy under the Col de Fréjus in Savoie. Mostly the Italians simply melted away, a rag, tag and bobtail army scattering arms and equipment and even uniforms in its wake, careering back to Italy. For them the war seemed over. It was a rout.

The Italian high command had spent weeks planning the defence of these Alpine choke points against the anticipated German ambush. It had not had the will to put the plans into action. Goebbels commented in his diary that had the Italians blown the Alpine bridges and tunnels, the forces engaging Eisenhower's armies in Sicily would have been trapped.[3] How fortunate that the Italians were Italian!

2

And the Italians were not the only ones to be caught out by Eisenhower's broadcast.

One of the first things on the Germans' agenda in the old Italian zone was the Jews. The most vulnerable were those in the communities perched along the Alpine Franco-Italian border. These were the five thousand or so refugees in Megève, St Gervais, Barcelonnette, Vence, Venanson, Saint-Martin-Vésubie and Nice: those enjoying assigned residence under the protection of Guido Lospinoso, Il Duce's Inspector General of Racial Policy.

Six weeks earlier in the last week of July, the news of Mussolini's fall had been received by these refugees in the Alps with outbursts of joy. The wildest of hopes sprang up that the collapse of the whole Axis was at hand. In Nice, a young refugee recorded that 26 July 1943 'was a night of delirium. People celebrated the event as though it was 14 July [Bastille Day, when the French celebrate the storming of the prison-fortress in Paris], the cafés remained open all night. It seemed that the nightmare was nearing an end and the war would be over any moment.'[4]

Over the following few days in early August 1943, more sober counsels prevailed. The Italians had been the bulwark between the Jewish communities and the combined anti-Semitic forces of the Vichy French and the Germans in the interlocking and overlapping administration of the Italian zone. Now it was said that the Italians would withdraw and leave the Jews to fend for themselves. In the first few hours of his administration Badoglio had tactfully declared that 'The war continues on the side of our Germanic ally.'[5] Who knew how long this might last?

On 15 August 1944, a deal had been struck in Bolzano between Generals Rommel and Gloria, between the German and Italian forces. The Regio Esercito would cede the territory to the west of the Var and Tinée rivers to the Germans and continue to hold the

Alpine foothills and the Alpes-Maritimes themselves to the east. This meant not much more than a small enclave around Nice itself and was obviously a fragile, temporary arrangement, and from Annecy and Megève in the north to Saint-Martin-Vésubie and Nice in the south there was growing panic. Those Jews who had prospects of legally entering neighbouring Italy or Switzerland desperately sought the necessary papers to do so. Those without such hopes made other arrangements. In Saint-Martin-Vésubie, the Alpine settlement high above Nice, the Movement of Zionist Youth defied the orders of the Italian authorities to stay within the confines of the town. It sent scouts eastwards from Saint-Martin up to explore the two high passes over into Italy, the 8,342-foot Col de Cerise and the 8,106-foot Col de Fenestre. How practicable were these tracks for the very young and very old? These were their escape routes should the need arise.

In Rome, there was also action. At the end of August 1943 a ministerial meeting took the decision that the Jews in the assigned residence settlements should be returned to the small Nice haven. Lospinoso was duly instructed to make the necessary arrangements. Some were to be taken by train, some by truck. Meanwhile, in Nice itself, the Comité d'Assistance aux Refugés had conceived an ambitious plan to rescue all 30,000 Jews in the Alps by chartering four ships – *Duilio*, *Giulio Cesare*, *Saturnia* and *Vulcania*. This was the brainchild of one of the less sung heroes of the war, a fifty-eight-year-old Jewish banker called Angelo Donati. These ships would ferry the Jews from all the assigned residence communities from the port of Nice to mainland Italy, thence to Allied North Africa. Here they would be placed in US and British camps.

Not knowing that the armistice between Badoglio and the Allies had already been signed, during the course of the second week of September, Lospinoso's Jews from the north – from Barcelonnette to Vence – set off. Many of them actually arrived in Nice on 8 September itself, returning – as they thought – to the Italian sanctuary. That evening they heard to their horror

Eisenhower's announcement of the armistice. They knew what it meant.

Within thirty-six hours of the broadcast – on 10 September 1943 – a commando unit of German security forces arrived in Nice. It was led by SS-Hauptsturmführer Alois Brunner. This brave fellow was the right-hand man of one of the principal architects of the Holocaust, Adolf Eichmann: he who had set up the office for Jewish emigration in Vienna. The thirty-one-year-old Brunner had already distinguished himself in his merciless treatment of Jews in Salonika, Greece's second city, and at the Paris holding camp at Drancy.

At 3.30 p.m. on the day of his arrival Brunner unleashed a manhunt. It was led by the Gestapo, energetically aided and abetted by the French fascists, the Parti Populaire Français. Word went round the Jewish community like wildfire. A few of the refugees – some of whom had only just arrived – gathered up their portable possessions, rushed to the railway station in the Avenue Thiers, and found places on the last train from Nice. This steamed slowly east along the spectacular Riviera coast, the azure seas glittering in the autumn sunshine, through the *belle époque* resorts of Beaulieu, Monaco and Menton, across the border at Ventimiglia into the Italian province of Cuneo. Other refugees, the less fortunate, were seized in their homes and hotels, on the roads to the north and east and in the city itself. According to one witness, Léon Poliakov, 'Those official black Citroëns cruised the streets of Nice, and passengers attentively scrutinized passers-by. At any moment, a pedestrian would be asked to get into a car . . . The car went to the synagogue. There the victim was undressed and, if he was circumcised, he automatically took his place in the next convoy to Drancy.'[6] Brunner's Gestapo also headed for the offices of the *département* prefect Jean Chaigneau and the Italian consul-general Augusto Spechel. These two men held the names and addresses of the Jews in Nice itself and all the assigned residence communities on the Alpine border. Prefect Chaigneau was a courageous man. He had burned his lists.

Spechel had taken the precaution of transferring his to Rome. The Gestapo left empty-handed and furious.

As the manhunt progressed over the following thirty-six hours, two other groups of Jewish refugees were still on their way to Nice. One was a party of two hundred elderly, children and young mothers from Megève. They had been brought by truck from the resort to Chambéry, there to take a train to Nice via Grenoble. As the train neared the Dauphiné capital, so too did the Wehrmacht approaching from the west. Somehow word was passed to the train and it was diverted to the relative safety of Turin, over the Italian border. The younger and fitter from the community in Megève were to undertake the whole journey by road. On the morning of 11 September 1943, a long line of charcoal-burning gazogènes could be seen heading east along the coast road from Cannes. As the convoy approached the Var to the west of Nice, a roadblock barred its way. At first no one could make out by which forces it was manned. Soon it became apparent. Field grey: it was the Wehrmacht. A few of the Jews had the energy and strength of will to jump out of the trucks and disappear into the stony Provençal countryside. The rest were captured.

For them it was Drancy, Auschwitz and the gas chambers.

Meanwhile, in Saint-Martin-Vésubie the contingency plan of escape over the border to Italy was put into effect. It had been an agonising decision for these benighted people. They could stay where they were: perhaps the Germans would not trouble themselves with such a remote place. They could seek refuge in the immediate – and inhospitable – surroundings. Or they could head for Italy: another country with another language and another people, where they had no idea of what they would find. Most chose to head over the two passes for Italy, perhaps feeling that it was better to act than to await events. Few had any experience of the high Alpine world: of hanging glaciers, loose screes, of precipices and rockfalls, of foot- and handholds that could crumble at a touch.

The first of them set out within hours of Eisenhower's

announcement, on the evening of 8 September 1943. Autumn was already closing its fist on the terrain, turning the leaves in the lower valley around Saint-Martin-Vésubie to russet and yellow, the light shading upwards to the evergreen spruce and fir, and then to the bare rock above the treeline. Snow was in the air, ibex and chamois grazing in the middle distance, birds of prey circling high above.

Through this epic landscape around a thousand Jews – the young and the old, the strong and the weak – headed for the Col de Cerise or the Col de Fenestre – the two routes established just days previously by the young Zionists. It was an exodus. Many carried in small fibre suitcases all that they owned. Most took two days to make the journey, some more. The first day on either route was relatively easy, along mule tracks. That night, the refugees slept under the stars. The second, where the trail – such as it was – ran through a boulder field, was much tougher. There were no yellow waymarks to point to the next mountain restaurant: rather a switchback climb with the rocks shifting underfoot and snow-clad peaks staring down. The two passes themselves were high, windy, bleak places, windows from one valley – one world – to the next. On the third day the exiles descended into the Gesso valley and what they believed might be sanctuary.

As the ill-shod, poorly clothed parties – in ones and twos and groups of half a dozen or so – straggled down the rugged paths clutching their suitcases, they were watched with gathering interest by the Italian locals. Men, women and children loitered on their doorsteps and hung around on street corners, observing the refugees with considerable curiosity. One of the footsore, William Blye, 'thought it was because the Jews were speaking languages other than Italian and wearing city clothes . . . Only later was he told that the peasants were looking for horns. They thought that Jews had horns on their heads, like Moses and other Old Testament characters they had seen in church.'[7] Full of hope and fear, the exhausted refugees wound their way down the paths leading to the communities of Entraque, Valdieri and Borgo

San Dalmazzo in the province of Cuneo. These were medieval villages hewn out of rock, where the peasant community gleaned a subsistence living out of the thin Alpine soil.

The haven the Jews had hoped for they did not find. As in Nice, Rommel's forces had got there before the persecuted could escape. On 12 September 1943 the a battalion from the 1st SS Panzer Division Leibstandarte Adolf Hitler had occupied the provincial capital of Cuneo, within a few miles of all the refugees fleeing from Saint-Martin. On 18 September the battalion commander, SS-Sturmbannführer Joachim Peiper, ordered the Jews in the area to assemble at the barracks close to the railway station in Borgo San Dalmazzo. Two months later, of the 349 who had gathered or who were subsequently captured, 328 were dispatched to Drancy. On 7 December 1943 they were entrained to Auschwitz. Twelve survived.

Most of those who remained in Saint-Martin-Vésubie were captured by SS-Hauptsturmführer Alois Brunner's police, who arrived in the mountain settlement on 21 September 1943. They were deported and gassed. A few remained in hiding, helped by the locals. Only when Allied soldiers reached Saint-Martin-Vésubie from the beachheads of the south of France landings on 2 September 1944 did they know they would survive.

3

Further south in Italy, Operation Achse had similarly momentous consequences for a large group of Allied prisoners of war.

On the day of the armistice between the Allies and Italy, there were around 75,000 British and Dominion POWs in Italian camps. They were mostly infantrymen who had surrendered at Tobruk in 1941, scattered in some fifty-two camps all over the Italian peninsula. One of the terms of the armistice between the Allies and the new Badoglio administration was that the prisoners should be transferred to the care of the Allies. Churchill had demanded 'the immediate liberation of all British POWs in Italian hands, and the prevention, which can in the first instance only be by the Italians, of their being transported north towards Germany'.[8] The chaos that accompanied the armistice and its announcement, and the rapidity of Rommel's advance into northern Italy, meant that this was far easier to demand than do. Moreover, some of the more fascistic camp commanders simply ignored Badoglio's orders and handed their charges over to the Wehrmacht. Others threw open the gates of their camps to let nature take her course. The more enterprising, tougher and more resolute prisoners saw their chance and took it. Ill-prepared, ill-equipped, often dressed only in their service clothes, and rarely speaking more than a smattering of Italian, in groups of two or three they headed for freedom.

Where that lay was open to question. Some hoped to join Tito's partisans to the north-east of Italy in neighbouring Yugoslavia; some to join the nascent Italian resistance; some to join the Allied forces in Sicily; some to throw themselves on the mercy of the Vatican in Rome. Still others decided to wait in hiding for the anticipated Allied landings further north on the Italian peninsula: there were rumoured to be assaults planned or actually taking place in Genoa, La Spezia, Leghorn and Trieste.

Switzerland, too, promised freedom, but it lay beyond the Alps. Not for nothing were they the natural frontier between the two countries. Those POWs trekking from Italy into Switzerland had far more on their hands and under their feet than the refugees from Saint-Martin-Vésubie, for the Alps on the frontier here were much higher than in the Alpes-Maritimes. In the Pennine Alps they would have to climb, not walk; here they had to face the challenges of glaciers and crevasses, not just steep mountain paths. Few of the escapers from Italy had any experience of such places and conditions, and many of them had never even seen snow. Fewer still were properly equipped with warm jackets, thermal underwear, tough mountaineering boots, alpenstocks and crampons: some even tried to cross 10,000-foot passes in shorts. Hazards were human, too. The men on the run often had to throw themselves on the mercy of the inhabitants of the uplands through which they journeyed. Many were treated with great humanity by their former enemies, who risked exemplary punishment from the new occupiers: their chalets burned, their menfolk deported or executed. Others were more venal. The Italian peasants on the frontier soon spotted the opportunity to guide the POWs over the border. These men, the *passatori*, were incentivised by the British government to ply their trade. Once the scale of POWs seeking safety was understood, a bounty of £20 was offered for every man taken to safety in Switzerland. The Germans at once countered this with an offer of a similar sum of 1,800 lire. At the time the weekly wage for industrial workers in Milan was 200 lire. Robert Thomson, a South African who escaped over the passes, remembered, 'Even though the Italian guides were being well paid to take us to Switzerland, they wouldn't think twice about handing us over, instead, to the Germans, who would also reward them.'[9]

Prisoners in the camps close to the border began to arrive in Switzerland within days of the September armistice. The weather was still relatively good. As the weeks drew on conditions became more difficult, the routes more clogged with snow. In Zermatt, where the Matterhorn straddles the Swiss–Italian border, the escapers' problems were compounded by the fact that the three closest towns on the Italian side of the frontier were garrisoned by SS forces. Nevertheless, in the month after the Badoglio declaration more than one thousand Allied POWs crossed the high border by the passes above Zermatt and neighbouring Saas-Fee. One of them was the senior officer at Camp 49, Fontanellato, near Parma: Colonel Hugo de Burgh of the Royal Horse Artillery. This veteran of the North-West Frontier in British India thanked the Swiss patrol that welcomed him. 'Why not?' was the reply. 'If it had not been for the Battle of Britain in 1940 there would be no Switzerland.'[10]

Paul Schamberger's *Interlude in Switzerland* tells the story of South African Commonwealth troops who escaped from the

POW camps over the Alps in the wake of Operation Achse.[11] William 'Billy' Marais was a thirty-four-year-old corporal in the 4th South African Armoured Cars. Seconded to the Eighth Army, he was captured by Rommel's forces in the Western Desert in November 1941 and sent to an Italian POW camp. When the armistice was signed, he was at once dispatched north to Germany. Two days after the armistice he escaped from a train close to the Brenner Pass and spent twelve days in the foothills of the Dolomites trying to find a way into Switzerland. He lived by stealing fruit from orchards. After a few days on the run he was recaptured by a Fascist border patrol. He escaped once again by jumping down a precipice. Surviving this desperate remedy, he hunted up and down the border for a crossing point. Everywhere it seemed closely guarded by Italian troops. At last, utterly at the end of his tether, frozen stiff and exhausted, he managed to cross the frontier at the unguarded Stelvio Pass. At 9,045 feet, this was the second-highest paved pass in the Alps, where Switzerland jutted out between Austria to the north and Italy to the south, north of Bormio in the province of Sondrio and south of Stilfs in South Tyrol. There Marais collapsed. Before doing so he left a note in his diary.

Red Cross – Roote Kreuz
No. 135480
Cpl W.T. Marais
South African Tank Corps

Should I be found Please take this and if Possible deliver to Red +. I attempted to escape from the Germans. I have had about 12 days freedom from Barb wire.

Please let my Mother know that my thoughts were of her always. It is cold, very cold.[12]

Marais was found alive by a Swiss border patrol. Hearing the German spoken by his rescuers, he took them to be the Wehrmacht. Marais bit, yelled and screamed, and had to be subdued by being sat upon. He was taken a couple of days' march to the Kreisspital in Samedan, four miles north of the skiing resort St Moritz. Here he was cared for for some weeks with what he later remembered as incomparable kindness and humanity. On his recovery he was dispatched to Berne. There he was interrogated on his escape by the British military attaché, our friend Colonel Henry Cartwright. On falling ill once again, Marais was returned to Samedan. At 2 a.m. on 25 December 1943, he noted in his diary that he had there spent 'the most wonderful Christmas eve of my life'.[13]

4

Marais was followed by more than 5,000 Allied escapers from Italy who found their way over the Alps into Switzerland in the autumn and early winter of 1943. The vast majority of these men were British and Commonwealth servicemen. Provided they were not in military uniform, they fell into the Swiss category of 'evaders', which meant they were not interned. The Swiss had agreed to accept these men at the time when they were still turning away Jews because of a deal struck just three days after the announcement of the armistice. On 12 September 1943, the British envoy Sir Clifford Norton and his opposite number, Marcel Pilet-Golaz (foreign minister now rather than federal president), had agreed that the POWs would be accepted on three conditions: that they left as quickly as possible; that they were subject to Swiss military law; and that they were paid for by the British. The Swiss called this episode the 'invasion' or Grosseinbruch.

To cope with the numbers of POWs who arrived that autumn of 1943 the Swiss Internment Commissariat set up a special headquarters for the Allies. This was conveniently close to the Italian border in the Schwaner Hotel in Wil, Canton St Gallen. The unit provided an occupation in itself for those POWs with office skills. Each escaper had to be interviewed: his unit, POW camp, means of escape and identity of those who had helped or hindered his passage were recorded, assessed and passed on. For the remainder of the POWs, handier with tommy guns than typewriters, something else had to be done. Once they had recovered from the rigours of the passage over the Alps, the men behaved as might have been expected of servicemen in the prime of life. They devoted themselves to sport, alcohol, fighting among themselves, and pursuing Swiss women. Norton and Pilet-Golaz were at one that this was best done as far as possible out of sight of Swiss citizens, and especially their Swiss military counterparts. Accordingly, like the Jews of south-eastern France in the happy days of Guido Lospinoso, the men were dispatched to the country's largely deserted skiing resorts.

Adelboden in the Bernese Oberland, only forty miles south of the capital, was one of the very first resorts developed by the British in the early years of the twentieth century. Perched on a sunny, south-facing terrace at the end of the Engstlige valley, it was high – 4,430 feet – and surrounded by the snowfields of the Lohner, Steghorn and Wildstrubel mountains. Its proximity to Berne, coupled with its remoteness, made it a good location for the evaders. Not all of them wished to forgo the struggle and a number still thought it their duty to try to rejoin their units. Escape from Adelboden – approached during winter by only one road – was exacting. The village of Frutigen was the only door in the wall and that was guarded. Under the terms of the Hague Convention, the Swiss were required to prevent the evaders' flight.

The camp was opened by an advance party on 8 November 1943, the evaders themselves following three days later. The first snows of the season had come more than a month before and for most their new quarters compared favourably with the Italian POW camps and the billets at Sandhurst and the Salisbury Plain. 'The men marvelled at the spring mattresses, linen sheets, pillows and feather duvets on all the beds. All bedrooms had hot and cold running water'.[14] They also took up skiing, a sport that – according to the pre-war skiing ace James 'Jimmy' Riddel – was 'the most fun you can have with your trousers on'. Yet it was still Switzerland. One evader in Adelboden was Rommel's future biographer, Desmond Young. Attached to the 4th Indian Division, he had been captured at the Battle of Bir Hacheim in the Libyan desert. He reflected, 'We were, in effect, still in prison, though the bars were golden.'[15]

5

Prison, too, had been the fate of Mussolini, albeit a jail of a less congenial sort than Desmond Young's.

General Badoglio's advisers realised that the former Duce might be a target for kidnapping by the Wehrmacht, and kept him on the move. He was first rumoured to be on the island of Ventotene on Italy's west coast; then on another island, Maddalena, close to Sardinia. Il Duce was apparently in a reflective mood, whiling away the time reading Giuseppe Ricciotti's classic *Vita di Gesù Cristo* (Life of Jesus) seeking inspiration. Eventually he was tracked down by the naval intelligence service of Grossadmiral Karl Dönitz in the Albergo Ritugi. This hotel formed the nucleus of a skiing resort some eighty-two miles north of Rome, on the Gran Sasso mountain. At 9,554 feet this was the highest peak in the Apennines, the range that forms the femur of Italy's leg. It could be reached only by funicular railway.

Here Mussolini seemed secure enough, but Badoglio's men overlooked the courage and imagination of the Waffen-SS and the paratroopers of the Fallschirmjäger (parachute) Division. These men conceived Operation Eiche (Oak), a plan that reads like a cocktail of Jack Higgins's *The Eagle Has Landed* and Alistair MacLean's *Where Eagles Dare*.

Photoreconnaissance suggested that it would be possible to land gliders on the plateau around the hotel. The commandos could then seize Mussolini from his 250 Carabinieri captors, using an Italian general as a human shield. Il Duce would then be flown off the mountain in a Fieseler Storch, a tiny high-winged monoplane not dissimilar to the Lysanders used by the RAF for dropping SOE agents in France. This was the scheme conceived by Major Otto Harald Mors and the daredevil scar-faced giant Obersturmbannführer Otto Skorzeny, a sort of Nazi Lawrence of Arabia.

On 12 September 1943 Operation Eiche was put into action. Most surprisingly, all went according to plan. Nine lightweight DFS 230 gliders were successfully crash-landed on the mountain. They were guided by Skorzeny, who had cut a hole in the fuselage of his own glider to see the landmarks below. The commandos were spotted by Mussolini, looking wistfully out of a second-floor window of his prison-hotel. Most of the Carabinieri guarding the Duce fled their posts. The remainder obeyed Mussolini's call to avoid shooting the Italian general Fernando Soleti – or indeed anyone else. Not a drop of blood was spilt. Skorzeny – shades of *Where Eagles Dare* – put the radio out of operation, leapt up the stairs three at a time and duly greeted Mussolini. 'Duce,' he cried, 'the Führer has sent me to set you free!' Mussolini also knew his lines: 'I knew my friend would not forsake me!'[16] With the pilot, Mussolini and Skorzeny all on board, the tiny Fieseler was overloaded and staggered perilously off the high plateau. Landing safely in Rome, Mussolini was transferred to a more dignified Luftwaffe transport Heinkel He 111, thence to Vienna and on to a touching reunion with the Führer in Rastenburg.

Hitler was not all heart. He wanted Mussolini to establish a new Fascist government in Alpine Italy and the Lombardy plain immediately to the south. This would ease the administrative burden of northern Italy and help pacify the nascent partisan resistance. It would also safeguard the Wehrmacht's supply lines to its forces in the south – not to mention its lines of retreat.

Mussolini had other ideas, more attuned to *On Golden Pond*. He had intended to retire from politics and live out the remainder of his life in the company of his mistress: to Hitler's annoyance he proved to have little appetite for the grand plan. Still, in the circumstances it was difficult for Il Duce to refuse. On 23 September he duly proclaimed the Italian Social Republic (Repubblica Sociale Italiana, RSI). Its unofficial capital was Salò, perched on the shores of Lake Garda under the shadow of Monte San Bartolomeo, on the southern slopes of the Alps.

Here most of the republic's ministries were housed. Just eleven days after his rescue, Mussolini found himself in residence nearby at Rocca delle Caminate, a medieval fortress. Only his mistress Clara Petacci was missing. Josef 'Sepp' Dietrich was one of Hitler's intimates, an SS general who had begun life as a butcher. He was duly detached from his hard-pressed I SS Armoured Corps in Russia to deliver Petacci into Mussolini's arms in Salò. Goebbels, no stranger to infidelity, noted tartly in his diary on 9 November 1944, 'The personal conduct of the Duce with his girl friend, whom Sepp Dietrich had to bring to him, is cause for much misgiving.'[17]

Indeed, Mussolini now cut a sorry figure. He was guarded by a detachment of the Leibstandarte SS, Hitler's personal bodyguard unit; his phone was tapped, and even his doctor – George Zachariae – was provided by the Führer. Hitler had already threatened the Duce with the destruction of Milan and Turin – the north's industrial heartland – and the crucial port of Genoa. These remained part of Mussolini's puppet republic, but even before the RSI was proclaimed he had lost the Alpine provinces of Belluno, the long-disputed German-speaking South Tyrol, and the Trentino north of Venice. These were regarded as too close to the borders of the Reich to be placed under anything other than direct Nazi control. On 10 September 1943 the provinces were dubbed the Operationszone Alpenvorland or OZAV (Operational Zone of the Alpine Foothills). The OZAV was administered by High Commissioner Franz Hofer, a notorious Nazi who also ran the Alpine Reichsgau of Tyrol-Vorarlberg to the immediate north.

In the autumn of 1943, with many of the Allied POWs from the Italian camps still trekking north towards Switzerland, these three Italian provinces were given a makeover. Italian magistrates were replaced by German-speaking mayors. Italian newspapers were shut down, the Italian Fascist party was outlawed, and – above all – the Jewish population was relentlessly pursued. On 16 September 1943, thirty-five Jews from Merano were entrained for Auschwitz. When they reached the camp, the six-year-old in the party was gassed. Two months later they were followed by the refugees from Saint-Martin-Vésubie, entrained at Borgo San Dalmazzo.

PART THREE

NINE

'Our predecessors made mistakes'

HANS MEYER, Schweizerische Nationalbank

I

Lugano was a place to holiday. Once the capital of Switzerland's southernmost canton of Ticino, it lay on the benign south-facing slopes of the Piedmontese Alps as they drifted down towards the Lombardy plain. To the south, east and west lay Italy, Ticino here just a finger of Switzerland in another country. Overlooked by the 3,035-foot Monte Bre and the 2,995-foot Monte San Salvatore, the city lay on the shores of Lake Lugano, one of the mirrored gems of the Alps that so glorify the surrounding peaks. It advertised itself as the sunniest place in Switzerland. In 1899 Baedeker's Guide observed that 'The environs possess all the charms of Italian mountain-scenery; numerous villages, churches, chapels and country-seats are scattered along the banks of the lake, and the lower hills are covered with vineyards and gardens, contrasting beautifully with the dark foliage of the chestnuts and walnuts in the background.' Little had changed in the intervening years. Even in the autumn of 1943, four years into the war, the waterfront with its steamboat pier had a *belle époque* charm. Despite the blackout and the rationing, with its spectacular scenery, soft light and benign climate, there were far, far worse places to be. Since 1882, when the St Gotthard railway tunnel had opened for traffic, the city had exploited its position on the main line between northern Italy and central and northern Europe. As well as a vacation (Baedeker said it was 'a very pleasant place for an extended stay'),[1] it was a good place for a rendezvous or brief encounter.

Alfredo Pizzoni and Ferruccio Parri and a handful of their compatriots arrived in Lugano on 2 November 1943. It was some three months since the fall of Mussolini, six weeks since his declaration of the Italian Social Republic at Salò and his installation in Rocca delle Caminate under the watchful eyes of the Leibstandarte SS. The two middle-aged Italians were not on holiday. They were leaders of the Italian resistance, the newly formed Comitato de Liberazione Nazionale (National Liberation Committee, CLN), and they were in Lugano to meet two men who had travelled south through the St Gotthard from Berne on the Strade Ferrate Federali. One was our old friend John McCaffery of SOE, the other the American newcomer: the pipe-smoking adulterer, Allen Dulles of the OSS.

The pair did not have high expectations of the meeting. Italy had been a Fascist state for twenty years, virtually a generation. It was very difficult for the Allies to discern what sort of political forces might emerge after the castration of Mussolini: much as in Libya or Egypt today. Moreover, progress to date in fostering resistance – setting Italy ablaze – had been modest. Although the SOE had been at work in the country since October 1941, it had achieved relatively little. J Section, set up under Lieutenant Colonel C. L. Roseberry, had confined itself largely to subversion; a scheme to traffic war materiel to the clandestine opposition to Mussolini had been penetrated by Italian Military Intelligence. The Italian war record, starting with the Franco-Italian Alpine campaign of June 1940, also suggested that the 'macaroni' – as the French liked to call them – had little appetite for combat of any nature: conventional or guerrilla. They were too busy with personal grooming and the pursuit of love: *la dolce vita*.

Still, the armistice signed in Sicily between the Allies and Badoglio's forces two months previously had turned the tables. Italy was no longer an enemy state: she had metamorphosed into an occupied country. In the south, battle was now raging between the Allied forces of General Eisenhower and the Wehrmacht divisions of Generalfeldmarschall Albert Kesselring, around the 'Winter Line'. 'Smiling Albert' – so called for his cheery demeanour – was the new Rommel: a hugely gifted commander who would have much to do as the Wehrmacht retreated grudgingly north towards the Alps. His winter line in the Apennines was just south of Rome, close to the medieval monastery of Monte Cassino. In the north the job of the SOE and OSS was to liaise with the nascent resistance movement in the Alps and the Apennines that might in due course support the US Fifth Army and the British Eighth Army as they pushed up towards the Italian capital, then north to Berchtesgaden and Berlin.

This all meant that Dulles and McCaffery were obliged to do their homework. Pizzoni, it seemed, was a rather surprising thing for an Italian: a decorated war hero, educated in London and Oxford to boot. He was also a Milanese banker with a clear understanding of what it took to run an insurgency: money. With his close-set eyes and forceful manner, he was not to be tangled with; later he would bill himself Il Banchiere della Resistenza: 'the Partisans' Banker'. The bespectacled Parri was also a decorated First World War soldier, and a founding member of the Action Party: a liberal socialist as opposed to the communism espoused by many Italian partisans. He once described himself as a common man (*uomo della strada*), a regular guy (*uomo qualunque*). Journalist, academic, freedom fighter and the first post-war prime minister of Italy, he was hardly these things. He did, though, have an empathy with the Italian common man that made him the exception to the rule of recent Italian history. Like Marie Antoinette, Mussolini was above all that nonsense.

As was so often the case in Allied liaison with national resistance movements in Europe, when the two sides met that day in November 1943, they found themselves at odds.

Like Tito in Yugoslavia, the Italians knew they needed outside help; like Tito, Parri and Pizzoni wanted to rid themselves of the Germans; like Tito, they also wanted to create a new society out of the ruins of the old. Dulles and McCaffery were less interested in the latter. Besides wishing the Germans *auf Wiedersehen*, they wanted King Victor Emmanuel to retain his position as head of state, rather than being supplanted by the brave new republican and socialist state advocated by many Italians. On 21 September 1943 Churchill had told the House of Commons:

It is necessary in the general interest as well as in that of Italy that all surviving forces of Italian national life should be rallied together around their lawful Government, and that the King and Marshal Badoglio should be supported by whatever Liberal and Left-wing elements are capable of making head against the Fascist-Quisling combination, and thus of creating conditions which will help drive this villainous combination from Italian soil, or, better still, annihilate it on the spot.[2]

At odds over ends, the parties in Lugano also differed over means. Parri and Pizzoni envisaged a major resistance movement operating in large formations, manned by tens of thousands of partisans: in effect the military wing of a provisional government. McCaffery and Dulles prescribed smaller groups undertaking relatively small-scale sabotage activity of the sort that were showing results in France, not least in the Savoie and Dauphiné.

Agreement was nevertheless reached in Lugano that the Allies would undertake four immediate airdrops and that the partisans would be given 50,000 lire. This reflected the fact that Dulles and McCaffery were more impressed than they had anticipated. In a telegram to his masters in Washington on 8 November 1943, Dulles declared, 'I have met Attom of Motta [Dulles's code for Parri and the CLN] . . . Zulu and I are convinced that Motta is a serious organization . . . Report by Attom places 20,000 to 30,000 scantily armed men as the total number of dependable fighting men that the resistance movement in northern Italy has available to it.'[3] This could be a useful force.

Dulles's confidence was not altogether shared in London and Washington, two administrations that had seen little evidence to place much faith in the heirs of the Caesars. It was left to the Labour MP and Italian expert Ivor Bulmer-Thomas in the House of Commons to sally that 'Italians have not really fought in this war because they were fighting a war which for them was hateful. Give them a good cause and they will show they can fight as well as any other soldier'.[4]

In the late autumn of 1943, this was an arresting proposition. Time would tell.

2

Meanwhile, Allen Dulles hurried back to Berne and his Herrengasse desk. He had been in post for just over a year, and had certainly done enough to annoy his British opposite number, Claude Dansey, in London's Broadway.

The American's network of spies already covered France, Italy and Austria, and had successfully penetrated, besides Germany itself, Yugoslavia, Czechoslovakia, Bulgaria, Hungary, Spain, Portugal and North Africa. He was already helping the maquis in France and – beginning with his work in Lugano – the partisans in Italy. He was also supporting those in Germany trying to assassinate Hitler. He had recruited the former Swiss President, Marcel Pilet-Golaz, as informant 518. Above all, his British reject Fritz Kolbe had proved a gold mine. Kolbe's intelligence, duly validated through the good offices of Kim Philby, was now regarded as entirely reliable. Kolbe had supplied material including the V-1 and V-2 programmes, details of the revolutionary Me 262 jet fighter, Japanese campaign plans for South-East Asia, and the identity of a spy working in the British embassy in Ankara. It was no wonder that he would come to be seen as the most important spy in the whole European theatre.

Now, on his return to the Herrengasse, Dulles found he had two intriguing issues closer to home. The first concerned a striking sandstone building in the Bundesplatz, a spy's glance from Dulles's Herrengasse apartment. Silhouetted against the Bernese and Valais Alps, the building's façade was graced by a likeness of Mother Helvetia, suitably armed with shield and spear. It was the Bundeshaus, headquarters of the Swiss National Bank, and was in many respects as emblematic of Switzerland as the Matterhorn. 'The Swiss,' declared Chateaubriand rather uncharitably, 'neutral during the great revolutions in the countries surrounding them, have enriched themselves on the destitution of others and founded a bank on the misfortune of nations.'[5] Just a year into his mission and ninety-five after the death of the French sage, it had become apparent to Dulles that the doings of the bank represented a major issue for the Allies. Wars cost money and it was the Swiss who were helping to pay for the Nazis' barbarous war. This was the now notorious matter of the Swiss and Nazi gold. Dulles's other diversion was the rather more laudable humanitarian activities of his hosts.

German industry, by 1943 increasingly focused on the war effort, had a prodigious appetite for raw materials: chromium alloys for gun barrels, aluminium for aircraft manufacture, stainless steel for ball bearings and shell cases, diamonds for machine tools, oil, coal and gas for energy, and even common or garden iron ore for steel. Besides coal from the Ruhr and Saar, Germany had indigenous supplies of few of these strategic raw materials. Some were obtainable within the Greater Reich, notably oil from Romania; much of the material needed to be sourced from further afield: iron ore from Sweden, manganese from Spain, wolfram from Portugal, stainless steel from Turkey, industrial diamonds from South America. On 26 July 1943, Hitler had promoted Albert Speer, placing all war production under his ministry. Four months later on 13 November 1943, Speer gave Hitler an inventory of the Reich's reserves of manganese, nickel, chromium and wolfram. As the Reich shrank from the east, supplies were in danger of getting short.

These goods had to be paid for. The Reich's trading partners abroad would not accept payment in Reich marks or German gold. They would, however, pocket Swiss gold or any other internationally accepted foreign currency. Swiss francs would do nicely. For the Nazis the solution was obvious enough. The Reichsbank had a deposit account with the Swiss National Bank. Dormant in September 1939, on 14 January 1940 the first gold from Germany was credited on the ledger. It arrived by rail from the border city of Basel, packed in boxes. At Berne station, high above the river Aare that ringed the city's old quarter, it was transferred to trucks to complete the journey to the SNB head-quarters on the east side of the Bundesplatz. The entrance to the bank's underground vaults was guarded by Swiss soldiers, who looked on unblinkingly as the bank officials unloaded the bullion onto handcarts and wheeled the gold tenderly down to the vaults. There the bars were counted and registered and stacked on shelves. It was Aladdin's cave, Shakespeare's 'Gold! Yellow, glittering, precious gold!'

The gold was from Germany but strictly speaking did not belong to the Nazis. Germany's gold reserves were much depleted by the beginning of the war and needed replenishing. Fortunately there was a ready source. First, the gold reserves of the countries that the Reich had occupied during the blitzkrieg years of 1939, 1940 and 1941. The Netherlands parted with $137m, Belgium $22.6m, Luxembourg $4.8m, Hungary $32m, about $100m *in toto* came from Albania, Greece, Yugoslavia and – eventually – Italy. Second, after 1941, a new source materialised: gold stolen not from large institutions but from the small banks, commercial companies and civilian populations living under Nazi control. Special teams euphemistically known as Devisenschutzkommandos (foreign exchange protection task forces) 'broke into savings banks, looted private banks, emptied jewellers' shops and private residences'.[6] In due course the concentration and extermination camps added to this store, a productive source of wedding rings, trinkets and the fillings of teeth. At the Nuremberg War Crimes Tribunal, Rudolf Höss, the notorious camp commandant of Auschwitz, helpfully explained how the gold was plundered after the camp's victims had been gassed. 'Once the bodies had been hauled out [of the gas chambers], our special squads removed their rings and extracted the gold from the teeth of these cadavers . . . Special trucks were employed to transport it, and we packed the rings, watches, and bracelets separately. Exceptionally valuable pieces were later sold in Switzerland.'[7] The total sum from these civilian sources was reckoned at a further $146m.

It was true that these sources declared their provenance – either by way of a stamp indicating ownership or the equally telling fact that a filling looks like a filling, a wedding ring a wedding ring. This gold was accordingly smelted in the Prussian mint in Berlin, given a new seal, new numbers, and pre-war dates that assured the guileless acquirer of the bullion's pristine pre-war provenance.

This was the gold that, from January 1941, arrived in Switzerland in an ever-increasing stream from Nazi Germany – conservatively totalling 1.3 billion Swiss francs in the course of the war. The Nazis were reimbursed in Swiss francs and with this convertible currency they duly bought manganese, wolfram, tungsten, aluminium, oil, iron ore and – doubtless – cheap tin trays.

The colloquial term for this is money laundering. Other expressions might be used of those who knowingly handled gold not only looted from those countries occupied by Germany, but scavenged from the concentration and extermination camps. 'While other neutrals limited or suspended their gold shipments from Berlin, the SNB obligingly left its doors open. Despite Allied accusations of German looting ringing in their ears, the SNB's blithe acceptance of German protestations of innocence, even when uttered by officials who were old acquaintances from before the war, is hard to credit, far less condone.'[8] It was, too, a practice condoned at the highest levels. The bank's board was chaired by Ernst Weber, who himself reported to the bank council, headed by Professor Gottlieb Bachmann. Both were appointees of the Swiss finance ministry. When Bachmann evinced concern about doing business with the Nazis, Weber was reassuring: 'The National Bank cannot have regard to the provenance of the gold that is sold it by the Deutsche Reichsbank.'[9]

Since the huge controversy over this story in the 1990s, the Swiss bank's complicity in the traffic has been put beyond question: it was conceded by Switzerland's own Bergier commission. This stated: 'It is hardly surprising that the SNB's decisions have – quite legitimately – been the subject of historical and moral assessment on frequent occasions, and that its decisions are judged as having been reprehensible.'[10] In 1996 a new SNB board president, Hans Meyer, displayed refreshing candour, declaring 'Our predecessors made mistakes.'[11]

3

With the opening of the Second Front against the Soviet Union in June 1941, the Reich's need for strategic war materials grew, and with it the requirement for foreign exchange. Two years later in the summer of 1943 – just as Dulles was getting to know the German Foreign Office spy Fritz Kolbe – the Allies' bombing campaign of Germany industrial centres was beginning to bite. Albert Speer, who had just become Reich Minister of Armaments and War Production, recorded:

our Western enemies launched five major attacks on a single big city – Hamburg – within a week, from July 25 to August 2. Rash as this operation was, it had catastrophic consequences for us ... Huge conflagrations created cyclone-like firestorms; the asphalt of the streets began to blaze; people were suffocated in their cellars or burned to death in the streets. The devastation of this series of air raids could be compared only with the effects of a major earthquake.[12]

The consequence was that the Reich turned more and more for its war materials to further afield. By 1943, it was importing three-quarters of its wolfram and virtually all its manganese and stainless steel. To fund this, the Reich that year delivered to the Swiss a record figure of gold bars and coins, amounting to 529 million Swiss francs. The guards, porters and bookkeepers in the Bundeshaus worked overtime.

This was not a secret that could be kept from the Allies. In Britain the Ministry of Economic Warfare had interested itself in the matter of German gold operations for some time. Still, it was not until early 1943 when, buttressed by a similar interest displayed by the US Treasury Secretary Henry Morgenthau, the Allies agreed on a set of metrics for the Reich's reserves. The implication of these figures was that the Reich was in considerable financial straits and was likely to be channelling a good deal of gold in the direction of Berne. Quite how much was less apparent. From his desk in the Herrengasse, Dulles had the resources to put enquiries in hand. He found our lanky friend Hans Bernd Gisevius a most useful source. Admiral Canaris's man in Switzerland was well up on the bankers, lawyers and all the various middlemen involved in money laundering. Soon Dulles tentatively concluded that the Allies were considerably underestimating the extent of Swiss conversion of Nazi gold into Swiss francs. The consequence was that the Allies began to put pressure in an increasingly concerted form on the Swiss.

In January 1943, three months after Dulles's arrival in Switzerland, Churchill took a hand. At his behest the 'Inter-Allied declaration against acts of dispossession committed in territories under enemy control' was signed. Known as the 'loot declaration', this was an attempt to prevent the Reich taking advantage of its booty. It committed the Allies to restoring stolen goods after the war and fired warning shots across the bows of those nations accepting such goods. In April 1943, Washington put direct pressure on the Swiss to cut their loans to the Reich. This Allied proposal was backed up by a threat. Switzerland was dependent – despite the Wahlen plan which had turned flower beds, football fields and public parks into vegetable gardens – for roughly two-thirds of her food on countries beyond her borders. Although some still came from her immediate neighbours, other foodstuffs came from overseas through nearby ports like Genoa and Monaco. As has been remarked, cargoes bound for Switzerland were turned away from these ports or confiscated unless blessed with a navigation certificate issued by the Allies. These certificates would – threatened the US – be withdrawn unless Switzerland complied with Allied wishes. Starvation beckoned.

The responsible Swiss minister was fifty-nine-year-old Walther Stampfli, chairman of the Federal Department of Economics (Morgenthau's counterpart). He took exception to the Allied proposal. 'Just imagine, the Allies are demanding that we join in the war against Germany! Germany has never treated Switzerland as badly as the Allies are doing now.'[13] Like the Swiss in general, Stampfli of course needed to keep a balance between the Reich on his doorstep and the Allies still some distance – a diminishing distance but a distance nevertheless – away. Over the course of the summer of 1943, the summer of Mussolini's fall, he played for time.

The same strategy was deployed by the top Swiss industrialist Hans Sulzer. Whilst Allied concerns about the gold trade had mounted, so too did their objections to Switzerland's growing contribution to the Nazi war effort in the form of war materiel: precision instruments, trucks, tractors, railway locomotives, ammunition, weapons and even wooden huts for concentration camps. Unlike their counterparts in the Reich, Swiss factories were not being bombed. In the summer of 1943, the British Ministry of Economic Warfare had told the Swiss minister to London, Walter Thurnheer, that the Allies were considering blacklisting companies that failed to restrain their exports to the Axis. Already hundreds of firms had earned this mark of distinction. These negotiations were handled by the sixty-six-year-old Sulzer in his capacity as proprietor of the family engineering concern Gebrüder Sulzer AG, president of the employers' federation the Verband Schweizerischer Maschinenindustrieller, and president of the Supervisory Committee for Imports and Exports. The British case was that since 1940 Swiss exports to the Axis outweighed those to the Allies by six to one. It was perhaps this figure that led to the saying that the Swiss worked for the Axis during the week and the Allies at weekends. In any case, according to Sulzer the figures were fiction; British estimates of Swiss exports to the Axis were grossly overestimated, an 'optical illusion', he declared. So negotiations continued for nine months.

On Dulles's return to his Herrengasse desk from meeting the partisans in Lugano in early November 1943, the American spymaster found these two matters – money laundering and Swiss exports to the Reich – still unresolved. Meanwhile gold deliveries to the Bundeshaus grew and grew.

4

Somewhat removed on the moral spectrum from the industrialists and bankers were the Swiss diplomats, the International Red Cross, and some individual Swiss citizens.

Switzerland was first known for its mountains and its mercenaries and subsequently for its money. In the interval it was defined by its diplomats. When countries sever diplomatic relations, the interests of their citizens still need to be represented, their institutions and their people based in another country looked after, lent money, extracted from jail, sent home. Third parties representing such interests are 'protecting powers'. The Swiss made a name for themselves in this role during the Franco-Prussian War, and it was a part they enlarged upon during the First World War. It culminated in the Second World War when – at the height of her responsibilities in 1944 – Berne represented thirty-five countries.

At the outbreak of war in 1939, the Swiss had been appointed to represent Germany throughout the British Empire. This they discharged conscientiously and successfully, though not very cheaply. In German territories, British interests were at first handled by the United States. When the US entered the war in December 1941, the Swiss took over. Berne accordingly found herself in the unique position of representing the principal belligerents on both sides of the conflict. Much as Berne worked hard on behalf of the Germans, so did they toil for the British. In the course of 1942 the diplomats visited civilian camps on twenty occasions, POW camps 174 times. They also talked their way into British civilian internment camps in France that had been closed to the Americans and the Red Cross. This was a cause for congratulation from Anthony Eden at the Foreign Office in Whitehall. In 1943 came controversy.

In August 1942 Canadian forces taken prisoner in the cross-Channel raid on Dieppe were found to be carrying orders requiring them to tie the hands of any prisoners they might take; some had actually done so. This was strictly against the Geneva Conventions, the international laws that enshrine the humanitarian treatment of victims of – and participants in – war. OKW at once retaliated. At Dieppe itself, 1,376 Allied prisoners were chained and it was announced that British and Commonwealth POWs would henceforth be shackled. Churchill reciprocated by ordering German prisoners in Britain and Canada to be chained. On 13 October 1942 the PM announced that Germany had been requested to rescind her action in shackling prisoners and that if she did so Britain would cancel her own reprisals. These requests were made through and by Berne. 'GERMANY TO CONTINUE CHAINING PRISONERS', ran a subsequent newspaper headline: 'Request for Negotiation Rejected'. Tit for tat continued until 27 November 1942, when the Germans declared that if the practice continued it would no longer respect any aspect of the Conventions in its dealings with the Allies.

At this point Churchill reluctantly asked Berne to take an active role in resolving the matter. The task fell to Marcel Pilet-Golaz, the former President of the Federal Council, who was already working on an exchange between the two warring nations of sick and wounded POWs. On 10 December 1942, he achieved a Christmas armistice. This was respected by both sides. In the New Year, Berlin resumed shackling, but in a half-hearted way. In the following months the affair slowly blew over and reached formal resolution in November 1943, not long after Italy had changed sides. This was a month after Pilet-Golaz's efforts to achieve a prisoner exchange saw 4,000 British and 5,000 Germans repatriated. Together, these two episodes combined to define Switzerland's position in British eyes as an exemplary protecting power.

If this seems a diplomatic nicety, it was not. At the time very soon to come – the Tehran Conference between Stalin, Roosevelt and Churchill – at which discussions were taking place at the most senior level between the Allies on the shape of post-war Europe, this stood the Swiss in very good stead. 'No other single issue [than the handling of POWs] had a more profound influence on the tenor of Anglo-Swiss relations.'[14] When Stalin proposed the invasion of Switzerland in the autumn of 1944 as a means of turning the Siegfried Line, Churchill remembered the shackling crisis.

Switzerland's other principal humanitarian effort was the Red Cross.

This was an organisation founded by the Swiss businessman Henri Dunant. In 1859 he had witnessed the aftermath of the Battle of Solferino in Lombardy between Austrian and French forces, and had been horrified by the sufferings of the 40,000 dead and dying. Four years later in 1863, at Dunant's suggestion, the Swiss government mounted an international conference on the issue in Geneva. The signatories of the First Geneva Convention dedicated themselves to the 'amelioration of the condition of the wounded in Armies in the field'. By 1876 this body had become known as the International Committee of the Red Cross (ICRC), was headquartered in Geneva, and was the co-ordinating body for national Red Cross societies that had formed themselves in most of the European countries and in the United States. In 1901 Dunant shared with a fellow pacifist the very first Nobel Peace Prize.

The Second World War proved the Committee's sternest test. The legal basis on which the ICRC operated was the Geneva Convention of 1929. Germany was a signatory, as were the other major Western powers. The Soviet Union was not. The notorious Soviet treatment of Nazi POWs, and vice versa, showed the value of the Convention. Yet the ICRC could only do its work in liaison with the national Red Cross committees. Germany had its own such committee but this would have no truck with the ICRC: it had been subsumed into the Nazi Party. This meant that for long the International Committee could not obtain agreement with the Nazis about the treatment of the prisoners in the concentration camps, let alone the the activities of the SS-Totenkopfverbände in the extermination camps. Only in November 1943, the month of Dulles's trip to Lugano, did the ICRC finally manage to obtain permission to supplement the rations of concentration camp detainees. That month, parcels began to flow to Dachau, Buchenwald, Ravensbrück and Sachsenhausen.

This was a victory but a heavily qualified one. The Red Cross aligned itself closely with the Swiss government and – like the Federal Council – was reluctant to press its monstrous neighbour too hard. A year previously, on 14 October 1942, several ICRC board members had proposed a motion condemning Nazi treatment of detainees in the concentration camps, in effect proposing to make a very public international appeal in support of Europe's Jews. It was vetoed by the Swiss Federal Council and the remaining members of the board.

As Caroline Moorhead judged in her history of the ICRC, this failure 'has caused the organization great and lasting damage, both immediately after the war and in recent years ... [Its failure] has haunted it ever since.' Yves Sandoz of the Committee wrote of 'the greatest defeat in the 125-year history of our humanitarian mission'.[15]

5

In any case, in November 1943, the ICRC found it had a good deal to do rather closer to home than Auschwitz.

Since the seizure of the Franco-Swiss border by the Seventh Army in November 1942 the democracy had become an oasis in a fascist desert, and there were accordingly many who aspired to drink at the well. As we have seen, the Swiss categorised those seeking sanctuary as evaders (military personnel in plain clothes), Internierten (military personnel clothed as such) and Flüchtlings – civilian refugees. We also saw how the drizzle of Jewish refugees became a downpour after the German occupation of the French occupied zone in 1942; and how Switzerland was flooded with escaped POWs after Italy changed sides in September 1943. To this line of rather unwelcome guests was added fresh impetus that same autumn in the form of visitors from the skies. On 24 August 1942, a damaged RAF Mosquito fighter-bomber became the first Allied aircraft to find refuge on Swiss soil. It was the first of thirteen RAF aircraft that formed the prologue to the big wing of the USAAF.

To complement the night-bombing campaign against Germany of Air Chief Marshal Arthur Harris's RAF Bomber Command, in August 1942 the United States Eighth Air Force under Major-General Carl Spaatz had started its own campaign of daylight raids on Continental Europe. By the spring of 1943 this had gathered momentum, with April seeing a huge raid of 115 heavy bombers on the North Sea port of Bremen. At first these raids concentrated on Germany; later Italy was added to the target list. Crews of aircraft damaged en route to these targets, over the targets, or on their return flights naturally regarded Switzerland as any port in a storm.

On 13 August 1943 the first USAAF aircraft crash-landed in Switzerland. The B-24 Liberator *Death Dealer* had left its base in North Africa on a mission to the industrial city of Wiener Neustadt, some thirty miles south of the sometime capital of Austria. Sustaining damage over the target and with only two of its four engines running, the pilot First Lieutenant Alva Geron realised he would never make it back to base. He headed for Switzerland and crash-landed his craft at Thurau near the city of Wil in St Gallen, in the east of the country. He set fire to the remains of the B-24 and surrendered himself and his crew to the Swiss police.

As the summer turned to autumn, such Allied violations of Swiss airspace became frequent. These infractions meant that General Guisan – with the Nazis breathing down his neck – was obliged to take action. On 25 October the commander of Swiss forces ordered the Swiss air force to shoot down all bombers in Swiss airspace not indicating their willingness to land. A handful were indeed destroyed by the republic's fighters or by Swiss flak; most were safely escorted to the neutral Swiss airfields. Some airmen also parachuted from their stricken planes. There were also rumours that, given the familiar attractions of Switzerland even during the war, there were some aircrews who landed in Switzerland in planes that were perfectly serviceable. William Joyce was the Irish propagandist who worked for the Nazis. Dubbed 'Lord Haw Haw' for his nasal 'Jairmany Calling' accent, he imaginatively suggested that such crews had their golf bags on board.

In reality, few of the young American airmen arriving in Switzerland found themselves on the tee reaching for their drivers. They were interrogated by the Swiss, briefly quarantined, then sent off into internment: a legal requirement, as they were of course wearing military uniform.

At first in that autumn of 1943, their numbers were such that they could be accommodated in a couple of hotels: the Bellevue at Macolin and the Hôtel Trois Sapins at Evilard, both close to Berne. By November it was apparent that something larger would be necessary. The remote resort of Adelboden, forty miles south of Berne, was already being used as a camp for British and Commonwealth POWs who had escaped from Italy. Now it seemed a good solution for the Americans too. There was a large, empty hotel with what might have seemed to a Swiss bureaucrat a suitable name: the Nevada Palace. This formed the nucleus of a camp which the Americans named Camp Moloney. Sergeant Clinton Norby recalled his first impressions:

When we reached the top, the bus took us right through town (one street about four blocks long) to the other end where The Nevada Palace was located. There was a 30 foot picture window about 15 feet high which looked out over a valley about 2,000 to 3,000 feet below us. You could see clouds move up the valley and then they would just stop below the hotel. In fact, one day when I was looking out the window, the sun was shining on us, but looking down the slope, you could see it snowing.[16]

Picturesque though this might be, the former farmhands from Alabama and clerks from Albuquerque failed to find the experience very congenial. It was a long way from home, Mae West, root beer and other staples of the 1940s American lifestyle; they were subjected to a daily roll-call, an evening curfew, restriction to the immediate surroundings of the village, and generally kept under observation by the Swiss authorities; they were given the same rations as the Swiss army – 1,500 calories – which few found adequate; and above all they did not have enough to do. Lieutenant James D. Mahaffey remembered, 'In Adelboden, about the only thing we had to do was drink, read a few books, and eventually they had movies twice a week. I did manage to get in about a month of skiing, which I enjoyed quite a bit.'[17] If this was not war, neither was it precisely peace.

Like all such camps, Adelboden was subject to ICRC inspection. The Committee helped the internees make contact with home, and checked up on their hygiene and health, their clothing, lodging and food. It arranged for such matters as dental treatment, medicines, spectacles, and the other incidentals of life beyond the interest or remit of the Swiss internment authorities. The inspectors were subjected to complaints about the facilities and duly passed these on to the central committee in Geneva. The ICRC then duly made enquiries: normally of another office in Geneva, or sometimes Zurich. It could do little about keeping the Americans suitably occupied, and a number of these idle hands tried to escape. Those that did and were recaptured were dispatched to the Swiss punishment camps. These included one that became notorious: Wauwilermoos in Lucerne. Here, as we will see, the ICRC really did have a job to do.

The final aspect of Switzerland's humanitarian story lies with individual Swiss citizens.

Samedan was the village close to St Moritz where the South African corporal Billy Marais had been taken after escaping from Italy. The pastor at Samedan was a remarkable man. Fortunat Guidon was born in 1910 in Latsch, a medieval hamlet seven hundred feet above the 4,485-foot railway village of Bergün, on the line between St Moritz and Davos. He had met his wife Trudi Manz in 1935 while studying theology at the University of Bonn. There, perforce, the couple also studied the Nazi movement: many of their friends were Jews. In 1939, Guidon was appointed to the benefice of the reformed Protestant church at Samedan. He was twenty-nine, and this was only his second job. A man with a rigorous sense of right and wrong, he heard that the Swiss government was contravening the terms of its own neutrality by letting arms pass from Germany to Italy through the St Gotthard railway tunnel. He denounced the authorities from his pulpit. A local girl whom he had confirmed wrote from Berlin announcing her engagement to an SS officer. She sought testimony from him of the purity of her Aryan descent, a necessary procedure under the Nuremberg Laws. He refused. When the request was repeated and again turned down, Fortunat was told that his family had been earmarked for extermination. It was not surprising that refugees of all stripes threw themselves on the mercy of this man. These included old friends from Bonn, who turned up on his doorstep having escaped the Reich over the border with Austria, some twenty-five miles north. Guidon and his wife were determined to do what they could to help these people reach the safety of the Swiss interior. This placed them in a vulnerable position with regard to the cantonal authorities. The Samedan apartment in which the family lived was in a block that also housed both the police station and the cantonal authorities themselves.

The pastor's eldest son was Matteus. Born in 1936, he was a strong, intelligent, lively boy. He had often accompanied his father up the tracks north of Samedan across the 9,419-foot Fuorcla Pischa (Pischa pass). This led to his grandfather's little farmhouse in Chants. Five miles east up the Val Tours from Bergün, this was a remote spot where the Swiss police never ventured. From the autumn, Matteus had new companions on his climbs in the form of his parents' old friends. Soon they found themselves guided towards the Swiss interior by a boy of an age that would surely not excite the interest of the authorities. It was a journey from jeopardy to safety that took about eight hours. From the farmhouse in Chants, the boy's grandfather would take the refugees to Latsch, then further north-west towards safety. Matteus, now seventy-six, comments:

Of course at the time I didn't know what I was doing. My father would just say that because my report was good, I could take a day off school and take some people over the Fuorcla Pischa to Chants. Then I would catch the train back from Bergün. He told me not to talk to anyone. If I was asked who I was or what I was doing, I was to say that I didn't understand. It was only after the war that my mother told me about it all. The Pass? Well, I knew the way but some of the ladies I took were very sportif, they could see the route better than I could. Of course there were no waymarks then. Sometimes, too, it was very cold and they had to pull me along, so really it wasn't very romantic, no.

6

As the year 1943 drew to a close, from his desk in the Herrengasse Dulles was able to note the progress of a number of affairs with some satisfaction.

Despite Sulzer's protestations, his own firm, Gebrüder Sulzer AG, had been added to the British blacklist in September. On 19 November, Washington had followed suit. As a consequence of this sort of pressure, a month later on 19 December 1943, Switzerland signed a landmark agreement with the Allies that went a very fair way to addressing the concerns of Washington and London over the Swiss financial and industrial contribution to the Nazis' war effort. Deliveries of arms and ammunition to Germany would be virtually halved; exports of optical instruments, rocket components and other items of precision engineering would be cut by 60 per cent, and Swiss loans would also be reduced. As the scholar Gerhard Weinberg interpreted, 'By this time it was obvious that the Allies would win the war, and the exclusion of Swiss firms from a world dominated by the United Nations would end the country's prosperity permanently. The policy of government changed.'[18]

Dulles also – at last – had a little good news for the Italian partisans. Despite the goodwill established at the meeting in Lugano and the promises made of immediate aid, nothing had materialised. The OSS as yet had little lien on the USAAF, and its dedicated Special Operations 801st Bombardment Group – the Carpetbaggers – had not yet been formed. SOE had a better relationship with the RAF, but not that much better. The plan also became embroiled in politics. Once the British Foreign Office had got wind of the SOE/OSS scheme to assist leftward-leaning partisans, the procrastination in which government departments excelled was deployed. The four immediate airdrops promised were reduced to one, and that would equip only a fraction of the partisans Parri and Pizzoni claimed to have at their disposal. The drop was eventually made by the RAF on 23 December 1943, just in time for Christmas. It comprised arms for just thirty men.

INSPIRATION: Hitler was enchanted by the Alps, settled in Bavaria in 1928, conceived and directed much of the war from the Berghof, his headquarters at Berchtesgaden. Here he is pictured in contemplative mood enjoying Bergfried, the 'peace of the mountains'.

SKIING AND THE SWASTIKA: the Nazis began the politicisation of mountain sports no sooner had they come to power. In February 1936, Christl Cranz put herself in the Führer's good books by winning gold in the winter Olympics at Garmisch-Partenkirchen.

THE HEIGHT OF POWER: the political set pieces that led to the outbreak of war in 1939 were frequently staged by Hitler at the Berghof. British PM Neville Chamberlain, champion of appeasement, arrives in Berchtesgaden for a summit on 15 September 1938.

BRIEF ENCOUNTER: the Alps were the most convenient trysting-place for Hitler and Mussolini. Here the dictators duet at Kufstein in the Austrian Tyrol, en route to the pivotal meeting with Chamberlain and Daladier at Munich on 29 September 1938.

PLOUGHSHARES INTO SWORDS: the unique demands of high-altitude warfare saw resorts like Chamonix and Zermatt turned into military training camps; others, in Switzerland – Wengen, Adelboden and Davos – were transformed into internment camps for downed Allied airmen; still others – Megève and St Gervais – became havens for Jewish refugees.

SWITZERLAND'S CHURCHILL: while Swiss politicians wavered in the face of the Nazi threat to their country, General Henri Guisan stood so firm that his countrymen likened him to the British leader. In August 1940 he visited Davos on a morale-boosting tour of what would have been the front line, should the Wehrmacht have invaded.

ON HITLER'S DOORSTEP: despite Swiss neutrality, Hitler and Mussolini both made plans to invade continental Europe's oasis of democracy. The Swiss response was to create an Alpine redoubt in the southern sector of the country, and to maintain troops on the borders at the highest state of alert throughout the war.

AMERICA'S MAN IN BERNE: Allen Dulles of the OSS vied with his British colleagues for the position of Europe's chief Allied spymaster.

WILHELM GUSTLOFF: leader of the Nazi party in Switzerland. He was assassinated in Davos on 4 February 1936 by a prescient Croatian Jew, David Frankfurter.

ALAIN LE RAY was the first man to escape from the legendary POW camp at Colditz and became the most dashing of the leaders of the French resistance in the Rhône Alps.

THE GOOD SHEPHERD: Matteus Guidon, the seven-year-old son of a pastor in Samedan in eastern Switzerland, was employed by his father to escort Jewish refugees fleeing to the safety of the country's interior. He is seen in 1946 on the Fuorcla Pischa, over which he guided the persecuted.

TWO OF THE JEWISH REFUGEES escorted by Matteus Guidon. One of them, Hilde (*above left*), lived to enjoy a career in the Israeli army; the other, Michelle, was shot dead by the Germans on the French border.

CABLE-CAR TO DEATH: two of the Nazis' most infamous concentration camps were under the knees of the Alps: Dachau in Munich and Mauthausen close to Vienna. Sub-camps included Ebensee, whose survivors are pictured on 7 May 1945, shortly after liberation.

TO THE VICTORS, THE SPOILS: Göring's art collection that he intended to rival the Louvre, found its way to the Alps and fell into Allied hands at the war's end.

MAY 1945: A column of American tanks screeches through the newly conquered Bavarian skiing resort of Garmisch-Partenkirchen.

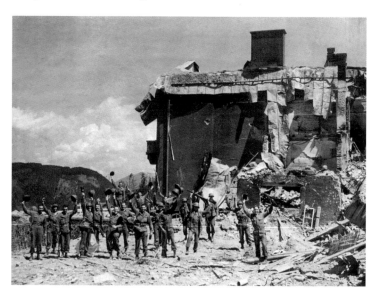

GÖTTERDÄMMERUNG: at the heart of Goebbels's vaunted Alpine redoubt, the victors grandstand for the cameras in the ruins of the Berghof, destroyed by the RAF bombing raid of 25 April 1945.

TEN

'A guerrilla à la Tito'

I am most anxious to see a guerrilla à la Tito started up in the Savoie and in the Alpes Maritimes.

WINSTON CHURCHILL

I

It was Christmas in Berchtesgaden. Snow had come early to Bavaria that year and would stay late. In the streets of the old town it lay deep, crisp and even, and at Obersalzberg itself the snow had drifted around the chalets of Bormann, Goebbels and Göring and about the Berghof itself. Here, preparations were in hand to welcome the Führer for the break from his labours in Rastenburg. It was his neighbour on the mountain, Albert Speer, who described the restorative effect of the Alpine headquarters on the Führer: 'After staying at Obersalzberg for a few weeks he would appear more relaxed. His eyes would be brighter, his capacity for reaction would have increased, and he would recover his pleasure in state business.'[1] It was the magic of the Alps that continues to cast its spell on all and sundry, even dictators.

Yet by Christmas 1943, Berchtesgaden had changed. Much as the Swiss were troubled by Allied overflights to targets east, south and north of their small democracy, so too were the more beleaguered citizens of Berchtesgaden. The Lockstein, a small steep mountain, rose virtually from the centre of the picture-postcard town. Into its roots a rough tunnel had been blasted to provide shelter for the inhabitants from hard rain. Irmgard Paul, who had been dandled on Hitler's knee six years previously, now found herself spirited away from school and taking cover in this mole hole for two, three or four hours every day.

Deep inside Lockstein we sat on crude, backless wooden benches lined up along the dirty, raw walls. The air-raid warden was impatient with our shuffling and cries of 'I want to sit next to Marianne and Anneliese!' or 'Save me a place, Annemarie,' and shouted repeatedly, 'Alles setzen!' (Everyone sit down). We planted our feet on wooden planks to avoid the deep puddles formed by the constant drip of water from the porous rock.[2]

Across the valley of the river Ache at Obersalzberg, similar precautions were now necessary. By the summer of 1943 – the months of the fall of Mussolini – it had become very apparent to the controller of the complex, the bull-necked murderer Reichsleiter Martin Bormann, that Hitler's sanctuary needed some form of air-raid protection. The skies were becoming all too crowded with Allied aircraft and the Luftwaffe was failing to do its job – even to protect the air force chief Hermann Göring's own luxurious Obersalzberg chalet. Under Bormann's direction anti-aircraft guns were installed on the Kehlstein mountain, a chemical system for creating artificial fog to shroud the complex was developed, Hitler's chalet was camouflaged, and the construction of a bunker system put in hand. This symbolism of impending attack compromised the calming atmosphere of the Nazis' private mountain.

Work on a shelter beneath Hitler's Berghof began in August 1943, just as the first USAAF Liberator crash-landed in Switzerland. It was planned to be completed on 24 December 1943, in time for Hitler's arrival and the exchange of presents traditional on Christmas Eve in Germany, Austria and Switzerland. In late October there was a crisis at Obersalzberg when movement of the surrounding soil caused the central corridor of the system to collapse. The only solution was to provide a concrete lining. Men had to be taken off dozens of other jobs to meet the deadline, yet met it was. On Christmas Eve the 400-foot bunker was ready for a gala opening. The steel blast doors swung smoothly on their hinges, the inlaid floor was polished, rugs garnished the floors, the air conditioning was running, the dog kennel had been sourced for Hitler's Alsatian, pictures graced the walls, tasteful furniture – or at least furniture regarded by Nazis as tasteful – was installed. It was home from home.

Of Hitler, though, there was still no sign.

After the recapture of the Ukrainian capital of Kiev by the Soviets on 6 November 1943, he had briefly left Rastenburg to visit Munich – for the annual celebration of the Beer Hall Putsch – and Breslau in western Poland. Then he returned to Rastenburg to direct operations on the Eastern Front. The outlook was poor. The winter was one such as only Russia can provide, and the line of the Dnjepr was proving impossible to hold. On Christmas Eve the First Ukrainian Front struck Generalfeldmarschall Ferdinand Schörner's Army Group South along the river Teterev. It was a signal for the beginning of a long retreat that would only end fifteen months later in Berlin. The grim news from the East was trumped on 26 December 1943 by another story filtering through to the gloomy woodland HQ. It was of the sinking of the 32,000-ton *Scharnhorst* at the Battle of North Cape, Norway. All but thirty of her two-thousand-strong crew perished when the convoy raider fell to the fourteen-inch guns of the British battleship *Duke of York*.

That Christmas there was no rest at the Berghof for the wicked. Hitler appeared neither for Christmas nor Silvester, the traditional New Year's Eve celebrations. Irmgard Paul remembered, 'On New Year's day, Mutti [her mother] wrote in her new diary for 1944: "We all look with a heavy heart to the future."'[3]

2

Churchill was now taking a very similar line on the likely outcome of the war. Five weeks earlier on 28 November 1943 he had met Marshal Stalin and President Roosevelt in Tehran. This was the first of the great wartime meetings between the three principal Allies. It was held to resolve uncertainties over a unified Allied strategy for victory, over the future of Europe after the war, and – particularly – over plans for the Second Front. After a good deal of wrangling, a date of May 1944 was agreed for the Allied invasion of France, for D-Day. The Big Three also discussed the breaking up of Germany after the war into a series of smaller states, from whence she came. Churchill, mindful of history, sought to isolate Prussia and its inveterate warmongers. He proposed merging Alpine Germany and Austria with Hungary to form a federation coalescing around the river Danube. It would, he said wistfully, be a 'broad, peaceful, cow-like confederation'.[4] Stalin and Roosevelt differed, but agreement was reached that the Reich would certainly no longer exist in her current bloated state.

Germany's hash having been settled, on 11 December 1943 Churchill arrived in Carthage for a meeting with General Dwight Eisenhower, then masterminding the Allies' push for Rome. On the following day the Prime Minister was diagnosed with pneumonia and on 15 December he suffered a mild heart attack. At the height of his illness he remarked to his daughter Sarah, 'If I die, don't worry – the war is won.'[5]

Unhappily for Hitler, Churchill did not succumb. By the morning of 18 January 1944 he was back in London, entirely recovered and answering Prime Minister's Questions in the House of Commons. The diarist 'Chips' Channon noted:

I went early to the House hearing that the PM was due back. The secret had been well kept, but I soon twigged that they wanted to stage a demonstration of enthusiasm and the surprise would add to it. It did. He came in just before 11.30 and smiled. The House cheered and rose, a courteous, spontaneous welcome which under the dramatic circumstances was legitimate, but curiously cold. Churchill is not loved in the House . . . and this morning's performance proved it. I thought he looked disappointed, but his health and colour have returned.[6]

*

Nine days later, on 27 January 1944, the PM was chairing a ministers' meeting to which he had invited Lord Selborne, head of the SOE.

Now that the date for the D-Day landings had been set, the PM was pondering the role that the French resistance might play in this great gamble. Hitherto, critics of SOE had been disappointed in the expectations that Churchill – amongst others – had entertained about its role in fostering resistance in Europe and overturning its Nazi occupiers. SOE, they said, had largely failed to set Europe ablaze and the resistance movements had done either less than was expected or – in the critical cases of Austria and Germany itself – nothing concrete at all. After all, Hitler was still in power, apparently unchallenged. The only exception to these conclusions was arguably in the Alps of France and certainly in those of Yugoslavia.

It will be remembered that it was Churchill's former historical research assistant Captain William Deakin who had been parachuted into Montenegro in May 1943. His mission had been to try to judge the rival claims of the communist Tito and the monarchist Mihailović: of the partisans and the patriots fighting to free Axis-occupied Yugoslavia. Deakin's admiration of the fighting spirit of Tito's forces in the course of the Battle of the Sutjeska had induced Churchill to dispatch a much more senior figure to resolve the matter once and for all. This was Brigadier Fitzroy Maclean, who was parachuted into Bosnia in September 1943. He was an astute choice, for the thirty-three-year-old Scot was the sort of derring-do adventurer who flourished in wartime.

Born into the Scottish landed gentry in 1911, Maclean was educated at Eton and Cambridge. He joined the diplomatic service in 1933, spent two and a half years in the Soviet Union, and when war broke out resigned to join the ranks in the Queen's Own Cameron Highlanders. Commissioned in 1941, he was sent to North Africa and at once distinguished himself with the newly formed Special Air Service (SAS). Later, in the Middle East, he kidnapped the pro-Axis commander of forces in Persia, Fazlollah Zahedi. The general was believed to be planning an uprising supported by the Germans. This hypothesis was supported by Maclean finding in his bedroom correspondence from a German agent, 'a collection of automatic weapons of German manufacture, a good deal of silk underwear, some opium [and] an illustrated register of the prostitutes of Isfahan'.[7] As to the mission in Yugoslavia, this, Maclean wrote candidly, was 'to find out who was killing most Germans and suggest means by which we could help them kill more'.[8]

He spent six weeks fact-finding in the autumn of 1943 in the whirligig of the Balkan Alps. Like Deakin, he was impressed by the firebrand Tito and his new form of warfare. He wrote after the war in his classic *Eastern Approaches*:

the Partisans constituted a military factor of first-rate importance against which a modern army was in many respects powerless. In the course of three years they [Axis forces] launched against them no less than seven full-scale offensives, each employing upwards of ten divisions with supporting arms. Once or twice large forces of Partisans came near to being surrounded and wiped out . . . But each time they succeeded in extricating themselves, fading away, reappearing elsewhere and attacking the enemy where he least expected it . . . the Germans . . . could do little more than garrison the large towns and try to guard the lines of communication between them . . . using a dozen or more precious divisions which they could with advantage have employed on other fronts.[9]

Naturally enough, this was a modus operandi and an outcome that greatly appealed to Churchill. It struck a chord with the man who had made his name in the Boer War, the conflict in which the guerrilla tactics of the Dutch settlers had proved so surprisingly effective against a lumbering and hidebound British army. Mafeking, Ladysmith and Colenso were hard lessons well learned by a leader who understood the meanings of history.

Having reached his conclusions in the late autumn of 1943, Maclean was extracted from Yugoslavia and hastily dispatched to British headquarters in Cairo. Here he could make his report before Churchill's summit with Stalin and Roosevelt in Tehran.

On 6 November 1943, Maclean duly presented his findings to the foreign secretary Anthony Eden. Naturally enough, he told Eden that the partisans' effectiveness could be considerably increased by Allied help. He also gave a caution: 'whether we gave such assistance or not, Tito and his followers would exercise decisive influence in Yugoslavia after the liberation'.[10] In short, although with Josip Broz would come victory over the

Wehrmacht, so would a communist state after the war. Churchill, a monarchist through and through, was as pragmatic here as he was in his dealings with Stalin. At a meeting with Maclean shortly after the Tehran Conference he asked first whether the Brigadier wore a kilt when he parachuted from a plane, subsequently of the government of post-war Yugoslavia. 'Do you intend', he asked Maclean, 'to make Yugoslavia your home after the war?' 'No Sir.' 'Neither do I. And that being so, the less you and I worry about the form of Government they set up, the better. That is for them to decide. What interests us is, which of them [partisans or patriots] is doing most harm to the Germans?'[11]

As part of the horse-trading at Tehran, Churchill, Roosevelt and Stalin had agreed that Tito's partisans in Yugoslavia should be supported with supplies and equipment to the greatest possible extent. At the beginning of December 1943, British support was also withdrawn from Mihailović. At much the same time the Wehrmacht opened the sixth anti-partisan offensive. Operation Kugelblitz was a drive by the V SS Mountain Corps to destroy partisan units in eastern Bosnia. Most of Tito's forces slipped through the closing SS ring, but at the price of some 9,000 casualties. Hard on its heels came Operation Schneesturm: two drives from Bosnia, one towards Italy and the other to the Adriatic coast. When the operation was called off in late December 1943 the partisans had lost another 2,000 men, but had still survived as a fighting force.

These events seemed to justify the wisdom of the British decision and the accuracy of Maclean's observations. Mihailović – and with him the young King Peter and the monarchy in Yugoslavia – would soon be consigned to the tides of history.

3

It was in the light of these lessons – both political and military – from Yugoslavia that Churchill chaired the London meeting on 27 January 1944.

The agenda was D-Day. When the Anglo-American forces landed in France, Churchill believed they would need all the help they could get. That month the PM had noted, 'It is to my mind very unwise to make plans on the basis of Hitler being defeated in 1944. The possibility of his gaining a victory in France cannot be excluded. The hazards of battle are very great. The reserves of the enemy are capable of being thrown from point to point with great facility.'[12] Plans for the Second Front called for two amphibious operations, Churchill explained to the meeting. The principal thrust was to be on France's Channel coast, the secondary on the Mediterranean coast in Provence. What help could the French resistance provide to support these operations?

From the fragmentary and largely spontaneous movement that had begun in 1941, the resistance in France had coalesced by 1943 into a body unified by the persuasive powers of General de Gaulle and the legendary resistance leader Jean Moulin. A senior civil servant, the forty-four-year-old Moulin had met de Gaulle in London in September 1941. The General had briefed him to fuse the various French resistance groups into what became the Conseil National de la Résistance (National Council of Resistance or CNR). Moulin succeeded. His arrest in Lyons in June 1943 and subsequent murder by the Gestapo monster Klaus Barbie was a major setback for the stripling CNR. Yet seven months later, by January 1944, the French resistance could smell victory. The advance of the Red Army on a 4,000-mile front, the steady progress of Eisenhower's forces in Italy, and the presumption that a great Allied army would soon return to the western shores of the Continent all whetted the appetite of those who had hitherto held back. Recruits flocked to the colours at every turn. Nowhere was this more so than to the east of the Rhône in the French Alps: in Savoie, Dauphiné and the Alpes-Maritimes.

It was here that in June 1940 the French Armée des Alpes, fighting on the border with Italy, had put to shame its peers caving in to Hitler's blitzkrieg further north; it was here, too, that the terrain played into the hands of the rural resistance or maquis. From Annecy, twenty-five miles south of the western tip of Lake

Geneva, in a line south via the hornets' nests of Chambéry, Grenoble and Barcelonnette to Nice, the resistance sprang up. Supplied from the Alpine towns and cities, the maquis secreted themselves in mountain redoubts. Their numbers had been swelled by the onset of Service du Travail Obligatoire in February 1943, and by the increasing levels of support in terms of both money and materiel from the SOE in Baker Street and – in 1943 – Allen Dulles's OSS. Despite the vicious attempts by the Italian OVRA – and subsequently its French and German equivalents – to smoke out the maquis, under leaders like Capitaine Alain Le Ray and Colonel Jean Vallette d'Osia, the work of subversion and sabotage mushroomed. The blowing of a bridge or railway junction, harassing troop movements, even simply cutting telephone lines were now beginning to pay dividends. Following massive demonstrations on 11 November 1943 – Armistice Day – on 13 November the maquis in the Dauphinois capital of Grenoble blew up the Polygon arsenal. The reprisal killing by the Seventh Army of eleven resistance members was called the city's Bartholomew's Day massacre. Now Grenoble was celebrated by de Gaulle and his Free French Forces as the 'capital of the maquis'. There was a similarly inspiring demonstration in Oyonnax in the Haut-Jura. Here, the maquis took possession of the town and paraded to the war memorial, laying a wreath of the cross of Lorraine, and singing the 'Marseillaise'.

The effect of all this activity was cumulative. In his memoirs, Generalfeldmarschall Gerd von Rundstedt, then in charge of the Wehrmacht's defence of the west, recorded that 'From January 1944 the state of affairs in southern France became so dangerous that all commanders reported a general revolt . . . Cases became numerous where whole formations of troops . . . were surrounded by bands for many days and, in isolated locations, simply killed off.'[13]

Obviously there was little scope for such maquis forces to support the D-Day Channel landings hundreds of miles north-west in the Pas-de-Calais or Normandy. The proposed landings in the south of France, where the Alpes-Maritimes ran right down to the Mediterranean at Nice, were quite another question. Here the strategic goal was of course not the coast itself, pleasant though it is to linger in Villefranche, Cannes, Antibes, St Raphael and St Tropez. The prize was the road north along the Rhône valley to the western marches of the Reich. Here the maquis really could help: or so claimed one of the participants at Churchill's January meeting, the splendidly named Emmanuel d'Astier de la Vigerie.

D'Astier was a dashing forty-three-year-old with a background in the French navy, in journalism, as a poet, as an opium-eater, and as the leader of the French resistance group Libération. A handsome, hawk-nosed charmer with a long face and a penchant for bow ties, in 1943 de Gaulle had made him Commissioner to the Interior of the Free French government in exile. This figure of fantasy reassured Churchill that properly arming the resistance would not exacerbate political rivalries – as it had done so unfortunately in Yugoslavia.[14]

For Churchill, this was the critical question. For surely to support the resistance was to point to de Gaulle as future leader of France, much as supporting the partisans meant endorsing Tito. Was this desirable?

To support the existing government, the Pétainists, was of course unthinkable, at least for Churchill. The Allies' intention, once France was rid of the Nazis, was to impose the formula of Allied Military Government of Occupied Territories (AMGOT). Mooted in Tehran, this would have to be discussed with de Gaulle in his capacity as leader of the Free French. The General had been a notable absentee from the top table at the conference. Although he now had a force of around 400,000 Free French servicemen at his disposal, he had no democratic mandate, he was notoriously intransigent, and he had made himself politically and personally unpopular with both Roosevelt and Churchill. 'He had to be rude to the British', Churchill later reflected, 'to prove to French eyes that he was not a British puppet. He certainly carried out this policy with perseverance.'[15] The Americans had had too many dealings with generals in politics in Latin America to find de Gaulle particularly palatable. Roosevelt himself preferred to deal with Pétain's Vichy administration: he supposed for some time that the Pétainists might be detached from the Reich.

After his illness in Carthage, Churchill had made his way to Marrakesh in Morocco. Here, on 31 December 1943, he had met Eisenhower and Rommel's nemesis, General Bernard Montgomery, to develop the plans for the French landings. On 12 January 1944 the Prime Minister entertained de Gaulle to a picnic lunch to discuss both these and post-war France. The General proved bitterly opposed to AMGOT and – as far as Churchill was concerned – recklessly divisive. The Prime Minister urged the General to avoid actions against former Vichy supporters that would see 'so wide a schism in France that the resultant friction in any territory that might be liberated would hamper our military options and therefore be a matter of concern to us'. Accommodation and at least a degree of conciliation were required. 'Look here,' Churchill declared over the couscous. 'I am the leader of a strong, unbeaten nation. Yet every morning when I wake my first thought is how I can please President Roosevelt, and my second is how I can conciliate Marshal Stalin. Your situation is very different. Why then should your first waking thought be how you can snap your fingers at the British and Americans?'[16] Yet as with Tito, it was perhaps in supporting de Gaulle and the maquis that lay the best chance of supporting the Riviera landings and freeing France. It was a conundrum.

At the 27 January meeting Churchill was certainly mindful of these considerations and so too was he mindful of Emmanuel d'Astier de la Vigerie. What was he to do?

Ever the Francophile, ever the romantic and ever struck by personalities as much as arguments, the conclusion of the conference was that Churchill would laud d'Astier and double the supplies of materiel to the maquis in the south-east of France, the area proximate to the site of the planned landings on the

French Riviera. As to d'Astier himself, Churchill enthused to Roosevelt:

This is a remarkable man of the Scarlet Pimpernel type . . . He has made very strong appeals to me to drop more arms by air for their resistance movements. I hope to be able to do more in February. He says that in Haute Savoie, south of Geneva between Grenoble and the Italian frontier, he has over 20,000 men all desperate, but only one in five has any weapon. If more weapons were available, very large numbers would take to the mountains. As you know, I am most anxious to see a guerrilla à la Tito started up in the Savoie and in the Alpes Maritimes.

In this way the die was cast – and was immediately to be tested.

4

For in the meantime, von Rundstedt and his colleagues in OKW had also been contemplating the impact of the maquis in the French Alps, the 'general revolt' as the Generalfeldmarschall called it. They decided that something concerted should be done. News of this leaked and on 2 February 1944 the BBC broadcast a warning:

Attention the maquis! Attention the Haute-Savoie! Calling the Haute-Savoie maquis, SOS, SOS. The Oberführer Joseph Darnand has decided to launch a massive attack tomorrow, 3 February, against the patriots hiding out in the mountains of the Haute-Savoie. There is not a minute to spare – you must take up your defensive positions.[17]

The forty-seven-year-old Darnand was a right-wing Frenchman with a taste for irregular warfare. A decorated veteran of the First World War, in 1941 he had set up a collaborationist militia, the Service d'ordre légionnaire, to do Vichy's dirty work. In January 1943 this evolved into the Milice. This was a vicious paramilitary force devoted to fighting the maquis. It worked under the formal leadership of the Vichy Prime Minister Pierre Laval, to whom Darnand was 'a fine soldier with about as much political intelligence as a kerbstone'.[18] In August 1943, Darnand joined the SS and was given the rank of Sturmbannführer (equivalent to major). By the French maquis, his men now became even more feared than the Gestapo: the Milice recruited the maquis' own compatriots who were fluent in the French language, and who also possessed the local knowledge that usually kept the maquis one step ahead of the Germans. In his new role Darnand threatened that the maquis themselves or anyone helping them would be court-martialled and executed; and he now believed that the maquis were a soft target because they were poorly supplied with arms, ammunition and the wherewithal of survival in the mountains and sabotage in the valleys. Hence the idea of a 'massive attack'.

By the time of Churchill's meeting with d'Astier in January 1944, plans were in fact already in hand to arm the Haute-Savoie maquisards. An SOE mission from London comprising Lieutenant Colonel Richard Heslop of the SOE itself and Captain Jean Rosenthal of the Free French Forces had been sent out to the Savoie in September 1943. They were given a good sense of progress in the *département* by Colonel d'Osia's maquis colleagues, the Colonel himself having just been seized by the Gestapo. On their return to London on 16 October, Heslop and Rosenthal reported very favourably on the possibilities of the Savoie: more than two thousand men were ready to fight. Of course they needed arms. The two of them had accordingly inspected half a dozen possible dropping zones, and selected the plateau of Glières, close to Annecy, as the most suitable. Returning on 18 October to the Alps, the pair got in touch with the head of the maquis in the *département* neighbouring the Haute-Savoie: Ain. This was Colonel Henri Romans-Petit, the forty-seven-year-old French army officer who had led the Armistice Day demonstration in Oyonnax in November 1943. He in turn appointed Lieutenant Théodose ('Tom') Morel to collect the parachute drops that would be made by the RAF on the Glières plateau in the New Year of 1944 – duly urged on Churchill.

Morel was a twenty-nine-year-old officer of the mountain light infantry. He had distinguished himself in the Alpine Franco-Italian campaign of June 1940, leading two operations around the tiny skiing resort of Val d'Isère and the nearby Little St Bernard Pass, winning decorations for both: the Croix de Guerre and Chevalier de la Légion d'honneur. He was a fine leader who established his authority with ease amongst those from the very varied social and political backgrounds that characterised the maquis. His motto was uncompromising: 'Vivre libre ou mourir' – 'Live in freedom or die.'

A man of his word, he led his men up to the Glières on the last day of the month, 31 January 1944. It was just four days after Churchill's meeting.

5

The Glières was a limestone plateau high above the Haute-Savoie capital of Annecy, much the size of the Isle of Wight. It was chosen for the airdrop because the lake at the head of which Annecy stood was a clear landmark for the RAF, and the ample size of the plateau meant it was easy to ensure the arms fell into the right hands: parachute drops are not very accurate.

Now it was also in the nature of these drops that they ran without the precision timing of the Great Western Railway. Wind, weather, low cloud, the waxing and the waning of the moon might all affect the ability of the RAF to make the drop. Morel and a number of maquisards – according to the differing accounts anything from 100 to 250 – were accordingly obliged to set up camp on the plateau in the first days of February and await events. This was easier said than done. With a mean altitude of around 4,000 feet, it was described by one of the maquis with some accuracy as an icy desert. It was a difficult place to survive, particularly in winter: all food consumed there had to be brought up from the valley or supplied by air. There was also very little shelter: a few mountain chalets fit for occupation only in the summer, and an old sawmill.

The very day of the maquis' arrival on the plateau – 31 January – Darnand declared a state of siege on the maquis in the Haute-Savoie. This made the refuge – of a sort – represented by the Glières the more attractive, and over the next few days Morel's forces were gradually supplemented by other maquis. They included eighty French communists and around sixty Spanish lumberjacks, a number of whom had seen action in the Spanish Civil War.

At the same time the Free French staff in Ain, possibly on the advice of Captain Rosenthal, came up with the idea that rather than simply collecting the arms dropped by the RAF, Morel's group should base itself on the plateau for a longer period and use it as a camp from which to sally forth on missions of subversion and sabotage. The argument was that as there were – clearly and justifiably – doubts in the Allied political and military high command about the value of the French resistance, the Glières group could be used for a strategic purpose: to demonstrate that the maquis could significantly disrupt the German military machine. This idea ran contrary to received resistance wisdom for its formations to stay in one place. Experience had proved it was wiser to give battle where the opportunity arose and then disperse: melt away into hills and valleys – much as Tito and the Yugoslav partisans had always done.

Ten days into his mission, the numbers of Morel's maquis had swelled to around 400, a motley force that needed food, arms and training. By this time the RAF had succeeded in finding a window in the weather that allowed its transports to drop some 220 containers of arms onto the plateau; on the other hand, the maquis were also coming under pressure from Darnand's Milice, supposedly numbering two thousand. The original idea was that the maquis should now withdraw to the valley with their arms. Instead they would have to give battle.

Honours at first were even. There were dozens of skirmishes around the plateau in which neither Darnand's Milice nor the maquis gained an upper hand. On 2 March 1944, Morel decided to take the battle to the enemy by raiding a Milice base at the Beau Séjour Hotel at Saint-Jean-de-Sixt, to the south of the plateau. This was a success, and spurred a more a more ambitious raid on the Hôtel de France at Entremont, four miles north of Saint-

Jean. The hotel was successfully seized by Morel's maquisards, and the Milice apparently disarmed. Their commander had in fact concealed a gun. He shot Morel dead and was at once shot dead himself by the maquis. Morel's body was brought back up to the plateau. In the presence of his parents, he was buried at the foot of a flagstaff from which streamed the defiant tricolour. 'Vivre libre ou mourir!'

Inexperienced and largely untrained, the maquis were ill-equipped to cope with his loss. Morel's replacement, the forty-three-year-old Capitaine Maurice Anjot, declared, 'On our side we will do our duty, but we must have help.'[19] Anjot, of the 27th Battalion Chasseurs Alpins, knew that his ill-fed and demoralised forces could not engage professional soldiers; he also knew that the evacuation of the plateau would be bad for the morale of the maquis locally and nationally, send the wrong signal to the Allied high command, and allow such weapons as had been dropped to fall into the hands of the Milice. From London, he heard the BBC proclaiming: 'Trois pays résistent en Europe: la Grèce, la Yugoslavie, la Haute-Savoie.'[20] The political stakes were high, and for the present Anjot felt he must remain rather than withdraw from the plateau. On 12 March the RAF dropped more supplies, and the maquisards beat off a series of Milice attacks.

OKW and von Rundstedt now lost patience with Darnand. The Glières was becoming a public embarrassment, a cause célèbre on the airwaves and in the local *estaminets* of the Haute-Savoie.

The end was swift and brutal. On 23 March 1944 OKW called in the 157th Reserve Division of the Wehrmacht and two German police battalions. Armed with heavy machine guns, mortars, howitzers and armoured cars, they were ordered to clear the plateau. Supported by ground-attack aircraft and artillery, three attack groups were organised into a pincer movement to attack both the rear and front of the plateau. Believing that upwards of a thousand maquis were holding the plateau, the Germans' own forces numbered 4,000. On 25 March the operation began with an artillery bombardment of the camps that lasted all day. The following morning the barrage opened up again and what remained of the camps was attacked by Stukas and Heinkel III and Junkers bombers. At two o'clock in the afternoon, the bombardment ceased and the Wehrmacht went into action. The Gebirgsjäger captured the two main routes of retreat from the plateau. The Spanish defended a hillock and held out to the last man and last round. All were killed, and by 10 p.m. that evening, Anjot was no longer in a quandary. There was no hope of reinforcements and no prospect of defeating the forces encroaching on the plateau. He had done everything possible, and retreat to the valley under cover of the night was the only reasonable course of action. His orders had to be carried to the forces dispersed over the plateau by skiers who struggled through the deep snow. Some of the groups did not receive their orders till the early hours of 26 March. Then, singly or in pairs, the exhausted maquis tried to find their way in the dark down into the relative warmth and safety of the valley. A few made it. Anjot died with five others on the descent of the west side of the plateau. Of the remaining four hundred or so maquis, more than 150 were killed; many of them showed signs of torture. The survivors were deported to the concentration camps, and the injured were shot out of hand. German losses were put at twenty-one.

General de Gaulle awarded Tom Morel the Croix de la Libération. The citation declared that 'He will remain the incarnation of French patriotism in the epic of the resistance, and one of the most prestigious martyrs of the Savoie'.[21] M. R. D. Foot, the SOE historian, had a different point of view that accorded with received wisdom on irregular warfare. He commented drily of the whole episode, 'This was magnificent, unforgettable; but tactically unsound.'[22] It was certainly nothing like the 'guerrilla à la Tito' that Churchill had hoped for as a result of the 27 January meeting, and it unconvincingly answered the question of the value of the maquis.

ELEVEN

Arbeit Macht Frei

*Don't worry about the victims. The work must
proceed and be finished in the shortest possible time.*
OBERGRUPPENFÜHRER HANS KAMMLER

I

It was 23 May 1944, six weeks after the Glières debacle, and
Albert Speer was attending a meeting at Obersalzberg. 'We were
all waiting', he remembered, 'in the inhospitable entrance hall
of the Berghof for Hitler.' The chalet itself now had a funereal
air, draped as it was in camouflage netting to conceal it from
marauding Allied aircraft. The party comprised the head of the
OKW, Generalfeldmarschall Keitel, the 'armaments' chief of the
air force, Generalfeldmarschall Erhard Milch, Reichsmarschall
Göring, Speer himself, and a handful of the Reich's leading industrialists: 'Krauch, Pleiger, Bütefisch, and E. R. Fischer'. Krauch
represented the chemical industry, Pleiger and Bütefisch coal and
oil. Fischer was the chairman of IG Farben, the company that
ran Germany's biggest synthetic oil plant at Leuna in Saxony-
Anhalt. Farben was also the patent-holder for Zyklon B, the
pesticide that the SS had turned to such imaginative use in the
Reich's extermination camps.

These great men were facing a crisis. Ten days earlier on
12 May 1944, General Carl Spaatz's US Eighth Air Force had
launched a mammoth raid of 935 bombers on Leuna and a series
of other fuel plants in central and eastern Germany. The results
were devastating. This was the opening hand of the Allies' 'oil
campaign' to cripple the Reich's armed forces. Should the Allies
persist in the tactic of attacking these plants, the whole German
military machine would grind to a halt. 'On that day', wrote

Speer with an eye to the gallery, 'the technological war was decided. Until then we had managed to produce approximately as many weapons as the armed forces needed . . . But with the attack . . . a new era in the air war began. It meant the end of German armaments production.'[1]

The meeting with Hitler at the Berghof was to brief him on precisely this point. It was difficult to predict how the irascible and capricious Führer would respond to this news. His senior advisers, leaders of men in their own right, were clearly nervous. Göring and Keitel were determined to put an optimistic gloss on the situation; the industrialists were as gloomy as Speer himself. Tension rose as the adjutant beckoned the party into the conference room with its spectacular views over the Berchtesgadener Alps, now sprinkled with the wild flowers of the season: the bistort, clematis and gypsophila, all the constituents of a daisy-chain. Hitler shook hands brusquely and the men took their seats. What, asked Hitler, were the results of the raids? The industrialists were firm, remembered Speer: 'They all testified as to the hopelessness of the situation if the raids were continued systematically.' Not so the military. Göring and Keitel tried to pooh-pooh the flinty Gradgrinds, according to Speer lest they themselves were blamed for the failure to protect the Reich's industry. Hitler, often susceptible to the rosy gloss of a sycophantic entourage, for once would have none of it. This was indeed a crisis. 'In my view the fuel,' he declared, 'Buna rubber and nitrogen plants represent a particularly sensitive point for the conduct of the war, since vital materials for armaments are being manufactured in a small number of plants.' Here, according to Speer, was Hitler the 'sober, intense man of keen insight'. Then the meeting concluded and the party retired to the Führer's teahouse on the hill opposite the Berghof: the Mooslahnerkopf. Here, *Kaffee und Kuchen* (coffee and cake) were served and – although it was late May – the fire crackled in the large fireplace. In the cosy domestic environment the Führer's uncompromising line softened. 'Hitler let himself be wafted to a friendlier world. It was all too clear how much he needed that. To me, too, he said

not another word about the danger hanging over our heads.'
D-Day was just a few days away, but it was still springtime for
Hitler.

Even so, despite the immense challenges posed by the ever-
increasing tempo of the RAF and USAAF air raids, Speer had contingency plans – indeed actions. He had proposed the dispersal
of the armaments industry away from the cities targeted by the
Allied air forces as early as 19 December 1942. This diaspora
was bitterly resisted by the Reich's forty-odd regional leaders,
the Gauleiters. Their concern was understandable. It was, as
Speer commented, that 'the almost peacetime quiet of their
small towns would be disturbed'.[2] Who wanted a munitions
factory on his doorstep? By autumn 1943 the intensity of Allied
bombing had caused the caution of the Gauleiters to crumble.
By the time of the crisis meeting in the Berghof, a good deal
of the German armaments industry had been scattered. Twenty-
seven central plants were dispersed into 729 fragments; fifty-one
engine factories became 249 smaller plants. The industry fled
from great industrial centres like Dortmund, Essen and Wiener
Neustadt to towns, and from towns to villages, from villages in
some instances to forest clearings. This was one measure. Hitler
had also long been urging Speer to transfer industrial production
to subterranean shelters. Here the armaments industry could
continue altogether unimpeded and unhindered by the attentions
of the USAAF and the RAF. It was this underground dispersal
scheme that had turned the eyes of the industrialists to the
Bavarian and Austrian Alps. Here the high mountains and deep
valleys made Bomber Command's job doubly difficult. Targets
were very tricky to identify and, when found, bomb with any
accuracy.

Besides fuel production, of the armaments themselves there
were two seen as of pivotal importance to the Reich. First the
Luftwaffe's revolutionary Messerschmitt Me 262 jet fighter;
second Wernher von Braun's V-2 rocket, the creation of which
would eventually write a new chapter in the history of mankind.
As the Battle of Narva on the borders of Estonia ebbed and

flowed between Generaloberst Johannes Friessner's Panzer Corps and Marshal Leonid Govorov's Leningrad Front, as the grey-coated guardians of the Atlantic Wall anxiously awaited the Allied invasion from Great Britain, these were two of the Wunderwaffen (wonder-weapons) that Hitler hoped might yet break the claws of the Allied pincer to the east and to the west.

2

Messerschmitt AG was the aircraft manufacturer that had won the favour of the Nazis by being rooted in the Party's Bavarian heartland. Heinkel was based in Warnemünde on the Baltic, Junkers in Saxony-Anhalt, Dornier at Friedreichshafen on the Bodensee (Lake Constance) and Focke-Wulf in Bremen on the North Sea coast. For the Austrian Hitler and his Munich-based Nazi movement, these places were nigh on enemy territory.

The man behind Messerschmitt, the forty-six-year-old Wilhelm Emil ('Willi') Messerschmitt, was the son of a wine merchant who had his eyes turned upwards on first seeing the grace and magic of a Zeppelin airship floating without visible means of suspension in the azure high skies above him. He had studied in Munich and set up his own aircraft company in 1923 in the Bavarian city of Augsburg. At a time at which some manufacturers were still designing open-cockpit, fabric-covered biplanes like the Fairey Swordfish, Messerschmitt had identified the advantages of all-metal monocoques. By 1934 he was working for the Bavarian Aircraft Works (Bayerische Flugzeugwerke, BFW). There he conceived the machine that became the famous Bf 109. It was a triumph of modernism: a closed-cockpit, low-wing monoplane with a retractable undercarriage and inverted V12 liquid-cooled engine. It looked like an angular Spitfire or Hurricane, and was more or less the match of the Royal Air Force's principal Battle of Britain fighters in terms of top speed, climb rate and manoeuvrability. In 1936 the 109 had beaten off competition from Arado, Heinkel and Focke-Wulf for a Reichs-luftfahrtministerium (Reich Air Ministry) brief for a single-seat fighter. It was a bid helped by Willi Messerschmitt's friendship with two leading Nazis: the beetle-browed deputy leader of the Nazi Party, Rudolf Hess, and the ever more portly head of the Luftwaffe and discerning art collector, Hermann Göring. In 1938 Messerschmitt himself became chairman and managing director of BFW and the company was renamed Messerschmitt in his honour. Up until 1943 Messerschmitt AG was supplying around half the Luftwaffe's fighters: principally the Bf 109 itself and the far less gainly twin-engine Me 110, which had proved easy meat for the Few. Messerschmitt's competitors grumbled of favouritism.

Like the British jet engine pioneer Frank Whittle, Willi Messerschmitt was also looking ahead. His compatriot Hans von Ohain's revolutionary turbojet had first run in September 1937, just five months after Whittle's own turbine. Ohain's ideas were developed by Heinkel, Junkers and the leading Bavarian engine manufacturer, Bayerische Motoren Werke or BMW. Willi Messerschmitt immediately saw the potential of this novel form of propulsion. His company started work before the outbreak of war on an airframe coded P3302. The result was a single-seater with high tailplane and a low main wing, on which were mounted two turbojets. This elegant and futuristic machine was dubbed the Me 262 or Schwalbe – the Swallow. The machine's development was much delayed by problems with BMWs new jets. It eventually flew under turbine power in July 1942. When the craft finally entered Luftwaffe service in March 1944 it was the world's first operational jet, pre-dating Whittle's Gloster Meteor by four months. With a top speed of 530 mph, the Schwalbe was very nearly 100 mph faster than any of the Allied piston-driven fighters operating in the European theatre. It clearly signalled their demise. For the Swallow, USAAF B-17 Flying Fortresses were sitting ducks. Not surprisingly, here was a weapon on which the Reich set great store. Speer described it as 'the most valuable of our "secret weapons"'. The general staff, he wrote, 'had been counting on this new type of fighter to bring about a decisive turning point in the air war'.[3] The challenge for Messerschmitt was to produce this revolutionary weapon in substantial numbers.

The company had major plants in the Bavarian cities of Regensburg and Augsburg itself. These were attended to by the RAF and the USAAF on 17 August 1943 and 25 February 1944 respectively. There was also a Messerschmitt factory in the eastern Austrian city of Wiener Neustadt, mainly producing Me 109s. This was subjected to a series of raids from August 1943 onwards. Dispersal was the obvious solution. As early as the summer of 1943 the company was producing its aircraft from twenty-five different locations. The Me 262 was put together from fuselages and tails in Regensburg, engines – eventually from Junkers – in Leipzig, wings and final assembly in Augsburg. Commonplace today in the airline industry, at the time the system was a novelty. After the war, an American inquiry into Messerschmitt reported:

Over an area from Stuttgart to Linz in northern Austria and from Nuremberg south into the Bavarian Alps, sub-assemblies were made in caves, tunnels in the Autobahn, clearings in the forests, small buildings etc. Many small assembly lines, just a small steel building with one pair of rails for conveying and an overhead crane, were set up in woods for final assembly. Some of these were near the Autobahn which was used as a runway after concreting the centre grass strip and painting it green.[4]

If dispersal solved one problem, it created another. In removing the industrial plants from major conurbations, it robbed the factories of their workforce. Fortunately from Messerschmitt's point of view, less so from that of others, a solution was at hand. There were Konzentrationslager (KZ) – concentration camps – all over the Reich, but there were three major ones in or close to Bavaria. Dachau, ten miles north-west of Munich, has been introduced. This was the very first of the camps in the Reich, opened in March 1933. Flossenbürg in eastern Bavaria had followed in May 1938. The third was 190 miles east in Austria, just where the northern fork of the Alps peters out at the Wienerwald. This was Mauthausen on the banks of the Danube, fourteen miles downstream from Hitler's childhood home of Linz.

Originally the concentration camps were what their name denoted: places in which those deemed undesirable by the state could be imprisoned, most obviously political dissidents. No sooner had the camps been taken over by Heinrich Himmler's SS than the role of a number of them changed and their inmates became sources of labour for the Reich. Sachsenhausen just north of Berlin (1936), Buchenwald near Weimar (1937) and Flossenbürg in Bavaria were sites all chosen because of their proximity to quarries. Mauthausen was such a camp from the very beginning, its inmates forced to labour in the granite quarry that adjoined it. Soon the use of forced labour – Zwangsarbeit – became much more widespread, in recognition of the simple fact that Germany alone lacked the population to win a war against the combined might of Britain and her Dominions, the United States and the Soviet Union.

As a consequence, the concentration camps spawned a series of subcamps for the purpose of providing slave labour at sites all over the Reich. Or, in the case of Mauthausen and Dachau (to a much lesser extent Flossenbürg), all over the Alps. By the early summer of 1944 the pair between them had more than 150 such subcamps smeared all over Austria and Bavaria. These included sites in the cities of Salzburg and Innsbruck, and in Alpine resorts including Ebensee, Bad Ischl, Oberammergau and Garmisch-Partenkirchen. For many of the Reich's industrialists, for the Krauchs, Pleigers and Messerschmitts, the camp inmates proved a godsend.

The first Dachau inmates arrived at the Messerschmitt works in Augsburg in March 1943. This was a critical time for the company as mass production of the Me 262 got under way. The company management – perhaps understandably – was sceptical of the merits of slave labour. How skilled would the workforce be? How hard would they work? Would they upset the other workers?

In practice all went well. The new system actually saw an increase in productivity at the Bavarian plant. It was also of course cheaper for Messerschmitt than paying wages, though the labourers were not supplied free of charge. The concentration camps were run by the SS along brisk commercial lines, and they charged Messerschmitt for the services of the prisoners. The great thing was that inmates themselves were either paid nominal amounts or nothing at all. Perhaps this gave meaning to the motto to be seen on the gates of a number of the concentration camps and first of all at Dachau: *Arbeit Macht Frei*. Work makes you free. Either way, on 20 July 1943 Willi Messerschmitt himself was moved to write to the camp commandant at Dachau, SS-Sturmbannführer Martin Gottfried Weiss, voicing his satisfaction with the arrangement and asking for more workers. He expressed the hope that this would lead to 'a larger mutual success in the future'.[5]

The increasing tempo of Allied bombing and the vulnerability of the Augsburg plant nevertheless dictated dispersal. The company's first solution was Sankt Georgen an der Gusen, a small town on the Danube a few miles upstream from Mauthausen. The inmates of the KZ camp started work on this site on 9 March 1944. Here they constructed a 50,000-square-metre tunnel system under the auspices of a joint venture set up between the Luftwaffe, Messerschmitt and one of the more imaginative enterprises of the SS: DESt, Deutsche Erde- und Steinwerke (German Earth and Stonework). Me 262 fuselages were produced in the complex for final assembly further north in Leipheim, Bavaria. The heat and dust of the tunnels added to the extreme brutality of the SS captors made Gusen 2 one of the worst of the work camps. According to Rav Yechezkel Harfenes, who had survived a number of such iron maidens, 'Compared to Gusen, however, one might almost say that those camps were paradises . . . It was unknown simply because very few of the tens of thousands of prisoners sent there remained alive to tell the story of its horrors.'[6]

The problem with this – other than gross inhumanity – was that it involved the movement of these aircraft assemblies at a time at which transportation problems caused by air raids began to stifle the dispersal system. A better idea seemed to be to move the entire manufacturing process underground, in effect a process of recentralisation. This was first mooted in 1943 but given greater impetus by the bombing by the USAAF of the main dispersed Me 262 assembly plant in Leipheim on 25 April 1944.

The destruction of nine jets almost ready for service concentrated minds. Huge bombproof bunker factories of 500,000 to 600,000 square metres were envisaged, around the size of sixty football pitches. Here the whole of the airframe as well as the engines would be manufactured and assembled in one place. Plans under the existing dispersal system were to produce a hundred Me 262s a month; a thousand would spew from these huge sites. Hitler, always interested in architectural schemes, was shown the plans on 14 April 1944, a couple of weeks before the Leipheim raid. He made several suggestions for their improvement. The underground factories were initially planned for Kaufering and Ottmarshausen, just outside Landsberg, the Bavarian town where Hitler had been imprisoned after his conviction for leading the failed Beer Hall Putsch. Yet more ambitious schemes were hatched for Landsberg itself. This was the Ringeltaube ('woodpigeon') project, comprising three huge bunkers of identical design. Here 90,000 workers were intended to produce 900 Me 262 fighters a month. These bunkers were five storeys (28.4 metres) high, 400 metres long, with a floor space of 95,000 square metres. Construction of the first (Weingut 2 – Vineyard 2) was beginning just as Speer and Hitler were taking *Kaffee und Kuchen* in the Obersalzberg teahouse on 23 May 1944.

No one could reproach the Reich, Speer or Messerschmitt for a lack of industry or initiative, merely of humanity. The only real difficulty was that any number of Me 262s would not fly very well without fuel.

3

Meanwhile, for its design centre and head office, Messerschmitt AG had settled on the 2,746-foot Alpine resort of Oberammergau. This was conveniently located in the Oberbayern region of the

Bavarian Alps, just sixty miles south of Augsburg, fifty south-west of Munich.

It was a resort of much Alpine charm, a medieval village where the houses were graced with the Luftmalerei frescos that were such a feature of Berchtesgaden. There was also a tradition of woodcarving. Here, an existing military emplacement could form the nucleus for the HQ. This was a barracks of the signals section of the 1st Mountain Regiment, the Gebirgs-Nachrichten-Abteilung 54. Overlooking a meadow and close to a pine forest, the surrounding peak of the 4,403-foot Kofel and dozens of higher peaks in the locality made it a very difficult target to Allied bombers – even if the RAF and USAAF intelligence staff discovered it was there. By way of cover, the HQ was given the suitably bland name of the Upper Bavarian Research Institute. As to the symbolism of Oberammergau, this the authorities ignored.

In 1633 the villagers had made a public vow. Should the bubonic plague raging in the region pass them by, they would stage in perpetuity a play of Christ's life. Oberammergau went sufficiently untouched for the villagers to believe they had been spared, and a great tradition was gradually established. Beginning in 1634, every ten years the villagers staged the Passion Play. Admission fees were instituted in 1790, package tours using the new railway line from Munich in 1870, and by 1930 the play was attracting something approaching half a million visitors from all over the world. In 1934, Hitler himself had attended the celebrations marking the 300th anniversary of the first performance. He was not enthusiastic. The play revealed, he declared, 'the muck and mire of Jewry'. Nine years later it was said that he felt the Passion Play theatre was peculiarly appropriate for armaments production, so – loosely – inverting the principle of turning swords into ploughshares.

The inhabitants of the village were naturally more cautious about their Christian resort cum shrine being turned into an armaments factory. None were more so than the mayor, Alfred Bierling. A local man who had himself performed in the play, he was determined to stand up for the Catholic traditions of the village. When the dispersal scheme was first mooted, a number of arms manufacturers had expressed interest in the Passion Play theatre. This was a building dating from 1890, originally capable of holding an audience of 4,000, in 1930 enlarged. BMW was amongst the enthusiastic bidders. The Munich works of the firm supplied engines for a number of the Luftwaffe's fighters and bombers. These included the rival of the Bf 109, the Focke-Wulf 190, together with prototype versions of the Me 262 itself. Bierling managed to discourage BMW, arguing that 'the theater is in its way a house of God; similarly, they could seize and desanctify a church'.[7] He failed with Messerschmitt AG, perhaps on account of Hitler's own influence.

By the autumn of 1943 there were already 1,000 Messerschmitt workers in the village; by the time of Speer's crisis meeting with Hitler in May 1944, 3,000. Work had by then begun on a twenty-three-kilometre complex of tunnels that would comprise production facilities that included sub-assemblies for the Me 262. On the design side Messerschmitt was working on the variants of the Me 262 that Hitler had recently insisted on, turning it from a fighter into a light bomber; on the Me 264, a four-engine bomber with a range to reach New York; on the Me 323, a six-engine heavy transport; on the Me 163 rocket-powered fighter; and on the Me P1101, a variable-sweep-wing ramjet fighter. It was a portfolio of futuristic projects that might well have excited the jealousy of Boeing, creators of that icon of US military power, the B-17 Flying Fortress.

As to Bierling, he was then saddled with the consequences of accommodating a workforce that tripled the population of the village. Needless to say, tensions arose. They boiled over just after Speer's meeting in the Berghof when two USAAF aircraft crashed in the vicinity of Oberammergau. Their American crews were seen as murderers pulverising the German cities, death-dealers that the company was working flat out to destroy. Feelings naturally ran high.

The first incident involved a fighter. The pilot of this aircraft was killed but the navigator parachuted down to the steep little fields of the village, where the hay grew high. Bierling was obliged to rescue the survivor from a mob intent on lynching him. The following day a bomber crashed in the vicinity, all the crew safely parachuting to earth. Once again the lynch mob assembled and once again Bierling was forced to intervene. 'If we in Oberammergau permit the fliers to be hurt,' he told the villagers, 'then we could never more play the Passion in good conscience.'[8] The aviators survived, Bierling was investigated by the Gestapo, and Messerschmitt's good work went on.

4

While Mayor Bierling played the good Samaritan in Oberammergau, 150 miles due east, his compatriot Obersturmführer Otto Riemer was taking a rather less charitable line.

The forty-seven-year-old was the commandant of another Alpine armaments centre. This was the resort of Ebensee in the Salzkammergut mountains, Upper Austria. Riemer was an enthusiast for wine, women and song in the popular Bavarian tradition. On 18 May 1944, just as Speer was inspecting the damage to the fuel plant in Leuna, Riemer was setting out on an evening session of carousing with a dozen younger and more virile members of the SS camp guard. The party finally returned to the camp the following morning, still roaring drunk and brandishing their pistols. As they entered the Ebensee precincts they fired wildly at the inmates, the shots forcing the prisoners to scuttle for cover. The echoes rang around the 5,331-foot Feuerkogel mountain, as – soon enough – did the screams and cries. Between eight and fifteen captives appeared to have died.

It was an incident that even the SS thought worthy of censure. Riemer was duly demoted and a marginally less brutal man put in his stead: SS-Lagerführer Anton Ganz.

Ebensee was a child of the V-2 rocket programme. In the late thirties a young German aristocrat called Wernher von Braun had persuaded the army to fund a research programme into a long-range rocket with a payload of high explosive. Born in 1912, von Braun was the second son of a high-ranking civil servant who had served as minister for agriculture in the Weimar Republic. The son was a visionary who dreamed of space travel. Attending a talk by the balloon pioneer Auguste Piccard, he remarked to the lecturer, 'You know, I intend travelling to the moon at some time.'[9] Official enthusiasm for his work, eventually carried out by the Heeresversuchsanstalt (Army Research Centre) at Peenemünde on the remote island of Usedom on Germany's Baltic coast, blew hot and cold. Speer described it as 'my favorite armaments project' and wrote of the rocket's ability to 'graze the frontiers of space' as 'like the planning of a miracle'.[10] Hitler at first was sceptical, pointing out with some justice that the rocket was really nothing more than a long-range artillery shell with a much higher cost. In the autumn of 1939, with his mind more on targeting Paris and London than the Sea of Tranquillity on the Moon, Hitler had axed the project's funding. Speer, by then a figure of some influence and power in the Reich, made tacit arrangements with the Heeresversuchsanstalt to continue the work. The result by late 1941 was the solution of the main technological challenges and a thirteen-ton, forty-five-foot rocket. Its official designation was A-4.

On 13 June 1942, Speer flew to Peenemünde to witness the first firing. He was joined by Hermann Göring, who sported for this special occasion an opossum-skin coat teamed with bright red riding boots tricked out with silver spurs. Speer noted,

Before us in a clearing among the pines towered an unreal-looking missile four stories high . . . Wisps of vapor showed that the fuel tanks were being filled. At the predetermined second, at first with a faltering motion but then with the roar of an unleashed giant, the rocket rose slowly from its pad, seemed to stand upon its jet of flame for the fraction of a second, then vanished with a howl into the low clouds.[11]

It was a splendid demonstration, only slightly marred by a malfunction in the guidance system that brought the rocket and most of its fuel quite noisily back to earth only half a mile from where Speer's party stood. The armaments minister was unnerved. Not so von Braun and his team. Speer continued, 'the technicians were satisfied, since the thorniest problem had been solved: getting it off the ground'. In October a second test flight took place during which the guidance system worked as intended, taking the rocket 120 miles down-range. On 22 December 1942, Speer induced Hitler to sign an order for the rocket's mass production. Seven months later on 7 July 1943, Speer presided over a meeting at which the thirty-one-year-old von Braun showed a colour film of an A-4 launch to the Führer. 'For the first time Hitler saw the majestic spectacle of a great rocket rising from its pad and disappearing into the stratosphere.' Now the Führer was completely won over, indeed quite ecstatic. 'The A-4 is a measure that can decide the war,' he enthused to his rising young minister. 'And what encouragement to the home front when we attack the English with it! This is the decisive weapon of the war.' Yet even on that happy day, Hitler added a caution: 'In this project we can use only Germans. God help us if the enemy finds out about the business.'

The difficulty was that they already had, courtesy of a series of intelligence sources, not the least of which was Allen Dulles in Berne. Just six weeks later on 17 August 1943 came Operation Hydra, the RAF raid on Peenemünde carried out by 600 heavy bombers. The production of the V-2s was delayed, and the implications of the raid were the same as those for the rest of the Reich's armaments industry. It was essential to move the production lines to somewhere less vulnerable to the Allied bombers.

A number of possible locations were identified, several of which seemed to share particular promise. One was an old anhydrite mine in the Harz mountains near Nordhausen in Thuringia. The other was a smaller site in the Salzkammergut tourist district of Salzburg. This was an Alpine region of outstanding natural beauty, now a UNESCO World Heritage Site. The location itself was just outside the market town of Ebensee on the southern tip of the Traunsee. Both sites had the potential for providing the great caverns needed to build the rockets. Both were within fairly easy reach of the concentration camps that would provide the labour: in the case of what came to be called Mittelbau-Dora, Buchenwald; in that of Ebensee, Mauthausen.

After the Peenemünde raid Hitler and Speer were even more sensitive to security issues, and the bespectacled – but not particularly learned – head of the SS Heinrich Himmler made an excellent point. If the entire workforce were concentration camp prisoners, all contact with the outside world would be eliminated. For despite the uncertain efforts of Switzerland's International Red Cross, such prisoners were almost completely isolated: they were not even allowed to send or receive mail. Himmler appointed SS-Obergruppenführer Hans Kammler to oversee the movement of the production facilities to the new sites. The forty-two-year-old civil engineer had already distinguished himself by managing the transition of Auschwitz-Birkenau from a concentration camp to an extermination camp, duly installing the cremation facilities for the industrialisation of death. His new role involved creating dispersed production facilities for various advanced weapons, including the Me 262.

Mittelbau was first to the starting gate. On 28 August 1943 the first 107 prisoners from Buchenwald arrived at the old anhydrite mine. As at Oberammergau, the first job was to create a work space by blasting out new tunnels: then to begin the assembly of the rockets. Progress was such that on 10 December 1943 the site was ready for an inspection by Albert Speer. Unlike most of Hitler's leaders, Speer was a well-educated and cultured man. He was horrified by what he saw – or so he later professed. 'As I learned from the overseers after the inspection was over, the sanitary conditions were inadequate, disease rampant; the prisoners were quartered right there in the damp caves, and as a result the mortality among them was extraordinarily high.'[12] The figure for that month of December was in fact 5.7 per cent, meaning that almost three-quarters of the workers would die in the course of a year. The bodies of the fallen were taken back to Buchenwald for cremation. The first rockets rolled off the assembly line on New Year's Eve 1943. By the early summer of 1944 more than a thousand had been completed. The cost was about a third of the 12,000 workers involved. Obergruppenführer Kammler reassured his colleagues, 'Don't worry about the victims. The work must proceed and be finished in the shortest possible time.'

Although Mittelbau-Dora has become a byword of the barbarity of the Nazi slave labour (Zwangsarbeit) programme, conditions in Ebensee in the Alps were, if anything, worse. Project Cement was begun in October 1943, supposedly to provide another haven for the construction of what Goebbels had decided should be called the V-2: Vergeltungswaffe 2 (revenge weapon 2), in retaliation for the bombing by the Allies of German cities. The first one thousand prisoners arrived from Mauthausen on 18 November 1943 and set to work blasting out two huge tunnels, A and B. The prisoners rose at 4.30 a.m. and were given a breakfast of half a litre of ersatz coffee. They then worked till 6 p.m. Lunch was three-quarters of a litre of hot water garnished with potato peelings, dinner 150 g of bread, the flour of which was bran mixed with sawdust. 150 g is not all that much, and it was generally reduced by those responsible for its distribution taking more than their fair share. The result was that most of the inmates got half as much as the allocation at Auschwitz, itself by no means the Ritz. Some of the prisoners supplemented this diet with coal, one thing with which the camp was well supplied. In *The Straits of Hell*, his account of his experiences in Ebensee, Moshe Ha-Elion, a Jew from Salonika in Greece, described it as 'sweetish, sufficiently brittle, and easy to chew, was apparently satiating too'. Still, there were snags:

Coal's influence on me was two-fold. Strong pressures on the stomach caused a violent desire to give off excrement. On the other hand, acute constipation, with a feeling that there was some sort of 'cork' in my anus preventing any possibility of excreting. One day, after my stomach-ache worsened to such an extent to be unbearable, I used my hands to draw the 'cork.' This incident led to the decision not to eat more coal.[13]

In the first few months at the 1,400-foot-high camp there was virtually no accommodation to protect the workforce from an exceptionally harsh winter. The inmates had to live in the storehouse of an abandoned mill. By day the temperature rarely rose above freezing; by night it could fall to −25 degrees Celsius. The mortality rate rose to become the highest of any of the Nazi labour camps. Bodies were piled in heaps for removal to the crematoria at Mauthausen, as the camp did not yet have such a very necessary facility of its own. When the SS finally provided wooden huts for the workforce that in the New Year of 1944 would average between 5,000 and 6,000, the bodies were left piled up in the huts themselves before collection. The living slept with the dead. Obersturmführer Riemer was appointed as camp commandant in early 1944. Besides the huts he also organised a crematorium, work on which started in March 1944. By the time of his rampage in May 1944 that led to the death of some of his charges, its chimney soared above the camp. When the crematorium opened for business on 31 July 1944, the smokestack proved not quite high enough to save the Ebensee villagers from now and then inhaling the remains of their neighbours.

By this time the two main tunnels were complete. However, rather than work starting on A-4 sub-assemblies, the camp was reportedly redesignated by Hitler himself to produce tank gears. A more intriguing alternative account is that von Braun had never intended Ebensee for A-4 production. It was destined for the A-9/A-10. This was a manned intercontinental rocket developed from the A-4, which would have sufficient range to hit New York. Conceived in 1940, work on the manned two-stage rocket was prohibited in 1943 so that von Braun would concentrate his energies on the production model A-4. In practice, he managed to continue his labours in secret on his most ambitious brainchild. So he developed the thinking that would ultimately put the intended victims of the rocket – the hated Americans – on the Moon.

Still, Ebensee was – and is – a beautiful place. Moshe Ha-Elion remembered his arrival at the camp from Mauthausen, the last part of the journey on foot.

We walked over the next three days: Wels-Lambach, Lambach-Gmunden, Gmunden-Ebensee . . . on the last day of the march, far in front of us one could see the snow-capped peaks of the Austrian Alps. Nearer up, mountain ridges sloped towards a long narrow lake, the Traunsee, at the side of which we walked for some distance . . . in spite of my poor condition I couldn't avoid paying attention to and being impressed by the beautiful scenery.[14]

5

In the weeks after Speer's crisis meeting at the Berghof, these long-standing endeavours in the Reich's Alps bore fruit. On 26 July 1944, Leutnant Alfred Schreiber of the new Me 262 squadron at Lechfeld just south of Augsburg went into action. He damaged an RAF Mosquito reconnaissance aircraft of No. 540 Squadron. It was the first victory for a turbojet fighter in aviation history. Five weeks later on 29 August 1944, the stockpile of completed V-2s was such that Hitler would order their operational deployment. At 6.43 p.m. on 8 September 1944, the first V-2 hit Chiswick in west London. It killed sixty-three-year-old Mrs Ada Harrison, three-year-old Rosemary Clarke, and Frank Browning of the Royal Engineers. The age of the ballistic missile, the weapon that defined the Cold War, had begun.

Yet by this time, these efforts smelled of too little, too late. Early on the morning of 6 June 1944, the leaders of the German Seventh Army on the Normandy coast had realised that two American and one British airborne division were in their midst. Word was passed at once to the Berghof, where Hitler was fast asleep. Speer was in the chalet about ten o'clock that morning: 'one of Hitler's military adjutants told me that the invasion had begun early that morning. "Has the Fuehrer been awakened?" I asked. He shook his head. "No, he receives the news after he has eaten breakfast."'[15]

Hitler's hunch had once been that the landings would indeed take place on the Normandy beaches. Now he had changed his mind. When the daily conference was finally convened that afternoon, the Führer maintained that the landings on the beaches designated by General Eisenhower – now Supreme Commander of the Allied Expeditionary Force – Utah, Omaha, Gold, Juno and Sword were merely a feint intended to divert attention from the main thrust across Dover Straits. By the time this trail had proved false, it was too late. The D-Day bridgehead had been established, and Allied armies were back in western Europe for the first time since Dunkirk.

Eleven weeks later on 15 August 1944 came Operation Dragoon. This was the Allied invasion of the French Riviera coast to the immediate west of the Alpes-Maritimes at Nice. Here, General Alexander Patch commanding the US Seventh Army and General Jean de Lattre de Tassigny commanding the French First Army confronted Generaloberst Johannes Blaskowitz's Heeresgruppe G (Army Group G). This provided little opposition to the *débarquement*. Churchill was observing the landings from the British destroyer HMS *Kimberley*. In the early afternoon, he wrote to his wife, 'we found ourselves in an immense concourse of ships all sprawled along 20 miles of coast with poor St Tropez in the centre. It had been expected that the bombardment would continue all day, but the air and the ships had practically silenced the enemy guns by 8 o'clock. This rendered the proceedings rather dull.'[16]

Soon after, the way north – the Route Napoléon, taken by the Emperor in 1815 on his escape from Elba – was open. This was the route that led from the Riviera to Grenoble, and from Grenoble to the high Alps. On 30 August 1944, US paratroopers liberated Nice, capital of the Alpes-Maritimes.

Twenty-one months earlier on 10 November 1942, Churchill had said of the Allied landings in North Africa and Rommel's defeat at El Alamein, 'Now this is not the end. It is not even the beginning of the end. But it is, perhaps, the end of the beginning.' For the Alps, Operation Dragoon really was the beginning of the end.

TWELVE

The Mayfly Republics

*The news is increasingly wonderful; and it is
important now not to be killed during the next
few weeks. There is still fighting in Paris, but
everywhere in France our troops are making
sensational advances. Rumania is on our side,
Bulgaria is asking for peace, Russia marches on . . .
The Marne, Chateau Thierry, the Allied Victories.
It is so like 1918, the same names and places and
forward triumphant march towards victory.*

HENRY 'CHIPS' CHANNON

I

This was the diarist and parliamentarian 'Chips' Channon, ten
days after the Allied landings in the south of France. The note
of euphoria in the wake of the initial success of Overlord in
Normandy, then Dragoon on the French Riviera was infectious.
There were many who thought the end of the summer of 1944
would bring the end of the war. The 20 July bomb plot to
assassinate Hitler, the Russian offensive that had brought the
Soviets to the steel doors of his Rastenburg HQ, General George
Patton's drive towards Paris, the pace of General Alexander
Patch's forces thrusting up from the Riviera – all had given
credence to the idea. Germany would collapse abruptly, just as
she had done in the autumn of 1918. It was a tempting notion,
and there were all too many who gave in to temptation. Some of
the Allied leaders themselves were no exception.

As a matter of long-agreed policy, in the first days of June
they had given a call to action to the Resistance throughout
France to support the imminent D-Day landings: to disrupt the

Wehrmacht's lines of communication, to derail reinforcements, to bomb, to sabotage, to do everything to support the Allied *débarquements*. The resistance was supported by SOE and OSS teams dropped in France for this purpose. Then, within twenty-four hours of the Normandy landings, there came more specific, targeted calls. These were from the Free French leader General de Gaulle, and from the Supreme Commander of Allied Forces in Italy, Field Marshal Harold Alexander. The pair broadcast separate calls to the maquis and the partisans, respectively in the French and the Italian Alps. On 5 June 1944, de Gaulle declared enigmatically from London on the BBC, 'Le chamois des Alpes bondit'.[1] This was the signal for the insurrection in the Vercors outside Grenoble, the 'capital of the maquis'. On 6 June itself, as the British, Canadian and American landing craft surged towards the Normandy beaches, Alexander broadcast from the radio station in newly liberated Rome: 'To those who have arms, use them . . . to workers and clerks, leave your work . . . to peasants . . . do all you can to help the patriots. The Allies are supplying patriot groups with thousands of automatic weapons. Find out whether there is one for you.'[2]

The results were momentous. They were also by no means what these two warlords had anticipated. The twenty Italian partisan republics declared during the 'partisan summer' – the largest Ossola – were an astonishing act of military and political courage from a people largely written off by the English-speaking Allies as cowards. Of the Vercors, de Gaulle's biographer Robert Aron wrote, 'Of all the episodes of liberation, none is more shocking, none more mysterious.'[3]

2

In early June 1944, the thirty-nine-year-old François Huet found himself the newly appointed military head of the Vercors, the great limestone table and natural fortress that lay immediately south-west of Grenoble in the Dauphiné. The plateau dominated the lines of communication, overseeing the routes through which an Allied force from the south of France from the long-heralded landings might drive up towards the Reich; likewise the lifeline along which the Wehrmacht would retreat. It was for this reason that Capitaine Alain Le Ray's original plans for Operation Montagnards proposed supplementing the maquis established on the plateau since early 1941 with a force of regular infantry and artillery. The Vercors might then play a strategic role in the defeat of the occupying forces in south-eastern France by sallying forth to attack its lines of communication. A rising might also provide a beacon for the country as a whole. In May, Colonel Marcel Descour had told Huet, 'The Vercors is the only maquis, in the whole of France, which has been given the mission to set up its own free territory. It will receive the arms, ammunition, and troops which will allow it to be the advance guard of a landing in Provence.'[4] Under General Marie-Pierre Koenig, Descour was Chief of Staff of the newly formed Forces Françaises de l'Intérieur (FFI). Created at de Gaulle's instigation, the French Forces of the Interior were an amalgamation of the resistance into properly organised light infantry units. It was a formulation that symbolised the changing status of France from an occupied country to a resurgent nation on the cusp of liberation, of which the Vercors would be an emblem. Descour's order meant something. The Vercors would not wait passively to be liberated. It would liberate itself. Vive la France!

Huet's orders were clear and the broadcast from de Gaulle himself was clarion. The commandant mobilised the Vercors on 9 June 1944, three days after the D-Day landings and just as the bridgeheads on Sword, Juno, Gold, Omaha and Utah were being established more than 500 miles north in Normandy. Huet called not only those on the plateau, but all in the immediate area. Wrote the eyewitness Roland Bechmann-Lescot: 'From all directions, from Grenoble, Romans and Die, from every district and by every means of locomotion, on foot, by car, by the busload ... the volunteers, on being summoned by the leaders of the Vercors, assembled, under the very noses of the Germans.'[5] To the 500 or so maquis on the plateau would soon be added twice that number; according to some sources many more. Setting up his headquarters in Vassieux-en-Vercors, Huet duly divided his forces into five companies. He needed to train, arm and suitably dispose his maquis.

The village of St-Nizier-du-Moucherotte lay almost at the north-eastern tip of the plateau, immediately overlooking the Grenoble basin. St-Nizier was the terminus of a narrow-gauge tramline that ran the fifteen miles up from the city. The ascent here was moderately steep but of a gradient manageable by the tram: it was the one flank of the Vercors on which it was vulnerable. From here the city below could be seen: the Bastille fortifications, the square tower of the cathedral, the silvery confluence of the tumbling Drac and Isère rivers. From the city – almost from the barracks of the Wehrmacht's 157th Reserve Division – the village could also be observed.

There, on the afternoon of 10 June 1944, the maquis under Huet's orders closed the tramline and raised a giant tricolour. The Vercors was declaring its freedom from the occupying forces. 'The weather', wrote Huet's Chief of Staff Pierre Tanant, 'was magnificent in this month of June. The sky was a resplendent blue. It felt deliciously good at 1,000 metres in altitude. And above all on those verdant hills one felt free.'[6] When the Grenoblois spotted the tricolour billowing lazily in the Provençal breeze, they might have been excused for thinking that the hour of liberation was itself at hand. It was intoxicating. Huet himself declared to the maquis under his command, 'The eyes of the whole country are fixed on us . . . We have faith in each other. We have right on our side.' For those who had lived through the bitter days of the Fall of France in June 1940 and endured the privation, repression, deportations and terror first of Vichy, then of the Italian Fourth Army, now of Generalleutnant Karl Pflaum's 157th Reserve, it was a day of unparalleled joy. It was a *jour de fête* that evoked the folk memories of the Revolution of 1789.

Commandant Huet was human: he shared the euphoria. Yet as a professional soldier he was aware how precarious was the plateau's position. The terrain certainly lent itself to defence.

There were just eight roads up to the Vercors. Two of these rose up to passes more than 3,000 feet high. Here a child could turn back an army. The remainder were easily blocked. There were around twenty mountain tracks that scrambled up its flanks, but these too were simply defended. Only St-Nizier itself was problematic. The difficulty lay more with the resources of defence. 'What is an army without artillery, tanks and air force?'[7] Stalin would ask this of the insurgency that would erupt on 1 August 1944 more than 1,000 miles north-east of Grenoble: the Warsaw Rising. Moreover, despite the efforts of Huet's predecessors as military commanders of the Vercors going back to Le Ray, many of the Vercors maquis were not even trained in handling light arms. They were civilians with guns. As to the weapons themselves, as the numbers of maquisards responding to Huet's call grew, as the news from the bridgeheads in Normandy reached happy ears, these too were in short supply.

The *patron* of the Vercors was its civilian leader, the fifty-year-old Eugène Chavant. Founder of the resistance group France Combat, he had been taken by the Free French submarine *Casabianca* to Allied headquarters in Algiers in late May 1944 to discuss the Montagnards plan. The French colony hosted the combined Allied guerrilla operations team, the Special Projects Operations Centre. This was a newly – and not very thoroughly – merged team uniting elements of SOE, OSS and their French equivalent, the Bureau Central de Renseignements et d'Action (BCRA). Chavant, son of a cobbler, was supposedly ill at ease amongst the international military top brass. He was nevertheless promised not only materiel in the form of arms and ammunition, but 4,000 paratroopers. As Le Ray had known, the maquis might be expected to hold the plateau and had a good record of conducting skirmishes and running sabotage operations. It could hardly take on a professional army, especially one as professional as the Wehrmacht. Finally, as the Alpinist Pierre Dalloz, one of the civilian architects of the original Montagnards scheme, had pointed out, the combined regular and irregular forces needed to be facing an army on the edge of defeat: preferably an army that was retreating headlong up the Rhône with the Allies snapping at its heels. In 1942 he had written, 'If the Vercors plan can be put into effect, it must be done by surprise and against a distressed and disorganized enemy . . . It will not be a matter of attacking an enemy in full possession of his resources'.[8]

Huet understood all these points. Chavant, though he had served in the 20th Battalion of Chasseurs in the First World War and was twice decorated, perhaps understood them less well. It was Chavant, though, who had been to Algiers. He assumed that Algiers and London grasped the operation and were committed to it, though at the time they had quite a lot on their hands: Operation Dragoon, the preparations for Operation Market Garden on the Rhine, and – soon – the Warsaw Rising. Certainly the operation had been endorsed formally by de Gaulle himself, the operational head of the SOE, Brigadier Colin Gubbins, and by David Bruce of the OSS in London. These were, Chavant felt, reassuring commitments.

3

The tricolour raised on the flagstaff at St-Nizier on 10 June 1944 was certainly provocative. Generalleutnant Pflaum's 157th Reserve Division was mountain light infantry, a Gebirgsjäger formation familiar with mountain warfare. Pflaum himself was a fifty-four-year-old born and brought up in Bavaria. He was a veteran of service in mountain regiments and had an excellent understanding of mountain engagements. He appreciated the strategic threat posed by the Vercors to his lines of communication, signalled by the French flag. On 13 June his forces attacked St-Nizier. Huet had done his work well, and a relatively small force of Germans was repelled by a force of 250 maquisards. The turning point of the engagement was the arrival of maquis reinforcements singing the 'Marseillaise'. The following day Pflaum returned with a larger force, this time to succeed. On 15 June Huet was forced to withdraw the maquisards towards the interior of the plateau. The Germans took fire-and-brimstone revenge on the village.

Pflaum, though, had been taken aback by the strength of the Vercors's maquis. He was also dealing with an insurrection led by the maquis, inspired by the SOE, in the neighbouring *département* of Ain. The General accordingly regrouped in Grenoble to consider his position, and to gather what forces he could: both air and land. Soon, reconnaissance aircraft from the local airbase of Valence-Chabeuil were overflying the Vercors, identifying concentrations of maquis and using any stragglers as machine-gun target practice.

Over the course of the next four weeks, as the Allies in the north under General Patton pushed slowly towards Cherbourg and Caen through the bocage country, Huet consolidated his defences. He was supported by no fewer than fourteen airdrops from Algiers, and the arrival of a party of French engineers to prepare a landing ground at the resistance HQ in Vassieux. This surely heralded the Allied regular forces, the 4,000 paratroops promised to Chavant. The BBC – alongside the regular bulletins on Normandy – broadcast the electrifying news of the liberation of the Vercors. It was part of a propaganda policy to destabilise the occupying forces throughout France.

Friday 14 July was Bastille Day. All France was celebrating the storming of the prison-fortress in Paris and the beginnings of the republic. The Vercors was no exception. There was a parade in Vassieux, parties all over the plateau, a gun salute, and – best of all – an airdrop. Seventy-two B-17 bombers from the Eighth Air Force overflew the half-finished airstrip in Vassieux and dropped no fewer than 860 containers of materiel. Only the Reich could rain on this parade and rain it did. No sooner had the roar of the B-17s' Pratt and Whitneys died away than another sound was heard. It was the Luftwaffe. Focke-Wulfs from Valence-Chabeuil had been alerted to the drop and strafed Vassieux with machine guns and incendiaries, diluting the best efforts of the USAAF. Huet's forces crept out after nightfall to scavenge what they could of the drop.

Scarcely had they recovered from Bastille Day when General-leutnant Pflaum attacked again. Huet's local intelligence was all too good. On 17 July he heard that German reinforcements were approaching both from Chambéry to the north and Valence to the west. By 19 July, Huet was surrounded by forces supposedly amounting to 10,000 men; some sources say 20,000. By the following day, intelligence suggested that Pflaum had turned the tables on the maquis. From a mountain fortress from which to harass a beleaguered enemy, Huet's forces had been entrapped. If there were few ways for attackers to get onto the table, so too were there few for the defenders to get off. Pflaum had blocked all the eight main roads with infantry and artillery. On Friday 21 July the Generalleutnant launched the operation to clear the plateau. Where were the 4,000 paratroopers promised to Chavant?

In the course of that morning, some 400 maquis in Vassieux were clearing the meadows around the village to complete the makeshift airstrip. In the Alpine summer it was slow, heavy, hot work, using sickles and scythes, spades and shovels. Given the events of Bastille Day, a close watch was kept for enemy aircraft. Suddenly a cry of joy went up. There, from the south, surely from Algiers, was a formation of transport aircraft towing perhaps forty gliders. The maquis shaded their eyes against the sun. The promise made to Chavant had been fulfilled! There were whoops and shouts of joy. 'It's the Yanks! It's the Yanks!' Someone ran to the village to bring the great news to Huet.

By the time the maquis realised that the insignia on the gliders were the black crosses of the Luftwaffe, not the Stars and Stripes roundel of the USAAF, it was too late. Someone yelled, 'It's the Boche!'[9] The Luftwaffe airlift group landed two companies of infantry on the ground painstakingly prepared for the Allied forces. In all there were over 500 troops, mixed units including some Russians fighting for the Reich. Soon they linked up with the Gerbirgsjäger mountain infantry units from Grenoble, Chambéry and Valence. The maquis were at bay.

When the news was brought to Chavant, his companion Father Martin said, 'He roared with pain. I have never seen him before in an extreme emotional state and it was a terrible sight. He pounded the café table with his fist, swearing he'd been betrayed.'[10] A desperate Huet radioed Algiers, 'We shall not forget the bitterness of having been abandoned alone and without support in time of battle.'[11] Chavant, to whom the commitments of regular forces had been explicitly and personally given, was even more vocal: 'If you do not take immediate action, we shall be at one with the local population in saying that you people in London and Algiers have entirely failed to understand the situation in which we are placed, and we shall consider you to be cowards and criminals. Repeat, cowards and criminals.'

The appeals were to no avail. The Wehrmacht ran amok through Vassieux and the other communities on the plateau. By 23 July Huet had no choice. He ordered the maquis to disperse in what had become drenching rain.

Pflaum's forces treated the inhabitants of the Vercors utterly without compassion, humanity or mercy. They tortured, maimed and killed without discrimination men, women and children, combatants or otherwise. They liquidated a makeshift hospital, killing all the patients and staff. They disembowelled one woman and left her to die with her entrails draped round her neck. Another girl was raped in turn by seventeen soldiers. A doctor held her hand, monitoring her pulse, lest she faint. 'They were terrible hours during the engagement,' wrote one German soldier. 'How savagely we massacred these people. We completely wiped out a hospital full of partisans, with all the doctors and nurses. The wounded were dragged out and killed with machine pistols. It may have been atrocious but these dogs deserve no better.'[12] When the 157th Reserve withdrew in the third week of August and the inhabitants of the plateau came out to bury their dead, they found some of the victims castrated, some with breasts sliced off, some with missing tongues, some with eyes gouged out. In all, around 630 maquisards were killed on the plateau and a further 200 from local towns and villages in subsequent Wehrmacht reprisals. German losses were put at 150. Huet and Chavant, both embittered, both survived.

As to the Allies' 'betrayal', no completely convincing explanation has ever emerged. Some say that Chavant overstated the level of commitment in Algiers; others that the maquis acted prematurely in declaring the republic, egged on by Colonel Descour. Yet others blame the liaison between Vercors and the nascent Special Projects Operations Centre in Algiers; others still ambivalence on the part of de Gaulle towards a republic for which he could take little credit. 'Were the Vercors' maquis left to their fate by an inflexible Allied command and did they fail to receive the massive help promised by Gaullist leaders in Algiers? The bulk of evidence suggests that the Vercors was indeed a victim of both Allied and Gaullist decisions not to send last-minute reinforcements despite the most moving telegrams from the beleaguered Resistance fighters.'[13]

4

While the Vercors was burying its dead in August 1944, three hundred miles to the east in the Italian Alps, the partisans were planning whole handfuls of republics. They were envisaged on disturbingly similar lines to those of their counterparts in France in the Glières and Vercors. Perhaps they would fare better. The autumn of 1944 would tell.

The progress of the resistance in the Italian Alps and Apennines had been entirely unexpected. The British MP Ivor Bulmer-Thomas had told the Commons in autumn 1943 that 'Italians have not really fought in this war because they were fighting a war which for them was hateful. Give them a good cause and they will show they can fight as well as any other soldier.'[14] At the time this remark had been entirely against the grain of opinion. It had turned out to be entirely correct.

The Alps in northern Italy – as elsewhere in the range – had proved the cradle of resistance because the mountains were a haven in which those with good local knowledge could conceal themselves with ease in makeshift camps. Here they would be difficult to find and, if found, difficult to rout out. The nucleus of the partisan brigades was remnants of the Italian Fourth Army; it had been garrisoned in the Alpes-Maritimes after the Franco-Italian campaign of June 1940, and its men were familiar with

Alpine conditions. Like their counterparts to the east and west in the Alps, the Italians were also inspired by the prospect of creating a new society out of the ruins of a failed political order: most leant to the left, the majority of those communists. They were also given a good deal of help by the Allies. The SOE and OSS were – albeit modest – contributors to the partisans virtually from their beginning; the Allies eventually sent more than 200 missions amounting to around 1,000 men and women to operate behind fascist lines in Italy; in 1944 the SOE delivered 513 tons of weapons to the partisans, the OSS a further 290.

Reaching out from London's Broadway, MI6 also played its part. Following a string of failures in the early years of the war, the service surprised itself with Major Brian Ashford-Russell. Born in England in 1907, educated in South Africa, a cattle buyer in Argentina then a civil administrator in Peru, he had joined 7 Commando in 1941 and was badly wounded in North Africa. Repatriated as unfit for military service, in 1941 he joined MI6: his future wife Elizabeth Todd worked for Claude Dansey in the service's secret Broadway offices.

From the autumn of 1943 Ashford-Russell set up a series of what eventually amounted to twenty networks in northern Italy. They provided critical intelligence on politics, propaganda, economics, military logistics, civilian and military morale, and – above all – the order of battle of German and Italian fascist forces. To Sir Stewart Menzies ('C'), the service's Mediterranean section head Captain Cuthbert Bowlby assessed Ashford-Russell's performance as 'astounding . . . As far as I can remember, during my 6 years in your organisation, nothing much has ever been produced from Italy, which makes the results achieved all the more meritorious.'[15] The Major did not entirely share the partisans' scarlet political views. When the author first met Ashford-Russell in 1978, his opening gambit was 'Don't you think the *Daily Telegraph* is getting very left-wing?'

The upshot of these combined Allied and Italian efforts was foreseen only by Bulmer-Thomas. Not long before his Rome broadcast of 6 June 1944, Field Marshal Alexander could tell

The Times that of the twenty-five German divisions in Italy, six were being held down by the partisans. There were three Allied armies fighting in Italy. The US Fifth Army and the British Eighth Army needed no introduction. The partisans, he declared, were the third.

They now numbered perhaps 100,000, and were on their way to becoming the largest resistance movement in western Europe. All the mountains – partly the Apennines, partly the Alps – in the lozenge formed by Genoa to the Po, to Bologna and down to the German front line, and the mountains south-east of Turin to the sea and south-west and north-west to the French frontier, were in partisan hands.[16] As in Yugoslavia, the Germans were largely reduced to holding the main lines of communication and the principal towns. When Rome had fallen on 4 June 1944, Generalfeldmarschall Kesselring's forces had retreated to defend the Gotenstellung (Gothic Line) in the Apennines just north of Florence. Here and to the north in the Alps his troops had nearly as much trouble with the partisans' irregular warfare as with the British and US armies. In his memoirs he recorded, 'It was clear to me by June 1944 that the Partisans might critically affect the retirement of my armies.'

In the summer of 1944 the partisans were spurred by the Normandy landings in June, Alexander's Rome proclamation, and the Dragoon landings on the Riviera in August. As Churchill said of the Warsaw Rising that was now erupting further east in Poland, 'The leaders of the Polish Underground Army [decided] to raise a general insurrection against the Germans, in order to speed the liberation of their country and prevent them fighting a series of bitter defensive actions on Polish territory and particularly in Warsaw itself.'[17] He might have added that the rising was also to ensure that the indigenous population rather than the Soviet 'liberators' were in charge of the post-war country. Similarly, it was tempting for the Italian partisans to exploit the advantages of the terrain and try to establish mountain republics, both in the Alps that formed the cap to their country and in the

Apennines that constituted its backbone. Rather than merely ridding themselves of the Germans, they would be pointing the way to a better post-war, post-Fascist and – for many of them – post-monarchist future. Of the twenty republics, the Ossola valley in the Alps was the keystone.

Lying to the north of Lake Maggiore, this valley's capital was Domodossola, a handsome town of some 10,000 at the confluence of the Bogna and Toce rivers. At 620 square miles, Ossola was sizeable, with a total population of around 82,000. It boasted Italy's only gold mine, quarries for marble and granite, engineering factories, and a hydroelectric station that lit Milan. The valley also carried the main railway line linking Switzerland with Milan through the Simplon tunnel. This gave the valley vital strategic significance as Kesselring sought to contain Alexander's forces pushing north from Rome; like the Rhône valley, Ossola was a line of retreat for the Wehrmacht, in this case for Kesselring's forces on the Gothic Line.

On 6 June 1944 the Alexander proclamation whipped up enthusiasm among the Ossola partisans for insurrection. The eruption of the republic would send just the right signal of defiance to Mussolini in Salò, to Badoglio's replacement Ivanoe Bonomi and the monarchists in Rome, and to the Allies in Washington and London. It did, though, need practical support in the form of arms, men and money from the SOE and OSS, from Allen Dulles and John McCaffery.

5

Writing after the event, Dulles and McCaffery seem to have been ambivalent about the operation. The idea was contrary to the general Allied policy of pursuing military rather than quasi-political objectives; it would be costly of lives and materiel; it would certainly provoke a response from the occupying Fascists. There was also the example of Glières from the spring and – ringing in everyone's ears – of the Vercors. Still, by August 1944 the partisans had considerable forces in the Ossola valley and in any case did not – as such – take orders from the Allies. McCaffery reported to his SOE superiors that the Comitato di Liberazione Nazionale Alta Italia (CLNAI) had been 'bitten by the bug' of the scheme and – supposedly reluctantly – he agreed with Dulles to provide the help of the SOE and OSS. At the time of the rising, at least McCaffery seems to have been rather more enthusiastic. Briefing Lieutenant George Patterson, a Canadian officer attached to SOE, McCaffery commented, 'It may all come to nothing I grant you, but there is a chance it could spread . . . if North Italy were to rise in rebellion it would cut the German Army's lines of supply and almost certainly force them into surrender . . . That's why we have to do all we can to help them.'[18]

At first all went well. A coalition of partisan forces of various political shades was put together, albeit one lacking a unified command. Initial partisan strikes on 23 August 1944 succeeded, and a week later the valleys north of Domodossola up towards the Swiss border lay in partisan hands. When partisan forces reportedly numbering 3,000 surrounded the railway town, the 500-strong Fascist garrison ran up the white flag to negotiate an armistice. On 9 September the Fascists withdrew to the south, deprived of their heavy weapons but complete with their lives and – unlike the maquis of the Vercors – their genitals. On 10 September 1944 the republic of Ossola was proclaimed and the celebrations got under way. The town centre was thronged with the sort of jostling, boisterous crowd that Italy does so well. A manifesto was read out in the Piazza Repubblica proclaiming the Free Republic of Domodossola; a constitution was drafted, printed on posters and daubed over town and country; a special train arrived from Berne bearing a figurehead president: Professor Ettore Tibaldi. Soon, a provisional government was appointed and quartered in Domodossola town hall; diplomatic recognition by the Swiss followed. Community leaders sympathetic to the Fascists were removed from their posts and an open society was encouraged by the publication of free news-sheets. Trade unions – banned by Mussolini – were encouraged to re-establish themselves. The schools reopened with new textbooks that honoured faiths other than Fascism. By mid-September a regular train service was running through the Simplon to Switzerland.

Yet autumn comes early in the Alps. There were around 85,000 mouths to feed and the industrial Ossola valley was not a subsistence community. Supported by the Swiss and Italian Red Cross, Dulles and McCaffery brought in food from Switzerland through the Simplon; their efforts were nullified by the Wehrmacht strangling supplies coming from the south. Bread ran out and the people were reduced to living on chestnuts and milk. On 28 September 1944 a Swiss political leader visited the republic and told a Swiss newspaper, 'The food situation is tragic . . . there is no winter clothing . . . there's nothing . . . children are starving.'[19] Dissent spread. The discovery of an arms dump led to a stand-off between the communist Garibaldi brigades and those partisans of more moderate persuasion. On 10 October 1944, a month after the declaration of the republic, the Wehrmacht launched Operation Avanti under the leadership of SS-Brigadeführer Willy Tensfeld. His forces supposedly comprised 20,000 well-armed men, supported by artillery. The fragmented forces of the several partisan brigades organised themselves as best they could. Blocks of granite from the quarries were used to obstruct roads, crops cut down to create open fields of fire, barbed wire spread.

On 14 October 1944, Domodossola once again fell. Two days later the partisans elsewhere in the valley were scattering in the face of Tensfeld's SS. The fairy tale was at an end, just as it had been in Vercors.

Here in the Italian Alps, though, there was a line of escape. Three special trains were chartered to take the republicans north through the Simplon to safety in Switzerland. About 2,000 partisans escaped and around 35,000 civilians – almost half of the permanent population. With some justice, the refugees feared reprisals. Earlier in the month in Marzabotto in the Apennines outside Bologna, 800 civilians who supported the partisans had been murdered by the Waffen-SS: the worst massacre in western Europe in the whole war. By 26 October 1944 the mayfly republic of Ossola was back in the hands of the Fascists. It had survived for thirty-five days.

The CLNAI at once blamed McCaffery and Dulles for failing to provide the promised airdrops of materiel and of regular forces. The pair responded that the USAAF and RAF had been all too busy in Warsaw and Arnhem and they had been against the rising in the first place. Some partisans attributed darker, political motives to the Allies. Churchill favoured the new monarchist Ivanoe Bonomi administration in Rome, and would naturally scotch the initiative of the communist brigades: Domodossola was much too close to Tito's Yugoslavia. The partisan leader Ferruccio Parri commented sourly that the episode was 'the most obvious and painful example of Allied lack of interest in liberating certain frontier areas'.[20]

6

Meanwhile, back in France, a miracle – of sorts – had come to pass.

To the north-east of the Vercors, the newly formed Forces Françaises de l'Intérieur under General Marie-Pierre Koenig had seized control of Annecy and the Haute-Savoie. On 19 August 1944, the *New York Times*' correspondent reported that

General Koenig's patriot army, after 36 hours' co-ordinated operations in Haute Savoie, have driven all Germans excepting the Annemasse garrison from a rough triangle 50 miles at the base and 40 in depth, and are still fighting ahead. The Maquis thus far have cleared up the districts between Bellegarde in the west, St. Gingolph in the east, and Chamonix in the south, in a series of 133 separate engagements surpassing anything yet executed by the French patriots.[21]

This triumph threatened General Pflaum's line of retreat, and he was obliged to withdraw the 157th Reserve from the Vercors and from Grenoble itself. The evacuation was completed by midnight of 21 August 1944, the division hightailing it over the passes on the Franco-Italian border to the relative safety of Fascist Italy, much harassed by the maquis.

In Grenoble the following morning, elements of the Forces Françaises de l'Intérieur and elements of the 36th Infantry Division of the US Seventh Army entered the city. This was the liberation of the first of the principal Alpine cities that had fallen to the Nazis; Grenoble erupted in joy.

This deliverance was far, far sooner than the planners of Operation Dragoon had expected or dared dream of; it was only a week after the Riviera landings, only ten weeks after the tricolour had been raised at St-Nizier. A recent historian of Dragoon put the breathtaking achievement of the advance on Grenoble and its early liberation down to two factors: the operation's planners in Washington and the maquis. Regarding the latter, he says:

The speed of the advance can also be credited in part to the exceptional role of the FFI in this theatre. While the Maquis was seldom strong enough to overcome the Wehrmacht in a deliberate battle, the Wehrmacht occupation units were so intimidated by the Maquis threat that they were unwilling and unable to set up blocking positions on the approaches to Grenoble even though the terrain favoured the defense.[22]

Yet the Vercors itself remains a source of controversy. Alain Le Ray, the Vercors's first military commander, thought that the revolt of the plateau 'induced in the German war machine a kind of paralysis, both moral and material ... The losses were too great, for sure. But Vercors is a page of history of which France can be proud.'[23] Others dwell on the death toll, the decimation of one generation of the plateau's inhabitants, the scarring of the next, and how soon after the tragedy came liberation. Max Hastings calls the Vercors simply 'madness'.

On 25 August, when Paris followed the Rhône-Alpes, the Vichy administration collapsed: with France falling to Allied control, Pétain and his ministers were seized by the Germans and taken to Sigmaringen on the Danube. The Free French, fearful of the Allied military control discussed with such ill temper by de Gaulle and Churchill during their picnic in Marrakesh in January 1944, hastily set up the Gouvernement provisoire de la République française (Provisional Government of the French Republic, GPRF). This was officially recognised by the British and the Americans on 25 October 1944.

Two weeks later, on 5 November 1944, de Gaulle, in his role as head of the new provisional government, visited Grenoble to bestow on the city a signal honour. It was the Compagnon de la Libération, so recognising the community as the inspiration of the resistance and kingpin of liberation. The General was received by the Grenoblois as a conquering hero. In his memoirs he recalled, 'The ardour that swept over the "Allobroges" [the ancient people of Dauphiné and Savoie] in the Place de la Bastille, which I covered on foot, and in the Place Rivet, where the crowd gathered to hear speeches was indescribable.'

As to the Ossola republic and its nineteen siblings, by early December 1944 all were back in the hands of the Fascists. This does not mean they lack political and historical significance as emblems of a people recovering their self-confidence, ambition and desire for autonomy, indeed far from it. This, though, is from the comfortable armchair of hindsight.[24] In the short term, the lesson for Alexander, Eisenhower at Supreme Headquarters Allied Expeditionary Force (SHAEF) and Churchill himself was sharper. Whatever was happening in France, the Wehrmacht would fight bitterly to keep open its lines of retreat for Kesselring's forces on the Gothic Line.

The mainspring was Hitler. The Führer had left Berchtesgaden on 17 July 1944. As the Red Army approached the borders of Germany to the east, and as the US generals Patton and Patch drove their forces up to the Reich from the west and the south of France, the Führer thought he could best direct events from Berlin. In some respects he recognised the inevitability of defeat, certainly in his orders to destroy the Reich's industrial and communications infrastructure ahead of the arrival of the Allies. (This was the 'scorched earth' policy, which has a bearing on the story henceforth.) In other respects he was obdurate. On the last day of August 1944 he told his warlords, 'If necessary we'll fight on the Rhine. It doesn't make any difference. Under all circumstances we will continue this battle until, as Frederick the Great said, one of our damned enemies gets too tired to fight any more.'[25] The message from Warsaw was a final echo of this determination to fight to the last. On 2 October 1944, Churchill was visited by Premier Mikolajczyk, the leader of the exiled Polish government in London. The news was bad. After sixty days of fighting, his compatriots in the Polish capital were about to surrender to the forces of Generaloberst Heinz Guderian. The Warsaw Rising was over.

Chips Channon's hopes for the collapse of the Reich and an early end to the war had been entirely dispelled.

PART FOUR

THIRTEEN

The Troops of Midian

*The slightest frontier incident could force us to
take such countermeasures as would set fire to the
powder keg and lead to far-reaching operations.*

GENERAL HENRI GUISAN

I

While the republic of Ossola was fighting for its life, one of its
supposed supporters, Allen Dulles, was whisked out of Switzerland for a month's conference with his operational and political
masters.

He was now altogether worthy of their attention as the key
player in what had become a 15,000-person, $52 million world-
wide operation. In the early days of September 1944, his trip
took him first over the newly opened Swiss frontier into the
Rhône valley – not far from the Vercors – and from there to
war-torn London. Then from 14 to 21 September he was in
Washington. Here he was reunited with his wife Clover and
his brother, John Foster Dulles. His wife quizzed him on his
mistresses, word of whom had been hurried to Washington; his
brother was working as chief foreign policy adviser to Thomas
E. Dewey, the Republican candidate challenging Roosevelt for
the presidency. Dulles himself, at the same time as being briefed
by his chief 'Wild Bill' Donovan, played the amused observer of
the election campaign, now in full swing. He found Capitol Hill
awash with facts, views, gossip, opinions and schemes less for
winning the war than the post-war reconstruction of Europe –
particularly of Germany.

These plans had many scribes. One of the earliest was Churchill,
who had proposed at the Tehran Conference in November 1943

a division of the Reich into two: between Prussia and the Alpine Austria-Bavaria; the industrial Ruhr and Westphalia would be under international control. In Washington, the proposals of Roosevelt's Secretary of the Treasury Henry Morgenthau naturally had greater currency. These called for a more radical demilitarisation, partitioning and deindustrialisation of Germany. This scheme was being vigorously debated by Roosevelt and Churchill at the Octagon conference in Quebec while Dulles was in Washington. Either would have nicely transformed the geopolitics of the Alps.

On the spymaster's return to Berne in early November 1944, Dulles discovered that all this planning had been somewhat premature. It was true that the reopening of the Swiss border made his journey to Switzerland a very different affair from his hair's-breadth arrival on 7 November 1942, just as Operation Anton snapped the border shut. But the war in Europe had yet to be won. In London, as Dulles had noticed both on his outbound and inbound visits, the euphoria of late August 1944 experienced by 'Chips' Channon had been much dampened by the perpetual whiff of cordite from the Vergeltungswaffen 'revenge weapons' raining on the capital. On the Continent itself, the Western Allied armies, having romped through southern and western France, were now finding the going far from good. They were at the end of their long supply chains, short of food and ammunition, slowed by winter weather that had arrived six weeks early, and by finding the rearguard of the Wehrmacht more entrenched every mile it was pushed closer to its home frontiers. Operation Market Garden, the attempt to short-circuit resistance and seize a key bridge over the Rhine at Arnhem, had failed just before Dulles's return to Switzerland. In Italy, Field Marshal Alexander's forces were making heavy work of Generalfeldmarschall Albert Kesselring's Gothic Line in the Apennines north of Florence. Just as Dulles got back to Berne, on 10 November 1944, Alexander made a controversial public announcement that suggested he was digging in for the winter and would resume hostilities in the spring. For the winter, he and his armies would be *en vacances*, it seemed.

The implications of Alexander's difficulties in the Apennines were lost neither in Washington, London nor Berne itself. The extent to which Kesselring had been able to hold up the Allies' advance first for five months at Monte Cassino and now at the Gothic Line was food for thought. The moral was simple. It was of the extreme difficulty of dislodging a determined defender in mountainous terrain that might have been designed for defence: where he who holds the higher ground can repel a much larger and better-armed force down below. If this was true in the Italian Apennines, it would be doubly so in the far more formidable mountain chain to the north: the 800-mile, 15,000-foot-high rock wall that divided Europe, the great edifice that lay between Alexander's forces and the Reich. It was for these reasons that the eyes of both General Patton and the Third Army in the west, and the Red Army in the east, were turning increasingly away from Berlin towards Berchtesgaden and Bavaria.

It was originally anticipated that the Red Army and the Western Allies would eventually join hands on the river Oder. This was the pre-war border between Germany and Poland, around a hundred miles east of Berlin. The Reich would accordingly be split in half by the Allies. For a regime that had already displayed its determination to fight on, this would dictate flight south by the Reich government to what was in any case recognised by the Allies as an established headquarters in Berchtesgaden. It now seemed self-evident that modest German forces could hold such a bastion for some time. According to the Allied headquarters, SHAEF, Kesselring commanded more than a million troops in northern Italy, Bavaria and the Tyrol. Who knew how long the war might last if he disposed his million troops in these Alps? Some Allied planners thought a year; others supposed still longer, perhaps till 1947.

Reichsführer Heinrich Himmler was in fact planning this retreat into the mountain fastness just as Dulles was getting his feet back under the desk in the Herrengasse in November 1944. The Reichsführer's staff worked up the detail with the Gauleiters of the areas concerned: Franz Hofer of the Tyrol, South Tyrol, Trentino and Vorarlberg, and Karl Rainer of Carinthia, Austria's most southerly and principally Alpine state. The citadel was dubbed the Alpenfestung – the Alpine Fortress.

Goebbels, seizing on rumours already circulating, then set up a publicity unit dedicated to ventilating an idea as yet confined to paper. Blueprints, construction plans, logistical arrangements and troop movements were all leaked to the credulous; sketchy plans were turned into concrete emplacements at absolutely no cost. On 13 December 1944, the readers of the *Evening Independent* in Florida were told: 'NAZIS PREPARED FOR FIVE YEARS' UNDERGROUND WARFARE'. The Associated Press correspondent Wes Gallagher told his readers:

Information from inside Germany indicates that Adolf Hitler's close followers have prepared for five years of underground warfare against the Allies after the German army collapses . . .

Himmler started laying the plans for underground warfare in the last two months of 1943 and these plans are now being carried out inside Germany.

The plans are threefold, embracing (1) Open warfare directed from Hitler's mountain headquarters; (2) Sabotage and guerrilla activity conducted by partisan bands organized by districts, and (3) Propaganda warfare to be carried on by some 200,000 Nazi followers in Europe and elsewhere . . .

Already picked S. S. (elite) troops have been established in underground strongholds and hospitals in the Austrian, Bavarian and Italian Alpine area and it is the plan of Nazi leaders to flee to that region when the German military collapse comes.[1]

Other papers with rather wider circulations carried similar stories. It was a clever campaign. It was widely believed.

For the Swiss in Berne this was obviously a matter a good deal closer to home than it was in either Washington or London. From the point of view of the head of Switzerland's armed forces, General Guisan, the risk of the Nazi Alpenfestung was that the Reich would invade Switzerland to secure its south-western flank, incorporating Switzerland's own fortified Redoubt into a larger Alpine defence system. This had been the fear behind the March Alarm of 1943.

This was not Guisan's only concern. As the Allied armies moved inexorably closer to the borders of the Reich from east, west and south there was little to prevent their onward march into his own country; and there was also some military logic. The principal barrier to General Patton's forces in the west was the Siegfried Line or Westwall. This was the Wehrmacht's Maginot Line, a defence system running 390 miles due south from Kleve on the Reich's border with Holland down to Weil am Rhein – close to Basel – on the frontier with Switzerland. Operation Market Garden was an attempt to leapfrog the Line.

At the Moscow Conference in October 1944, Stalin brightly proposed to Churchill the idea of the Allies invading Switzerland as a way to turn the southern end of the Line. This was firmly repudiated by Churchill. It would both contravene Switzerland's neutrality and be counterproductive. In the meantime, the idea had sufficient currency for him to write to Foreign Secretary Anthony Eden on 3 December:

I put this down for record. Of all the neutrals, Switzerland has the greatest right to distinction. She has been the sole international force linking the hideously sundered nations and ourselves. What does it matter whether she has been able to give us the commercial advantages we desire or has given too many to the Germans, to keep herself alive? She has been a democratic State, standing for freedom in self-defence among her mountains, and in thought, in spite of race, largely on our side . . . I was astonished at U.J.'s [Stalin's – in the phrase of the time, 'Uncle Joe'] savageness against her . . . He called them 'swine' . . . I am sure we ought to stand by Switzerland, and we ought to explain to U.J. why it is we do so.[2]

Kind words, Guisan would have thought. But words butter no parsnips nor deflect great armies. The war that had ranged all over the European continent, from Norway's North Cape to Gibraltar, from Helsinki to Istanbul, now seemed likely to culminate not in the Reich's capital of Berlin, but in the high Alps. That Christmas of 1944, Switzerland again had to be on its guard.

2

In these circumstances intelligence from the Austrian and Bavarian Alps was suddenly at a premium, so it was timely that a sunburnt young Austrian called Fritz Molden now made his appearance at Dulles's Herrengasse HQ. The twenty-year-old was a rare thing: a member of a successful resistance cell in the Reich.

By the time of the Normandy and Riviera landings in June and August 1944, resistance in Europe had become virtually a mass movement. There were thought to be 100,000 combatant partisans in Italy, a similar number in France, and perhaps five times that figure in Yugoslavia. Irrespective of the punitive actions of the Nazi occupying forces, resistance was now a major fact of daily life for the inhabitants of the occupied countries; it was an identified priority for the Wehrmacht; it was a focus for active support by the Allies. No such situation existed in the Reich itself, either in the Alpine regions of Austria and Bavaria or elsewhere.

This is not to say there was no dissent. It certainly existed: in the Church, the Left, in the intelligentsia, above all in the Wehrmacht. 'There was always resistance, both open and covert, in all social and occupational strata.'[3] It was muted for three reasons: the fact that most Germans accepted that Hitler's government was legally legitimate; the fact that it had rescued many of its people from the desperate economic straits of the early thirties; the fact that the Reich's security services made resistance tantamount to suicide. It was only in the closed society of the armed services that the Gestapo found it difficult to keep the lid on the words, thoughts and deeds of the opponents of the Nazi regime. And of course it was only here that there was resistance of any substance. Before the tragedy of Claus von Stauffenberg's 20 July 1944 attempt on Hitler's life, the White Rose movement had been virtually the only eye-catching effort to repudiate Nazism.

This had erupted in the Nazis' heartland, the Bavarian capital of Munich.

Here a handful of students at the university produced and distributed a series of leaflets denouncing the regime and calling for active opposition to tyranny. They were supported by their philosophy professor Kurt Huber. In the first appeal in June 1942 they presciently wrote: 'Isn't it true that every honest German is ashamed of his government these days? Who among us has any conception of the dimensions of shame that will befall us and our children when one day the veil has fallen from our eyes and the most horrible of crimes – crimes that infinitely outdistance every human measure – reach the light of day?' The leaflets – there were six in all – were distributed in the Alpine cities of Austria and Bavaria: Bregenz, Innsbruck, Salzburg, Klagenfurt, Graz and of course Munich itself. The defeat at Stalingrad in February 1943 inspired the last and most vitriolic denunciation. The 'day of reckoning' had come, it announced. It described Hitler as 'the most contemptible tyrant our people has ever endured'.[4]

The leaflets had been passed on by the Gestapo to Paul Giesler, the Gauleiter of Bavaria, and their source as the university of Munich had been identified. It was outrageous that this should happen in the capital of the Nazi movement, indeed within a rifle shot of the site of the legendary Beer Hall Putsch. A call to order was essential.

According to our old friend the American war correspondent William Shirer, that February of 1943 Giesler assembled the student body in Munich. He suggested that the men not already drafted into the Wehrmacht should undertake work supportive of the war, and that the women should bear a child each year to boost the population of the Fatherland. He added tactfully, 'If some of the girls lack sufficient charm to find a mate, I will assign each of them one of my adjutants . . . and I can promise her a thoroughly enjoyable experience.'[5] The Munich students, once enthusiastic Nazis, were incensed, threw out Giesler's SS and Gestapo minders, and – that afternoon – demonstrated openly against the Reich. This was utterly unprecedented.

On 19 February two of the key members of the group, siblings Hans and Sophie Scholl, were seen by a university caretaker distributing leaflets. They were arrested, interrogated by the Gestapo, tortured, and tried for political offences in the Volks-gerichtshof. This was the people's court, where justice was the last thing dispensed. The Scholls and a handful of others were found guilty of treason in trials on 22 February and 19 April 1943. All – including Huber – were beheaded. Hans Scholl commented during his interrogation: 'I knew what I took upon myself and I was prepared to lose my life by so doing.'⁶ The Scholls' parents were invoiced for court and execution expenses.

Across the old border from Bavaria in Austria, there were also some pockets of resistance in the Alps.

The original Austrian dissenters comprised a motley crew of Catholics – like the Scholls – monarchists, Christian Democrats and communists. All had gone to ground after Anschluss in 1938, the demonstration in Vienna's Stefansplatz in October 1939 excepted; all were subsequently enthused by the Allies' Moscow Declaration of 30 October 1943. Signed by the foreign secretaries of the Big Three – the USA, UK and USSR – this declared Anschluss null and void, and guaranteed that the union of Germany and Austria would be reversed: that the Alpine state would recover her independence from Germany. This stimulated the development in Austria of 'O5', a military resistance move-ment based in Vienna, the Tyrol and the Vorarlberg, the name standing for OE, i.e. Österreich, Austria (E being the fifth letter in the alphabet).

One of the leaders of O5 was the Viennese publisher and historian Ernst Molden. His son Fritz, born in 1924, was a counterpart of the Scholls in Vienna: a member of an anti-fascist student group. Rather than beheading, Molden's reward for dissent was to be sent to a punishment battalion on the Eastern Front. He deserted, convinced the military authorities that he was dead, assumed a new identity, got himself sent to the Italian front and eventually crossed into the Swiss canton of Ticino in March 1944. Just as he was settling down in a railway carriage to enjoy the Swiss newspapers, he was picked up by the Swiss border police. When he eventually persuaded his interrogators of his bona fides as a member of the Austrian resistance, a deal was struck.

Much as General Guisan was concerned with the Allies trespassing on Swiss territory, so too he remained on his guard against the Wehrmacht. Leaving aside the threat of being incorporated into the rumoured Nazi Alpenfestung, there was also the danger of German troops taking a short cut home from Italy. As Molden himself put it in his memoirs, 'The further the Allies advanced in Italy, the greater was the danger that the German forces, and in particular the German South West Army Group in Italy, would simply ignore Switzerland's neutrality and march across the country.'[7] After all, for Kesselring's Heeresgruppe C (Army Group C), the country was the shortest and most direct route between north-west Italy and Germany. Guisan was accordingly hungry for information on German troop movements to the west, south and east: in France, Italy and Austria. The agreement made between Molden and the head of Swiss intelligence Colonel Max Waibel was simple. The Swiss would facilitate the movement of Molden and his O5 associates across the Alpine border into Switzerland in exchange for military intelligence. This, Molden held, 'marked a crucial turning point in the history of the Austrian resistance movement. For it provided us with our first opportunity of maintaining regular and reliable contact with the free world.'[8]

For Molden this was the beginning of a desperately dangerous year. In the guise of Sergeant Hans Steinhauser of the Wehrmacht's 133rd Infantry Regiment he undertook a series of trips into Austria. His task was to establish a network of O5 recruits to assist the passage of the Western Allies when they reached the southern and western borders of Austria. Over the summer and autumn of 1944, as the Allies landed in Normandy and the Riviera, Molden set up links in Vienna. He also established cells in the more westerly Alpine cities of Salzburg and Innsbruck, both of which were major communication hubs and therefore strategic targets for the Allies. Just before Dulles's trip to London and Washington, Molden was introduced to the pipe-smoking US spymaster in the Herrengasse. 'My first impression of Allen Welsh Dulles was that of a somewhat delicate but wiry grey-haired man, broad featured, with a trim moustache and a lofty forehead. Behind his steel-rimmed glasses his clear, grey-blue eyes were alive with interest'.[9]

Like the Swiss, Dulles was certainly interested in forging links with the Austrian resistance, not least because of the prospect of the Nazis decamping south from Berlin to the Reich's Alps. According to Molden, 'Like everyone else, whether in the Allied, the German or the Swiss camp, he [Dulles] believed that the Nazis would make a last stand in the "Alpine redoubt".'[10] At the same time, Dulles was a spymaster who regarded an Austrian army deserter with a degree of reserve. He cautiously commissioned Molden to seek out intelligence on behalf of OSS. 'First,' Molden said of his talk with Dulles, 'we must show we could produce results.'[11]

On Dulles's return from London in November 1944, the pair met again. Dulles was now convinced of Molden's integrity and proposed sending him to SHAEF headquarters to be debriefed – and then to be briefed – on Austria. This would reveal the doings of MI6 in the country. Claude Dansey was still number two to Sir Stewart Menzies at MI6 headquarters in London's Broadway. 'Colonel Z' strenuously objected to disclosing such intelligence to an 'Austrian deserter'. He continued to regard Dulles as naive.

This was another nice inter-Allied row, one that appears to have culminated in the proposal by Dansey of an acid test. According to Molden,

I know, because Allen [Dulles] told me much later, that the British wanted to let me go back into Austria on a mission and then they would tip off the SS. If the Germans let me go back across the border into Switzerland then that would be proof that I was a Nazi agent. And the British would shoot me. If the Germans shot me immediately, it would be proof that the British had been wrong about me but – poof – that was not such a big loss.[12]

Dulles led Molden to believe that he himself had scotched the plan. In the meantime Molden became OSS source K28.

On 12 December 1944, Molden was in the Tyrolean capital of Innsbruck. This was the medieval city set in the wide valley of the river Inn, dominated by the peaks of the Nordkette, the Patscherkofel, and the Serles. There, in the university, in the strictest of secrecy, a complex political agreement was being hammered out. Present were seven Austrian men: liberals, monarchists and Christian Socialists – soon to be joined by communists. At last the deal was struck. The work to which Molden had been contributing had culminated in the foundation of the political wing of O5, the Provisorisches Österreichisches National-kommitee (Provisional Austrian National Committee or POEN). This was fifteen months after the creation of its equivalent in Italy, Comitato di Liberazione Nazionale, and two and a half years after its counterpart in France, Conseil National de la Résistance. It was, though, within the Reich itself. Molden perhaps not unreasonably regarded this as a 'glorious achievement'.[13]

Three days later, Innsbruck received its twelfth visit from the USAAF. The B-24 Liberators from the 336th Heavy Bomb Group were targeting the marshalling yards that served the line over the Brenner Pass. Soon Inge Rainer, the teenager from Kitzbühel, found herself drafted to the city. 'I was sent to near Innsbruck, to learn to shoot small-bore weapons. In the morning we went to Innsbruck to clear the bombing and in the afternoon to shoot. If they sent children back to Innsbruck and taught girls to shoot, this made me think, "The war is over, we have lost." It was a terrible shock.'[14]

3

As Christmas 1944 approached, the situation on and around Switzerland's borders became more and more tense.

To the west, the Germans were making a stand just on the Swiss border at the Belfort Gap. This was one of the Achilles' heels in the republic's defences, a corridor of flat terrain between the Vosges mountains in France and the north-western corner of

Switzerland. It was the gateway to the Rhine, one of Germany's most important natural defences.

Here in mid-September, the 11th Panzer Division, led by Generalleutnant Wend von Wietersheim, found itself confronted by the I French Army Corps. This force, led by Lieutenant General Emile Béthouart, had been part of the 15 August landings on the French Riviera. Béthouart had pushed steadily up the east bank of the Rhône, slowed by adding other formations to the Corps and by the unseasonably poor weather. His thrust into south-western Germany along the northern Swiss border was now blocked. The Panzer division could be bypassed only by attempting the Vosges mountains on his left flank or by breaching Swiss territory – and neutrality – on his right. As General Guisan appreciated, the Vosges were virtually impenetrable; he saw how tempting Switzerland must have looked to his French opposite number. In 1946, Guisan wrote:

In case we were attacked, even if it was only in this small projection of our territory, we had the duty to reply immediately with very effective measures. Our reaction at this very place was of great symbolic value for our own position vis-à-vis the world and for our own domestic situation. The slightest frontier incident could force us to take such countermeasures as would set fire to the powder keg and lead to far-reaching operations.[15]

By which he meant that open warfare with the Allies might have undesirable political consequences.

In practice Guisan had little choice. To add to the French and the German forces around Belfort he brought up a whole division of his own men, dug in just inside Switzerland's border. Béthouart himself waited until the supply situation had improved before giving battle. Responding to Eisenhower's autumn call from SHAEF for a general offensive, on 13 November 1944 Béthouart launched his attack. Believing that the French I Corps had dug in for the winter, the Panzer division was under strength. Caught by surprise, the Panzer forces retreated to the fortified city of Belfort. Respecting the Swiss border, Béthouart pushed through the German lines. On 19 November, the French I Corps reached the Rhine at Huningue, a northern suburb of Basel, where France, Germany and Switzerland met. The journalist-turned-soldier Urs Schwarz was a witness:

I watched as the last German trucks departed in an easterly direction. A group of German officers and soldiers had been left behind; they came across the border, at first refused to lay down their arms, and then surrendered to the Swiss soldiers. I watched as a French flag went up at the customs-house at the border, while the shells still exploded over the roofs.[16]

The 11th Panzer Division was by no means finished. It retreated only to Colmar, forty miles north of Basel on the Alsatian plain. Guisan's troops remained on guard, mindful of the danger of a counter-attack.

This was the first of the General's problems.

On the border with Italy, the situation was similarly precarious. Here the country's natural defences, the Alps, were far better. Here, too, was Switzerland's own Alpine redoubt: completed; stored, manned and ready for war; yet not necessarily a match for the German armies desperate to return to the Fatherland, anxious to get home.

Here Guisan's de facto allies were the partisans, but the Italian resistance was enduring the bitterest of winters. Autumn had seen the collapse of the high hopes inspired by the twenty free republics of a mass rising that would see the early end of the war. Then had come Alexander's broadcast of 10 November 1944, suspending major operations. The partisan leader Roberto Battaglia commented:

This was a grave set-back for the Resistance. To the Germans, on the contrary, it was a tonic. Having received the assurance that they would not be subjected to a major attack by the Allies during the winter, they decided to make the most of the respite and deal the Partisans a crushing blow.[17]

The Wehrmacht and its Fascist allies in northern Italy were very largely successful. They seized a number of prominent partisans including Ferruccio Parri, committed wide-scale atrocities against the civilian population supportive of the partisans, and smoked out tens of thousands from the partisan mountain camps, both in the Apennines on Italy's spine and further north in the Alps themselves. Bletchley Park decrypts in January 1945 suggested that as many as 70,000 partisans surrendered; an SOE report gives a similar flavour of the winter. 'Enemy activity has continued to be forceful,' noted No. 1 Special Force. 'Communications with the field have been irregular and many missions have been forced to change location frequently and to live and work in conditions of extreme hardship.'[18] For Guisan, here too lay danger.

Finally, to the east of Switzerland beyond the buffer of the Italian Alps lay Yugoslavia. Given Stalin's modest proposals about the Alpine republic, the news for Guisan from the far eastern Alps was in some respects the most alarming of all.

Since the failure of the Axis's Fifth Enemy Offensive in June 1943, Tito's partisans had gone from strength to strength; they now numbered perhaps half a million, and Tito was formally recognised by the Allies as the commander-in-chief of Yugoslav armed forces. On 17 June 1944 the Treaty of Vis attempted to merge Tito's administration with that of King Peter, still exiled in London; on 12 September 1944, just as Dulles reached Washington, the King called for his people to rally round Tito's leadership. Then, three weeks later on 28 September 1944, an announcement was made that Tito had agreed to 'temporary entry' of Soviet troops into north-eastern Yugoslavia. Their role was officially to support the partisans' effort to drive out the Wehrmacht. By 20 October the Red Army had occupied Belgrade.

For the Swiss the message was clear. A crimson tide was fast rising towards their tiny democracy, a tide that might reach anywhere.

Of Guisan's three potential crises, in France, Italy and Yugoslavia, it was the one to the west that erupted.

In his last great throw of the dice, Hitler had assembled a total of seventy divisions comprising four armies: the Sixth and

Fifth Panzer Armies, the Seventh Army and the Fifteenth Army. They were earmarked for the Ardennes offensive. This was Unternehmen Wacht am Rhein (Operation Watch on the Rhine, named after a popular German song). 'This great force,' Churchill recounted, 'led by its armour, was intended to break through our weak centre in the Ardennes to the river Meuse, swing north and northwest, cut the Allied line in two, seize the port of Antwerp, and sever the lifeline of our northern armies.'[19] The ultimate hope was that the Western Allies would sue for peace, enabling the Wehrmacht to about-face and to concentrate all its forces on the Eastern Front. Hitler's plan in the proximity of Belfort on the Swiss border was to smash through the lines of the US Seventh Army and the French First Army in the Upper Vosges mountains.

At 5.30 a.m. on 16 December 1944 the storm broke with a ninety-minute artillery barrage on an eighty-mile front. Who could tell how this would pan out for Switzerland – and indeed the West?

4

That Christmas of 1944, while the Swiss in Berne and on the borders of Switzerland were discovering that Hitler's war was not yet over, so too were the Allied guests of the Swiss in the republic's interior.

As Allied air activity increased over the beleaguered Reich, we have already seen how the number of airmen who ended up landing, crash-landing or parachuting into Switzerland increased accordingly. As the Hague Convention required, the crews ended up in Swiss internment camps. Following the downing of the B-24 *Death-Dealer* in August 1943, the USAAF airmen had been dispatched to Adelboden. Here they shared the Canton Berne skiing resort with British and Commonwealth internees, many of whom had escaped from the Italian POW camps. As the numbers of US servicemen swelled in the first months of 1944, they outgrew the resort.

In Adelboden, officers and enlisted men were all interned at Camp Moloney. In the spring of 1944 the Swiss internment committee agreed with the US military attaché, Brigadier General Barnwell Legge at the American legation in Berne, that two additional camps should be set up: a new officers' camp in Davos, and a new camp for enlisted men in Wengen. The facilities in the two proposed resorts – Davos in Canton Graubünden and Wengen in the Bernese Oberland – were underutilised because of the collapse of international tourism; the relative remoteness of the resorts also made escape difficult. Camp Davos was opened in June 1944, its equivalent in Wengen two months later in August. From this famous old resort the internees would be able to enjoy the prospect of the Alps' best-known trio of peaks: the Eiger, Mönch and Jungfrau.

As it turned out, Davos was immediately a cause of friction. The resort had a long-standing German community, was the original seat of the German Nazis in Switzerland, and was the site of the assassination of their leader Wilhelm Gustloff in February 1936. Now, alongside the civilian German community, there were hundreds of convalescent Reich servicemen in the town, making use of the sanatoria that in peace had ministered to victims of tuberculosis. When Davos's German community heard of the imminent arrival of the American officers, its leaders immediately lodged a protest with the Swiss – to no avail. The Germans then spread the rumour that the airmen were no better than Chicago gangsters. When the first USAAF men arrived on 22 June 1944, they found the shops closed, shutters bolted and the streets deserted. The town returned to normal when the US airmen showed themselves friendly and open-handed. The inhabitants of Davos were then treated to the intriguing sight of uniformed servicemen from the Allies and the Reich rubbing shoulders with a due circumspection on the wide promenade between Davos Dorf and Davos Platz.

Camp Davos was located in the Palace Hotel on this road between Dorf and Platz. This was barely a hundred yards from the German consulate. It was hardly surprising that on US Independence Day on 4 July 1944 a couple of high-spirited US officers should let off a few fireworks outside the consulate. On the evening of 7 August – a month after the D-Day landings – another pair of officers removed the consulate's badge of office, a large eagle clutching a swastika that garnished the building's entrance. The Germans protested, the swastika was recovered, the perpetrators identified, and demands were made to send the guilty men to the Swiss punishment camp at Wauwilermoos. Tipped off, the two officers escaped over the Swiss border into France – with the help of sympathetic Swiss civilians.

Such diversions aside, life in Camp Davos was not unduly onerous. James Goings had crash-landed near Knutwil, Canton Lucerne, on 27 May 1944. He remembered:

The days were spent in many various ways. We could walk through the town down to the lake of Davos, up to Parsenn, Schatzalp, Strela-Pass or Jakobshorn, for example. Baseball teams were selected and a playing field set up in the valley below the Belvedere. When the cold weather came, many of us joined ski-classes and went skating . . . There were five moving picture houses in Davos, two in Platz and three in Dorf. In the late afternoon the finer hotels held tea dances, where many men went to meet local ladies, and built lasting friendships . . . others did nothing other than plan to escape from Switzerland into France to meet the American troops as they pushed back to Germany.[20]

Under the Hague Convention the Swiss were obliged to prevent such escapes. Those guardians in Davos took their duties seriously. The internees were subjected to two daily roll-calls, had an evening curfew, and were forbidden to go further than two miles from the town without express permission. While Switzerland remained an oasis, bordered on all sides by the Axis, escape, in any case, remained next to impossible. Once the border with France reopened in August 1944 and in particular when the US armies reached Geneva, the situation changed drastically. 'Escape became the first priority for all officers at Davos as well as all enlisted men in the other camps.'[21]

The paradox was that Brigadier General Barnwell Legge had announced that those who succeeded in doing their duty by escaping would be court-martialled on their return to the US. This masked delicate negotiations he was undertaking for the wholesale release of all the US internees in Switzerland in exchange for the release of their German counterparts to the Germans. Despite this threat, in the course of the autumn and early winter of 1944, those US internees who could be dragged away from the ski slopes and the women of Adelboden, Wengen and Davos escaped in a very steady stream. About two-thirds of them made it to their own lines, the remainder being recaptured. It was a few of these unfortunates who were destined to spend Christmas of 1944 in the Swiss Straflager (punishment) camps. The most notorious of these was Wauwilermoos, where the airmen were under the care of 'Captain' André-Henri Béguin.

In 1937, Béguin had been dismissed from the army on various counts including financial fraud occasioned by the charges of keeping four mistresses; now in his new guise at Wauwilermoos he sported Nazi uniform and signed his correspondence 'Heil Hitler'. His camp in Lucerne was surrounded by barbed wire and watchtowers and guarded by dogs, its inmates a mixed bunch of Swiss criminals and Allied internees: French, British, Italians, Poles, Russians, Americans. The Allied servicemen were kept without due legal process, representation, trial, sentence or indication of the time of their likely release. They were allowed no mail, and they slept on dirty straw along with the lice and the rats. The camp had no proper sanitation facilities – showers or lavatories – and the food was atrocious: it was served from slop pails into tin cans, sometimes into a trough. There was little medical attention: dysentery, pyorrhoea and boils went untreated and unchecked. When the men complained to members of the International Red Cross on the Committee's occasional visits, no action was taken. The US mission in the form of Barnwell Legge was of little help, supposedly because he felt the camp's notoriety discouraged escapes. The US airman James Misuraca commented, 'The guards were coarse and crude. The officials treated us like scum. This was purely and simply a concentration camp.'[22]

A handful of Allied servicemen spent Christmas of 1944 and celebrated the New Year of 1945 as guests of Béguin. It was not their happiest festive season.

5

By Christmas, the likely fate of Operation Wacht am Rhein had become apparent. 'On December 23,' wrote Speer, 'Model [Generalfeldmarschall Walter Model, one of the architects of the operation] told me that the offensive had definitely failed – but Hitler had ordered it to continue.'[23] Churchill, who on Christmas Day had flown from London to Naples, then from the southern Italian city to Athens, was drawing similar conclusions. Shortly before flying out of the Greek capital on 28 December 1944, he received a telegram from Field Marshal Montgomery in France confirming the collapse of the operation.

The same day, in Berne, Fritz Molden once again met Allen Dulles. Besides the good tidings from the Ardennes, the spymaster had some news of more personal interest for the young Austrian. The United States had decided to give provisional recognition to POEN, the Provisional Austrian National Committee. Molden himself was to be appointed liaison officer between the Allies and POEN. Dulles said, 'You are the first Austrian to be accredited as liaison officer at Allied HQ.' It was, recorded Molden, 'a solemn moment'.[24]

For Speer, who had been close to the German front in the Ardennes until 30 December, diplomacy dictated that he deliver his New Year wishes personally to the Führer. Although Hitler had intended to spend Christmas in Berchtesgaden, Wacht am Rhein required his presence at a more westerly headquarters at Kransberg Castle in Hesse. When Speer eventually reached Hitler's bunker in the castle, it was already two hours into the happy new year of 1945. The armaments and war production minister was relieved to find he was not too late to wish the Führer glückliches neues Jahr.

Hitler was looking his age, indeed rather more. The five years of war – not to mention the 20 July 1944 bomb – had aged him brutally. He was suffering from spells of dizziness, shaking of limbs he could not control, and periodic fits of deafness. Soon the once worshipped leader, the man who had mesmerised the

Nuremberg rallies and struck fear into the hearts of European leaders, would be seen by all as a physical wreck. 'All witnesses of the final days agree when they describe his emaciated face, his grey complexion, his stooping body, his shaking hands and foot, his hoarse and quavering voice, and the film of exhaustion that covered his eyes.'[25] On that New Year's Day of 1945, Speer remembered:

adjutants, doctors, secretaries, Bormann – the whole circle except for the generals attached to the Fuehrer's headquarters, were gathered around Hitler drinking champagne. The alcohol had relaxed everyone, but the atmosphere was still subdued. Hitler [for long teetotal] seemed to be the only one in the company who was drunk without having taken any stimulating beverage. He was in the grip of a permanent euphoria.

Although the beginning of a new year in no way dispelled the desperate situation of the year past . . . Hitler made optimistic forecasts for 1945.

Speer thought otherwise. 'The failure of the Ardennes offensive meant that the war was over. What followed was only the occupation of Germany, delayed somewhat by a confused and impotent resistance.'[26]

FOURTEEN

The Redoubt That Never Was

Strictly speaking the idea of an Alpine Fortress was more a creation of American Intelligence than of Germany's leaders.

DOUGLAS BOTTING AND IAN SAYER

I

Speer was right, but this was with the benefit of hindsight. In the first few weeks of 1945 this collapse of the Reich was not seen as a likely outcome by the Allied high command.

Although Wacht am Rhein had failed, there was a definite sense that the Allies' own campaigns both in Italy and on the western borders of Germany had stalled. On 3 January 1945, Churchill had told Roosevelt, 'There is this brutal fact: we need more fighting troops to make things move.'[1] The Western Allied armies were also running very short of ammunition, victims of long supply lines from ports working – largely as a consequence of the Wehrmacht – at very much less than full capacity. Moreover, the final meeting early in February of Churchill, Stalin and Roosevelt at Yalta on the Black Sea clearly foreshadowed not so much victory over the Reich as the Cold War. As military issues receded, political ones loomed. Churchill continued, 'As the victory of the Grand Alliance became only a matter of time it was natural that Russian ambitions should grow. Communism raised its head behind the thundering Russian battle-front. Russia was the Deliverer, and Communism the gospel she brought.'[2] The alliance to destroy Hitler was now dissolving at frightening speed, and Churchill justifiably feared that the results of his Herculean labours would see one totalitarian regime in Europe replaced by another: the Red Army was only forty miles from Berlin.

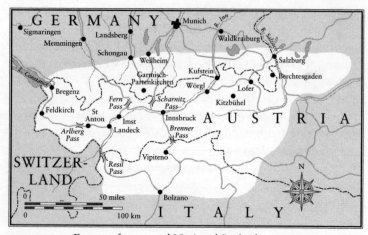

Extent of supposed National Redoubt, 1945

At SHAEF Eisenhower's responsibility was to address these problems. Having lost around 80,000 US troops in the Ardennes, his military imperative was to strike quickly to still the Nazis' lifeblood. About this objective there was no question. It had been set out by the Combined Chiefs of Staff with admirable brevity: 'You will enter the continent of Europe and, in conjunction with the other United Nations, undertake operations aimed at the heart of Germany and the destruction of her armed forces.'[3] Eisenhower's problem was that the heart had moved.

The whispers of the Alpenfestung had been circulating since the autumn. From then there had been an ever-increasing stream of intelligence reports from Germany herself, from neutral countries and from the battlefields of central Europe. Hitler would make the Nazis' last stand in the crags of Berchtesgadener Land. There had even been stories in the press. On 12 February 1945, the day after the conference in Yalta broke up, the US War Department issued a memorandum that declared: 'Not enough weight is given to the many reports of the probable Nazi last stand in the Bavarian Alps . . . The Nazi myth which is important when you are dealing with men like Hitler requires a *Götterdämmerung*. It may be significant that Berchtesgaden itself, which would be the headquarters, is on the site of the tomb of Barbarossa who, in Germany mythology, is supposed to return from the dead.'[4] A month later, on 11 March, another SHAEF intelligence report echoed: 'German defence policy is to safeguard the Alpine Zone ... Defences continue to be constructed in depth in the south, through the Black Forest to Lake Constance and from the Hungarian frontier to the west of Graz ... In Italy ... defence lines are built up in the foothills of the Italian Alps.'[5] There was even a story of a frightening new Geheimwaffe (secret weapon) sited in the Redoubt that – even now – would turn the course of the war. Returning to his post of Supreme Commander in Italy following a car crash, 'smiling Albert' Kesselring had joked to his staff, 'I am V3.'[6]

The drip, drip of such intelligence had now begun to influence military thinking at SHAEF. On 21 March 1945 the principal army group on the Western Front, General Omar Bradley's Twelfth, issued a note headed 'Re-Orientation of Strategy'. This stated that the existence of the Redoubt had rendered 'obsolete the plans we brought with us over the beaches'. Should the focus really be on Berlin? it asked; 'all indications suggest that the enemy's political and military directorate is already in the process of displacing to the "Redoubt" in lower Bavaria'.[7] Clearly this required the Allied forces to think again. Bradley's proposal was that rather than pushing on to Berlin, the Twelfth Army Group should dip south and cut through the centre of Germany. This would prevent the forces around the capital retreating south into the Redoubt; rather, it would push them northwards. The Twelfth would then pivot south, meet up with General de Lattre de Tassigny's French First Army coming in from the west and with Alexander's forces advancing over the Italian Alps from the south. These three forces would clear up any Wehrmacht forces remaining in the Redoubt.

Bradley, a friend and classmate of Eisenhower from West Point, could hardly be ignored. The Supreme Commander's immediate superior, the US Chief of General Staff, General George Marshall, had to be obeyed. He had made the same point. It was true that not all the Allied staff were convinced about the redoubt – either US or British. It was a story largely unsupported by Bletchley's Ultra decrypts, radio intercepts, agents in Austria and Germany, and a simple assessment of the known locations of the Wehrmacht's remaining forces. Still, intelligence had largely failed to spot the massive preparations for Wacht am Rhein in the Ardennes. In the end SHAEF's head of intelligence, Major General Kenneth Strong, took what might have seemed a reasonable line. 'The redoubt may not be there, but we have to take steps to prevent it being there.'[8]

Eisenhower was in any case obliged to act with the information he had to hand at the time. On 29 March 1944 he drafted three cables. One was directly to Stalin, one to General Marshall, and one to Field Marshal Montgomery – the latter leading the 21st Army Group on the thrust of the Western Allies to Berlin. The Supreme Commander copied Churchill on his cable to Stalin.

The substance of the messages was that, as the principal military target of the Western Allies, Berchtesgaden had to be substituted for Berlin. Churchill, on his way to spend Easter weekend at his own Berchtesgaden, the Buckinghamshire country retreat of Chequers, was appalled. He had spoken directly to the Supreme Allied Commander on the scrambler telephone the previous evening. Leaving aside the gross breach of protocol of the simple soldier trespassing in the forbidden country of high political strategy by communicating directly with Stalin, there were the practical consequences for Berlin. On the secure phone line Churchill had not raised the issue of protocol with Eisenhower. Rather, he had ventilated the political importance of the German capital and the imperative of Montgomery's forces reaching there before the Red Army. At the time Eisenhower, despite his subsequent presidency, was unschooled in high politics. He was obdurate. 'Berlin', he had told Churchill, 'is no longer a major military objective.' It had been replaced by what the Supreme Commander called 'the mountain citadel'.[9]

Churchill could do nothing. As Supreme Allied Commander,

Eisenhower to date had delivered everything demanded of him. The Normandy and Riviera landings, the early joining hands of Patton's and Patch's forces in Dijon, the drive towards the Rhine, the scuppering of the Ardennes counteroffensive. The United States forces were in the ascendant, the British an increasingly junior partner. In the past three years, Churchill's final court of appeal would have been Roosevelt. The President, ailing at Yalta, was now dying. Arriving at the Little White House in Warm Springs, Georgia, on Good Friday, he had to be carried from the train by one of his secret service aides. Replies to Churchill's cabled concerns over the fate of Berlin appeared over the President's name, but were the work of other hands. The row kindled, poisoning the relationship between the English-speaking Allies. On 31 March 1945, the US military chiefs in Washington gave Eisenhower their unqualified support.

So too did the kindly Marshal Stalin. Meeting in Moscow with the British and American ambassadors, he endorsed Eisenhower's plan to attack central Germany, and expressed the view that the Nazis' 'last stand would probably be in western Czechoslovakia and Bavaria'. Dismissing the ambassadors, the Soviet leader picked up the phone, sent for his top warlords – Marshals Georgy Zhukov and Ivan Koniev – and set them a simple task. Eisenhower's averred plan was a decoy, he told the two marshals: a pretence, a red herring. The Red Army must race to be first in Berlin. He told his western allies at the same time that only second-rank, inferior and reserve Red Army forces would head for the German capital. This was misleading. Antony Beevor comments: 'It was the greatest April Fool in modern history.'[10]

By 7 April 1945, the whole matter was resolved. Eisenhower cabled to Churchill, 'Quite naturally, if at any moment collapse should suddenly come about everywhere along the front we would rush forward, and Lübeck and Berlin would be included in our important targets.'[11] This was the best Churchill would get. In these circumstances he cabled to the ailing Roosevelt that he regarded the matter as closed. In a characteristic flourish, he added: 'to prove my sincerity I will use one of my very few Latin quotations: *Amantium irae amoris integratio est*' (Lovers' quarrels are a renewal of love).[12] Whether Eisenhower's decision about the Alpenfestung was momentous – as some hold – is a matter of debate. James Lucas asserts that it 'altered the course of post-war European history'.[13] Max Hastings writes: 'It is hard, however, to make a plausible case that any of this changed the post-war political map of Europe, as the Supreme Commander's detractors claimed.'[14]

A week later, on 15 April 1945, the commander of the US Ninth Army, General William Hood Simpson, was recalled by Omar Bradley to Twelfth Army Group headquarters in Wiesbaden, Hesse. Bradley was waiting for Simpson at the airfield. 'We shook hands, and there and then he told me the news. "You must stop on the Elbe. You are not to advance any farther in the direction of Berlin."' Simpson was flabbergasted. He had led his army from Brest on the French Atlantic coast to within reach of the Reich. 'All I could think of was, How am I going to tell my staff, my corps commanders and my troops? Above all, how am I going to tell my troops?'[15]

While Simpson was obliged to hold fire, the Allied forces in Italy were pushing up towards the Alpenfestung.

In December of 1944 Alexander had been replaced as Supreme Allied Commander in Italy by Mark W. Clark. (Alexander himself had been promoted to Supreme Allied Commander Mediterranean.) The forty-eight-year-old US general had distinguished himself by ignoring Alexander's orders in the aftermath of the capture of Monte Cassino. Clark had thereby captured Rome, but a number of German units had escaped to fight another day – as it so happened on the Gothic Line in the Apennines that was now causing him such trouble. A week before Simpson's interview with Bradley, Clark had launched the Allies' final offensive in the Italian peninsula. He sent the British Eighth Army in the east on a drive towards the Argenta Gap just north of Ravenna, and the US IV Corps up from the

Apennines to encircle the strategic centre of Bologna. By 15 April, Clark's offensive was making good progress, a spearhead heading due north for the Alps.

Also heading for the Alps – though southwards rather than northwards – were two trains, *Adler* and *Dohle*, that had set out that same day from the rubble of Berlin. They carried an intriguing cargo. A few days earlier at the town of Merkers in Thuringia, the Allies had discovered $238 million in the form of gold and currency. It was hidden in a mine. These were the bulk of the Reichsbank's reserves, sent there for safe keeping on the orders of the Reichsbank chief, Walther Funk. The trains heading to Bavaria carried the remaining reserves: a smaller but nevertheless useful sum of $15 million.

2

It was at this point that Allen Dulles in Berne appeared to make a contribution to the culmination of the war in the Alps. This was Operation Sunrise, according to his biographer James Srodes 'one of the most dramatic and controversial intelligence triumphs of his career and his last major coup of World War II'.[16]

Since the autumn of 1944, Dulles had been getting feelers for peace from Kesselring's forces in Italy. This was scarcely surprising. The Wehrmacht was between a rock and a hard place. The rock was the southern flank of the Alps and the hard place was Mark Clark's US Fifth and British Eighth Armies, which were poised to embark on their assault on the Gothic Line in the Apennines. In theory, the Alps represented the lifeline of the German Tenth and Fourteenth Armies that together constituted Kesselring's Heeresgruppe C, its escape route back to Germany. In practice, the story of the partisan republics of the autumn of 1944 had shown that safe passage through the high Alpine passes infested with partisans now looked an increasingly remote possibility. The alternative was a pitched battle between these four armies on the plain of Lombardy that lay between the foothills of the Alps to the north and the northernmost ridges of the Apennines in the south.

As the prospect of Clark's inevitable spring assault neared, German appetite for a negotiated surrender increased daily. Professional soldiers like the Wehrmacht would not deign to parley with the partisans, whom they regarded as bandits and criminals and against whom they had committed numerous atrocities. They would negotiate with the regular Allied forces, members of which at least would not shoot them on sight, castrate them, gouge their eyes out or lock them in burning churches: all brutalities that the Wehrmacht and SS had visited on the partisans and their supporters. For their part, the Allies themselves were far from averse to a surrender that would avoid either a German retreat into the supposed Redoubt or a bitter battle in Lombardy with a battle-hardened and far from demoralised opponent. The lives of hundreds of thousands of men were at stake.

Nothing concrete had materialised from the expressions of interest from the Germans floated over the New Year. Then, through the good offices of the Swiss intelligence chief Colonel Max Waibel – Fritz Molden's contact – in early February came a fresh approach. The whole thing was done very nicely. There were no hurried phone calls or clandestine meetings in Berne's Herrengasse. Waibel and Dulles had dinner together at an excellent restaurant close to Lake Lucerne, in fact quite close to the punishment camp of Wauwilermoos. They ate trout washed down with hock and discussed the virtues of the Italian partisan movement, possibly of women too. Dulles enjoyed his evening but thought Waibel's proposal that he should meet yet another couple of go-betweens, an Italian and a Swiss, was unenticing. When he eventually met the pair, he was even more sceptical of their claims to be in touch with Obergruppenführer Karl Wolff. This was the SS general in charge of all the SS forces in Italy and – it was to be assumed – a diehard Nazi. All such officers in Heinrich Himmler's thug force had taken personal pledges of allegiance to the Führer. They were surely the last people to give peace a chance. Dulles was most surprised when the go-betweens returned within the week with two real live Waffen-SS officers: Standartenführer Eugen Dollmann and Obersturmführer Guido

Zimmer. They were in Lugano, the charming lakeside resort where, in November 1944, Dulles had first met Ferruccio Parri, the CLNAI partisan leader.

It was now that Dulles showed his mettle. Dollmann claimed he was an emissary from Wolff, and that his superior officer wanted a face-to-face meeting with Dulles to negotiate a surrender. Unlike his compatriot General Eisenhower, Dulles was attuned to political nuances and fully aware of the delicacy of any such negotiations. The relationship between the Eastern and Western Allies was now such that Stalin would – and very soon did – take a jaundiced view of a surrender that could speed the passage eastwards of the Western Allied armies. As Churchill said later of these early contacts, 'I realised at once that the Soviet Government might be suspicious of a separate military surrender in the South, which would enable our armies to advance against reduced opposition as far as Vienna and beyond, or indeed towards the Elbe or Berlin.'[17] So if Dulles was to risk such contacts, he needed, in his own words, 'concrete evidence both of their seriousness and of their authority'. He needed proof positive.[18]

Now Ferruccio Parri was one of the many partisans who had been seized by the Gestapo in the winter breathing space so unhappily granted to Kesselring's forces by Field Marshal Alexander's 10 November 1944 broadcast. So too had Parri's lieutenant, Antonio Usmiani. The pair were not being at all well treated by their captors, not least because of a bungled attempt by the partisans to rescue Parri from Gestapo HQ in Milan. Wrote Dulles:

I proposed, therefore, that General Wolff, if he wanted to see me, should give evidence of the seriousness of his intentions by releasing these two prisoners to me in Switzerland. In asking for Parri I realized that I was asking for probably the most important Italian prisoner the SS held . . . I knew that in asking for his release I was asking for something that would be very difficult for Wolff to do, and in fact I was putting the stakes high – almost too high, as it later turned out. Yet if these men could be released, the seriousness of General Wolff's intentions would be amply demonstrated.[19]

Dulles did not trouble himself to go to Lugano on 4 March 1945. He was suffering from gout. Thoughtfully, he delegated the initial negotiations to an American Jew with the telltale name of Paul Blum. When Dollmann asked whether Dulles would meet Wolff on the neutral territory of Switzerland, Blum set out Dulles's conditions. He handed the Waffen-SS officers a slip of paper. It bore two names: Ferruccio Parri and Antonio Usmiani. Dollmann blenched.

After a few moments' consideration he said he would see what he could do. Dollmann and Zimmer returned to Milan, Blum to Berne to report to Dulles. The American in turn passed on what he thought fit to Colonel Max Waibel. The Swiss were not entirely disinterested. Their principal lifeline was the Ligurian port of Genoa, through which such essentials as the Allies thought fit to grant them were shipped. The speedy cessation of hostilities before the port was wrecked by the Germans under Hitler's 'scorched earth' policy was, Waibel thought, desirable.

Chiasso, four days later. Picture the scene at the windswept Alpine town on the Ticino border where Switzerland stretches an arm into Italy. An SS car is seen approaching the border checkpoint. It bears the familiar lightning logo of the SS. It draws up rather sharply. Smartly, an officer dressed as a captain alights from the car. It is Captain Zimmer. His arrival has been anticipated. One of Waibel's representatives steps forward. Passwords are exchanged. 'I have two men for you,' announces Zimmer, with the air of a conjurer. 'Please take them to Allen Dulles with the compliments of General Wolff.' Zimmer returns to the car. From the rear doors he helps two dazed and dishevelled figures onto the tarmac. Uncertainly, encouraged by Zimmer, half expecting a shot in the back, they shuffle across the border. Parri and Usmiani are free, a couple of characters out of a John le Carré thriller.

Two hours later the car returns. Captain Zimmer emerges once again, followed by Colonel Dollmann. Then comes an SS adjutant, Sturmbannführer Wenner. They form a guard of honour for a man of the notably 'Aryan' features so favoured in the Reich: tall, bronzed, blue-eyed, blond-haired. The hawklike nose is his signature. It is Heinrich Himmler's personal representative in Italy, Obergruppenführer Karl Wolff. Within hours Wolff and Dulles are chatting in front of the log fire in the OSS Herrengasse apartment in Berne, the spymaster puffing away at his pipe. He liked to put his guests at ease.

Up until this time, Dulles had not troubled Washington or indeed anyone outside the immediate circle of those concerned with these developments. Now he called Allied Forces Headquarters (AFHQ) in the Royal Palace at Caserta, some twenty-five miles north of Naples. He outlined Wolff's proposals. These included the public disavowal of Hitler and Himmler by all senior German officers in Italy, and the release of hundreds of Jews interned at Bologna. AFHQ was electrified by this news, dispatched the British and US Chiefs of Staff to talk to Dulles and Wolff and – in the way of a bureaucracy – gave the operation a name: Sunrise. With the prospect of the surrender of Heeresgruppe C – around 200,000 men – Dulles seemed to be on the brink of a huge coup. He was told to pursue the talks. '[O]n March 19,' wrote Churchill, 'a second exploratory meeting was held with General Wolff.' Here the idea of calling off General Mark Clark's spring offensive was tabled. During the remainder of March the negotiations proceeded. Dulles even rented a chalet in the lakeside resort of Ascona in Canton Ticino. It would act as a convenient and secure base for the talks, a 'safe house'. The shores of Lake Maggiore would surely prove conducive to surrender.

Then three things went wrong. Wolff's superior Generalfeld-marschall Kesselring suddenly moved headquarters and distanced himself from negotiations of which he had tacitly approved. Second, Himmler got word of the talks and threatened Wolff with holding his wife and family hostage against his loyalty to the Reich; unbeknownst to Hitler, the former chicken farmer was pursuing his own surrender negotiations with the Allies, using the Swede Count Folke Bernadotte as a middleman. Third, Stalin, well served by his own intelligence service, abruptly accused Roosevelt and Churchill of negotiating a separate surrender with the Reich behind his back. The Marshal demanded the talks be called off. In his last message to the Soviet leader, Roosevelt firmly rebuked his ally. Harry S. Truman, his successor, was less robust. Lobbied by the Joint Chiefs of Staff (JCS), who – apparently correctly – felt that both Dulles and AFHQ in Caserta were being economical with the truth about the talks, the new president bowed to Stalin's demands.

Dulles, having nursed the negotiations with imagination and tenacity, turned up at the Herrengasse on 20 April 1945 to be confronted by a telegram from Washington. It read in part, 'especially in view of complications which have arisen with the Russians, the U.S. and British governments have decided OSS should break off [Sunrise] contacts; that JCS are so instructing OSS; that the whole matter is to be regarded as closed and that Russians be informed.'[20] It was a bombshell.

3

And despite the fact that for practical purposes the war was now virtually over, in the Alps the fighting went on.

When the German occupying forces in the French Alps had withdrawn in the face of the Allied armies forcing their way up the Rhône valley from the Riviera landings in August 1944, they had left a rearguard in place. This was at the northern end of the Alpine frontier between France and Italy, where in June 1940 the Armée des Alpes had successfully resisted Mussolini's forces. In the Tarentaise valley in the Savoie lay the village of Val d'Isère. Before the war it was barely acknowledged as a skiing resort, boasting just one primitive drag lift. Eight or nine miles south towered the 9,252-foot Mont Froid. Here in some of the old Petit Ligne Maginot casemates were around 1,500 fascist troops: the 3rd Battalion of the 100. Gebirgsjägerregiment, and a company of the Italian Folgore Regiment. They guarded the route over the frontier ridge between France and Italy: the Col du Mont Cenis into the Susa valley and beyond into Piedmont.

To support the last push of General Mark Clark's Fifth and Eighth Armies into northern Italy, the French planned an assault. Around 3,000 men were assembled by Alain Le Ray. This was the former military head of the Vercors, now a thirty-five-year-old lieutenant colonel. His forces were members of the 27th French Mountain Division, largely former maquisards, now the FFI. On 5 April, the *chasseurs* seized the middle and western strongpoints despite bitter winds and snow. The following day the eastern casemate fell, and with it Mont Froid. Then came counter-attacks, three in all.

A short time before midnight, after a violent shelling, an enemy detachment (one German company and two Italian platoons), composed of five groups, silently approached the eastern casemate: while three groups made a frontal attack, the two others tried to outflank the position. Apocalyptical scene with flashes of fire and tracer bullets, bursts of gunfire, mortar shells, grenades and Panzerfaust projectiles in a hell of a row ... The small French garrison was overwhelmed and on the verge of being annihilated. Under the command of Chief Warrant Officer Jeangrand, a platoon of the 4th company of the 6th BCA (with Sergeant Roger Cerri and Senior Corporal Jean Gilbert) came immediately to the rescue ...

... Jeangrand, Warrant Officer Gay and a private were killed, three others wounded. All the groups withdrew under fire and took refuge in the center block. The attackers screamed and charged with submachine guns and hand grenades. The French chasseurs alpins defended themselves energetically. Facing a volley of bullets, the enemy had to step back, but it attacked quickly again and arrived at close range. Several French soldiers were killed or wounded, but the others, singing the Chant du départ, opened a running fire. As dawn was breaking, the attackers retired ... Shortly afterwards, a snowstorm raged. It was freezing hard. Most men were exhausted, many men had frozen feet, the weapons were frozen ... On the 9th of April, the 4th company of the 6th BCA was relieved at last.[21]

Three days later, the 3rd Battalion briefly recaptured the bitterly contested redoubt. Le Ray's men were later described as 'forcing the Germans from their last mountain-top strongholds' in the French Alps.[22] The war had less than a month to run.

4

20 April 1945. It was Hitler's birthday, his fifty-sixth. Hitherto, the Führer's intention had been to withdraw to Berchtesgaden as the Soviet army closed on Berlin. Ten days earlier his domestic staff had followed in the wake of many of the Reich ministries, various senior officials, camp followers and the $15 million Reichsbank's reserves to the relative safety of Bavaria. In the Berghof, Hitler's staff busied themselves with spring-cleaning the chalet to make the place fit for a king. In the circumstances they were particularly careful to dust down the extensive bunker complex. Air raids were anticipated.

Hitler, though, was wavering. On the eve of his birthday he had quietly given in to Goebbels's request that such military reserves as the Wehrmacht still possessed should be committed to the defence of the capital, deployed around the very gates of Berlin. On his birthday itself, in the Führerbunker under the Chancellery dutifully designed by Speer for a contingency never seriously anticipated, congratulations seemed slightly misplaced. 'No one knew quite what to say,' remembered the 'armaments' minister. 'Hitler received the expressions of good wishes coolly and almost unwillingly, in keeping with the circumstances.'[23] All the leading Nazis were there, including Speer himself, Göring, Goebbels, Himmler, Ribbentrop, Bormann and the military chiefs Dönitz, Keitel, Jodl and Krebs. Göring, doubtless anticipating events, was wearing a rather surprising new uniform plastered across his broad frame. It was olive-green. One of the entourage whispered to Speer, 'Like an American general!' Discussion eventually turned to the military situation. The sounds of Soviet artillery could be heard all too clearly, even fifty-five feet under the Chancellery garden. When Hitler announced his decision to defend Berlin there was an outcry. 'At once everyone began clamoring that it was essential to shift the headquarters to Obersalzberg, and that now was the last moment remaining.' Göring then chimed in. There was only one route still open south to Berchtesgaden, he said. It might be lost at any moment; now was surely the time to stage a retreat south. This inflamed Hitler: 'How can I call on the troops to undertake the decisive battle for Berlin if at the same moment I myself withdraw to safety! . . . I shall leave it to fate whether I die in the capital or fly to Obersalzberg at the last moment!'[24]

For the present, Hitler would stay.

Göring thought it best – wisest – to do otherwise. Once the conference was over he turned to Hitler and explained that he had a lot to do in Bavaria. He would leave for the south that very evening. Speer says, 'I was standing only a few feet away from the two and had a sense of being present at a historic moment: The leadership of the Reich was splitting asunder.'[25]

It was in fact the night of the final exodus to Bavaria. Bormann as usual had been efficiency itself. He had arranged for a motorcade of cars, buses, armoured vehicles and trucks to take the leaders' closest ministers, aides and their families south to safety. His attention to detail went right down to the allocation of seats. Göring himself left with a large escort and a truck full of booty from Carinhall, his country estate to the north of Berlin. Two trainloads of other treasures – paintings, sculptures, tapestries, fine wines, cigars, morocco-bound books – had preceded him.

Meanwhile, the two other trains, *Adler* and *Dohle*, carrying the $15 million of Reich reserves, trundled slowly south along what remained of the Reich's railway network.

The military situation discussed in the Führerbunker conference was utterly irretrievable. The Allied vice had now so tightened on the Reich that its frontiers were largely defined by the Alps. It held the west of Czechoslovakia, Austria west of Vienna, northern Italy, north-western Yugoslavia and southern Bavaria. From all points of the compass the Allies were now closing on the mountains.

To the west, the Allied forces approaching the Alps were General de Lattre de Tassigny's First French and the US Seventh Armies, together comprising General Jacob Devers's Sixth Army

Group. This was tasked with forcing its way through Bavaria into Austria to destroy the Alpine Redoubt. The French, setting out from Lake Constance, were to confront the enemy forces in the western Austrian province of Vorarlberg, at the west end of which lay the resort of St Anton. The US army was to head further east to Innsbruck, capital of the Tyrol, the province adjoining Vorarlberg to the east. A third thrust was to take the form of Patton's Third Army, on loan from General Bradley. This was to head for Salzburg, rather over a hundred miles east of Innsbruck. It, too, was thought to be part of the Alpine Redoubt.

Coming up from the south towards the Italian Alps were General Mark Clark's US Fifth and British Eighth Armies. By 18 April, the Eighth Army was now through Argenta and its armour was racing to meet the US forces advancing from the east. The objective was to stop SS-Obergruppenführer Karl Wolff and Army Group C in Bologna at the northern foot of the Apennines, the southern edge of the Po plain. By 23 April both Allied armies had reached the river Po, in Italy a natural barrier of similar significance to the Rhine. Beyond lay the foothills of the Italian Alps. The Italian partisans – the National Liberation Committee – called for a general rising. At long last, the hour of liberation really had come.

To the east, Tito's forces in Yugoslavia amounted to 800,000. They were now dubbed the Yugoslav Army of National Liberation (JANL), and were a formidable threat. Tito's ambitions for the Fourth Army of the JANL were not restricted to driving out the remains of Generaloberst Löhr's Heeresgruppe E from the old borders of Yugoslavia. His plan was to go beyond those frontiers and seize the southern provinces of Austria, including the cities of Fiume, Trieste and Pola. The Yugoslav leader also had ambitions for joining forces with the communist partisans to the west in Italy, even those in France.[26]

The JANL offensive opened on 12 April 1945. Ten days later, just as the British Eighth and the US Fifth Armies reached the Po, and just as the US Seventh Army headed for Innsbruck, the JANL was within reach of Trieste. It was also casting its eyes towards

Klagenfurt, capital of the eastern Austrian Alpine province of Carinthia.

It was also on that day of 23 April that Speer returned to the bunker under the Chancellery to say goodbye to Hitler. Stepping down into that Stygian world, Speer came across Reichsleiter Martin Bormann, who had masterminded the creation of the Nazi headquarters at Berchtesgaden. Like Göring and the other high party officials who had already fled to the 'redoubt', Bormann thought the caution represented by Berchtesgaden better than the valour embodied in the shambles that remained of Berlin. He urged Speer to persuade Hitler to fly – even at this eleventh hour – to Obersalzberg.

When Speer was ushered into Hitler's presence deep in the bunker, the Führer was busy with the succession planning now so much the vogue amongst business chief executives. He cross-questioned Speer on the merits of Grossadmiral Karl Dönitz, a submariner who in happier days had conceived the devastatingly successful 'wolf-pack' U-boat tactics in the Battle of the Atlantic. Speer might have been excused for thinking the question academic. Germany's principal cities lay in ruins, her industry was shattered, her armies overrun, her population on the point of starvation. What the Germans later called Stunde Null (zero hour) of the complete and unconditional surrender was only a fortnight away. With Germany cut in two by the Allies, Dönitz – Hitler explained – would be charged with setting up an administration in the north from his headquarters in Plön, Schleswig. The loyal Kesselring was to be Dönitz's opposite number in the south. Then Hitler turned to his own fate. 'What do you think? Should I stay here or fly to Berchtesgaden? Jodl has told me that tomorrow is the last chance for that.' Speer advised Hitler to remain in Berlin. 'It seems to me better, if it must be, that you end your life here in the capital as the Fuehrer rather than in your weekend house.'

Hitler concurred: 'I too have resolved to stay here. I only wanted to hear your view once more.' Perhaps there were other reasons. As Antony Beevor comments, 'The Fall of Berchtesgaden did not have quite the same ring as the Fall of Berlin.'[27]

5

Hitler, though, had not quite done with Berchtesgaden, the resort where all his great thoughts had germinated. Scarcely had the matter been settled when the omnipresent Bormann scuttled in. He was bearing a telegram from Göring. The General-feldmarschall had been as good as his word. He had now reached Berchtesgaden with his looted goods and opened up his chalet at Obersalzberg; the mountain complex was still deep in the late winter's drifting snow. There he had indeed been busy. He had scrupulously reviewed the arrangements for the safe storage of his collection from Carinhall, including works by Botticelli, Rembrandt, Dürer, Gobelin and Picasso. He had then returned to his chalet, opened his safe in the study, and drawn out a steel box. Within this lay a copy of Hitler's decree of 29 June 1941. This had been the upshot of Rudolf Hess's strange flight to England on 10 May 1941. As Hitler's deputy could no longer discharge his duties from confinement in England (initially in the Tower of London), Göring had then been promoted to replace him. Göring had this in writing.

In the chalet's study the Marshal pondered the document. It designated Göring himself – creator of the Luftwaffe, Reichs-minister of aviation, Reichsminister of forestry and President of Prussia – as Hitler's successor. It was to come into effect should the Führer die or become incapacitated. Even at this late hour, Göring's appetite for power was unbounded. Given the imminent fall of the capital to the Soviet forces, Göring's telegram posed an innocent question. On the assumption that Hitler was to remain in Berlin – therefore to be captured or die a Heldentod, a hero's death – should Göring assume the leadership of the Reich? This missive was followed by another cable addressed to Joachim von Ribbentrop but copied to Hitler.

I have asked the Fuehrer to provide me with instructions by 10 p.m. April 23. If by this time it is apparent that the Fuehrer has been deprived of his freedom of action to conduct the affairs of the Reich, his decree of June 29, 1941, becomes effective, according to which I am heir to all his offices as his deputy. [If] by 12 midnight April 23, 1945, you receive no other word either from the Fuehrer directly or from me, you are to come to me at once by air.[28]

Speer was now at a loose end, for he had no armaments industry to manage. As a result of the toils of the USAAF, RAF and various Allied armies, there was none. All 'the good Nazi' could do was to try to sabotage Hitler's 'scorched earth' policy. He followed these dramatic events as a disinterested observer. Bormann and Göring had never agreed. Here was Bormann's opportunity to worst – preferably annihilate – the portly air marshal. Göring, claimed the bull-necked Bormann to Hitler, was launching a coup d'état. This latest cable was obviously an ultimatum. 'Goering is engaged in treason!' he raged to Hitler and Speer, his face empurpled. 'He's already sending telegrams to members of the government and announcing that on the basis of his powers he will assume your office at twelve o'clock tonight, *mein Führer.*' Hitler, hitherto calm, was incensed. Bormann had played his cards well. 'I've known it all along,' Hitler blazed. 'I know that Goering is lazy. He let the air force go to pot. He was corrupt. His example made corruption possible in our state. Besides he's been a drug addict for years. I've known it all along.'[29]

With that, Hitler at once had Göring stripped of his succession to the Third Reich and gave orders that he should be arrested for high treason. This carried the death penalty. In the light of Göring's long services to the Nazi Party, this – Hitler decreed – would be commuted: provided he at once resigned from all his offices. He was to answer yes or no, *nein* or *ja*. Immediately.

Bormann himself kindly drafted the cable to Obersalzberg to this effect. This was excellent. The outcome was predictable. But the Reichsleiter felt it wise to go one step further entirely on his own initiative. The SS detachment based at Obersalzberg was still on guard in its barracks. These were at the Hotel zum Türken, a few hundred yards uphill from the Berghof. By this time perhaps little could have surprised the leaders of the detachment, Obersturmbannführer Hans Frank and Obersturmführer von Bredow. In ten years Berchtesgaden had changed from a remote resort in the Bavarian Alps to the epicentre of a movement that defined the first half of the twentieth century and gave a new twist to the term 'civilisation'. The cable the pair received from Bormann on the evening of 23 April 1945 ordered them to arrest Göring for high treason. They would answer with their lives if they failed.

Frank and von Bredow hastily buckled on their pistols and routed out the SS guard. It was a cold night. Göring's chalet was uphill, through the snow. At shortly after midnight there was a thunderous knock at the door of the chalet and Göring found himself under house arrest. The Generalfeldmarschall was apparently unperturbed, confident, serene. To his wife Emmy, he remarked, 'Everything will be cleared up by tomorrow. It's simply a matter of a misunderstanding. Sleep peacefully, as I am going to do. Can you imagine for a single moment that Adolf Hitler would have me arrested today – I who have followed him through thick and thin for the last twenty-three years? Come now! It's really unthinkable!'[30]

The Reichsbank gold and currency reserves dispatched from Berlin on the trains *Adler* and *Dohle* had now finally reached their destination.

This was Mittenwald in the Bavarian Alps, a short way south of the secret Messerschmitt factory in Oberammergau, itself the neighbour of Garmisch-Partenkirchen. The reserves had been transferred to Opel Blitz trucks, a convoy of which drew up at the officers' mess of the Mountain Infantry Training School on the afternoon of 23 April. It was here that the late General-feldmarschall Rommel – a victim of the aftermath of the 20 July bomb plot – had sought advice about Operation Achse, the seizure of the Italian Alpine passes. Now his adviser, General der Gebirgstruppe Valentin Feurstein, was commanding the defence of Bregenz, the city just inside the Austrian–Swiss border, 125 miles west. The matter of the Reichsbank's reserves was placed in the hands of the school's current commanding officer, the forty-year-old Oberst Franz Wilhelm Pfeiffer. The responsibility for the reserves lay ultimately with the Reichsbank chief, Walther

Funk. His officials accompanying the booty told Pfeiffer they were putting him in charge of concealing the reserves until the whirlwind of the Allied advance had passed by. When a new Bavarian state rose from the ashes of the Reich, it could then be financed. This was foresight. Pfeiffer, a tall, balding and dutiful career army officer, was not best pleased with the enormity of the task that had been foisted on him. Nevertheless, he found somewhere to store the reserves: the bowling alley of the officers' mess. Then, under the watchful eyes of the Reichsbank officials, Pfeiffer and his men duly unloaded the sacks of currency and 364 bags of gold.

6

Meanwhile, the story of the surrender of the Wehrmacht and SS forces in Italy continued to unfold. Just as Hitler in the Berlin bunker was dealing with Göring's high treason, Dulles in the Herrengasse in Berne received a phone call. It was his friend Colonel Max Waibel, the Swiss intelligence chief. It placed Dulles in a conundrum. 'He had astounding news,' remembered Dulles.

General Wolff, his adjutant, Major Wenner, and one of Vietinghoff's [Generaloberst Heinrich von Vietinghoff, who had now replaced the promoted Kesselring] high staff officers, Lt. Col. Viktor von Schweinitz, were on their way to Switzerland. They were coming to surrender . . . Wolff and Schweinitz were ready to go to Caserta immediately to arrange for the capitulation of all the German forces, Wehrmacht and SS, in North Italy. They proposed an immediate meeting with me in Lucerne to arrange the details of the trip to Allied headquarters. And I was under the strictest military orders to have no dealings with them![31]

Dulles at once cabled AFHQ in Caserta to allow him to reopen the negotiations that he had so reluctantly closed. AFHQ cabled Washington. Truman, still fearful of compromising relations with Stalin, refused. The Joint Chiefs of Staff could only suggest to Dulles that Wolff should be kept in play by using Waibel as an intermediary.

Like Hitler in his bunker, Dulles was incensed. He broke two of his best pipes in his anger. In jeopardy were the lives of tens of thousands of Mark Clark's Allied troops, similar numbers of Vietinghoff's Germans, and his own great coup. The JCS's suggestion also placed Waibel in an impossible situation. The Swiss were keen enough to see a brokered armistice, but as a statutory neutral it was difficult for them to be seen to engage in peace negotiations on behalf of one of the belligerents. Waibel knew that his political masters would be aghast at the prospect. Nevertheless, he agreed to meet Wolff in Lucerne and start talks. He could not reveal that Dulles himself was under orders not to treat with them. On meeting Waibel on 24 April, the hawk-nosed Wolff not unreasonably enquired, 'Where is Herr Dulles?'

*

The following morning, 25 April 1945, shortly after dawn, 359 Lancasters from Bomber Groups 1, 5 and 8 in Lincolnshire could be seen to the north of the Alps over Basel, carefully skirting Swiss airspace. They were heading east, escorted by RAF and USAAF Mustang long-distance fighters and an RAF Mosquito Pathfinder squadron. One of the bomber pilots logged:

The Alps were crossed at 16,000 feet, just over the peaks. It began to get light at this altitude and the mountaintops jutted out more and more vividly from the darkness below. As the sun rose, the details of the scene appeared more clearly: the views and landscapes were so varied and beautiful in the rosy dawn that one's attention was fully occupied in admiration.

The navigator recalled me to the task in hand by suddenly exclaiming: 'Ten minutes to go, Skipper. See anything?'

There wasn't anything I could see apart from the mountain slopes covered with foliage and the bombers before and around us. It was now broad daylight and I began to look about for Berchtesgaden. There was still one minute to go when a batch of colored marker flares appeared – the Pathfinders had located the target. Fairly intensive flak broke out in the distance. Amidst the flares, I could see the flashing explosions of bombs dropped by the Lancaster before me.

I steered to port and began to run up to the target. I could see Berchtesgaden [actually Obersalzberg] clearly in the light of the markers: it looked like a wall built into the steep rocky slope . . . the flak became thicker and the shells burst closer to us, some quite near. The bomb-aimer got busy. 'Open the door [bomb bay], Skipper,' he began. 'Skipper, steady, port, a little more – steady –' and finally: 'Bombs gone!'[32]

Irmgard Paul was at school in Berchtesgaden. Over the past three months the air-raid sirens had screamed no fewer than forty-eight times to clear the pleasant streets of the Bavarian resort of humanity. This time, at 09:30, Irmgard and four of her school friends – Else, Wiebke, Barbel and Ingrid – were caught out in the open on the slopes of Obersalzberg. 'Let's run to my house, it's the nearest!' she shouted to her friends. They dashed up the sandy, tree-lined road toward Haus Linden, still covered in patches of snow. They were too late. The bombs were already plummeting down towards them. After each detonation of the 500-kilogram bombs a Pentecostal blast funnelled down the narrow valley. The five girls had to grab the spruce trees to avoid being blown off their feet. 'The earth shook, and the air was filled with the rumble of airplane motors, the whistle of falling bombs, the detonations, and the wind that followed.'

After forty-five minutes of terror, it was all over. Irmgard was able to see how fortunate – blessed – the town of Berchtesgaden itself had been.

Usually when the sirens wailed the Obersalzberg complex was shrouded in the acrid smoke of the chemical smokescreen system installed in 1943. With the Reich's industry and communications in ruins, the supplies of the chemical had run out. The RAF Lancasters were able to bomb Obersalzberg with – for 1945 – pinpoint accuracy and to avoid collateral damage to the town of Berchtesgaden on the far side of the river Ache. The town and its inhabitants were all safe. Irmgard commented, 'There were those who considered this a miracle; the Lord Himself had protected us, evidenced by the sign of a cross they saw in the sky. I, however, was puzzled, and would be for a long time. Why of all places should He protect Berchtesgaden, when all of Europe was in ashes?'[33]

Obersalzberg itself was quite another story. 'The plateau had become a chaotic brown and black mess of tree-stumps resembling charred matchsticks, irregular dark craters and ruins that still smoked.' Remembered Irmgard: '"It's all gone", I said to no one in particular.'[34]

The Berghof lay in ruins. Hitler's mountain headquarters, the haven where he had conceived the European war, where he had entertained the Duke of Windsor, berated Schuschnigg, Daladier, Halifax and Chamberlain, where he had toyed with Mussolini, where he had given the directives for the invasion of Great Britain, Yugoslavia and the Soviet Union, where he had developed Operation Achse with Rommel, where he had been told of the impending siege of Stalingrad, where he had first heard the news of the Normandy landings, where he had so enjoyed Bergfried – the peace of the mountains – was no more.

Only the Kehlstein itself, the great Watzmann and – still capped with snow – the Untersberg remained. It was surprising that Barbarossa had not been awakened from his long sleep.

FIFTEEN

Storming the Eagle's Nest

*We had seen terrible sights from combat across
Europe but what we were observing was a climax
to the things human beings do to their fellow man.*

ROBERT B. PERSINGER

I

In the aftermath of the bombing of Obersalzberg, the inhabitants of Berchtesgaden ventured out to pick over the ruins of the Nazi headquarters.

Hitherto much of the plateau had been sealed off, closely guarded and discouragingly designated the Führersperrgebiet ('leader's territory'). Now these arrangements were no longer enforced by the SS. They seemed pointless. The locals edged past the gates swinging idly on their hinges, past the empty guard-houses and into the forbidden land. Everywhere was a smell of burning, of scorched earth, of cordite. Obersalzberg had been devastated. Besides the Berghof, the Hotel Platterhof, three farms, the chalets of Bormann and Göring, and the SS headquarters at the Hotel zum Türken had received direct hits. Around forty people had died. The wooded mountainside looked like a tornado had swept through: the trees uprooted, smashed and tossed aside. In the remains of the SS barracks, Irmgard Paul found some of the SS troops demob-happy, distributing 'champagne, cigars, and specialty foods we had not seen in years' to the astonished villagers. Yet in the barracks yard, 'a group of diehards was still practicing goose-stepping to an officer's commands'. The community was in flux, not knowing which way to turn. 'I asked Mutti [her mother] again what would happen to us when the war was over. She didn't answer – how could she when she didn't know? Suddenly my fear gave way to an intense anger at her ignorance, impotence and sadness. She should not have let all this happen.'[1]

Hermann Göring and his family had survived the air raid, sheltered in the Obersalzberg bunker. When the dust had settled he had emerged from the shelter and looked around. The sight was displeasing, indeed it was all too reminiscent of Berlin. Feeling that the complex no longer offered the comforts of the past, the Marshal thought he should move to another property of his nearby, Mauterndorf Castle. He raised the matter with Obersturmbannführer Frank, head of the SS guard, his captor. Frank had just received another cable from Bormann. It was threatening. 'The situation in Berlin is more tense. If Berlin and we should fall, the traitors of April 23 [Göring and his complicit ADCs] must be exterminated. Men, do your duty. Your life and honour depend on it.'[2] Frank felt on consideration that Berlin and Bormann were far way, the Allies were nearer, and Göring was closer still. The Generalfeldmarschall was surely the best man to strike a deal with the Allies. Frank glanced at the ruins of the SS barracks, latched the safety catch on his pistol and told Göring that he thought Mauterndorf an excellent idea.

Not far away in Mittenwald, preparations were also in hand for a move. Although the Allies knew nothing of the Messerschmitt factory at Oberammergau or the location of the Reich's gold reserves, the road and rail communications through the region of Garmisch-Partenkirchen ran south into the Inn valley to Innsbruck itself and the Tyrol, thence across the Brenner Pass into Italy. They were of strategic importance, and they were now in the sights of the 10th Armored Division of General Patch's Seventh Army. Between sunrise and sunset of 23 April the Division had captured twenty-eight towns. Garmisch-Partenkirchen was next stop. Forewarned by the local commander at the resort, Oberst Pfeiffer scratched his bald head. The bowling alley in the officers' mess scarcely passed muster as a place of concealment for the reserves. On the afternoon of 25 April a fatigue party was once more at work in Mittenwald, loading the Opel trucks. The next destination for the gold was a remote spot called Ensiedl, some fourteen miles north of Mittenwald. As Göring set off for Mauterndorf, Pfeiffer jumped aboard the leading truck and headed north.

Meanwhile, 280 miles to the west in Lucerne, Colonel Max Waibel had been having trouble with Obergruppenführer Karl Wolff. There was the SS general, anxious to come to terms with the Allies, and the chief Allied negotiator – Allen Dulles – was nowhere to be seen. After twenty-four hours, Wolff and his fellow officers were becoming testy, suspicious. General Mark Clark's two armies were pushing into the Alps and – in a bitterly contested ten-day battle – had now taken the regional capital and communications hub of Bologna. This was 225 miles south from the vital Brenner Pass, Wolff's principal remaining line of escape back to the Reich. The general began to suspect that he was being strung along to prevent him achieving any sort of managed retreat for the Army Group C forces. As he pointed out to Waibel, the Allies were also hazarding all the major industrial complexes in northern Italy, including the port of Genoa – Switzerland's lifeline. This was earmarked for destruction under Hitler's 'scorched earth' policy. Where the hell was Dulles?

Actually, the spymaster was remarkably close. Anticipating that Truman's order banning the negotiations would be lifted, he had shifted camp to Lucerne. He was being briefed daily, sometimes hourly, by Waibel. Dulles was pressurising AFHQ in Caserta and AFHQ in turn pressurising the Chiefs of Staff in Washington. On the day of the Berchtesgaden bombing, 25 April, Wolff's patience ran out and he caught the train back to the Italian frontier. According to Dulles, he returned 'to keep order and avert ruthless violence and destruction in northern Italy'.[3]

If the Wehrmacht's Army Group C in Italy was fighting on, so too were the forces to the north in Austria. This was the challenge for General Devers's Sixth Army Group, comprising General de Lattre de Tassigny's First French Army and General Patch's Seventh US Army.

On 29 April 1945, units of the French Eighth Armoured Division crossed the border from Germany into Austria. German resistance was stiff. First there was Bregenz on the eastern shores of the Bodensee. Attempts at negotiating an armistice with the city commander Generalleutnant Valentin Feurstein failed, and the capital of the Vorarlberg was heavily bombed. It had survived six years of war unscathed. After this westernmost Austrian city fell, the French were able to advance eastwards only very slowly into the Alpine Vorarlberg itself. The German rearguard, sometimes comprising only machine-gun groups, slowed the French enough to allow other Wehrmacht forces to reinforce the front to the north-east. Here Patch's Seventh Army was pushing into Munich. On 29 April the 45th Division was engaged in house-to-house fighting against the Munich SS Standarte in the grounds of the university – the home of the White Rose martyrs. Meanwhile the French, following the valley of the Inn east down towards Innsbruck, were so hampered by the rearguard that Fritz Molden's O5 resistance forces were brought into play. They led General de Lattre de Tassigny's forces through the Wehrmacht positions by mountain paths, high passes still knee-, waist- and shoulder-deep in snow, to cut off the Germans from behind.

To the east of the French, some units of Patch's Seventh Army then headed south from Munich towards Innsbruck. Others were driving due south towards Berchtesgaden. Both spearheads found the country descending into chaos. There were legions of surrendering German troops, there were villages where the Austrians and Bavarians broke into applause, waved flags and showered kisses on the advancing troops, and yet there was also sporadic and in some cases fanatical resistance to the onward march of the Allies. This came from the German equivalents of the French maquis and the Italian partisans, dubbed by Goebbels the Werewolves. A Seventh Army GI observed:

At the time I could not understand it, this resistance, this pointless resistance to our advance. The war was all over – our columns were spreading across the whole of Germany and Austria. We were irresistible. We could conquer the world; that was our growing conviction. And the enemy had nothing. Yet he resisted and in some places with an implacable fanaticism. I know now what it was that animated the enemy although I didn't then, in 1945. The world of those children of the Hitler Youth was coming to an end. Soon there would be nothing left. No parades, no songs, no swastikas, no marching and no fighting for the Faith – for the belief in Hitler. The roof was falling in on those children's ideals. Denied the opportunity to be real soldiers, to wear a proper uniform and to fight as soldiers in a formal unit, those kids were determined to show us that they knew how to sacrifice themselves.[4]

Dulles, at least, was determined to stop the slaughter. On 27 April his calls to AFHQ in Caserta and thence to Washington were at last answered. Churchill and Truman had conferred. The Prime Minister had then carefully cabled Stalin.

The German envoys, with whom all contact was broken by us some days ago, have now arrived again on the Lake of Lucerne. They claim to have full powers to surrender the Army in Italy. Field-Marshal Alexander is therefore being told that he is free to permit these envoys to come to AFHQ in Italy ... Will you please send Russian representatives forthwith to Field-Marshal Alexander's headquarters.[5]

For his part, President Truman had girded himself and given Dulles permission to resume negotiations with Wolff. The SS Obergruppenführer still had his own ideas. Taking his life in his hands, he flew north to the little that remained of Berlin to seek a final audience with Hitler. The Führer, Wolff said, 'seemed in low spirits but had not given up hope'. He told Wolff, 'We must fight on to gain time; in two more months, the break between the Anglo-Saxons and the Russians will come about and then I shall join the party which first approaches me. It makes no difference which.'[6]

Wolff returned to his headquarters in Bolzano, the capital of the South Tyrol seized nineteen months earlier by Rommel in the course of Operation Achse. Here wiser counsels prevailed. Hitler, as he had told Speer, had now put Kesselring in charge of the whole of the defence of the Reich's west. This had left Italy to Generaloberst Heinrich von Vietinghoff. This change in leadership and – in Churchill's words – 'the force of facts overcame German hesitancies'.[7] On 29 April at AFHQ in Caserta, two of Vietinghoff's representatives effected the final, formal and unconditional surrender of the General's forces in Italy. So ended Operation Sunrise, and with it the prospect of a full-scale confrontation in the Italian Alps between Army Group C and the Allies' Fifth and Eighth Armies. Now, for Eisenhower at SHAEF, the prospect of a general surrender seemed ever closer.

Dulles was invited to witness the ceremony at AFHQ in Caserta. He refused, claiming that 'My presence at the surrender ceremony might well have been discovered by the press and have blown the security of the operation we had so carefully preserved up to this point.'[8] The truth was that he was once again suffering from gout. As to this being a major coup for Dulles, it was all a little late. 'The main impact of the surrender negotiations . . . was to be on relations between the Allies.'[9]

2

That same day Hitler married Eva Braun in Berlin. The thirty-three-year-old had had to wait some time: the couple had been lovers since 1932. Addressed by one of the bunker staff as 'Gnädiges Fräulein' (gracious lady), Braun corrected, 'You may safely call me Frau Hitler.'[10] The Führer then busied himself with dictating a political testament and his will. The testament placed the blame for the debacle of the previous few years firmly in the hands of 'international Jewry'. In thanking his secretaries for this work, Hitler said that he wished his generals had been equally reliable.

The following morning was 30 April 1945. The news was bad. Mussolini was dead – he who, in Hugh Trevor-Roper's words in The Last Days of Hitler, was the Führer's 'partner in crime, the herald of Fascism, who had first shown to Hitler the possibilities of dictatorship in modern Europe'.[11] Il Duce had been captured by Italian partisans of the 52nd Garibaldi Brigade at the village of Dongo near Lake Como. He had abandoned the collapsing Italian Social Republic in Salò and was attempting to escape over the Alps to Switzerland. Badoglio's 'Dictator Number One' was shot the following day. He and his mistress Clara Petacci were strung up in an Esso petrol station in Milan's Piazzale Loreto for the edification of the newly liberated Milanese. Closer to home in Berlin, the situation was no better. Soviet forces had now reached the Potsdamer Platz, the Weidendammer Bridge over the river Spree, the Tiergarten and the underground railway tunnel in the Vossstrasse. The Chancellery itself was within hours of being broached. Mussolini's end was now smiling at the Führer himself.

After lunch that day, Hitler and Eva Braun withdrew into their suite. Their purpose was obvious, disclosed, agreed. On hearing a single shot, the remaining members of Hitler's court discovered the pair lying dead. Hitler had shot himself, his wife had taken poison. 'Dictator Number Two' was presumably on his way to Valhalla, the Teutonic 'hall of the slain'.

It was the early evening of 30 April 1945 and the loyal Reichsleiter Bormann had a job. He cabled Grossadmiral Karl Dönitz in Plön in Schleswig with the news that, in place of Göring, Hitler had appointed the Grand Admiral himself his successor. This came as a complete surprise to Dönitz. At 10.20 the following evening, he broadcast on Hamburg radio. Hitler had died fighting at the head of his troops in Berlin, he said. In Washington, President Truman, asked about the reported deaths of Hitler and Mussolini, commented, 'I am very happy they are out of the way.'[12] Churchill, asked in the House of Commons whether he wished to comment, replied drily, 'No, other than that the situation is more satisfying than it was five years ago.'[13]

Back in Berchtesgaden, it was first rumoured that Hitler had died leading his troops in defence of the Chancellery. It was a Heldentod – a hero's death; the German people expected nothing less. A later rumour was more widely credited: that the creator of the Third Reich had taken his own life. Radio reception was poor, remembered Irmgard Paul. 'A rare clear voice on the radio confirmed Hitler's death. Profoundly shocked, Mutti absorbed the news, not so much because she mourned

Hitler but because she felt so deeply betrayed. Our only hope now was that the Führer's suicide would speed up the end and stop the bloodshed.'[14] The question now was whether the Red Army or the Western Allies would be the first to reach Berchtesgaden. The prospect of the Soviets petrified the people. They had been taught by Goebbels that the Red Army were little better than animals. This was entirely borne out by the Soviet troops' behaviour in Vienna – which they had reached on 13 April – and subsequently Berlin. In both the capitals looting was the order of the day, the inhabitants were shot at random, and rape was endemic. 'Our fear mounted when we heard that the Russians were approaching from Vienna at about the same rate as the U.S. troops from the northwest.'[15]

3

It was May Day, and in Mittenwald Colonel Pfeiffer had endured a vexing seventy-two hours. On the night of 25–6 April he had safely supervised the movement of the Reichsbank's $15 million to Einsiedl under cover of darkness. For twenty-four hours the reserves had been under armed guard in a chalet on the wooded slopes of the Steinriegel above the village. A fatigue party had then prepared a cache further up the mountain: on the Steinriegel itself and the adjoining Klausenkopf. The Mittenwald mountain warfare school was – for obvious reasons – less mechanised than the armoured units that had brought blitzkrieg to western Europe precisely five years previously. Pfeiffer had at his disposal 5,000 mules – smarter and more sure-footed in the Alps than men, horses or indeed Panzers. Eight of these beasts were shepherded over from Mittenwald and loaded up. 'By dawn on 28 April the gold and currency reserves . . . lay snug in their watertight holes in the frost-rimed ground of the Bavarian Alps'.[16] Although the OSS now had a scent of the plunder, they would be there for some time.

If Pfeiffer expected congratulations for a difficult job well executed in double-quick time, he was disappointed. On 29 April Patch's 10th Armored Division reached Oberammergau, and the valley down to the Tyrol and the vital Brenner Pass – via Mittenwald – was at its mercy. Pfeiffer's orders from on high were abrupt. 'Do everything possible to block the route between Garmisch and the Tyrol . . . the fate of the Alpine Fortress lies in your hands!'[17]

It was too late. Not only was the 10th Armored an unstoppable force, the USAAF was thundering down in support. The local commander in Garmisch-Partenkirchen was a Gebirgsjäger officer called Sturmbannführer Michael Pössinger. Recognising the inevitable, he went to meet the Americans at Oberammergau. All he could do now was to try to save the valley, not least the 80,000 wounded and refugees now crowded into Garmisch-Partenkirchen. The American commander was obdurate. A 200-bomber strike force was – as he spoke – on its way to flatten everything between Oberammergau and Innsbruck. The bombers could not be turned back. At his wits' end, Pössinger went down on his knees to the American. At last a message was patched through to the USAAF, the strike force turned back, and the valley was saved. Pössinger was then seized as a hostage and tied to the turret of the leading US tank. At 6.45 on the evening of 29 April, Garmisch-Partenkirchen fell to the Allies.

Four days later on 3 May, a curious scene was enacted at the bulging twin town. It was a photo opportunity with captured German rocket scientists, led by Wernher von Braun. As part of the dispersal programme that had followed the RAF raid on Peenemünde in August 1943, the research station's wind tunnel and much of the technical support staff had been removed to Kochel am See, forty-five miles south of Munich. In the first two months of 1945, von Braun and his team were even more mindful than the Nazi leaders of the approaching end. Hitherto the Nazi Party had been an admirable supporter of von Braun's appliance of science to his rocket ambitions. Now it seemed he might have to find new benefactors.

Following the liberation of the Mittelbau-Dora V-2 works in the Harz mountains by US forces on 11 April, von Braun's team was hastily dispatched from Kochel by Obergruppenführer Hans Kammler to Oberammergau. The Allies might be interested in the man whose rocket plant had consumed 20,000 lives – leaving aside the rather more modest numbers of the victims on the receiving end of the weapon, mainly in London and Antwerp. In Oberammergau, where the Passion Play had once been staged, von Braun persuaded the SS guards that his valuable team would be safer somewhere less conspicuous than the Messerschmitt works. He settled at Haus Ingeburg in Oberjoch on the old border between Germany and Austria, a once fashionable skiing resort about thirty miles west of Garmisch-Partenkirchen. Here, right at the end of the skiing season, von Braun's group enjoyed a pleasant limbo between one life and the next: Kammler had finally abandoned the scientists to their own devices, concerning himself with his own safety. On 2 May, two days after Hitler's death, with the US forces everywhere, von Braun thought it time to surrender to the Allies. He sent out his young brother Magnus, who spoke a smattering of English, to surrender. Cycling down the hill from the resort on a fine spring morning, Magnus – looking like he had just come off the piste – came across a unit of an Anti-Tank Company, 324th Infantry Regiment, 44th Infantry Division. He claimed that the inventor of the infamous V-2 was within hailing distance and wanted to surrender. The interpreter Private First Class Fred Schneikert was sceptical of this sunburned young man: 'I think you're nuts,' he told von Braun, 'but we'll investigate.'

Very soon the scientists found themselves in front of the cameras of the world's press in Garmisch-Partenkirchen.[18]

4

There were now no fewer than three Allied armies heading for Innsbruck, capital of the Tyrol. The city was still supposed by SHAEF to be the headquarters of the Alpine Redoubt. There was the French First Army still driving south-east from Bregenz, and the US Seventh Army advancing south from Munich (the latter knocking on the door of Mittenwald). Then there was the British

Eighth Army coming up from Italy and the south.

In Italy, the surrender at Caserta on 29 April engineered by Dulles had certainly not brought an immediate end to hostilities in the country's Alps. Vietinghoff's Army Group C units were scattered, communications were poor, and there were still SS and Wehrmacht officers who felt their loyalty to Hitler stretched beyond his shallow grave. Moreover, the surrender of forces in Italy did not apply to Army Group G in neighbouring Austria, imminent though a surrender there – and indeed a general surrender of all German forces – might well be.

Accordingly, General Mark Clark ordered the 88th Division of the British Eighth Army to head for Innsbruck through the Brenner Pass – the gateway from Italy to Austria, where Mussolini and Hitler had been wont to meet to discuss the dismemberment of Europe in the early months of the war. The Eighth had crossed the river Po on 25 April and now had the southern flanks of the Brandenberg Alps in its sights. The Brenner was around two hundred miles due north, and the second half of the route would be literally and figuratively an uphill struggle. Bill Morgan of the 351st Infantry Regiment commented:

We all knew that the Brenner was the German Army's lifeline and that the Tedeschi [Germans] would not sit idly by as we cut it. The Brenner is about twelve miles long and goes through the mountains. There was only one road and God knows what Kraut troops there were ready to oppose us. It shook me the casual way in which it was put to us. The 88th will penetrate the Brenner with the objective of capturing Innsbruck. I would love to meet the Staff Colonel who picked that one out of the hat for us.[19]

As it so turned out, the 88th was saved the trouble – at least in the Tyrolese capital – by the Austrian resistance, O5. Led by thirty-six-year-old Karl Gruber, this was a force in Innsbruck of only eighty-five men. On 2 May Gruber's partisans seized the Wehrmacht's Innsbruck HQ, capturing the commander of the whole southern front, General Johannes Böheim. Gruber then took the city's radio station by the ruse of pretending to be German reinforcements. In the bright dawn of the communications age,

Final operations, 1945

this was one of the levers of power.

By way of forcing the pace of events, O5 announced that at 17:00 on the following day, 3 May, a regional armistice would come into effect in the Tyrol and Vorarlberg, Salzburg, parts of Carinthia and the Steiermark. This was virtually the whole of Alpine Austria. The populace was to offer no resistance to the advancing Allied forces, to placard their houses with the old Austrian flag or white sheets, and to wear armbands in the old colours of Austria: red and white. The Nazi salute so deplored by Maria von Trapp was henceforth abolished. The finale in the broadcast was the trumpet call that had brought down the walls of Jericho: 'The hour of liberation has come'.[20]

The wording was interesting. The US Seventh Army had been told to treat Austria as a conquered country. The Austrians saw the Western Allies as liberators, buoyed as they were by the Moscow Declaration of 1943 that promised Austria a return to independence. On the evening of 3 May units of the US 103rd

Infantry Division, guided by liaison officers from O5, entered the Alpine city. It was snowing heavily, but Innsbruck was *en fête*, the US forces embraced by the Tyrolese. There was a good deal of yodelling and singing of Austrian folk songs. O5 had diplomatically hoisted the Stars and Stripes over the town hall, one of the buildings to have survived the concerted Allied raids on the city. Here it fluttered alluringly in the breeze.

For Innsbruck, the bridge on the river Inn, the war was over.

To complete the rout of the Germans, the US 411th Regiment was then ordered by General Patton due south from Innsbruck twenty-five miles to the Brenner Pass. The Seventh Army's last combat mission in Europe was to link up with the 88th Division of the British Eighth Army. At 10:51 on 4 May 1945 units of the 411th ran across the 88th at Sterzing, about twelve miles south of the Brenner. This was Bill Morgan's unit. The Tyrol was free.

So too – or very nearly – was Europe. As Churchill put it, 'And so all three "fronts", Western, Eastern, and Southern, once thousands of miles apart, at last came together, crushing the life out of the German armies. Their encirclement had been completed by Montgomery in the north . . . The end was near.'[21]

On 5 May, another of the O5 liaison officers reached Innsbruck. This was Fritz Molden, Dulles's agent K28. The streets were full of partying Tyrolese, and the government offices safely in the hands of Molden's old friend, Karl Gruber.

Our sense of euphoria was tremendous. After seven years we had a country of our own once more; Austria had risen out of the ashes . . . it seemed scarcely conceivable, and months would go by before I could even begin to take everything in. Here I was at Innsbruck in Austria, sitting in the Dollinger [a famous old inn] with my friends, and we – they and I – were free men. We could go out into the street and look everyone in the eye, without having to show our papers or worry about saying Austria instead of Ostmark; nor would we ever again have to utter the words 'Heil Hitler'.

Molden's work with Dulles, his midnight tramps over the high Alps dodging SS patrols, had borne fruit.

And that same day – Saturday 5 May – units of General Devers's Sixth Army Group reached Berchtesgaden in force.

By now it was beginning to be accepted by Eisenhower and his staff at SHAEF that there was little substance to the Alpine Redoubt and that, in the aftermath of Hitler's death, only fragments of the Wehrmacht and SS retained the will to fight. On 22 April Goebbels had broadcast Hitler's decision to remain in Berlin. The claim might or might not be true. Dönitz's announcement of the Führer's death fell into the same category of a statement unverified. More persuasive was the intelligence both from captured German officers and from the Allied armies in the Redoubt area. The Germans denied the existence of the Alpenfestung and the Allies had found the Bavarian and Austrian Alps only sporadically defended. This all meant that the importance of Berchtesgaden as a strategic objective was diminishing day by day.

It was still one of immense prestige. It was a location far more personally associated with Hitler than Berlin, it was the second HQ of the Reich, and it was the one remaining plum as the capital fell to the Soviets. Every military unit in the immediate area on the old border between Austria and Bavaria wanted to capture Berchtesgaden.

SHAEF had actually designated two units for the purpose: the French 2nd Armoured (part of the French First Army) and the American 101st Airborne (part of the US Seventh). At the eleventh hour, the fall of the city of Salzburg to the 3rd Infantry Division of VI Corps thrust Major General John O'Daniel's forces into the frame. Mozart's city had surrendered without much of a fight, and Berchtesgaden was only twenty miles away to the south-west. General Patch ordered O'Daniel to make a dash for the Berghof.

The General found little resistance en route, and his troops reached Berchtesgaden at 15:58 on 4 May. The commander of L Company, Lieutenant Sherman Pratt, seems to have been the first Allied officer to enter the town. He was surprised to find the Bavarian resort so untouched by the hand of war, and relieved to discover no signs of resistance: the buildings were festooned with white flags of surrender, most of them bed-sheets. 'Berchtesgaden', he declared, remembering the snow-capped Kehlstein, Untersberg and Watzmann, the evergreen woods, the gingerbread houses with their colourful frescos, and the peasants in their lederhosen and dirndls, 'looked like a village from a fairy tale.'[22]

Kesselring, having been charged with keeping the advancing Allied forces at bay on the Western Front, had established a main base at Pullach, close to Munich. He had been persuaded by Berchtesgaden's Landrat (mayor) Karl Theodor Jakob that defence of the town would be inhumane given the numbers of civilian and military hospitals and children's homes that he had managed to introduce to the valley in the course of the war. Resistance would be only symbolic, and Jakob was allowed by Kesselring to simply surrender the town to the Allies.

On the evening of 4 May 1945, O'Daniel's 3rd Infantry Division was followed by the French (partly composed of French colonial forces from Morocco). Paratroopers of the 101st Airborne arrived at about 10:00 the following day. They had come from the Normandy beaches to wake up to a sunny spring day, fresh, sharp, clear, and full of hope. Here in Berchtesgaden, in the aftermath of Hitler's death, and with a general surrender of the Third Reich's forces imminent, morning had broken in the Alps. After nearly five and three-quarter years of war, peace had finally dawned on Berchtesgaden, the Bavarian township that had played such a strange part in Hitler's war.

Irmgard Paul crept out of Haus Linden in Obersalzberg to spy on the Allied occupiers. She had never seen an American before, and watched curiously as the tanks and armoured cars rumbled and screeched watchfully up and down the steep roads and narrow streets of the mountain town. She thought the Americans looked very young. Meeting her friend Wiebke, with whom she had sheltered from the RAF bombs ten days earlier, the same thought hit both girls at once. 'On an impulse we took each other's crossed-over hands and began to whirl around on the gravel road, singing and shouting, "Der Krieg ist aus! Der Krieg ist aus! Der Krieg ist aus!" (The war is over!) We were giddy with happiness, swirling in a wild dance until we fell to the ground.'[23]

5

The French and US forces had some clearing up to do.

On their arrival they had to take charge of a motley collection of around 2,000 German military personnel: Heer, Waffen-SS and Luftwaffe, all anxious to surrender and prepared to be relieved of their valuables. Harvard-educated David Webster of the 101st Airborne wrote unapologetically to his parents, 'We obtained pistols, knives, watches, fur-lined coats, camouflaged jump jackets. Most of the Germans take it in pretty good spirit, but once in a while we get an individual who does not want to be relieved of the excess weight of his watch. A pistol flashed in his face, however, can persuade anybody.'[24] This was small change, complemented by a collection of silverware from the town's main hotel, the Berchtesgadener Hof. It was here that Neville Chamberlain had stayed on the night of 15 September 1938 when deploying Plan Z at his first, momentous meeting with Hitler. Although the ruined Obersalzberg had already been ransacked by the locals, the Allied troops wandering around the Nazis' holy mountain, the homes of Göring, Speer, Goebbels and Bormann, still found a few souvenirs: Hitler's photo albums featuring fine studies of visiting dignitaries like David Lloyd George and the Duke of Windsor; a Mercedes fire engine, one of Göring's bulletproof Mercedes, and all sorts of other vehicles; the contents of the wine cellar at the officers' club. 'It looks to me', said a wide-eyed infantry colonel, 'like they were expecting to defend this place with wine bottles.'[25] Contemporary photos show battle-stained GIs gaping at the blackened terrace of the Berghof where once Hitler had lorded it over his General-feldmarschalls.

The bigger game in Berchtesgaden was Göring's booty. Although the Allies would soon discover a stupendous cache of more than 6,500 paintings in a salt mine at Altaussee in the Salz-kammergut (the nucleus of Hitler's planned national collection in Linz), the Reichsmarschall's collection was still worth writing home about.

The trains carrying most of the treasures of Carinhall had safely reached Berchtesgaden on 11 April. Then there had been a hitch in the safe and secret disposal of the valuables. Göring's original intention had been to store the treasures in the unfinished underground command post at Schwab, a village on the road from Berchtesgaden to Königsee. The job was only half completed when news of the Allies' approach brought a halt to the curatorship and the hasty sealing of the entrance to the cache with cement. As the Allies neared on 3 May some of the remaining railway cars were sent a couple of stops down the line to Unterstein. Here – and it was an indication of how far the orderly Austrian society had broken down – the cars were ransacked by the villagers. The locals may have found few uses for the paintings but gold coins, cigarettes, sugar and all sorts of alcohol were quickly given new homes. When the Allies arrived, some of the more responsible officers had been briefed to keep their eyes open for significant caches of Nazi loot. They saw the number of empty, heavily gilded picture frames lying around the town as a clue. Captain Harry Anderson of the 101st Airborne made some local enquiries and soon trotted down to Schwab. He found the tunnels of the concrete emplacement empty but surmised that there might be some sealed chambers. These his men located using a sounding device. Loath to use explosives, the sappers spent three days chipping away at a sealing wall that proved to be eighteen inches thick. Within was an Aladdin's cave of antique furniture, rare gramophone records, Old and New Masters – including a Renoir, a van Gogh and five Rembrandts. Anderson's men erected a placard over the cache: 'Hermann Goering's Art Collection Through the Courtesy of the 101st Airborne Division'.[26]

Other valuables found by the Allies in Berchtesgaden were the head of the Reich Chancellery Dr Hans Lammers, the former

Nazi governor general of Poland Hans Frank, the propagandist Julius Streicher, the German Labour Front leader Robert Ley, various members of the Führer's personal staff including his physician Dr Theodor Morell, the RSHA security chief Ernst Kaltenbrunner, Himmler's wife and daughter, and – reportedly – the family of Albert Speer. It was quite a bag.

The Allies also found some women. The eleven-year-old Irmgard Paul had been armed by her mother with pepper as a deterrent to the soldiers' attentions. Some of the Western Allied troops were certainly not above using force. According to Paul, a sixteen-year-old Berchtesgaden girl was gang-raped by US troops, and French and Moroccan forces were given free licence by their officers, 'because this was Berchtesgaden'.[27] Comments Max Hastings, 'The American and British armies in Germany looted energetically and raped occasionally, but few men sought explicit revenge from the vanquished. The French, however, saw many scores to be paid.'[28] Webster of the 101st remarked, 'In Austria, where the women were cleaner, fairer, better built, and more willing than in any other part of Europe, the G.I.s had their field day.'[29]

Meanwhile, 'smiling Albert' Kesselring had more serious matters in hand.

He had sought the advice of SS-Obergruppenführer Karl Wolff, a man now familiar with the Allies' surrender procedures. Kesselring reluctantly accepted that the time had come for him to surrender the ever fewer troops under his command, principally Army Group G. He delegated the job to General Hermann Foertsch. An arrangement was made for Foertsch and General Dever's Sixth Army Group to meet on the outskirts of Munich. Foertsch arrived in the course of the night of 4–5 May at the Thorak estate in Haar. US forces in the area were alerted to watch out for for a vehicle bearing a white flag and with its bonnet covered in white. At about 15:30 on 5 May 1945, Foertsch and General Devers formally signed the surrender terms. They were to come into force from noon of the following day, and would see the surrender of about 100,000 square miles of territory.

It was very nearly over, very nearly Stunde Null.

6

The 80th Infantry Division was part of General George Patton's Third Army. It had landed at Utah Beach on 4 August 1944, a month after D-Day, helped created the Falaise pocket that saw the surrender of perhaps 50,000 troops from Army Group B, crossed the Rhine on 27–8 March 1945, and in late April pushed into Bavaria – to Nuremberg and Regensburg. On 6 May, units of the Division reached the Ebensee concentration camp in the Salz-kammergut mountains, a few miles due east of Berchtesgaden.

It will be remembered that Ebensee was a subcamp of Maut-hausen. The main camp on the Danube just downstream from Linz was now the last remaining major concentration camp in the ever smaller area controlled by the Reich. In the first months of 1945 it was flooded with the inmates of those camps evacuated by the SS before they could be overrun by the Allies. Some of the overflow from Mauthausen was pushed on to Ebensee. The wooden-hutted barracks in the Salzkammergut were designed to hold around a hundred prisoners. Within a few weeks of the end of the war, the actual figure had risen to 750; the total in the small camp to around 18,500. By no means all the prisoners survived the continuing brutality of their captors, the barbarity of their working conditions, and their ever shorter rations. Deaths peaked at about 380 a day. At this level the crematorium, opened in June 1944 by the dutiful Obersturmführer Otto Riemer, was unable to keep up with the rate of mortality. The bodies – some inmates not quite dead – were piled up inside and outside the furnace building.

On 1 May 1945 the camp's work of constructing tank gears and lorry parts was suspended: a rumour had flown round that Hitler was dead. No work was done over the next forty-eight hours. On Friday 4 May, the day US forces reached Berchtes-gaden, the inmates were told by some of the leaders amongst the prisoners that there would be a roll-call the following morning. They would be instructed by the SS guards to go into the great tunnels they had themselves excavated to shelter from Allied bombs and shells. They were to refuse.

The following day the Appell (roll-call) was duly held. According to the inmate Moshe Ha-Elion, the camp commander SS-Obersturmführer Anton Ganz announced, '"The Americans are approaching the camp and we have decided to deliver you into their hands . . . You are in danger of being hurt by shelling or enemy planes. We propose that you should go into the tunnels." Before he finished ending his words, all of us shouted in one loud voice. "We don't want to go! We don't want to go!"' Ganz, at the end of his reign of terror, appeared to concede. The following night the tunnels were blown up. The intended fate of the inmates was clear: an attempt by the SS guards to conceal their dirty work from the Americans, from the forces of a justice that was rough.

On Sunday 6 May 1945, at a little after noon, two or three tanks rumbled through the open gates of the camp. The SS guards – Ganz included – had fled during the night. A cry went up. 'They are Americans. They are Americans!'[30]

Robert B. Persinger was a platoon tank sergeant of the 3rd Cavalry Reconnaissance Squadron.

As we approached on the gravel road to the camp we saw masses of human beings that appeared almost like ghosts standing in mud and filth up to their ankles behind the high wire fence. They were dressed in their filthy striped clothes and some in partial clothing, barely covering their bodies. They appeared so thin and sickly, it was evident that they were starving . . . We were taken . . . to the crematorium where there were stacks of bodies piled like cordwood one on top of the other completely around the inside walls . . . We had seen terrible sights from combat across Europe but what we were observing was a climax to the things human beings do to their fellow man.[31]

In scenes repeated at other concentration camps across what was left of the Reich, the inmates of Ebensee then turned against those who remained of their captors. Moshe Ha-Elion recounted that one of these was a Kapo – a prisoner in charge of supervising the camp labour. Gypsy Kapo – as he was known – was notorious for his cruelty. He was captured by a group of Russian-Ukrainian Jews who were then joined by a lynch mob. They beat the Kapo to the ground and stoned him till he seemed dead. They then set off carrying him to the camp's crematorium through the cordon of cadavers. The Kapo regained consciousness and began to struggle. Someone shouted, 'Let's burn him alive!' He cried in horror, seeing the end that awaited him. He was dragged to the crematorium and thrown onto the iron stretcher used for offering up the bodies to the furnace, shouting and screaming at the top of his voice. 'Someone took a long bar, which served for the purpose of pushing the corpses from the carriage into the oven and thrust the hook into the Capo's groin and pushed his body into the oven . . . the door of the oven was shut. The cries were no more heard.'[32]

Mauthausen itself was liberated by the 11th Armored Division of the US Seventh Army on the same day as its subcamp. The death toll here has been put as high as 320,000. The other major camp in the foothills of the Alps was of course Dachau – the very first of the camps – in Munich. Here, in accordance with Hitler's orders that none of the Dachau inmates should be left to the Allied armies, on 26 April a party of 7,000 Russians, Poles and German Jews set out south on a Todesmarsch (death march) into the Tyrol. Thousands died on the route south to Tegernsee, some freezing to death.

The camp was liberated three days later, on 29 April, by the 42nd Infantry Division of XV Corps of the US army: 32,000 prisoners were freed. On the outskirts of Dachau, the 42nd discovered an abandoned train that had arrived two or three days earlier bringing 2,300 evacuees from Buchenwald, the camp on the Etter Mountain near Weimar. All were dead.

7

The day after Ebensee was liberated. In Kufstein, a medieval Alpine town in the broad valley of the Inn, some fifty miles downstream from Innsbruck. It is dominated by a symbol of impregnability, a magnificent thirteenth-century fortress set on a rock above the fast-flowing river, swollen with meltwater from the Vorarlberg and Tyrol. The cellars of the castle have been pressed into service as air-raid shelters for the last eighteen months. Three days earlier the city, the second-largest in the Tyrol, surrendered to the US Seventh Army's 12th Armored Division. Now it is Monday 7 May. In Rheims in the early hours, the instrument of general surrender has been signed by a representative of the Reich's new leader, Grossadmiral Dönitz, by Generaloberst Alfred Jodl on behalf of the OKW, by General Walter Bedell Smith on behalf of the Western Allies, and by General Ivan Susloparov for the Soviets. The armistice is set to come into force at 23:01 on the following day, Tuesday 8 May: Victory in Europe Day, VE Day.

Kufstein is now a command post of the US 36th Infantry Division of the Seventh Army. Part of Operation Dragoon, the 36th has fought its way up from the Riviera landings, past Grenoble and the Vercors, and is now battling with the retreating German forces in western Austria. That Monday morning the assistant division commander, Brigadier General Robert Stack, is brought a letter. It comes by hand of officer and purports to be from Reichsmarschall Göring. It has been delivered under truce through the German lines by Göring's ADC, Oberst Berndt von Brauchitsch. Addressed to General Eisenhower himself, it is Göring's misplaced attempt to come to terms with the Supreme Allied Commander: 'to arrange for me to have a man-to-man, soldier-to-soldier talk . . . as one Marshal to another'.[33] Göring wants to negotiate a surrender, and then use his standing to set Germany back on its feet. The letter is duly copied and dispatched by plane to headquarters of XXVI Corps, thence to SHAEF and Eisenhower's bulging 'in tray'.

Shortly afterwards, Stack's divisional commander appeared, General John Dahlquist. As part of the Allied plan to capture the perpetrators of the war, the General's unit had already seized Generalfeldmarschall Gerd von Rundstedt and Generalfeld-marschall Hugo Sperrle. Now Stack proposed to Dahlquist that they should go after Göring himself, by far the most important remaining prize amongst the Nazi leaders. Said Stack, 'John, let's go get him.' Dahlquist replied, 'You go get him', so Stack, as he recounted, was stuck with the job.[34]

Since leaving his ruined chalet at Obersalzberg in the aftermath of the bombing on 25 April, Göring and a considerable entourage had been on the move. He had first been driven by the SS some seventy miles south-east to Mauterndorf Castle. This was a picture-postcard Bavarian schloss that the Reichsmarschall had inherited in 1939. Here Göring had enjoyed an ambiguous position with SS-Obersturmbannführer Frank, halfway between captive and host. Here, too, news had reached the ill-assorted house party of the death of the Führer. Göring was galled. 'Now I'll never be able to convince him I was loyal to the end!'[35] Still, for Frank this turn of events put a fresh complexion on things. If actually freeing Göring seemed injudicious, his rescue by the Americans now swarming all over the supposed Redoubt might not be altogether inconvenient. Providing the whole thing was not too blatant. It would never do for Himmler to hear of such disloyalty, should he still be in power!

To this end, with Frank's agreement, Göring now tore a page out of the script of Jack Higgins's *The Eagle Has Landed*. He sent first his wife's niece, and then Emmy Göring herself out through the castle's secret passages. These led to the town of Mauterndorf. Here, disappointingly, the ladies found no one who could help them. Accordingly, with an eye to the less than friendly Soviet forces advancing from the east, Göring thought he might shift base again. He could go seventy-five miles west to Fischhorn, another castle fit for a Reichsmarschall in Zell am See. This enchanting resort on Lake Zell, surrounded by a horseshoe of mountains – the Schmittenhöhe and the Hundstein – owed its popularity to the opening of the Salzburg–Tyrol railway in 1875. In spring 1945 it was the furthest point south possible for the Nazis to reach before the high passes to Italy were clear of snow; some 25,000 troops would soon surrender there. In the meantime Göring dispatched Oberst von Brauchitsch to find the Supreme Allied Commander. Brauchitsch had eventually found his way through the German and into the US lines to Kufstein. In the absence of Eisenhower he accepted as a substitute Brigadier Stack.

The Brigadier's headhunting party duly set out from Kufstein, making for Mauterndorf. For obvious reasons this was a hazardous operation. The general surrender of all German forces had been signed in Rheims but was not yet in force. German troops might perfectly reasonably take exception to a small US party on a manhunt. Care – and good luck – would be needed.

The party comprised a staff car, a jeep, and the Divisional Reconnaissance Troop in a handful of other jeeps and cars, led by Oberst von Brauchitsch in an army vehicle. Brigadier General Stack's group crossed from US into German lines just south of the resort of Kitzbühel. The posse was much delayed by the poor mountain roads, the remains of the winter snow, and never-ending streams of refugees and retreating troops. In the absence of petrol, many of the conveyances were horse-drawn.

Meanwhile, Göring had got bored waiting and had decided to effect his own rescue. He joked to his wife, 'If the mountain will not come to Mahomet, then Mahomet must come to the mountain!'[36] After some confusion, Stack eventually caught up with Göring's twenty-five-car convoy stuck in a traffic jam on the road from Mauterndorf to Zell am Zee. The convoy was facing west, seemingly on its way to the fashionable lakeside resort and Fischhorn Castle. According to the Brigadier, what with his wife, sister-in-law, daughter, guards, butler, aides and chef, Göring had an entourage of seventy-five. Göring himself was seated comfortably in his bulletproof Mercedes. The Reichsmarschall saluted, Stack returned the salute, and asked the Marschall if he wished to surrender. Göring agreed, with the proviso that he was brought back to US – not Soviet – lines. Brigadier Stack said that this was just where he would like to go himself.

The 36th Division headquarters had now moved forward to Kitzbühel, basing itself at the Grand Hotel. Wrote Stack,

I questioned Goering at length . . . particularly about the "Austrian Redoubt." Our Intelligence, including Supreme Headquarters Allied Expeditionary Force, were convinced that the die-hard Nazis had constructed underground factories, hangars, armories, etc., in the Austrian Alps and that they would carry on a last ditch stand there, perhaps for years. Goering said, "No, there had been some talk of such a plan a year before but that nothing at all had been done to implement the plan." He was telling the truth although our Intelligence had been completely taken in by the story.[37]

Göring was given chicken for lunch at the Grand Hotel and photographed with the US top brass in convivial poses soon reproduced in the world's press. The pictures made his captors unpopular. There was a storm of protest over such fraternisation with the Nazi leader. One American who had lost two sons in the war wrote to Dahlquist, 'Why don't you resign the Army and stay over there and suck the hind tit of Goering??'[38]

The US Seventh Army was then headquartered in the Bavarian city of Augsburg. Thence Göring was dispatched in a two-man spotter plane, a Piper L-4. Wrote Stack, 'We had doubts he would fit in the miniature plane but we stuffed him in.' According to the pilot, Captain Mayhew Foster, when asked when the Reich began manufacturing jets, Göring joked, 'Too late.'[39]

As to Kitzbühel in those early May days, a holiday mood seemed already to have returned to the famous Tyrolese resort. Inge Rainer had returned there in April to find her parents' pension full of Luftwaffe personnel on crutches. They were turned out to make room for the US servicemen, the victors then demanding nothing but the best. The Seventh Army's 36th Signals Company soon found itself set up in the Grand Hotel. This

served free drinks for two days, which did not improve our efficiency, but made the work more pleasant by far . . . Air Marshal Goering was wheeled into town following his capture, for interrogation and a chicken dinner. It was easy to tell that the war was over, sunbathing signalmen on the Kitzbuhl porches could look down into the streets and see German M.P.'s [military police] directing our military traffic. Finie, la guerre.[40]

If this made the war in the Alps indeed seem over, nothing could be further from the case in the south-eastern ranges of Austria and the adjoining areas of Italy and Yugoslavia. Here, General-oberst Löhr's Heeresgruppe E was staging a retreat north-west into the Austrian province of Carinthia. The corps was hotly pursued by Tito's Yugoslav Army of National Liberation. This was intent on redressing the injustices of the past and rewriting national frontiers in the country's favour.

Löhr had done well enough until his right flank was exposed by the surrender on 29 April of Vietinghoff's Army Group C – the surrender so painfully negotiated by Allen Dulles with SS-Obergruppenführer Wolff. The British, all too well aware of Tito's ambitions, took this opportunity to get their retaliation in first. Units of the British Eighth Army headed across Istria into Alpine Carinthia. Löhr and his staff were in a quandary.

We had not been advised that negotiations were in progress and when the capitulation came, suddenly we had nobody covering our right flank. The situation had other, more political, considerations, namely, were we of Army Group 'E' bound by the surrender in Italy? If we were then further resistance to the Jugoslavs could be interpreted as breaking the armistice conditions. If we were not so bound, how were we to act against those British and American troops who were crossing our Army Group boundary line in north-eastern Italy?[41]

With Hitler dead and the OKW command structure dissolving, Löhr personally took the decision to fight on – not least because he believed a managed retreat into Carinthia was the only way of saving his 400,000 men. His army was in any case at the end of its tether. Leaving aside the absence of overall political and military direction, the collapse of the Reich meant the dissolution of the logistics chain for supplying armies in the field. Löhr was desperately short of food, fuel and ammunition. The first week of May was here one of heavy rain. As Group E slowly retreated towards Carinthia, the British Eighth in the west and the JANL in the south closed at its heels.

Underlying Löhr's ever-changing military position lay the

shifting sands of post-war politics. Vienna had fallen to the Red Army on 13 April 1945 and Austria's eastern provinces were under Soviet domination. The provisional government in the capital was attempting to reunite the remaining provinces, with the Soviets pushing for a communist Austria. Carinthia had already declared in favour of the provincial government. This was the Red Tide that Churchill had feared. Now the British ambassador in Belgrade hastily called the PM with some disturbing news. 'A Jugoslav Division is under orders to move into Austria and to take Klagenfurt.'[42] This was Carinthia's capital, Austria's sixth-largest city, one dominated by the Karawanken Alps that divided Austria from Italy and Yugoslavia. At once the British Eighth Army was ordered to push into Carinthia with all speed. At much the same time the JANL crossed the Austrian border into the province. The race for Klagenfurt – and for the future of eastern Europe – was on. The battle had morphed from one between the Grand Alliance and the Reich to one between elements of the Grand Alliance.

In Klagenfurt itself on Tuesday 8 May – just as Göring was being entertained to chicken dinner in Kitzbühel's Grand Hotel – there was chaos. Political power was still nominally in the hands of the Reich Gauleiter Rainer. Told by Kesselring in Graz on 6 May that the war – or at least this war – was over, Rainer was prepared to cede power to what amounted to the local resistance. This was a left-leaning, although not completely communist, group.

These political virgins now had on their hands two ardent and powerful suitors, each with designs on Klagenfurt: the JANL pushing up from the south and the British Eighth Army from the west. It was assumed that the JANL would impose not only a communist regime in the city but one that would incorporate Carinthia into Yugoslavia. On the other hand, it was by no means clear – as in the Tyrol – whether the British would act as conquerors or liberators. One Austrian put it rather presciently: 'Even if the British are harsh, at least one day they will leave Austria. It does not matter how accommodating the Jugoslavs may be to us, they will be with us for ever. The choice is clear. It is essential to do everything to speed the British entry.'[43] Happily the decision was made on the Carinthians' behalf. The British Eighth Army beat the JANL to Klagenfurt by a short head. Its units then occupied all the town's principal buildings. When the JANL arrived it had to make do with such two- and one-star accommodation as was left.

The following day was Wednesday 9 May. The Rheims surrender document committed all German forces to a complete capitulation – unconditional surrender – by 23:01 on Tuesday 8 May. This midnight hour found Löhr's Army Group still in limbo, and Carinthia occupied by two armies. When the capitulation came into force, Field Marshal Alexander requested Marshal Tito to withdraw the JANL. The Marshal refused, arguing that the Germans had invaded Yugoslavia in April 1941 and that his armies were merely pursuing them back to their own territory.

In the face of this impasse and as relations between the JANL and the British Eighth deteriorated, plans were made to turn the forces of the Anglo-Saxon Allies on the JANL. An amphibious assault of Istria was put in hand, RAF and USAAF bomber groups were briefed, and Churchill asked Alexander, as Supreme Allied Commander Mediterranean, whether his armies would be prepared to fight the JANL. It was by no means an open-and-shut case. Eventually Alexander cabled Churchill: 'My soldiers will obey orders, but I doubt whether they will fight against Tito with as much enthusiasm as they did against the hated Germans.'[44] Churchill attempted to resolve the matter through President Truman and Marshal Stalin. The former stated that the US would not support territorial claims pursued by force; Stalin advised Tito to withdraw his troops. The Yugoslav leader was by now his own man, less mindful of Moscow. He artfully offered to place the JANL troops under British command. Meanwhile, tension grew on the ground between the British and Yugoslav forces.

There had been an English tank positioned outside the Landhaus [a picturesque medieval government building] since the English arrived.

The Jugoslav soldiers were very excited and when their two dusty tanks arrived they began to cheer. An English officer went across and spoke to the Titoist commander. It was clear that an argument had developed.

The English officer stopped talking, turned round, climbed onto his tank and disappeared inside it. He reappeared and stood up in the turret. I can see him now, with earphones on and a microphone round his throat. He spoke into this and very slowly the gun on the English tank, which had been pointing up towards the sky, began to lower and then the turret began to turn towards the first Jugoslav vehicle. There was an absolute silence. The gun was brought right down and was aimed directly at the Jugoslavs. Suddenly the partisans started their tank engines and drove out of the square. We Austrians went wild and we all applauded as if it had been an entertainment. Looking back I realize how naive we all were. A war might have broken out in that square on that day.[45]

Churchill refused to take the JANL under Eighth Army command, and Tito thought better of pushing the point. On 18 May 1945, the JANL trooped out of Klagenfurt, defiantly singing partisan songs. They headed south, and had soon crossed the river Drau and the frontier with Yugoslavia. A similar impasse between Alexander's and Tito's forces in the Adriatic city of Trieste was settled when JANL forces left on 12 June 1945. Both incidents are sometimes billed as the last battles of the Second World War and the first of the Cold War.

Yet it was not quite over. If an expansionist policy in the Alps was to be expected of Tito, it was not entirely anticipated of de Gaulle. As the General – now very much in charge in France as Prime Minister of the provisional government – had remarked when conferring the Compagnon de la Libération in Grenoble, he had plans for his Alpine specialists. These turned out to be the seizure of the Italian province of Cuneo in the Alpes-Maritimes. It was from here in December 1943, from Borgo San Dalmazzo, that the 328 refugees from Saint-Martin-Vésubie had been sent to their deaths in Auschwitz.

In the closing days of the fighting in early May 1945, de Gaulle had ordered units of the French First Army to cross the Alpine border into Cuneo. The frontier here between France and Italy had long been disputed, not least in June 1940 when Mussolini's troops had invaded the Alpes-Maritimes. Here, towards the end of the month of May 1945, the French were surprised by the US IV Corps. This was charged with setting up military government in north-west Italy. Lieutenant General Paul-André Doyen, the commander of the French Armée des Alpes, was most put out. He wrote a surprising letter to the commander of the IV Corps, Major General Willis D. Crittenberger, objecting to the US Corps's presence in Cuneo.

France cannot consent that a modification against her will should be made in the existing state of affairs in the Alpes-Maritimes. This would be contrary to her honour and her security. I have been ordered by the Provisional Government of the French Republic to occupy and administer this territory. This mission being incompatible with the installation of an Allied military agency in the same region, I find myself obliged to oppose it. Any insistence in this direction would assume a clearly unfriendly character, even a hostile character, and could have grave consequences.[46]

On 2 June 1945 the moustached Doyen followed this with another letter to Crittenberger in which he stated that he had been ordered by General de Gaulle to prevent the setting up of an Allied military government in Cuneo 'by all necessary means without exception'. Meaning that – like the case of JANL and the British Eighth Army in Carinthia – the supposed Allies were poised to become foes.

In Cuneo the job of resolving the matter once again fell to Alexander. The Field Marshal called in Churchill. The Prime Minister wrote to President Truman with nice understatement, 'Is it not rather disagreeable for us to be addressed in these terms by General de Gaulle, whom we have reinstated in liberated France at some expense of American and British blood and treasure?' Truman wrote at once to de Gaulle. The General climbed down, Doyen withdrew the French First Army and Cuneo remained Italian.

9

Endsieg at last had come, final victory, but not for the Third Reich. In Germany, Victory in Europe Day was Stunde Null: zero hour. A vivid picture has been painted of this German apocalypse:

It was a land of ruins peopled by ghosts, a land without government, order or purpose, without industry, communications or proper means of existence, a nation that had entirely forfeited its nationhood and lay entirely at the beck and call of foreign armies . . . The almost complete cessation of the means of communication . . . seemed to have brought civilised life itself to a halt.[47]

Out of the 18.2 million men in Germany's armed services, 5.3 million had died: a million more than the total population of Switzerland.

London was a rather different story. 'Chips' Channon recorded the occasion of VE Day – 8 May 1945 – in the House of Commons:

Every seat was occupied; the Ambassadors were all present, peers queued up. At three o'clock, in the Whips' Room, I heard the PM make the official announcement over the wireless that the war in Europe was at an end . . . At last Winston, smiling and bent, appeared, and had a tremendous reception. Everyone (except the recently elected cad for Chelmsford) rose and cheered and waved handkerchiefs and Order Papers . . . Winston smiled and half bowed – as he often does, and turning towards the Speaker, read out the same short announcement of the surrender of Germany which he had already given over the wireless. The House was profoundly moved, and gave him another great cheer . . . Then Winston, in a lower voice, added his personal thanks and praise for the House of Commons and the Democratic System: some Members wept, and the PM moved that we repair to St Margaret's to offer thanks to Almighty God using the identical phraseology employed by Lloyd George in 1918.[48]

One final task in Europe remained for Churchill as war leader. This was to attend the last of the great Allied war conferences, held two and a half months after VE Day in Potsdam on the outskirts of Berlin. The ambitions of Hitler for a new European order were perfectly symbolised by the smoking rubble and human detritus of the Reich's sometime capital. A new order had arisen nonetheless. As President Truman's secretary of state Dean Acheson would later put it, 'The whole world structure and order that we had inherited from the nineteenth century was gone.'[49] The United States – as Truman himself observed – 'emerged from this war the most powerful nation in the world';[50] and both Great Britain and France had been reduced to the rank of second-class powers. Potsdam was not a rerun of Versailles, where Lloyd George for Great Britain, Georges Clemenceau for France, and Woodrow Wilson for the United States had between them divided up Europe's plum pudding. To Potsdam the French were not even invited.

Two topics dominated the July conference: the war with Japan and the post-war future of what was once the Reich – within which lay her Alps.

At Potsdam the three principal Allies agreed on the aims of their joint occupation of Germany. She was to be demilitarised, denazified, democratised, decentralised and decartelised – the last the process of replacing monopolies with a free-market economy. In short, Germany was to be turned into a liberal democracy, based on the models of Great Britain and the United States. At the same time all her annexations in Europe were to revert to their former identities, these including Austria. Both Germany and Austria would be partitioned into four, thence to be governed by the Americans, the British, the Soviets and the French. The Reich's Alps, Bavaria and Alpine Austria, were to exchange totalitarianism for occupation, albeit largely under democratic governance.

As to the rest of the Alps, those in the east in Yugoslavia were now firmly under Tito's communist control, those to the south in Italy under Allied military control, and those in France under the impress of General de Gaulle's provisional government.

This left Switzerland, the heart of the Alps. The great stone walls that formed her eastern, western and southern borders had been the shields of her democracy. In July 1945, as Churchill left London for Potsdam, General Henri Guisan finally demobilised the Swiss citizen army. For the Swiss, the war that in some sense had never begun was over.

That same month the British Alpinist Arnold Lunn returned to Switzerland for the first time since May 1940. He was travelling to Zermatt to celebrate the eightieth anniversary of the first ascent of the Matterhorn by the Englishman Edward Whymper. It was Lunn who in 1940 had been horrified by the prospect of the swastika flying over the roofs of Berne. Five years had passed:

I walked to the terrace at Berne, and against the ebbing twilight I saw my beloved mountains Wetterhorn, Eiger, Mönch and Jungfrau, serene and untroubled, untainted by the cruel and evil things which we had been fighting, and still bearing witness to the eternal loveliness which man cannot mar, and which time cannot diminish.[51]

The shadow of the swastika had been lifted from the Alps. The Third Reich, as William Shirer would later put it, had passed into history.

Epilogue

Fifteen months later, Winston Churchill was himself in Switzerland. He was staying in the Villa Chiosi on the northern shores of Lake Geneva. 'For centuries', said Baedeker, the great lake on the border between Switzerland and France had 'been a favourite theme with writers of every nationality (Byron, Voltaire, Rousseau, Alex. Dumas, etc.). On the N. side it is bounded by gently sloping hills, richly clothed with vineyards and orchards, and enlivened with smiling villages . . . The banks of the lake are clothed with rich vegetation and studded with charming villas.'[1] The Villa Chiosi was just one such sequestered retreat. Here, on 23 August 1946, Churchill arrived to work on his memoirs – to be called simply *The Second World War* – to paint the idyllic autumn land- and lakescape around him, and to prepare a speech.

He had been dismissed as Prime Minister by an ungrateful British electorate in the khaki election of July 1945, with Hitler defeated but the war with Japan still lingering. The Swiss – or at least some of them – were happier than the British to honour their debts. It was one of the former Prime Minister's compatriots, Colonel Hugo de Burgh of the Royal Horse Artillery, who had thanked Swiss officers for their help when he had escaped from Italy into Switzerland over the high passes into Zermatt in the autumn of 1943. 'Why not?' had been the reply. 'If it had not been for the Battle of Britain in 1940 there would be no Switzerland.' General Guisan's men had had a point. The survival of freedom in Switzerland and elsewhere in the Alps was not principally a consequence of the efforts of the Alpine people themselves, either in Switzerland herself or in the Alps of France, Italy, Austria, Bavaria or even Yugoslavia. Freedom, where it had been maintained or restored, was the carefree child of events in London's Downing Street, Baker Street and Broadway, in the skies over England in the epic summer of 1940, in the White House in Washington, in the Kremlin in Moscow, and in places like Berne's Herrengasse, the bitter suburbs of Stalingrad, and the sands of El Alamein. The dwellers in the Alps had reason for gratitude.

So the University of Zurich had asked the architect of the West's salvation, the greatest statesman of the twentieth century, Hitler's nemesis – now merely Leader of His Majesty's Opposition – to talk about the future of Europe. In a speech less well known than the 'Iron Curtain' lecture of six months earlier in Fulton, Ohio, the seventy-one-year-old grandfather sought to draw a line not under one war but under a series of conflicts that had convulsed Europe over more than a century. He was to make proposals that he hoped would prevent another European war in his audience's lifetime; that, too, of their children and their children's children. After the First World War it was said with much vehemence, 'Never again!' Churchill, as a survivor of the trenches, could hardly have felt this more keenly at the second time of asking, sixteen months after the end of the second war to ruin Europe and decimate her people in thirty years.

On 19 September 1946, Churchill told his listeners at the university that 'In this last struggle crimes and massacres have been committed for which there is no parallel since the invasions of the Mongols in the fourteenth century and no equal at any time in human history.' Forty million people had died in Europe and perhaps the same number were now refugees, displaced persons. '[O]ver wide areas a vast quivering mass of tormented, hungry, care-worn and bewildered human beings gape at the ruins of their cities and homes, and scan the dark horizons for the approach of some new peril, tyranny or terror.' Europe, 'home of all the great parent races of the western world . . . fountain of Christian faith and Christian ethics . . . origin of most of the culture, arts, philosophy and science both of ancient and modern times', had been laid waste. But for the succour of the 'great Republic across the Atlantic Ocean' the Dark Ages would have returned. 'They may still return,' Churchill warned.[2]

In the Alps, matters as yet were not that much better. Switzerland had survived militarily and materially but by no means morally unscathed. The rapacity of her bankers and the failures of her humanitarian mission would gradually emerge to stain and sully her once lofty reputation. In 1946 the Bavarian and Austrian Alps still laboured under Allied military rule: AMGOT – Allied Military Government of Occupied Territory. Bavaria was under US control, and the western Alpine areas of Austria with its better-known resorts like Kitzbühel, Lech and St Anton were in the hands of France; she had thoughtfully provided an abortion service for those inhabitants of the two provinces raped by her armed forces. In the eastern Tyrol, the British occupying forces in Lienz forcefully repatriated more than 2,000 Cossacks to the Red Army – most to their deaths. Bavaria and Austria were also well supplied with displaced persons camps, and Vienna was in the era of Carol Reed's masterpiece *The Third Man*. With anti-Semitic persecution still lingering in Europe, in 1947 the Krimmler Tauern Pass close to Zell am Zee saw the extraordinary escape of 5,000 Jews from Austria into Italy, en route to a nascent Israel. The Italian Alps were gingerly emerging from AMGOT, coming to terms with the legacy of Mussolini, Salò, of more than twenty years of Fascism: Ferruccio Parri was briefly Prime Minister. Bavaria, Austria and Italy were all subsisting on US aid. In the Alps of France, the Third Republic and then the Etat Français – Vichy – had of course collapsed. The Provisional Government of the French Republic (GPRF) was still struggling to come to terms with the Fall of 1940, the years of widespread collaboration, and the purges – one spontaneous and the other sanctioned by the state – that followed Liberation in the late summer of 1944. These had seen the execution of almost 10,000, including the author of the Glières tragedy, SS-Sturmbannführer Joseph Darnand. In Yugoslavia, on 29 November 1945, King Peter had been deposed to usher in a communist republic. Marshal Tito and the iron forces of communism he represented were the 'new peril, tyranny or terror' to which Churchill alluded.

For this desecration and destruction of the pre-war order in Europe – its Alps included – the guilty must be punished. So Churchill declared in Zurich. Hitler, Himmler, Goebbels and Bormann were already dead, the first three by their own hands. Reichsleiter Bormann had apparently been killed in Berlin on 1 May 1945, trying to filter his way through Soviet lines as the Red Army closed on the Führerbunker and Hitler's charred remains. As Churchill was speaking in Zurich in September 1946, Hermann Göring, Albert Speer, Joachim von Ribbentrop and Alfred Jodl were amongst those being tried at the International Military Tribunal at Nuremberg. In Berchtesgaden, Irmgard Paul was

glued to the large black radio in Haus Pfeilbrand, listening to broadcasts of the International High Tribunal for German War Crimes . . . Our everyday worries and family dramas paled before the nearly incredible revelations contained in the daily reports from Nuremberg . . . This was the first time that the vast majority of the German public heard about the enormity of the crimes the Nazis, and therefore Germany, had committed. Albert Speer . . . hoped that the trial of the 'real' criminals might avert wholesale condemnation of the German people. He was not the only one to be so naïve.

The guilt of genocide would be upon all of us for generations. Nothing could undo what had happened – the victims would not come back to life, the survivors would never forget and probably never forgive, and I would never make sense of it. Who had we become under the Nazi regime, and how was it accomplished?[3]

Of Hitler's inner circle, only Speer would escape the death sentence; only Göring would cheat the hangman by swallowing poison within hours of his intended execution.

Churchill in his speech looked back not just to Hitler's war, but to the First World War in which he had been a lieutenant colonel in the Grenadier Guards; and before that to the 1870–71 Franco-Prussian War that had ended three years before his birth. All three great conflicts had been rooted in the nationalistic rivalries between the peoples of Europe. If yet another war was to be prevented, Churchill was not the only statesman to see a solution in a political and economic union of Europe. As he put it,

Yet all the while there is a remedy which, if it were generally and spontaneously adopted, would as if by a miracle transform the whole scene, and would in a few years make all Europe . . . as free and as happy as Switzerland is today. What is this sovereign remedy? It is to re-create the European Family . . . with a structure under which it can dwell in peace, in safety and in freedom. We must build a kind of United States of Europe.

It was the boldest of ambitions. It proposed reconciliation between two great European nations that had been at best rivals and at worst at each other's throats since before the Franco-Prussian War. 'I am now going to say something that will astonish you,' continued Churchill. 'The first step in the re-creation of the European family must be a partnership between France and Germany . . . There can be no revival of Europe without a spiritually great France and a spiritually great Germany.' This was akin to a joint venture between Israel and Hamas. Still, as Churchill remarked, the leader of the free world, President Truman, 'had expressed his interest and sympathy with this great design'. Moreover, one of the President's underlings, the former Berne spymaster Allen Dulles, was working on a complementary project to rebuild Europe with US aid, soon to be known as the Marshall Plan. (Dulles's OSS – for some 'Oh So Social' – had been disbanded by Truman on 20 September 1945. It had been a little profligate. A US government report on the intelligence organisation had uncovered 'poor security, incompetence, waste, nepotism, inadequate training, extravagance, corruption, alcoholism, orgies, foreign penetration'.[4] The indictment might have been written by Dulles's British counterpart and old rival, Claude Dansey, who would die in 1947.)

At first Churchill's proposals fell like frost in May. General de Gaulle, briefly out of power, wrote to him to say that the idea had been badly received in France. Countries desperately in need of such basics as food, clothing and medical supplies found it difficult to raise their eyes to the horizon.

The work of the United Nations Relief and Rehabilitation Administration (UNRRA), subsequently that of the Marshall Plan, nevertheless encouraged imagination. As the former US Chief of Staff George Marshall – now Truman's secretary of state – said in June 1947, 'It is logical that the United States should do whatever it is able to do to assist in the return of normal economic health in the world, without which there can be no political stability and no assured peace.' The Plan became known as the European Recovery Programme. It bred a series of agencies devoted to the cause of reconstruction, the most important of which was the Organisation for European Economic Co-operation (OEEC). In 1949 this was complemented by the creation of the Council of Europe that Churchill had proposed in Zurich. That same year AMGOT in Germany – including Bavaria – ended with the creation of the Federal Republic of Germany. This was followed in 1951 by the creation of the European Coal and Steel Community, the principal members of which actually were West Germany and France. The twain had met.

This organisation was intended to be a first step towards the federation of Europe. In 1957 the six members of the Coal and Steel Community signed the Treaty of Rome. This created the European Economic Community, or EEC. Twenty years after the momentous visit of Viscount Halifax – the 'Holy Fox' – to Hitler in the Berghof, the meeting that ushered in Chamberlain's policy of appeasement, an organisation had been founded that really would mean 'peace for our time'.

This template for European political and economic union meant peace and freedom in western Europe. It also meant manna in the Alps of France, Switzerland, Austria, Bavaria and Italy – if not Yugoslavia.

By the time of the creation of the EEC, Italy was enjoying what was actually described as an economic miracle. The counterpart in France under the Fourth Republic was *les trentes glorieuses*. Switzerland, which had enriched rather than pauperised itself during the war, was sufficiently prosperous to contribute to rather than benefit from the Marshall Plan. Austria rebuilt her economy under Allied occupation and regained her independence in 1955. All these states were now democracies and most – in the immediate aftermath of the war – had even given women the vote. God was once again in his heaven and all was right with the world.

The Alps and their principal resorts were indices of this stability and prosperity. In 1956 Cortina d'Ampezzo, briefly the capital of the mayfly republic of Carnia, hosted the Winter Olympics. Over the border in France, Val d'Isère – close to the site of the Battle of Mont Froid – was being rapidly developed into one of France's most successful skiing resorts, albeit the most architecturally depraved. Megève, in the war the temporary haven for Jewish refugees, soon forgot its past. Easier to reach than many of its competitors, the resort had become so popular with the French capital's socialites, said Jean Cocteau, that it was 'the twenty-first arrondissement of Paris'. In Kitzbühel in the Tyrol, the golden vein of the Hahnenkamm downhill race had been reopened as early as 1945. Ten years later, with the ending of AMGOT and the restitution of the republic, the old mining village was once again attracting the wealthy and fashionable, some of whom skied. In Switzerland, St Moritz had enjoyed a post-war revival and found its slopes studded with stars, amongst them Audrey Hepburn, Aristotle Onassis and the Aga Khan. Zermatt, which had been so welcoming to POWs escaping from Italy, was attracting 200,000 visitors a year; the village elders had induced the cellist Pablo Casals to broaden its appeal beyond the philistine and – like many of the resorts – the community was investing in new cable car systems. Adelboden, in the absence of its US enlisted airmen at Camp Moloney, was exploring the possibilities of opening up the Silleren as a skiing area. Davos, bereft of its US officers, would soon be establishing its annual World Economic Forum. In Bavaria, Garmisch-Partenkirchen had found itself the repository for the Reich's $15 million reserves, secreted away in nearby Einsiedl and eventually discovered by the Allies on 6 June

1945. By 1953 the town was sufficiently rehabilitated to host the world bobsleigh championships. Its neighbour Oberammergau once again staged the Passion Play in 1950, albeit only with the permission of the US occupying forces. St Anton, once so busy with SS troops guarding the Arlberg Pass, in 1953–4 turned its energies to constructing the Vallugabahn cable way up to the Valluga Grat. As to Obersalzberg itself, in some strange way it once again became Führersperrgebiet, 'leader's territory'. It was turned over to the US occupying forces, its buildings were requisitioned by the US army, and the old Hotel Platterhof was rebuilt as the Hotel General Walker to form the centrepiece of the US Armed Forces Recreation Center. The remains of the Berghof were demolished in 1953.

By 1957 Europe – the Eastern Bloc excepted – and the Alps had once more achieved what the Germans called Bergfried, the peace of the mountains. 'Therefore I say to you,' Churchill had concluded in Zurich in 1946: 'let Europe arise!' Europe had arisen from the ashes of the eagle that smouldered in the Berlin and Berchtesgaden of May 1945. The Alps were once again, in Mark Twain's words, 'the visible throne of God'. It had taken twenty years, the Holocaust and forty million lives.

Acknowledgements

Creating any book is a voyage of discovery enlivened by unexpected landfalls, uncharted reefs, the calms of the Sargasso Sea, the storms of the South Atlantic, fine passages with following winds, the odd waterspout and – sadly – ships that pass in the night. This particular trip took – in all – twelve years, and was eased by a host of fellow seafarers, many of whom went out of their way to help a lone sailor, occasionally in distress.

My thanks in the first instance go to Gail Pirkis, who commissioned four of my books in the closing years of John Murray's Albemarle Street era, a *belle époque* we will not see again. It was Gail who conjured into being *How the English Made the Alps*; and it was her enthusiasm for a sequel that saw the idea survive the demise of Albemarle Street, and brought it – nascent, amorphous, but heart still beating – into the tempestuous new world of publishing in the 2000s. Then, as is the way with books, it was set aside whilst the clamour of small children reigned on our north Norfolk estate.

The idea was – miraculously – revived by John Seaton of Faber and Faber. He asked me to heave to and discharge a cargo of paperback rights to my Murray books to the publishing house that still basked in the halo of T. S. Eliot, W. H. Auden, Jean Cocteau, Ezra Pound, Lawrence Durrell, William Golding, Ted Hughes, Silvia Plath, John Osborne and Tom Stoppard. Not only would Faber republish *Erskine Childers*, *We Come Unseen*, *Riviera* and *How the English Made the Alps* itself, they would also consider the book that was now taking shape amid the wood-shavings in the boathouse under the working title of *Alps*

Under the Swastika. When Julian Loose, Gail Pirkis's opposite number at Faber, expressed serious interest in the book – by then a good ten years after its conception – I had come across a Spanish galleon adrift on the high seas.

It is to Julian that I owe the current thrust of the book, for at his suggestion it was given a much sharper focus and far finer lines than I had originally drafted; to Julian, too, goes the credit of the final, far more telling title.

My research then took me to the Alps themselves, often following paths that I had first trodden in the previous century in pursuit of the English in the Alps. Here I was not entirely surprised to discover those who felt the story of the Alps during the war was one best forgotten, that concentration camps and deportations and rocket factories and the Gestapo detracted from the rosy hue and crackling banknotes of tourism. Of the many, many exceptions I would like particularly to thank Timothy Nelson of Bibliotheken der Landschaft Davos, Corina Huber of the Bibliothek St Moritz, the scholar Alois Schwarzmüller of Garmisch-Partenkirchen, and three quite remarkable living witnesses: Frau Inge Rainer of Kitzbühel, Marko Feingold of Salzburg, and Matteus Guidon of Bergün, Canton Graubünden. These people told a truth that was far from invariably comfortable.

Thereafter, when the book was actually in draft, a handful of specialists troubled themselves to wade through the Dead Sea of typographical errors and non sequiturs in an attempt to generally set the ship to rights. These were the Alpinists David Pirkis and Philip Hawes, the scholar Clive Jenkins, the wizard of the Man Booker Prize David Waller, the iconoclast Alan Page, the Second World War historian Bill Purdue, and the diplomat Michael Zimmermann. I am grateful equally for their patience, their scholarship, and for their insistence that only certain vintages would change hands. In the usual way, I myself bear responsibility for the errors and omissions that remain.

At the same time a galaxy of others have provided moral and practical support for the book. Prominent amongst them are my very old friend and colleague Tim Lefroy of the Advertising

Association, the head of the commentariat Peter York, the business guru Murray Keith, Elisabeth Dyck and Ruth Morgart of the United Nations, Mary Palmer of the NHS, and my business partner Richard Kennan of Gig House Films.

In a sense most importantly, it is my family that has borne this long voyage with fortitude, humour and even patience. It is a great sadness that my mother Stella, a generous and constructive critic of the book's early chapters, did not live to see the work completed; my sister and two brothers have been unwaveringly encouraging; and it is with great pleasure that I was able to dedicate this book to my father, hale and hearty in his ninety-first year. To my wife Kate I owe a great deal of typing, fact-checking and childcare; to my son Ashmole time that would otherwise have been spent building his own boat; and to my daughter Jessie the energy that would surely have been devoted to augmenting her wardrobe. All in all, although they have coped with the passage very well, they are pleased it is over. I have yet to tell them that another is about to begin.

Finally, my thanks go to Faber's Kate Murray-Browne, who has seen the book through the press so expertly and sympathetically; to my copy editor Merlin Cox, whose eye for detail, English grammar and even maths proved so much better than my own; and to my typesetter, Donald Sommerville, who has added more than just style to the book.

Notes

1 Plan Z

1. David Paroissien (ed.), *Selected Letters of Charles Dickens* (London: Macmillan, 1985).
2. John Ruskin, *Modern Painters* (New York: Wiley, 1888).
3. Mark Twain, *A Tramp Abroad* (London: Chatto & Windus, 1880).
4. Winston S. Churchill, *The Second World War, Volume I: The Gathering Storm* (London: Cassell, 1948).
5. Graham Macklin, *Chamberlain* (London: Haus, 2006).
6. Robert Rhodes James (ed.), *Chips: The Diaries of Sir Henry Channon* (Weidenfeld & Nicolson, 1967).
7. Macklin.
8. Norman Cameron and R. H. Stevens, *Hitler's Table Talk, 1941–1944: His Private Conversations* (London: Phoenix, 2000 [1953]).
9. Cameron and Stevens.
10. Cameron and Stevens.
11. Andrew Roberts, *The Holy Fox: A Biography of Lord Halifax* (London: Weidenfeld & Nicolson, 1991).
12. Roberts.
13. Churchill, *Second World War, Volume I*.
14. William L. Shirer, *The Rise and Fall of the Third Reich: A History of Nazi Germany* (London: Book Club Associates, 1969).
15. Macklin.
16. Churchill, *Second World War, Volume I*.
17. Roberts.
18. Nerin E. Gun, *Hitler's Mistress* (Coronet, 1976).
19. Keith Feiling, *The Life of Neville Chamberlain* (London: Macmillan, 1946).
20. Nevile Henderson, *Failure of a Mission: Berlin 1937–1939* (London: Hodder & Stoughton, 1940).
21. Cameron and Stevens.
22. Macklin.
23. Ralph F. De Bedts, *Ambassador Joseph Kennedy 1938–1940: An Anatomy of Appeasement* (New York: Peter Lang, 1985).

24. De Bedts.

25. Shirer, *Rise and Fall*.

26. Cicely Williams, *Zermatt Saga* (London: Allen & Unwin, 1964).

27. Arnold Lunn, *The Story of Ski-ing* (London: Eyre & Spottiswoode, 1952).

2 'I need a few thousand dead'

1. William L. Shirer, *Berlin Diary: The Journal of a Foreign Correspondent, 1934–1941* (Baltimore, MD, and London: Johns Hopkins University Press, 2002).

2. Urs Schwarz, *The Eye of the Hurricane: Switzerland in World War Two* (Boulder, CO: Westview, 1980).

3. Jon Kimche, *Spying for Peace: General Guisan and Swiss Neutrality* (London: Weidenfeld & Nicolson, 1962).

4. Winston S. Churchill, *The Second World War, Volume II: Their Finest Hour* (London: Cassell, 1949).

5. Stephen P. Halbrook, *Target Switzerland: Swiss Armed Neutrality in World War II* (New York: Sarpedon, 1998).

6. Halbrook, *Target Switzerland*.

7. Halbrook, *Target Switzerland*.

8. Cicely Williams, *Zermatt Saga*.

9. Shirer, *Rise and Fall*.

10. Richard Lamb, *Mussolini and the British* (London: John Murray, 1997).

11. Lamb, *Mussolini and the British*.

12. Richard Collier, *Duce! The Rise and Fall of Benito Mussolini* (London: Collins, 1971).

13. Pietro Badoglio, *Italy in the Second World War* (*L'Italia nella seconda guerra mondiale*), tr. Muriel Currey (Oxford: Oxford University Press, 1948).

14. Badoglio.

15. Conrad Black, *Franklin Delano Roosevelt* (London: Weidenfeld & Nicolson, 2003).

16. Claire Eliane Engel, *Mountaineering in the Alps: An Historical Survey* (London: Allen and Unwin, 1971).

17. Galeazzo Ciano, *The Ciano Diaries 1939–1943*, ed. Hugh Gibson (New York: Fertig, 1973).

18. Neville Stephen Lytton, *Life in Unoccupied France* (London: Macmillan, 1942).

19. Ciano.

20. Winston S. Churchill, *The Second World War, Volume V: Closing the Ring* (London: Cassell, 1952).

21. Shirer, *Berlin Diary*.

22. Kimche.

3 Triumph of the Will

1. Churchill, *Second World War, Volume II*.
2. Shirer, *Rise and Fall*.
3. Shirer, *Rise and Fall*.
4. www.winstonchurchill.org/learnspeeches/speeches-of-winston-churchill/128-we-shall-fight-on-the-beaches.
5. Shirer, *Rise and Fall*.
6. *Strand Magazine*, 1894.
7. Alan Morris Schom, *A Survey of Nazi and Pro-Nazi Groups in Switzerland: 1930–1945* (Los Angeles: Simon Wiesenthal Center, 1998).
8. Shirer, *Berlin Diary*.
9. Stephen P. Halbrook, *The Swiss and the Nazis: How the Alpine Republic Survived in the Shadow of the Third Reich* (Staplehurst: Spellmount, 2006).
10. 'Schwerin, Gustloff's Funeral: Speech of February 12, 1936'. www.hitler.org/speeches/02-12-36.html.
11. Peter Bollier, quoted in Halbrook, *Swiss and the Nazis*.
12. Kimche.
13. Jean-Jacques Langendorf and Pierre Streit, *Le Général Guisan et l'esprit de résistance* (Bière: Cabédita, 2010).
14. Kimche.
15. *New York Times*, 25 July 1999.
16. Halbrook, *Target Switzerland*.
17. Halbrook, *Target Switzerland*.
18. Halbrook, *Target Switzerland*.
19. Kimche.
20. Kimche.
21. Shirer, *Rise and Fall*.
22. Shirer, *Rise and Fall*.
23. Shirer, *Rise and Fall*.
24. Joachim C. Fest, *Hitler*, tr. Richard and Clara Winston (London: Weidenfeld & Nicolson, 1974).
25. Shirer, *Berlin Diary*.
26. Cicely Williams, *Zermatt Saga*.

4 The Alps under the Swastika

1. Shirer, *Berlin Diary*.
2. Shirer, *Berlin Diary*.
3. Shirer, *Berlin Diary*.
4. Maria Augusta Trapp, *The Sound of Music: The Story of the Trapp Family Singers* (London: White Lion, 1976).
5. Fritz Molden, *Exploding Star: A Young Austrian Against Hitler* (London: Weidenfeld & Nicolson, 1978).

6. Shirer, *Rise and Fall*.
7. Trapp.
8. Interview with author, 2012.
9. Molden.
10. Trapp.
11. Gordon Brook-Shepherd, *The Austrians* (London: HarperCollins, 1996).
12. Shirer, *Berlin Diary*.
13. Irmgard Hunt, *On Hitler's Mountain: My Nazi Childhood* (New York: William Morrow, 2005).
14. Hunt.
15. Hunt.
16. Shirer, *Berlin Diary*.
17. Ian Ousby, *Occupation: The Ordeal of France, 1940–1944* (London: John Murray, 1997).
18. Ousby.
19. Pierre Giolitto, *Grenoble 1940–1944* (Paris: Perrin, 2001).
20. Peter Leslie, *The Liberation of the Riviera* (London: Dent, 1981).
21. Jim Ring, *Riviera* (London: John Murray, 2004).
22. Shirer, *Berlin Diary*.
23. Paul Ladame, *Defending Switzerland: Then and Now* (Caravan Books, 1999).
24. Ladame.
25. Shirer, *Berlin Diary*.
26. Ladame.
27. Shirer, *Berlin Diary*.
28. Raymond Flower, *The Palace: A Profile of St Moritz* (London: Debrett's Peerage, 1982).
29. Rhodes James (ed.).
30. Shirer, *Rise and Fall*.

5 'The lifeboat is full'

1. Martin Gilbert, *Churchill: A Life* (London: Heinemann, 1991).
2. Wilhelm Deist, *Germany and the Second World War* (Oxford: Oxford University Press, 1990).
3. Albert Speer, *Inside the Third Reich* (New York: Macmillan, 1970).
4. Alexander Rotenberg, *Emissaries: A Memoir of the Riviera, Haute-Savoie, Switzerland, and World War II* (Secaucus, NJ: Citadel Press, 1987).
5. Independent Commission of Experts Switzerland – Second World War (ICE), *Switzerland, National Socialism and the Second World War: Final Report* (Munich: Pendo, 2002)
6. Christopher Sykes, *Crossroads to Israel* (Bloomington, IN: Indiana University Press, 1973).
7. Sykes.

8. ICE.
9. Kimche.
10. Kimche.
11. ICE.
12. Rotenberg.
13. Rotenberg.
14. Rotenberg.
15. Daniel Carpi, *Between Mussolini and Hitler: The Jews and the Italian Authorities in France and Tunisia* (Hanover, NH, and London: Brandeis University Press, 1994).
16. Gilbert, *Churchill: A Life.*
17. Susan Zuccotti, *Holocaust Odysseys* (New Haven, CT, and London: Yale University Press, 2007).
18. Speer.
19. Hunt.
20. Deist.
21. Halbrook, *Swiss and the Nazis.*

6 Setting the Alps Ablaze

1. Mark Wheeler, *Britain and the War for Yugoslavia, 1940–1943* (Boulder, CO: East European Monographs, 1980).
2. David Stafford, *Britain and European Resistance, 1940–1945: A Survey of the Special Operations Executive, with Documents* (London: Macmillan, 1980).
3. Neville Wylie, *Britain, Switzerland and the Second World War* (Oxford and New York: Oxford University Press, 2003).
4. M. R. D. Foot, *SOE: The Special Operations Executive 1940–46* (London: BBC, 1984).
5. Kim Philby, *My Silent War* (London: Grafton, 1989 [1968]).
6. Malcolm Tudor, *Special Force: SOE and Italian Resistance 1943–1945* (Newtown, Powys: Emilia Publishing, 2004).
7. Michael Pearson, *Tears of Glory: The Betrayal of Vercors, 1944* (London: Macmillan, 1978).
8. R. J. B. Bosworth, *Mussolini's Italy: Life Under the Dictatorship, 1915–1945* (London: Allen Lane, 2005).
9. Shirer, *Rise and Fall.*
10. Bosworth.
11. John Pimlott, *Rommel and His Art of War* (London: Greenhill, 2003).
12. David Irving, *The Trail of the Fox* (London: Papermac, 1977)
13. Irving.
14. Basil Davidson, *Special Operations Europe: Scenes from the Anti-Nazi War* (London: Gollancz, 1980).
15. Marko Attila Hoare, *Genocide and Resistance in Hitler's Bosnia* (Oxford: Oxford University Press, 2006).

16. Hoare.
17. Fitzroy Maclean, *Eastern Approaches* (London: Penguin, 1991 [1949]).
18. Bosworth.
19. Shirer, *Rise and Fall*.

7 Spy City Central

1. James Srodes, *Allen Dulles: Master of Spies* (Washington: Regnery Publishing, 1999).
2. Keith Jeffery, *MI6: The History of the Secret Intelligence Service* (London: Bloomsbury, 2010).
3. Jeffery.
4. Jeffery.
5. Anthony Read and David Fisher, *Colonel Z: The Life and Times of a Master of Spies* (London: Hodder & Stoughton, 1984).
6. Philby.
7. Wylie.
8. Wylie.
9. Wylie.
10. Read and Fisher.
11. Leonard Mosley, *Dulles: A Biography of Eleanor, Allen, and John Foster Dulles and Their Family Network* (New York: Dial Press/James Wade, 1978).
12. Mosley, *Dulles*.
13. Mosley, *Dulles*.
14. Winston S. Churchill, *The World Crisis, Volume V: The Aftermath* (London: Thornton Butterworth, 1929).
15. Srodes.
16. Srodes.
17. Dulles, Allen W., *Germany's Underground* (New York: Da Capo Press, 2000).
18. Dulles, *Germany's Underground*.
19. Read and Fisher.
20. Read and Fisher.
21. Mosley, *Dulles*.
22. Mosley, *Dulles*.
23. Philby.
24. Philby.
25. Philby.
26. Philby.
27. Mary Bancroft, *Autobiography of a Spy* (New York: William Morrow, 1983).
28. Bancroft.

8 Operation Achse

1. Bosworth.
2. Bosworth.
3. Joseph Goebbels, *The Goebbels Diaries, 1942–43*, ed. Louis P. Lochner (New York: Doubleday, 1948).
4. Zuccotti, *Holocaust Odysseys*.
5. Bosworth.
6. Zuccotti, *Holocaust Odysseys*.
7. Zuccotti, *Holocaust Odysseys*.
8. Malcolm Tudor, *British Prisoners of War in Italy: Paths to Freedom* (Newtown, Powys: Emilia Publishing, 2000).
9. Paul Schamberger, *Interlude in Switzerland: The Story of the South African Refugee-Soldiers in the Alps during the Second World War* (Parkhurst, South Africa: Maus Publishing, 2001).
10. Cicely Williams, *Zermatt Saga*.
11. Schamberger.
12. Schamberger.
13. Schamberger.
14. Schamberger.
15. Schamberger.
16. Collier.
17. Shirer, *Rise and Fall*.

9 'Our predecessors made mistakes'

1. Karl Baedeker, *Northern Italy* (Leipsic: Karl Baedeker, 1899).
2. Gilbert, *Churchill: A Life*.
3. Allen W. Dulles, *From Hitler's Doorstep: The Wartime Intelligence Reports of Allen Dulles, 1942–1945*, ed. Neal H. Petersen (University Park, PA: Pennsylvania State University Press, 1996).
4. Tom Behan, *The Italian Resistance* (London and New York: Pluto Press, 2009).
5. Ziegler, Jean, *The Swiss, the Gold and the Dead* (New York and London: Harcourt Brace, 1998).
6. Ziegler.
7. Ziegler.
8. Wylie.
9. Ziegler.
10. ICE.
11. Ziegler.
12. Speer.
13. Ziegler.
14. Wylie.

15. Caroline Moorehead, *Dunant's Dream: War, Switzerland and the History of the Red Cross* (London: HarperCollins, 1998).
16. Tanner, Stephen, *Refuge from the Reich: American Airmen and Switzerland During World War II* (New York: Sarpedon; London: Greenhill, 2000).
17. Tanner.
18. Gerhard Weinberg, *A World at Arms: A Global History of World War II* (Cambridge: Cambridge University Press, 2005).

10 'A guerrilla à la Tito'

1. Speer.
2. Hunt.
3. Hunt.
4. Gilbert, *Churchill: A Life.*
5. Gilbert, *Churchill: A Life.*
6. Rhodes James (ed.).
7. Maclean.
8. Maclean.
9. Maclean.
10. Maclean.
11. Maclean.
12. M. R. D. Foot, *SOE in France: An Account of the Work of the British Special Operations Executive in France, 1940–1944* (London: HMSO, 1966).
13. Charles Messenger, *The Last Prussian: A Biography of Field Marshal Gerd Von Rundstedt* (London: Brassey's, 1991).
14. Churchill, *Second World War, Volume V.*
15. Churchill, *Second World War, Volume V.*
16. Gilbert, *Churchill: A Life.*
17. Patrick de Gmeline, *Tom Morel, héros des Glières* (Paris: Presses de la Cité, 2008).
18. Ousby.
19. De Gmeline.
20. De Gmeline.
21. De Gmeline.
22. Foot, *SOE in France.*

11 Arbeit Macht Frei

1. Speer.
2. Speer.
3. Speer.
4. Daniel Uziel, *Arming the Luftwaffe: The German Aviation Industry in World War II* (Jefferson, NC: McFarland, 2011).

5. Frank Vann, *Willy Messerschmitt* (Yeovil: Patrick Stephens, 1993).
6. Yechezkel Harfenes, *Slingshot of Hell* (Spring Valley, NY: Feldheim, 1989).
7. Helena Waddy, *Oberammergau in the Nazi Era: The Fate of a Catholic Village in Hitler's Germany* (New York and Oxford: Oxford University Press, 2010).
8. Waddy.
9. Wayne Biddle, *Dark Side of the Moon: Wernher von Braun, the Third Reich, and the Space Race* (New York and London: Norton, 2009).
10. Speer.
11. Speer.
12. Speer.
13. Moshe Ha-Elion, *The Straits of Hell: The Chronicle of a Salonikan Jew in the Nazi Extermination Camps, Auschwitz, Mauthausen, Melk, Ebensee* (Mannheim: Bibliopolis; Cincinnati, OH: Bowman & Cody, 2005).
14. Ha-Elion.
15. Speer.
16. Gilbert, *Churchill: A Life.*

12 The Mayfly Republics

1. Pearson.
2. Tudor, *Special Force.*
3. Robert Aron, *Charles de Gaulle* (Paris: Librairie académique Perrin, 1964).
4. H. R. Kedward, *In Search of the Maquis: Rural Resistance in Southern France, 1942–1944* (Oxford: Clarendon Press, 1993).
5. Aron.
6. Aron.
7. Churchill, *Second World War, Volume V.*
8. Aron.
9. Pearson.
10. Aron.
11. Aron.
12. Kedward.
13. Kedward.
14. Behan.
15. Jeffery.
16. Tudor, *Special Force.*
17. Winston S. Churchill, *The Second World War, Volume VI: Triumph and Tragedy* (London: Cassell, 1954).
18. David Stafford, *Mission Accomplished: SOE and Italy 1943–1945* (London: Bodley Head, 2011).
19. Stafford, *Mission Accomplished.*

20. Stafford, *Mission Accomplished*.
21. *New York Times*, 19 August 1944.
22. Steven J. Zaloga, *Operation Dragoon 1944: France's Other D-Day* (Oxford: Osprey, 2009).
23. Kedward.
24. Laurence Lewis, *Echoes of Resistance: British Involvement with the Italian Partisans* (Tunbridge Wells: Costello, 1985).
25. Speer.

13 The Troops of Midian

1. www.newspaperarchive.com.
2. Churchill, *Second World War, Volume VI*.
3. Peter Hoffman, *German Resistance to Hitler* (Cambridge, MA: Harvard University Press, 1988).
4. Dumbach, Annette E., *Sophie Scholl and the White Rose* (Oxford: Oneworld, 2007).
5. Shirer, *Rise and Fall*.
6. Dumbach.
7. Molden.
8. Molden.
9. Molden.
10. Molden.
11. Molden.
12. Molden.
13. Molden.
14. Interview with author, 2012.
15. Schwarz.
16. Schwarz.
17. Roberto Battaglia, *The Story of the Italian Resistance* (London: Odhams Press, 1957).
18. Stafford, *Mission Accomplished*.
19. Stafford, *Mission Accomplished*.
20. Tanner.
21. Fredy Peter, *Jump Boys Jump* (Ilfracombe: Arthur H. Stockwell, 2003).
22. Tanner.
23. Speer.
24. Molden.
25. Hugh Trevor-Roper, *The Last Days of Hitler* (London: Papermac, 1995).
26. Speer.

14 The Redoubt That Never Was

1. Churchill, *Second World War, Volume VI*.
2. Churchill, *Second World War, Volume VI*.

3. Cornelius Ryan, *The Last Battle* (London: New English Library, 1980).
4. Ryan.
5. Ryan.
6. James Lucas, *Last Days of the Third Reich: The Collapse of Nazi Germany, May 1945* (London: Cassell, 2000).
7. Ryan.
8. Ryan.
9. Ryan.
10. Antony Beevor, *Berlin: The Downfall 1945* (London: Viking, 2002).
11. Churchill, *Second World War, Volume VI*.
12. Churchill, *Second World War, Volume VI*.
13. Lucas, *Last Days*.
14. Hastings, Max, *All Hell Let Loose* (London: HarperPress, 2011).
15. Ryan.
16. Srodes.
17. Churchill, *Second World War, Volume VI*.
18. Dulles, *Germany's Underground*.
19. Mosley, *Dulles*.
20. Mosley, *Dulles*.
21. Alain Cerri, 'The Battle of Mount Froid', http://worldatwar.net/article/mountfroid/index.html.
22. *Daily Telegraph*, 3 July 2007.
23. Speer.
24. Speer.
25. Speer.
26. Halbrook, *Target Switzerland*.
27. Beevor.
28. Speer.
29. Speer.
30. Leonard Mosley, *The Reich Marshal: A Biography of Hermann Göring* (London: Weidenfeld & Nicolson, 1974).
31. Mosley, *Dulles*.
32. 'Raid on Berchtesgaden', www.polishsquadronsremembered.com/300/Berchtesgaden.html.
33. Hunt.
34. Hunt.

15 Storming the Eagle's Nest

1. Hunt.
2. Mosley, *The Reich Marshal*.
3. R. Smith, *OSS: The Secret History of America's First Central Intelligence Agency* (New York: Lyons Press, 2005).
4. Lucas, *Last Days*.
5. Churchill, *Second World War, Volume VI*.

6. Srodes.
7. Churchill, *Second World War, Volume VI.*
8. Mosley, *Dulles.*
9. Weinberg.
10. Trevor-Roper.
11. Trevor-Roper.
12. Harry S. Truman Library and Museum, 'The President's News Conference' (2 May 1945), http://trumanlibrary.org/publicpapers/view-papers.php?pid=29.
13. Gilbert, *Churchill: A Life.*
14. Hunt.
15. Hunt.
16. Sayer and Botting.
17. Sayer and Botting.
18. Biddle.
19. Lucas, *Last Days.*
20. Molden.
21. Churchill, *Second World War, Volume VI.*
22. John C. McManus, 'World War II: Race to Seize Berchtesgaden', *World War II*, May 2005. www.historynet.com/world-war-ii-race-to-seize-Berchtesgaden.htm.
23. Hunt.
24. Stephen E. Ambrose, *Band of Brothers* (New York: Simon & Schuster, 1992).
25. Kenneth Alford, *Nazi Plunder: Great Treasure Stories of World War II* (Cambridge, MA: Da Capo; London: Eurospan, 2001).
26. Lynn H. Nicholas, *The Rape of Europa: The Fate of Europe's Treasures in the Third Reich and the Second World War* (London: Macmillan, 1994).
27. Hunt.
28. Hastings, *All Hell Let Loose.*
29. Ambrose.
30. Ha-Elion.
31. Robert B. Persinger, 'Remembering Ebensee 1945'. www.memorial-ebensee.at/english/persinger.html.
32. Ha-Elion.
33. Mosley, *The Reich Marshal.*
34. Robert I. Stack, 'Capture of Goering'. www.kwanah.com/36division/ps/pso277.htm.
35. Mosley, *The Reich Marshal.*
36. Mosley, *The Reich Marshal.*
37. Stack.
38. Alford.

39. 'Hermann Goering "too heavy" for US plane transport after capture', *Telegraph*, 31 January 2011. www.telegraph.co.uk/news/worldnews/europe/germany/8291253/Hermann-Goering-too-heavy-for-US-plane-transport-after-capture.html.

40. '36th Signal Company: May 1945'. www.texasmilitaryforcesmuseum.org/gallery/signal/signal11.htm.

41. Lucas, *Last Days*.

42. Lucas, *Last Days*.

43. Lucas, *Last Days*.

44. Lucas, *Last Days*.

45. Lucas, *Last Days*.

46. Churchill, *Second World War, Volume VI*.

47. Sayer and Botting.

48. Rhodes James (ed.).

49. Richard Overy, *Why the Allies Won* (New York: Norton, 1996 [1995]).

50. Overy.

51. Wraight, John, *The Swiss and the British* (Sailsbury, Wiltshire: Michael Russell, 1987).

Epilogue

1. Karl Baedeker, *Switzerland* (London: Dulau, 1901).

2. 'Mr Winston Churchill speaking in Zurich, 19th September 1946'. www.churchill-society-london.org.uk/astonish.html.

3. Hunt.

4. Srodes.

Select Bibliography

Absolom, Roger, *Strange Alliance* (Florence: Leo S. Olschki, 1992)

Alcorn, William, *The Maginot Line* (Oxford: Osprey, 2003)

Alford, Kenneth, *Nazi Plunder: Great Treasure Stories of World War II* (Cambridge, MA: Da Capo; London: Eurospan, 2001)

Allinson, Mark, *Germany and Austria 1814–2000* (London: Arnold, 2002)

Ambrose, Stephen E., *Band of Brothers* (New York: Simon & Schuster, 1992)

Aron, Robert, *Charles de Gaulle* (Paris: Librairie académique Perrin, 1964)

Bach, Steven, *Leni: The Life and Work of Leni Riefenstahl* (New York: Knopf, 2007)

Badoglio, Pietro, *Italy in the Second World War* (*L'Italia nella seconda guerra mondiale*), tr. Muriel Currey (Oxford: Oxford University Press, 1948)

Baedeker, Karl, *Northern Italy* (Leipsic: Karl Baedeker, 1899)

——, *Switzerland* (London: Dulau, 1901)

Balfour, Michael, *Withstanding Hitler* (New York: Routledge, 1988)

Bancroft, Mary, *Autobiography of a Spy* (New York: William Morrow, 1983)

Barker, Noel, *The Week France Fell* (New York: Stein & Day, 1976)

Battaglia, Roberto, *The Story of the Italian Resistance* (London: Odhams Press, 1957)

Beevor, Antony, *Berlin: The Downfall 1945* (London: Viking, 2002)

Behan, Tom, *The Italian Resistance* (London and New York: Pluto Press, 2009)

Biddle, Wayne, *Dark Side of the Moon: Wernher von Braun, the Third Reich, and the Space Race* (New York and London: Norton, 2009)

Black, Conrad, *Franklin Delano Roosevelt* (London: Weidenfeld & Nicolson, 2003)

Bolle, Pierre (ed.), *Grenoble et le Vercors: De la Résistance à la Libération, 1940–1944* (Grenoble: Presses universitaires de Grenoble, 2003)

Bonjour, Edgar, *A Short History of Switzerland* (Oxford: Clarendon Press, 1952)

Boone, J. C., *Hitler at the Obersalzberg* (Xlibris, 2008)

Bosworth, R. J. B., *Mussolini's Italy: Life Under the Dictatorship, 1915–1945* (London: Allen Lane, 2005)

Bower, Tom, *Nazi Gold: The Full Story of the Fifty-Year Swiss-Nazi Conspiracy to Steal Billions from Europe's Jews and Holocaust Survivors* (New York: HarperCollins, 1997)

Brook-Shepherd, Gordon, *The Austrians* (London: HarperCollins, 1996)

Buckmaster, Maurice, *They Fought Alone: The Story of British Agents in France* (London: Odhams Press, 1958)

Bullock, Alan, *Hitler: A Study in Tyranny* (London: Odhams Press, 1952)

Burleigh, Michael, *The Third Reich: A New History* (London: Pan, 2001 [2000])

Cameron, Norman, and R. H. Stevens, *Hitler's Table Talk, 1941–1944: His Private Conversations* (London: Phoenix, 2000 [1953])

Carpi, Daniel, *Between Mussolini and Hitler: The Jews and the Italian Authorities in France and Tunisia* (Hanover, NH, and London: Brandeis University Press, 1994)

Chapman, Guy, *Why France Collapsed* (London: Cassell, 1968)

Churchill, Winston S., *The World Crisis, Volume V: The Aftermath* (London: Thornton Butterworth, 1929)

_____, *The Second World War, Volume I: The Gathering Storm* (London: Cassell, 1948)

_____, *The Second World War, Volume II: Their Finest Hour* (London: Cassell, 1949)

_____, *The Second World War, Volume III: The Grand Alliance* (London: Cassell, 1950)

_____, *The Second World War, Volume IV: The Hinge of Fate* (London: Cassell, 1951)

_____, *The Second World War, Volume V: Closing the Ring* (London: Cassell, 1952)

_____, *The Second World War, Volume VI: Triumph and Tragedy* (London: Cassell, 1954)

_____, *The Second World War, Abridged Edition with an Epilogue on the Years 1945 to 1957* (London: Pimlico, 2002)

Ciano, Galeazzo, *The Ciano Diaries 1939–1943*, ed. Hugh Gibson (New York: Fertig, 1973)

Cobb, Matthew, *The Resistance: The French Fight Against the Nazis* (London: Simon & Schuster, 2009)

Codevilla, Angelo M., *Between the Alps and a Hard Place* (Washington: Regnery Publishing, 2000)

Collier, Richard, *Duce! The Rise and Fall of Benito Mussolini* (London: Collins, 1971)

Colville, John, *The Fringes of Power. Downing Street Diaries Volume Two: 1941–April 1955* (London: Hodder & Stoughton, 1985)

Cooke, Philip (ed.), *The Italian Resistance: An Anthology* (Manchester: Manchester University Press, 1997)

Crowdy, Terry, *French Resistance Fighter: France's Secret Army* (Oxford: Osprey, 2007)

Davidson, Basil, *Special Operations Europe: Scenes from the Anti-Nazi War* (London: Gollancz, 1980)

Dear, Ian, *Sabotage and Subversion: The SOE and OSS at War* (Stroud: History Press, 2010)

De Bedts, Ralph F., *Ambassador Joseph Kennedy 1938–1940: An Anatomy of Appeasement* (New York: Peter Lang, 1985)

de Gaulle, Charles, *The Complete War Memoirs of Charles de Gaulle* (New York: Simon and Schuster, 1971)

de Gmeline, Patrick, *Tom Morel, héros des Glières* (Paris: Presses de la Cité, 2008)

Deist, Wilhelm, *Germany and the Second World War* (Oxford: Oxford University Press, 1990)

Donaldson, Frances, *Edward VIII* (Weidenfeld & Nicolson, 1974)

Draper, Theodore, *The Six Weeks' War: France May 10–June 25, 1940* (London: Methuen, 1946)

Drummond, Anthony Deane, *Return Ticket* (London: Collins, 1967)

Dulles, Allen W., *From Hitler's Doorstep: The Wartime Intelligence Reports of Allen Dulles, 1942–1945*, ed. Neal H. Petersen (University Park, PA: Pennsylvania State University Press, 1996)

——, *Germany's Underground* (New York: Da Capo Press, 2000)

Dumbach, Annette E., *Sophie Scholl and the White Rose* (Oxford: Oneworld, 2007)

Ellwood, David, *Italy 1943–1945* (Leicester: Leicester University Press, 1985)

Engel, Claire Eliane, *A History of Mountaineering in the Alps* (London: George Allen and Unwin, 1950)

——, *Mountaineering in the Alps: An Historical Survey* (London: Allen and Unwin, 1971)

Feiling, Keith, *The Life of Neville Chamberlain* (London: Macmillan, 1946)

Feldman, Alfred, *One Step Ahead: A Jewish Fugitive in Hitler's Europe* (Carbondale, IL: SIU Press, 2001)

Fest, Joachim C., *Hitler*, tr. Richard and Clara Winston (London: Weidenfeld & Nicolson, 1974)

Flower, Raymond, *The Palace: A Profile of St Moritz* (London: Debrett's Peerage, 1982)

Foot, M. R. D., *SOE in France: An Account of the Work of the British Special Operations Executive in France, 1940–1944* (London: HMSO, 1966)

——, *SOE: The Special Operations Executive 1940–46* (London: BBC, 1984)

——, and J. M. Langley, *MI9: Escape and Evasion 1939–1945* (Boston, MA: Little, Brown, 1980)

Fortune, G., *Hitler Divided France* (London: Macmillan, 1943)

Fowler, William, *The Secret War in Italy: Operation Herring and No 1 Italian SAS* (Hersham: Ian Allan, 2010)

Funk, Arthur, *Hidden Ally: The French Resistance, Special Operations and the Landings in Southern France, 1944* (Westport, CT: Greenwood Press, 1992)

Garliński, Józef F., *The Swiss Corridor: Espionage Networks in Switzerland during World War II* (London: Dent, 1981)

Garnett, David, *The Secret History of PWE: The Political Warfare Executive, 1939–1945* (London: St Ermin's, 2002)

Garrett-Groag, Lillian, *The White Rose* (New York: Dramatist's Play Service, 2007)

Gilbert, Martin, *Churchill: A Life* (London: Heinemann, 1991)

——, *The Righteous: The Unsung Heroes of the Holocaust* (London: Doubleday, 2002)

Ginsborg, Paul, *A History of Contemporary Italy: Society and Politics, 1943–1988* (London: Penguin, 1990)

Giolitto, Pierre, *Grenoble 1940–1944* (Paris: Perrin, 2001)

Goebbels, Joseph, *The Goebbels Diaries, 1942–43*, ed. Louis P. Lochner (New York: Doubleday, 1948)

Goulthard, Adolphe, *The Battle of France, 1940* (*1940: la guerre des occasions perdues*), tr. A. R. P. Burgess (London: Frederick Muller, 1958)

Grandjacques, Gabriel, *La Montagne-Refuge: Les Juifs au Pays du Mont-Blanc: Saint-Gervais, Megève . . . 1940–1944* (Montmélian: La Fontaine de Siloé, 2007)

Gregory, Barry, *Mountain and Arctic Warfare: From Alexander to Afghanistan* (London: Stephens, 1989)

Griffiths, Frank, *Winged Hours* (London: Kimber, 1981)

Grose, Peter, *Gentleman Spy: The Life of Allen Dulles* (London: André Deutsch, 1995 [1994])

Gun, Nerin E., *Hitler's Mistress* (London: Coronet, 1976)

Ha-Elion, Moshe, *The Straits of Hell: The Chronicle of a Salonikan Jew in the Nazi Extermination Camps, Auschwitz, Mauthausen, Melk, Ebensee* (Mannheim: Bibliopolis; Cincinnati, OH: Bowman & Cody, 2005)

Halbrook, Stephen P., *Target Switzerland: Swiss Armed Neutrality in World War II* (New York: Sarpedon, 1998)

——, *The Swiss and the Nazis: How the Alpine Republic Survived in the Shadow of the Third Reich* (Staplehurst: Spellmount, 2006)

Halpenny, Bruce Barrymore, *The War in Italy 1942–1945* (Lincoln: L'Aquila Publishing, 2009)

Harfenes, Yechezkel, *Slingshot of Hell* (Spring Valley, NY: Feldheim, 1989)

Hastings, Max, *Finest Years: Churchill as Warlord, 1940–45* (London: HarperPress, 2010)

——, *All Hell Let Loose* (London: HarperPress, 2011)

Henderson, Nevile, *Failure of a Mission: Berlin 1937–1939* (London: Hodder & Stoughton, 1940)

Hoare, Marko Attila, *Genocide and Resistance in Hitler's Bosnia* (Oxford: Oxford University Press, 2006)

Hoffman, Peter, *German Resistance to Hitler* (Cambridge, MA: Harvard University Press, 1988)

Horne, Alastair, *To Lose a Battle: France 1940* (London: Macmillan, 1969)

Hunt, Irmgard, *On Hitler's Mountain: My Nazi Childhood* (New York: William Morrow, 2005)

Independent Commission of Experts Switzerland – Second World War (ICE), *Switzerland, National Socialism and the Second World War: Final Report* (Munich: Pendo, 2002)

Irving, David, *The Trail of the Fox* (London: Papermac, 1977)

Jeffery, Keith, *MI6: The History of the Secret Intelligence Service* (London: Bloomsbury, 2010)

Jörgensen, Christopher, *Hitler's Espionage Machine: The True Story Behind One of the World's Most Ruthless Spy Networks* (Guilford, CT: Lyons Press, 2004)

Jowett, Philip S., *The Italian Army 1940–45* (Oxford: Osprey, 2001)

Kedward, H. R., *In Search of the Maquis: Rural Resistance in Southern France, 1942–1944* (Oxford: Clarendon Press, 1993)

Keegan, John, *The Second World War* (London: Hutchinson, 1989)

Kershaw, Ian, *Hitler* (Harlow: Longman, 2001)

_____, *The End: Hitler's Germany 1944–45* (London: Allen Lane, 2011)

Kesselring, Albert, *The Memoirs of Field-Marshal Kesselring* (London: Greenhill, 1997)

Kimche, Jon, *Spying for Peace: General Guisan and Swiss Neutrality* (London: Weidenfeld & Nicolson, 1962)

Knight, Frida, *The French Resistance, 1940 to 1944* (London: Lawrence and Wishart, 1975)

Ladame, Paul, *Defending Switzerland: Then and Now* (Caravan Books, 1999)

Lamb, Richard, *War in Italy: 1943–45: A Brutal Story* (London: John Murray, 1993)

_____, *Mussolini and the British* (London: John Murray, 1997)

Langendorf, Jean-Jacques, and Pierre Streit, *Le Général Guisan et l'esprit de résistance* (Bière: Cabédita, 2010)

Lawson, Don, *The French Resistance* (London: Piccolo, 1985 [1984])

Leeds, Christopher, *Italy under Mussolini* (London: Wayland, 1972)

Leslie, Peter, *The Liberation of the Riviera* (London: Dent, 1981)

Lett, Brian, *SAS in Tuscany 1943–45* (Barnsley: Pen & Sword Military, 2011)

Levendel, Isaac, and Bernard Weisz, *Hunting Down the Jews: Vichy, the Nazis and Mafia Collaborators in Provence 1942–1944* (New York: Enigma, 2011)

Lewis, Laurence, *Echoes of Resistance: British Involvement with the Italian Partisans* (Tunbridge Wells: Costello, 1985)

Longden, Sean, *T-Force: The Race for Nazi War Secrets, 1945* (London, Constable, 2009)

Lucas, James, *Alpine Elite: German Mountain Troops of World War II* (London: Jane's, 1980)

____, *Hitler's Mountain Troops: Fighting at the Extremes* (London: Cassell, 1999 [1992])

____, *Last Days of the Third Reich: The Collapse of Nazi Germany, May 1945* (London: Cassell, 2000)

Lunn, Arnold, *The Story of Ski-ing* (London: Eyre & Spottiswoode, 1952)

Lytton, Neville Stephen, *Life in Unoccupied France* (London: Macmillan, 1942)

Mabire, Jean, *La Bataille des Alpes 1944–1945* (Paris: Presses de la Cité, 1992)

Mackenzie, William, *The Secret History of SOE: Special Operations Executive, 1940–1945* (London: St Ermin's, 2000)

Macklin, Graham, *Chamberlain* (London: Haus, 2006)

Maclean, Fitzroy, *Eastern Approaches* (London: Penguin, 1991 [1949])

McManus, John C., 'World War II: Race to Seize Berchtesgaden', *World War II*, May 2005. www.historynet.com/world-war-ii-race-to-seize-Berchtesgaden.htm

Marnham, Patrick, *The Death of Jean Moulin: Biography of a Ghost* (London: John Murray, 1999)

Messenger, Charles, *The Last Prussian: A Biography of Field Marshal Gerd Von Rundstedt* (London: Brassey's, 1991)

Millar, George, *Maquis* (London: Heinemann, 1945)

____, *Horned Pigeon* (London: Heinemann, 1947)

____, *Road to Resistance: An Autobiography* (London: Arrow, 1981 [1979])

Molden, Fritz, *Exploding Star: A Young Austrian Against Hitler* (London: Weidenfeld & Nicolson, 1978)

Moorehead, Caroline, *Dunant's Dream: War, Switzerland and the History of the Red Cross* (London: HarperCollins, 1998)

Mosley, Leonard, *The Reich Marshal: A Biography of Hermann Göring* (London: Weidenfeld & Nicolson, 1974)

____, *Dulles: A Biography of Eleanor, Allen, and John Foster Dulles and Their Family Network* (New York: Dial Press/James Wade, 1978)

Neave, Airey, *They Have Their Exits* (Barnsley: Leo Cooper, 2002 [1953])

____, *Saturday at MI9: A History of Underground Escape Lines in North-West Europe in 1940–5* (London: Coronet, 1971)

New, Mitya, *Switzerland Unwrapped: Exposing the Myths* (London: I.B.Tauris, 1997)

Nicholas, Lynn H., *The Rape of Europa: The Fate of Europe's Treasures in the Third Reich and the Second World War* (London: Macmillan, 1994)

O'Brien-ffrench, Conrad, *Delicate Mission* (London: Skilton & Shaw, 1979)

Ousby, Ian, *Occupation: The Ordeal of France, 1940–1944* (London: John Murray, 1997)

Overy, Richard, *Why the Allies Won* (New York: Norton, 1996 [1995])

Parker, R. A. C., *Chamberlain and Appeasement: British Policy and the Coming of the Second World War* (Basingstoke: Macmillan, 1993)

Paroissien, David (ed.), *Selected Letters of Charles Dickens* (London: Macmillan, 1985)

Paxton, Robert O., *Vichy France: Old Guard and New Order 1940–1944* (New York: Columbia University Press, 2001 [1972])

Pearson, Michael, *Tears of Glory: The Betrayal of Vercors, 1944* (London: Macmillan, 1978)

Percy, Philip, *France in Defeat* (London: Frederick Muller, 1941)

Persinger, Robert B., 'Remembering Ebensee 1945'. www.memorial-ebensee. at/english/persinger.html

Peter, Fredy, *Jump Boys Jump* (Ilfracombe: Arthur H. Stockwell, 2003)

Philby, Kim, *My Silent War* (London: Grafton, 1989 [1968])

Pimlott, John, *Rommel and His Art of War* (London: Greenhill, 2003)

Poirier, Jacques R. E., *The Giraffe Has a Long Neck* (Périgueux: Editions Fanlac, 1992)

Poznanski, Renée, *Jews in France in World War II*, tr. Nathan Bracher (Hanover, NH, and London: University Press of New England, 2001)

Read, Anthony, and David Fisher, *Colonel Z: The Life and Times of a Master of Spies* (London: Hodder & Stoughton, 1984)

Reid, Patrick R., *The Colditz Story* (London: Coronet, 1962 [1952])

——, *Latter Days of Colditz* (London: Coronet, 1972)

Rhodes James, Robert (ed.), *Chips: The Diaries of Sir Henry Channon* (Weidenfeld & Nicolson, 1967)

Rickard, Charles, *La Savoie dans la Résistance* (Rennes: Ouest-France, 1986)

Ridley, Jasper Godwin, *Tito* (London: Constable, 1994)

Ring, Jim, *Riviera* (London: John Murray, 2004)

Rings, Werner, *Schweiz im Krieg, 1933–1945: ein Bericht* (Zürich: Ex Libris, 1974)

Roberts, Andrew, *The Holy Fox: A Biography of Lord Halifax* (London: Weidenfeld & Nicolson, 1991)

Rotenberg, Alexander, *Emissaries: A Memoir of the Riviera, Haute-Savoie, Switzerland, and World War II* (Secaucus, NJ: Citadel Press, 1987)

Rowe, Vivian, *The Great Wall of France: The Triumph of the Maginot Line* (London: Putnam, 1959)

Ruskin, John, *Modern Painters* (New York: Wiley, 1888)

Ryan, Cornelius, *The Last Battle* (London: New English Library, 1980)

Sayer, Ian, *America's Secret Army: The Untold Story of the Counter Intelligence Corps* (London: Grafton, 1989)

——, and Douglas Botting, *Nazi Gold: The Story of the World's Greatest Robbery and Its Aftermath* (London: Panther, 1984)

Schamberger, Paul, *Interlude in Switzerland: The Story of the South African Refugee-Soldiers in the Alps during the Second World War* (Parkhurst, South Africa: Maus Publishing, 2001)

Schoenbrun, David, *Maquis: Soldiers of the Night: The Story of the French Resistance* (London: Robert Hale, 1990 [1980])

Schom, Alan Morris, *A Survey of Nazi and Pro-Nazi Groups in Switzerland: 1930–1945* (Los Angeles: Simon Wiesenthal Center, 1998)

Schwarz, Urs, *The Eye of the Hurricane: Switzerland in World War Two* (Boulder, CO: Westview, 1980)

Shennan, Andrew, *De Gaulle* (London: Longman, 1993)

Shirer, William L., *The Rise and Fall of the Third Reich: A History of Nazi Germany* (London: Book Club Associates, 1969)

____, *Berlin Diary: The Journal of a Foreign Correspondent, 1934–1941* (Baltimore, MD, and London: Johns Hopkins University Press, 2002)

Silvestre, Paul, and Suzanne Silvestre, *Chronique des maquis de l'Isère, 1943–1944* (Grenoble: Editions des 4 Seigneurs, 1978)

Smith, R., *OSS: The Secret History of America's First Central Intelligence Agency* (New York: Lyons Press, 2005)

Spears, Edward, *Assignment to Catastrophe* (London: Heinemann, 1954)

Speer, Albert, *Inside the Third Reich* (New York: Macmillan, 1970)

Spiller, Harry, *American POWs in World War II: Twelve Personal Accounts of Captivity by Germany and Japan* (Jefferson, NC: McFarland, 2009)

____, *Prisoners of Nazis: Accounts by American POWs in World War II* (Jefferson, NC: McFarland, 1998)

Srodes, James, *Allen Dulles: Master of Spies* (Washington: Regnery Publishing, 1999)

Stack, Robert I., 'Capture of Goering'. www.kwanah.com/36division/ps/ps0277.htm

Stafford, David, *Britain and European Resistance, 1940–1945: A Survey of the Special Operations Executive, with Documents* (London: Macmillan, 1980)

____, *Secret Agent: The True Story of the Special Operations Executive* (London: BBC Worldwide, 2000)

____, *Mission Accomplished: SOE and Italy 1943–1945* (London: Bodley Head, 2011)

Stone, Norman, *Hitler* (Sevenoaks: Coronet, 1982)

Sweets, J. F., *Choices in Vichy France: The French under Nazi Occupation* (New York: Oxford University Press, 1986)

Sykes, Christopher, *Crossroads to Israel* (Bloomington, IN: Indiana University Press, 1973)

Tanner, Stephen, *Refuge from the Reich: American Airmen and Switzerland During World War II* (New York: Sarpedon; London: Greenhill, 2000)

Tilman, H. W., *When Men and Mountains Meet* (Cambridge: Cambridge University Press, 1946)

Trapp, Maria Augusta, *The Sound of Music: The Story of the Trapp Family Singers* (London: White Lion, 1976)

Trevor-Roper, Hugh, *The Last Days of Hitler* (London: Papermac, 1995)

Tudor, Malcolm, *British Prisoners of War in Italy: Paths to Freedom* (Newtown, Powys: Emilia Publishing, 2000)

———, *Special Force: SOE and Italian Resistance 1943–1945* (Newtown, Powys: Emilia Publishing, 2004)

———, *Prisoners and Partisans: Escape and Evasion in World War II Italy* (Newtown: Emilia Publishing, 2006)

Twain, Mark, *A Tramp Abroad* (London: Chatto & Windus, 1880)

Uziel, Daniel, *Arming the Luftwaffe: The German Aviation Industry in World War II* (Jefferson, NC: McFarland, 2011)

Vann, Frank, *Willy Messerschmitt* (Yeovil: Patrick Stephens, 1993)

Volkman, Ernest, *Spies: The Secret Agents Who Changed the Course of History* (New York and Chichester: Wiley, 1994)

Waddy, Helena, *Oberammergau in the Nazi Era: The Fate of a Catholic Village in Hitler's Germany* (New York and Oxford: Oxford University Press, 2010)

Waugh, Evelyn, *The Diaries of Evelyn Waugh*, ed. Michael Davie (London: Phoenix, 2009)

Weinberg, Gerhard, *A World at Arms: A Global History of World War II* (Cambridge: Cambridge University Press, 2005)

West, Nigel, *MI6: British Secret Intelligence Service Operations, 1909–1945* (London: Weidenfeld & Nicolson, 1983)

Wheeler, Mark, *Britain and the War for Yugoslavia, 1940–1943* (Boulder, CO: East European Monographs, 1980)

Whitlock, Flint, *Soldiers on Skis: A Pictorial Memoir of the 10th Mountain Division* (Boulder, CO: Paladin, 1992)

Wilhelm, Maria de Blasio, *The Other Italy: Italian Resistance in World War II* (New York and London: Norton, 1988)

Williams, Cicely, *Zermatt Saga* (London: Allen & Unwin, 1964)

Williams, John, *The Ides of May: The Defeat of France, May–June 1940* (London: Constable, 1968)

Wiskemann, Elisabeth, *The Europe I Saw* (London: Collins, 1968)

Woods, Rex, *Night Train to Innsbruck: A Commando's Escape to Freedom* (London: Kimber, 1983)

———, *Special Commando: The Wartime Adventures of Lt-Col Robert Wilson, DSO and Bar* (London: Kimber, 1985)

Wraight, John, *The Swiss and the British* (Sailsbury, Wiltshire: Michael Russell, 1987)

Wylie, Neville, *Britain, Switzerland and the Second World War* (Oxford and New York: Oxford University Press, 2003)

Zaloga, Steven J., *Operation Dragoon 1944: France's Other D-Day* (Oxford: Osprey, 2009)

Ziegler, Jean, *The Swiss, the Gold and the Dead* (New York and London: Harcourt Brace, 1998)

Zuccotti, Susan, *Holocaust Odysseys* (New Haven, CT, and London: Yale University Press, 2007)

____, *Under His Very Windows: The Vatican and the Holocaust in Italy* (New Haven, CT, and London: Yale University Press, 2002)

Index